# BATS

*Biology, Behavior*
*and Folklore*

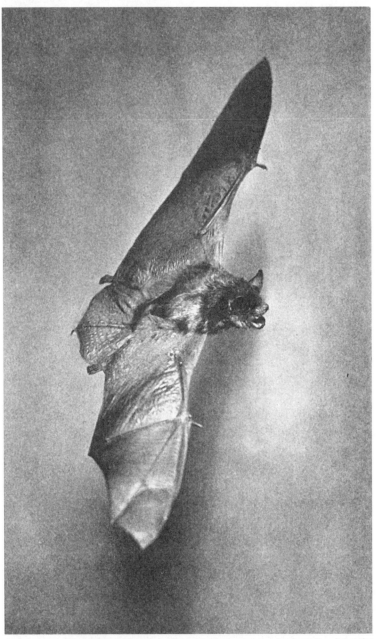

A little brown bat (*Myotis lucifugus*) in flight, banking on a turn, showing tail curled under and mouth open. Courtesy of Prof. Harold E. Edgerton.

# BATS

*Biology, Behavior and Folklore*

## Glover Morrill Allen

DOVER PUBLICATIONS, INC.
Mineola, New York

*Bibliographical Note*

This Dover edition, first published in 1962 and republished in 2004, is an unabridged republication of the second printing of the work, originally published by Harvard University Press, Cambridge, Massachusetts, in 1939 under the title *Bats*. The Harvard University Press edition was made possible by a grant from the Museum of Comparative Zoology of Harvard University. This Dover edition is published by special arrangement with the Harvard University Press.

*Library of Congress Cataloging-in-Publication Data*

Allen, Glover M. (Glover Morrill), 1879–1942.
    Bats : biology, behavior, and folklore / Glover Morrill Allen.
        p. cm.
    Originally published: Cambridge, Mass. : Harvard University Press, 1962.
    Includes bibliographical references and index.
    ISBN 0-486-43383-8 (pbk.)
        1. Bats. I. Title.

QL737.C5A375 2004
599.4—dc22

2004056021

Manufactured in the United States of America
Dover Publications, Inc., 31 East 2nd Street, Mineola, N.Y. 11501

# PREFACE

MANY millions of years before our own race appeared on the earth, bats were flying o' nights, just as now. For, once they had changed their fore feet into wings by lengthening their fingers and spreading a wide skin between them, bats entered the realm of the air, wherein they have continued to this present. No other mammals have ever attained the power of flight. In their kingdom of the air, bats have few competitors, for most birds fly by day. Their line has proved highly successful and at the present era shows a great variety of species, the larger number of which are dwellers in the warmer regions of the earth. From early times bats have aroused the wonder and interest of men, yet since to most of us they are still nearly as unknown as the stars, it seems worth while to present in the following pages some account of these extraordinary creatures. Notwithstanding their great diversity in species, very few common names have been given the many different kinds, so that it has been necessary often to employ the Latin names given to them by naturalists. It is hoped, however, that this will prove no hindrance to the general reader.

To the many friends and correspondents who have most generously permitted the use of photographs here reproduced, the author's grateful thanks are due, especially to the following: Dr. Thomas Barbour, Dr. Frank M. Chapman, Dr. Herbert C. Clark, Professor H. E. Edgerton, Dr. and Mrs. Joseph Grinnell, Mr. A. Brazier Howell, Mr. Wharton Huber, Mr. George L. Kirk, Herr Ernst Krause, Mr. J. G. Meyers, Mr. F. Ramsay, Dr. James Birch Rorer, Mr. M. W. F. Tweedie, Mr. Otho Webb, Professor William H. Weston, and Dr. Herbert P. Whitlock. For kind permission to reproduce figures of the teeth of certain bats from his monograph on the *Families and Genera of Bats* (1907) I am much indebted to Mr. Gerrit S. Miller, Jr., and the Smithsonian Institution. Acknowledgment is also gladly given to Dr. J. Bequaert for a critical reading of the chapter on parasites, and to Miss Mary B. Cobb, Librarian of the Boston Society of Natural History, for much help in looking up the extensive literature.

GLOVER MORRILL ALLEN

CAMBRIDGE, MASSACHUSETTS

# CONTENTS

# ILLUSTRATIONS

# BATS

*Biology, Behavior
and Folklore*

# CHAPTER I

## BATS IN FOLKLORE

All the charms
Of Sycorax, toads, beetles, bats, light on you.
— *The Tempest*, i: 2.

FROM earliest times the peculiar traits of bats have aroused the imagination and interest of humankind. Folklore abounds in superstitious fancies about them. Creatures that fly like birds, bite like beasts, hide by day, and see in the dark, surely could be neither "flesh, fowl, nor good red herring." Much interest attaches to folk tales and ancient beliefs of men in regard to the natural objects around them, for these represent the very beginnings of science, our first attempts to interpret observations of creatures other than ourselves and to explain the familiar occurrences about us in some more or less rational way. Frequently the observations are correctly made but quite as often their interpretation is wholly fanciful, for among simple people credulity is large and critical analysis rare. In earlier days, when good Sir Thomas Browne wrote his book exposing "Vulgar Errors," the scholarly of Europe based their knowledge mainly on authority, so that the older works on natural history were chiefly collections of quotations from Aristotle, Pliny, and others with a minimum of first-hand observations.

Bats typify a curious duality of nature, reflected in many an ancient folk tale, the origin of which no doubt goes far back in prehistory. Two of Aesop's well-known fables depict this ambiguous state. In the one, a bat, having fallen to earth, is seized by a weasel, who, when the bat pleads for his life, replies that he is by nature an enemy of all birds. The bat, however, assures the weasel that he is no bird, but a mouse, and on this plea is given his liberty. Shortly after, the bat is in a similar predicament, having been caught by another weasel whom again he entreats not to eat him. The weasel, however, tells the bat that mice are his special prey, whereupon the bat assures his captor that he is no mouse but a bird, and so is a second time released. The second fable relates to an ancient tradition of a war between the birds and the beasts, in which each party was by turns victorious. A bat, fearful of the outcome of the struggle, always associated with the stronger side. But when peace was at length declared, neither of the opposing parties would receive him because of his deceitful conduct, so that he was driven from the light of day and ever afterward forced to hide in dark places, whence he might issue only at night and alone. The moral of course is that "those who practice deceit must expect to be shunned."

Aesop is reputed to have been born about 620 B.C. and by his wit and learning raised himself from the rank of a slave to the privileges of a freedman in Greece. No doubt he drove his moral precepts home without offense by cleverly making the actors of his tales various familiar animals instead of human beings. This story of the animals and birds at war is perhaps one borrowed from still more ancient sources, for R. H. Nassau (*Where Animals Talk*, 1914) gives it in substantially the same form, as he found it current at the present day among one of the Negro tribes of southern Nigeria. In this version the bat (jemage) could not decide, in the battle between the beasts of the forest and the birds of the air, with which side to ally himself — whether as a mouse on the side of the beasts, or, because of his wings, on the side of the birds. The final result was that he became discredited by both and must even to this day avoid them by hiding in the daytime when the birds are abroad and by flying at night above the reach of the beasts. Gesner (1555) repeats the same tale in modified form from ancient Latin lore — "Avibus cunctis exulare aliquando jussis edicto, vespertilio dixit se murem esse; rursus alio super exilio murium promulgato, avem se esse dixit" (when the birds in council passed an edict to exile a certain one, the bat said he was a mouse; again, when another law was proclaimed against mice, he declared that he was a bird).

Curiously, a striking parallel to this tale is found among some of the North American Indians. In his account of the myths of the Cherokee, Mooney (1900) narrates a folk tale of a contest in which the animals challenged the birds to a great ball game. They met on the appointed day, the animals on a smooth grassy bottom near the river, the birds in the tree tops on the ridge. The bear as captain for the animals boasted and made show of his strength, and the fleet-footed deer was also there, who could outrun any of his side. The birds had the eagle for their captain, while the hawk and other swift fliers were also there; yet they were still somewhat afraid of the outcome. As Indian ball games are preceded by a ceremonial dance, a similar function was now performed by the birds and the animals, after which the former retired to the trees, preening themselves for the contest. Presently two "little things" hardly bigger than field mice came climbing up the tree in which the eagle captain sat, and begged to be allowed to join in the game. But the eagle, seeing that they were four-footed, asked why they did not go on the animals' side where they belonged. They replied that the animals had made fun of them and driven them off because they were so small. The eagle, pitying them, agreed, but was at a loss to know how they could join the birds if they had no wings. At last, after consulting with the hawk, it was decided to make them some. But of what? Then, remembering the drum they had used at the dance, with its head of groundhog skin, they took two pieces of this leather, cut them in the shape of wings, stretched them with cane splints, and fastened them on the forelegs of one of the little creatures. Thus Tlámeha, the bat, joined in the game. They now threw the ball to him, and so adroit did he prove in dodging and turning, yet never letting it fall, that the birds soon saw he would be one of their best players. There was no more leather to make wings for the second little creature, but, following the suggestion of one of the birds, they stretched the skin along its sides and thus made a flying squirrel. When all were ready, the signal was given and the game began. Almost at the first toss, the flying squirrel caught the ball and, carrying it up a tree, threw it to the birds, who kept it in the air for a long time before it dropped. The bear rushed to get it, but the martin darted after it and threw it to the bat. The bat was flying near the ground and by his clever dodging and doubling kept it away even from the deer, until he finally succeeded in throwing it between the goal posts and won the victory for the birds. In this game, which is much like lacrosse, the Cherokee player still invokes the aid of the bat and the flying squirrel in the preliminary dance and ties a small piece of a bat's wing to his ball-stick or fastens it to the frame over which the sticks are hung during the dance the night before. This story, according to Mooney, is one of the best-known animal tales and is found also among the Creeks and the Seminoles. In another version the bat is at first rejected by both sides. Finally accepted by the animals because of its teeth, it wins the victory for them.

Among the Pomo Indians of California there is a myth, recorded by S. A. Barrett (1933), which explains how fire was obtained by the animals. It seems that the bat, though having such small eyes and poor eyesight, insisted that he could see fire only a short distance away, but the people would not believe him, for it was dark. Finally, however, he was able to point it out to Oak-ball, who had climbed a tall tree to look off and could see it in the east (the sun, of course). Thereupon the swift-footed Jack Rabbit set off to procure it. In another Pomo myth the bat is one of the important characters in arrow-making, at which he was the most expert of them all. Having been given a large piece of obsidian, he put it into his mouth, chewed it up, and swallowed it. Presently he vomited forth a great quantity of excellent arrowheads, for which the others prepared shafts and feathers. Possibly in this case the association of a bat with arrowheads refers to the big-eared species of southern California, *Otopterus californicus*, which has on the end of the snout an erect and prominent nose-leaf, the shape of which recalls that of an arrowhead.

In his great work on natural history published in several volumes late in the seventeenth century, Aldrovandus brought together a wealth of folklore from ancient Latin sources. He repeats a time-worn tradition of the enmity existing between bats and storks. According to Aelianus, the bats hated the storks, who reciprocated this feeling ("ciconia non modo vespertilionis odio tenetur: sed hac etiam illius"). The bats, dying, took vengeance upon the storks by bringing disaster to their nests — indeed, one author avers that by merely touching a stork's egg the bat renders it sterile! For this reason the storks bring the green leaves of the plane tree and place them in their nests, so that when the bats come (as saith Zoroastres in Geoponicus) they are unable to destroy the eggs. Here one sees an evident attempt to explain the stork's habit of adding green leaves to the nest lining from time to time, a habit common to certain herons and hawks as well. Possibly some watchful person, seeing bats flying about a stork's nest, attributed to them the subsequent failure of the eggs to hatch and so had connected the observations in this way.

Bats seem to have harbored enmity not only against storks but against ants and locusts as well. Pliny tells of a certain kind of poisonous ant, called by Cicero *solifuga* (sun-fleer), against the sting of which the heart of a bat is a remedy as well as an antidote against all kinds of ants. It is for this reason, according to Oppian, that when owls wish to protect their young from ants, they place a bat's heart in their nest — again, perhaps, a hasty conclusion from finding part of an owl's meal in a nest cavity free from those insects. The antipathy between bats and locusts is more difficult to explain. At all events Democritus tells us that where a plague of these insects is on, they will never fly across that place where someone has hung a dead bat in the higher trees, but pass by leaving the field unravaged — again perhaps a case where the observed facts were explainable from some other cause.

A deep-rooted tradition in Europe held that bats were very fond of fat and frequently gnawed the hams and bacon which in former times were often hung to cure in the old-fashioned chimneys of houses or kept in well-aired rooms. It is said that the style of roof formerly in common use, with its short, steep pitch in front and long slope at the back, was designed to give easier access to the spacious chimney tops for hanging these meats. Aldrovandus assures us that if a ham be suspended from a ceiling without touching the floor, it will be found to show gouges where the bats have eaten from it. All the older natural-

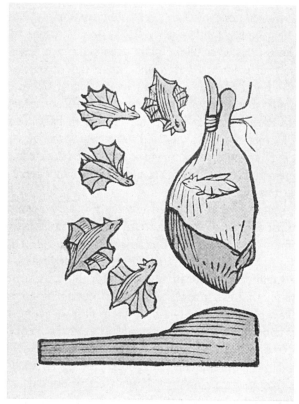

FIG. 1—Bats feeding on a "leg of bacon." As pictured in the *Hortus Sanitatis* ("Garden of Health"), a medieval work on natural history, printed in 1491 (from the copy in the British Museum).

history books mention this supposed fondness of bats for bacon, a taste reflected in their German name of *Speckmaus*. No doubt, too, the same thing is implied in our traditional nursery rhyme,

> Bat, bat, come under my hat,
> And I'll give you a side of bacon.

In a rare old work, *Hortus Sanitatis* ("The Garden of Health"), printed at Mainz in 1491, the author even goes so far as to include a picture of a large ham hanging up, with five bats fluttering about it and a sixth already alighted on it, about to enjoy the feast. It never occurred to anyone to test this belief until the German naturalists Kuhl and, shortly before him, Hermann, early in the nineteenth century, tried the experiment of feeding bacon (Speck) to captive bats; but they steadfastly refused it and finally died from starvation rather than eat it, thereby refuting the charge. I suspect that the real culprits were either the black or the roof rats, which climb readily, even passing from one building to another along modern telegraph cables, and that the innocent bats, having been discovered by day sleeping in the chimneys or storerooms, were given all the blame.

There is a firm belief among women that bats delight to become entangled in their hair, so that the appearance of one of these harmless creatures in a room or on the porch of a summer's evening is enough to cause immediate alarm. In rare instances small bats have swooped too near some heads and have caught their wings, but such cases seem too few to account for the widely held tradition. I knew of one such mishap. The lady was sitting alone at the time, and a passing bat caught in her hair, becoming so thoroughly enmeshed that she was unable to extricate it. Not daring to handle the creature, she sat quietly with admirable fortitude, waiting until help arrived! Rennes (1924) is authority for the statement that in Mayenne, France, the country folk believe that a bat flies near one's head with the evil plan of transferring lice to one's hair, and that for a bat to be caught in a woman's headdress presages a disastrous love affair for the victim or death within a year.

Anciently the figure of the wing of a bat together with that of an ant was used to signify a man who stays away from his home at night — a connection not difficult to see, the bat's wing standing for night habits and the ant for activity. In the days of the Greeks and Romans people were sometimes called Bats who thus transferred their activities to the night. It is said that the Egyptians used the figure of a bat to depict a weak and at the same time rashly bold man, because the bat, even though it is small and without feathers, nevertheless essays to fly. Gesner (1555) repeats the tale that Chaerephon, a Socratic philosopher, was aptly styled "the Bat," for, he writes, "not only does this animal not appear by day as with philosophers, but both hide and philosophize."

The Ancients seem to have collected debts by personally importuning the debtor. At all events, it was customary to speak of certain persons as "Bats" who stayed in all day, in fear lest, owing money, they should meet with their creditors. This may, in part, be the origin of a folk tale related by Aldrovandus (1681), who in turn accredits it to one Apologus, identical possibly with Aesop or an imitator. It seems that a bat, a diver (species of loon), and a bramblebush formed a partnership to carry on business together. The bat was to collect the moneys, the diver to sell certain articles, while the bush had clothes (?to sell). While they were all in a boat they became shipwrecked and barely escaped with their lives. Ever since, the bat has been forced to remain hidden by day lest it meet creditors; the diver may often be seen to this present swimming alongshore, frequently putting its head under the surface to look for its lost merchandise, while the bramble stands by the side of a path, plucking at passers-by to ask if they have seen its clothes. The interest of this, as of other folk tales, lies in its offering a perfectly rational explanation of the characteristic behavior of the three partners as we know them!

While the wings of birds are feathered like their bodies, the "leathery" wings of bats are naked or bald in contrast, a fact that even the unobservant must have noticed long ago. Thus the French word for bat is *chauve-souris*, or bald mouse. Yet, contrary to what one might expect, there is little in the way of folk tales to explain this fact. Among the Mordvines of Russia, however, the following legend is told, as quoted by Dähnhardt (*Natursagen*, 1:95). It appears that Satan, wishing to create man, took sand and mud from seventy-seven different lands and fashioned this material into human form. Unable, however, to give his product a divine nature, he called the bat to him, saying, "Fly up to Heaven; there you will find the towel of the Almighty

FIG. 2—The oldest known pictures of bats. The originals are wall paintings by the Egyptians and are in Tomb 15 at Beni Hasan. They date from the Twelfth Dynasty, about 2000 B.C. The top and bottom figures probably represent the Egyptian rousette (*Rousettus aegyptiacus*), one of the smaller fruit bats, still common in Egypt, and characterized by the short tail and lack of a membrane connecting the hind legs. The middle figure shows a bat with wings folded and with what appears to be a membrane between the upper sections of the hind legs. It probably represents the tomb bat (*Taphozous perforatus*), frequently found by day in the chambers of ancient tombs. (The figures are reproduced from Rosellini's *I Monumenti dell'Egito e della Nubia*, part 2, plate 14, 1834, by courtesy of the Boston Museum of Fine Arts.)

(Tscham-pas). Bring forth your young in one end of the towel, thus making it heavier so that it will fall down to me on the earth." The bat obeyed, and Satan, taking the towel, wiped off the man he had made, which thus received God-like form; but he could not of himself give it life. When, therefore, Tscham-pas vivified the effigy, he became a partner with Satan in the possession of Man: to Satan belonged his life, to God his soul. But the bat was punished. Its wings were taken away (probably it had feathered wings before), its tail became naked, and its feet were fashioned like Satan's.

Weather lore was always interesting to the agricultural peoples of Europe, and "signs" were believed to be furnished by various actions of animals. Although bats seem to have had little significance in prognostication, Aristotle tells us that if bats leave their retreats in numbers it is a sign of hot and calm weather to follow next day, but if they hide away and do not come forth in the evening, it presages storm or a cloudy sky. And it is often true that bats are less active on windy or threatening evenings, for they seem to prefer calm mild nights.

Because of its uncanny bloodletting habits, one would suppose that the vampire bat of tropical America would find frequent place in the folklore of the peoples inhabiting the regions where it occurs, but of this there seems to be little record. Among the Indians of Guiana, Roth (1924) found the belief current that if the seeds from the four-sided pod of a certain forest liana are scraped and rubbed on the toes, they cause any bat attacking that part of the body to fall down dead! For this reason the Creoles call the plant "bat's bane," but its efficacy may well be doubted. The same author (Roth, 1915) tells a legend he encountered among the Arawaks, one of whose traditions held that their old stone axes came from a distant country whither men journeyed, sometimes taking years. Once on a time, such a party at nightfall reached the bat country and prepared to sling their hammocks for the night. But the old man of the group warned them to build an enclosed camp as a protection from the giant bats which here were as large as cranes. One of the younger men, a slothful fellow, declared he would sleep outside, for he had no fear of the bats in spite of their size. Late that night, when the others had retired within their shelter, they heard him begging for admission, but he was told that he must remain outside and take the consequences. This he evidently did, for in the morning when they opened the door his companions found nothing of him but a heap of bones. The bats had sucked him dry! From the same source comes an Arawak legend that strongly reminds us of tales of the Thunderbird, once current among certain tribes of the West Coast. According to the story, there once lived on Bat Mountain (Muragayeng, in Arawak) of the Pakarama range in Guiana an immense bat, which, as soon as the sun had set, would swoop down on the village, carrying off and devouring anyone found out-of-doors. Often two or sometimes even three persons would be missing of a morning, and terror spread among the people. In vain the hunters of the tribe sought to find the creature's lair by day, until at length an old woman of their village declared that she was ready to sacrifice her life for the good of the others. So at nightfall she stationed herself in the middle of the village with her smoldering fire-stick covered, while the others hid in terror in their huts. At length a flutter of wings was heard, as the bat, seizing her in its claws, bore her off to its den. Uncovering her fire-stick, she caused a trail of light to appear, showing the hunters the direction they must take in the morning to find the lair. Next day, high flames from its burning nest led the people to its hiding place, where they succeeded in killing it. But whether or not they rescued the heroic old woman is not related.

It seems that among the Arawaks it is a bad omen to find bat's droppings on a pathway, but the island Caribs regarded bats as their guardian spirits, and whoever killed them would fall ill.

Another vampire story related by Roth concerns the night owl, Boku-boku, who married the bat's sister and often took her brothers at night to rob people's houses, frightening them with his weird cry. Once when the owl was otherwise busied, the bats went thieving by themselves, but being unable to call so loudly as the owl, they failed to frighten the people, and the village master with a blunt arrow shot and stunned one of them. His companions, however, succeeded in reviving him, and they flew away together. The next night they were less fortunate, for again the bat was wounded and this time did not recover. Ever since then the surviving bat continues to avenge his brother by sucking the blood of men and of their fowls, as well as inflicting other damage.

CHAPTER II

# BATS, GODS, AND MEN

Naturae vespertilionis congruere naturam Diaboli.
— Divus Basilius.

THE strange likeness of bats to human beings was long ago noticed among primitive men. Even the learned naturalists of
two centuries ago pointed out that, among the mammals then
known, only bats and elephants, besides man and apes, suckled
the young from a pair of breast nipples, a fact that led Linnaeus
to associate them near human beings in his classification. No
doubt, too, their bright little faces and prominent ears enhanced
the similarity to men, while their nocturnal habits combined to
add a supernatural element to their nature. It is hardly strange
then that human kind the world over have connected bats in
some mysterious way with the manifestations of the unseen
world, or regarded them as having some peculiar connection
with ourselves. In the open temples of the East, bats of various
species frequently take up their abode by day, and in parts of
China they are looked upon with favor as bringing good luck.
In other places they are less regarded, but at least some explanation of their predilection for these sacred places had to
be discovered. Thus Shortridge (in Ryley, 1913) learned that
the Kanarese believe that anciently bats were a sort of bird,
but that, becoming dissatisfied with their estate, they resorted to
the temples to pray to be made like men. At length, in answer
to their petitions, they did undergo change but only in part,
becoming nondescript, with the teeth, hair, and faces of men,
but in other respects remaining birdlike. Thereafter, too
ashamed to meet other birds, they went abroad only by night;
but by day they still resort to the temples to pray that they may
be changed back again into birds!

In describing the troglodytes of northern Africa, Herodotus

declares that they had a form of speech unlike any other, but squeaked after the manner of bats. In the mythology of the Ancients the bat, because of its nocturnal habits, was sacred to Proserpina, the wife of Pluto, the ruler of the underworld. In his account of this region Homer gives a vivid picture of the shades disturbed by Ulysses, fluttering like roosting bats from a tree and following after him with weird gibbering:

> Hae autem frementes sequebantur
> Sicut autem quando vespertiliones.

It is perhaps in keeping with this batlike appearance of the souls of the departed that among the Votiaks, a Finnish people, there is a belief that during sleep the soul frees itself from the body and may then appear in various forms, often as a bat. Holmberg (1927) relates that an aged Votiak told him, in explanation of the bats' disappearance by day, that it is because men are then awake and their souls at home; hence it is that bats appear only at night when men are sleeping. Should a bat come near anyone, it is believed to be in fact the spirit of some kinsman or acquaintance. In proof of this the same person related as tradition how a certain man one day went to rest while his companions sat in the yard. Presently, as he slept, a bat appeared and they watched it as it flew from one place to another. When the sleeper awoke and was asked what he had dreamed, he declared that in his sleep he had wandered to the very places where they had seen the bat fly. Obviously, then, the bat they had seen was none other than the soul of the sleeping man! It is a common belief among many peoples that the soul at death takes wing in the form of a bird. Of a similar sort is the belief held by the peasants of Sicily at the present day, that persons who have met a violent death, as by murder, mishap, or suicide, must pass a certain time as God may determine, in the form of a bat, a lizard, or other reptile (Keller, 1909). The origin of such tenets is not difficult to conceive. Indeed, I myself knew of an eminent naturalist who dropped dead one winter's night while on his way to a scientific meeting in Boston. That very evening a bat roused from hibernation was captured as it fluttered in the office room to which the deceased gentleman had been proceeding. We call it a coincidence, but the less tutored mind sees a mystic connection.

Among those of our race the bat has always a somewhat sinister significance through its association with darkness and caverns. As Divus Basilius, an old Latin writer, put it, the nature of the bat is kin with that of the Devil; but doubtless his acquaintance with the former was the less intimate! Artists of medieval Europe and of later times were accustomed to represent imps and devils with batlike leathern wings and pointed ears, while angels and other beneficent spirits had feathered pinions growing from their shoulders (though quite without obvious musculature for their use). So familiar was this presentation of the satanic form, that in 1770, when one of the sailors on Captain James Cook's first expedition to Australia came unexpectedly upon what must have been a large fruit bat, he rushed back to the others of the landing party, terror-stricken, declaring that he had met with a real live devil!

In a famous three-panel painting of the Annunciation, a valued relic known as the "triptych of Aix," the Virgin is shown kneeling before the lectern of the chapel, while from a small window above a beam of light falls upon her face — at first glance a sincere and beautiful treatment of a familiar subject. Yet it has been pointed out that a minute examination of the details indicates that the artist was filled with unholy thoughts, for he has introduced various features of an evil significance, though so unobtrusively as to escape any but a discerning eye. Thus, the wing of the announcing angel is that of an owl with a characteristic dark marking on the larger feathers, while hidden in a small triangular space above is the hovering figure of a bat peering down, and there are other symbols of a malefic nature. A writer in the *London News*, noting these details, believes the work is by an unidentified fifteenth-century artist.

The undeserved stigma placed upon the bat goes far back in the traditions of our culture. We learn from Ovid that Mineides and his sisters Alcithoë and Leuconoë, because their orgies displeased Bacchus, were turned into bats and gave their shrill

FIG. 3—Bats and bamboos. From a Japanese print. The species represented is probably the long-fingered bat (Miniopterus).

cries in the night air; while Buffon even supposes that the
harpies were intended to represent huge bats of terrifying
appearance.

It is good to find that other races of men than our own have
shown less prejudice toward the harmless wingèd bat. Among

FIG. 4—A carved Chinese bowl of white jade, with the *wu-fu* or design of the five bats.
Courtesy of the American Museum of Natural History.

the Chinese, who so often see the other side of the shield, bats
are held in high regard and by the Buddhists are sometimes
considered sacred. In the Chinese language the word for bat is
*fu,* which also is the name of the character meaning "happiness,"
just as with us the word bee has the same sound as the second
letter of the alphabet. By substitution, the figure of a bat
thus comes to stand for happiness or good luck and is frequently

seen worked into designs in Chinese handicraft. But again contrary to our usage, it is always represented with head pointing in and from above instead of head up and from below, spread-eagle or "spread-bat" style. Two bats written upon a gift signify good wishes from the donor, and a talisman widely used in China consists of a disk about the size of a dollar, enclosing the symbol of life (a tree with roots and branches), and surrounded by five bats with spread wings, facing in. This talisman of the five bats — or *wu-fu* — is worn for the five great happinesses sought by all men, namely, health, wealth, long life, good luck, and a desire for virtue or, as sometimes put, tranquility. So frequently is the bat symbol used in Chinese work that it becomes highly conventionalized and, far from having any sinister significance, is a favorite design. Dr. Bushell, an authority on the subject, points out that the patterns used in Chinese art are rather few and these highly conventionalized, consisting essentially of favorite designs of symbolic value. Thus the plants are chiefly the peony, the lotus, the plum blossom, sometimes the rose, the peach as the "fruit of life," and the magic fungus that grows overnight. Of animals, the deer, the tortoise, and the stork are Taoist emblems of longevity, for some reason a great desideratum; while in very many decorations the bat plays a prominent part.

In the splendid collection illustrating Chinese art in the Victoria and Albert Museum, London, one is impressed with the frequency with which carved or painted bats are worked into the design in order to carry "good fortune," for the Chinese are philosophers and realize how large a part luck plays in life. As the guidebook points out, a bat and two peaches together form a rebus to be read, "Happiness and longevity, both complete"; and what more could one desire? Of the many beautiful carvings in red lacquer exhibited, there is a round bowl and cover, the decoration of which consists of a bewilderingly intricate pattern of peony blossoms and leaves, the former with five-petaled centers, while carved around the rim of the bowl is a complete ring of little bats, their spread wings touching, their heads looking inward, and their tails three-lobed pointing outward all around. The possessor of such a treasure would indeed be lucky! Another beautiful lacquer box is shaped like a large peach with a design of peaches made of differently colored stones on its cover and two flying bats on opposite sides. Still another red box is actually in the conventionalized form of a bat, with bent wings, its eyes consisting of eight-petaled rosettes, perhaps symbolic of the "eight precious things." A smaller figure of a bat forms part of the pattern of the box cover. Still another piece, a carved round plate of red lacquer, has in its center a peach blossom fully blown, surrounded by a circle of eight bats facing in, and outside them eight sprays of flowers, again the mystic number, not only of ancient Chinese lore but also of the Buddhist philosophy, in which there are eight emblems of happy augury, or as in the Taoist symbols, eight attributes of the immortal genii. These pieces date from the early 1700's. Among the treasures of the collection are two thrones, one in carved red lacquer, the throne of the Emperor Ch'ien Lung (middle eighteenth century); the other of flat lacquer in black and gold (early seventeenth century). The former has a large bat in the middle of each side arm, while on the back is the design of the five bats, symbolic of the five great blessings. The other throne is a veritable cave of bats, for here, their small figures, instead of forming part of a principal design, are bestowed liberally in every conceivable nook of the carving, painted chiefly in gold along the arms or on the scrolls and in corners. Still another type of decoration is illustrated in a red-lacquer Buddhist scepter, the head of which is inlaid with small bats cut from some pearly shell. This emblem of authority is of relatively recent date and is said to be used by the priests of that religion. So a hunt for bats among the Chinese designs proved a delightful occupation.

The appearance of certain species of small bats, like pipistrelles, just at sunset, is perhaps the basis of the Mohammedan legend concerning the creation of the bat by Christ. While keeping the fast of Ramadaham, during which no food may be taken between sunrise and sunset, Jesus retired to a secluded spot among the hills, where the mountains about Jerusalem against the western sky shut out the sunset view. It was thus impossible for him to ascertain the moment when the sun sank below the horizon. So, by God's permission, he fashioned the clay image of a wingèd creature, prayed and breathed upon it. Immediately it opened its wings and fled into one of the dark caverns of the mountains. Thereafter it emerged every night just at the sunset hour and, by fluttering about Isa (Jesus), apprised him of the close of day. He then prepared to pray and partake of food let down by the All Merciful from Heaven on a table of shining silver that illumined the darkness and disclosed by its light a large roasted fish, five loaves, salt, vinegar, oil, pomegranates, dates, and salad (a hearty meal!). Thus Jesus broke his fast while the angels ministered at the table (J. G. Wood, 1870). Nevertheless, in spite of this divine origin, the bat seems to have been held in opprobrium by Jewish peoples, for in the apocryphal Book of Baruch it is used as the symbol of something abhorrent, as where he describes the smoky idols in the darkened temples — "upon their bodies and heads sit bats, swallows and birds . . . by this ye may know they are no gods." It is believed also that the admonition in Leviticus (xi:20), "All fowl that creep, going upon all four, shall be an abomination unto you," refers to bats; while in Isaiah (ii:20) the idols are cast to bats and moles as symbols of loathing and darkness. Bats still haunt the rock temples and ancient tombs of the Pharaohs, but the Egyptians seem to have taken relatively small interest in them. It is said, however, that they used the figure of a bat as the symbol of a nursing woman, for it is the only flying creature that has teeth and two nipples and nurtures its young with care.

Among primitive peoples bats occasionally have a totemic significance, perhaps for no special reason except as one of the familiar animal types. Thus in the Samoan Islands it is usual for a family to have a household god who appears in one case as a fowl, in another as an eel or an octopus. Sir J. G. Frazer (1910, II, 158) mentions one such deity named Tongo, who became incarnate in different animals for different families; in one family he appeared in the guise of a bat "and had a partiality for turmeric," a ginger-like root. The same author quotes C. H. Harper as to a bat clan, the Asini, on the Gold Coast of West Africa, in which the bat was the tribal totem. The usual implication is that the members of such a clan refrain from eating the bat, perhaps a more difficult feat of self-control than one would suppose for meat-hungry natives.

The Bat God was a powerful deity with the ancient Mayas of Central America, whose extraordinary temples and picture writing have excited the wonder of travelers and students. The name for bat in various Maya dialects is *zotz*, whence is derived the word *Zotzil*, the Bat People, who from pre-Columbian times to the present have lived in southern Chiapas, Mexico, about the city known as Tzinacantlan — "the Bat City"; and there is another place of the same name in southern Guatemala. Seler (1908) mentions an early account of the tribe of the Toltecs who "drew fire from fire sticks" and whose God was Zotzilaha Chamalcan and the bat (zotz) his image. He was therefore the God who controlled fire and was conceived of in the likeness of a bat. Seler corrects this by saying that Zotzilaha means "bat's house" and suggests that this implies a mountain cavern, hence a god of caverns and realms of darkness. According to other passages from the same source, Zotziha ("bat's house") is the name of a region to be traversed on the way to the depths of the earth's interior, hence the Kingdom of Darkness and Death, where dwells Cama-Zotz, the "death bat," he who kills those that venture into his realm and who bit off the head of the hero Hunahpu when he descended into the regions of the lower world. Seler says that such images of death play a large part in the mythical beliefs of the Mexican and Central American races.

This deity seems to have been peculiar to the Maya peoples and is unknown in the Mexican hierarchy. Several extraordinary representations of the god have been preserved in the fragments of books and of sculptures that have come down to us from these ancient races, as well as a famous one painted on a pottery urn discovered in the Ulloa valley. These agree in representing the deity in human form with batlike wings extending

from his arms and a large lancet-shaped nose-leaf surmounting
the muzzle. The mouth is usually open, exposing a set of teeth.
In one of the figures the nose-leaf has the form of a stone
knife with which the god slays his victims. He is shown in the
picture here copied, decapitating a man whose dripping head
he holds in one extended hand, while with the other he grasps
what is probably intended for a stone or obsidian sacrificial
knife. The glyph or conventionalized symbol for the god occurs
frequently in some Mayan texts or on the stone columns or
other carvings. It consists of the head in profile, always with
the ear and a prominent nose-leaf. Often a series of beadlike
circles hangs before the mouth, which Seler interprets as a
stream of blood flowing from the god's mouth and symbolizing
the destruction of life and the devouring of light. What is
probably to be regarded as proof of the identity of the Bat
God with a species of Artibeus, the common large fruit-eating
bat of Central America, comes in an interesting way. For Dr.
J. Ricketson in the course of his excavations in Petén, Guatemala, discovered an ancient altar on which was a slab of stone
sealed with plaster. On raising this, he found a quantity of
small bones in a layer about five inches long, an inch wide, and
one or two inches deep. These he submitted to me for identification, and they proved to be chiefly the skulls of two species of
leaf-nosed bats, Artibeus and the smaller Carollia, together with
those of a few small rodents and the ulna of a small bird. Thus
carefully protected, they had remained for centuries intact,
long after the flesh and fur had gone to dust. In this connection
it is interesting to mention that Aldrovandus (1681, 9:1) refers
to the veneration in which, according to Paulus Grysaldus, the
native Mexicans held bats because of a "certain divinity" (*pro
numine quodam*) evidently noticed by the early conquistadores.
Herrera (1889–90) tells us that in former times the Aztecs of
Mexico killed great numbers of bats, probably the free-tailed
"guano bats," using their tiny skins to make robes!

Bats are said to enter also into the religious life of the Australian blacks, or perhaps among only certain groups of them, but
what kind of bat, whether the edible flying foxes or some small

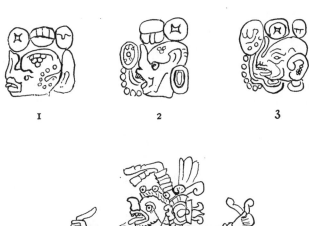

I                2                3

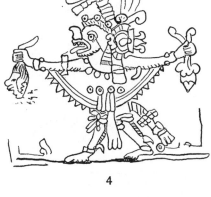

4

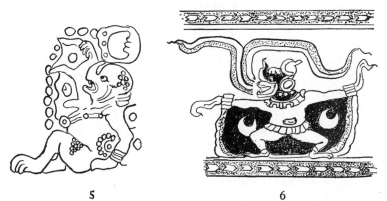

5                        6

Fig. 5—The Bat God of the Central American Indians. The three upper figures show in side view the conventionalized head of a leaf-nosed bat, probably an Artibeus, used as a glyph or symbol. The central figure shows the Bat God, identified by the nose-leaf and wing-like robes, slaying a human victim, whose head he holds in the right hand. The lower figures represent the Bat God with head and wings of the bat and body of human form.

species, is not recorded. In former days at least, the Ta-ta-thi group of tribes in New South Wales had, in addition to clan totems, a pair of sex totems, a bat for the men and a small owl for the women, so that often men and women addressed each other as bat or owl. Should a woman chance to kill a bat or a man a small owl, a fight immediately ensued. While exploring the lower Murray River in earlier days Krefft was warned not to kill a bat, for this animal was "brother belonging

Fig. 6—A bat "displaied proper."
From a fifteenth-century work on
heraldry.

to black fellow," and the blacks would never kill one, for to do so, they said, would mean that one of their women would surely die.

But the use of bats as totems is perhaps not altogether confined to the more primitive races, if, as some suppose, the use of animal figures in heraldic devices is in some degree derived from a previous totemic system. At all events, notwithstanding the usual association of bats with evil and sorcery, they play a small part in armorial bearings, though the reason for their selection is not always clear. I am indebted to Dr. Harold Bowditch, an authority on the subject, for some interesting notes. Thus, it appears that bats were displayed upon the coats of arms of several old families in Great Britain. In an ancient work by John Guillim, *A Display of Heraldrie* (1610–11, p. 182), illustrating the coats of arms of English families, that of the Baxters (itself a feminine form of Baker) is described as a black bat on a silver ground — "He beareth *Argent*, a

Reremouse displaied [i.e., with spread wings, facing], Sable, by the name of Baxter." Here there is probably a pun intended on the word bat or bakke and a baker of bread. He adds: "Sometimes you shall find the bird borne in form of some *Ordinary*; for so shal you see them borne displaied in *Pale*, three of them one aboue another. As in the Ensignes of the Kingdome of India sorted amongst the *Coat-armours* of the innumerous multitude of the great assembly holden at the *Councill* of *Constance*, Anno Dom. 1414" (this last a great religious conference attended by delegates from the churches throughout the Christian world). Another early writer, Sylvanus Morgan, in his book *The Sphere of Gentry* (1661), in describing the animals used in coats of arms, says that "The Batt may signifie Men of quick and secret execution, and bringing his strategems to passe in the night without hatching of Cockatrices Eggs" (?i.e., without miscarrying).

Among English coats of arms having a bat as the device were also those of the families Heyworth or Heiworth, Stainings, Atton, Josue, and Blake, as well as a Dublin family by the name of Wakefield; while the arms of the families Bate, Backkombe, Colyra, and Bostock displayed three bats. A possible connection is again seen in the similarity of the sound of the word "bat" or "bakke" and its older form "blakke" to some of these patronymics, but in the case of others (like Josue and Colyra) the implication is not apparent. The wakefulness of the bat by night may have led the Wakefields to adopt it as their symbol. In France the arms of the family Coo were a golden bat on a blue shield, while the Trippel family of Schaffhausen, Switzerland, bore a golden shield with a black bat above and a green pomegranate below. Perhaps in the latter case the old custom of impaling a bat above the door of a sheepfold (*Schaffhausen*) led to its adoption by this family of that place. In its usual conventionalized form the bat was shown with long ears, the belly facing forward, and the spread wings with a varying number of ribs. The feet were either hooklike or with three claws, birdlike. The long ears indicate that the common long-eared bat (*Plecotus auritus*) of Europe was the one intended to be shown.

# CHAPTER III

# SOME STRANGE USES FOR BATS

Wool of bat and tongue of dog. — *Macbeth*, iv: 1, 15.

In former times bats were much used as amulets or as ingredients of magical concoctions either for good or for evil. No doubt some of these uses go very far back into antiquity and later became part of the materia medica of the doctors and wise men of Greece and Rome, and of the Middle Ages in Europe. Among primitive peoples it is widely held that a person may acquire certain attributes of others by eating or in some other way utilizing the characteristic part, just as the African natives vie with one another for pieces of the heart of a slain lion, so that the lion's strength and courage may be transferred to them. By a like process of substitution, the characteristic qualities of bats were thus believed capable of transference through the use of their various parts either alone or as ingredients with other materials selected for a similar reason. Thus we find the traits of watchfulness and wakefulness, as well as the ability to see in the dark, among the qualities to be imparted directly or subjectively, and there are various charms based on these attributes. Another obvious trait of bats is the absence of hair on the wings; hence there must be some inherent quality that suppresses its growth locally, making the bat a desirable ingredient of a depilatory. Curiously, too, the converse may often obtain; for bats have hair on their bodies and so may come in with washes for encouraging its growth! Other purposes for which bats were used medicinally have a less obvious basis, which may have been the mere peculiarity of their appearance. It will be interesting to review some of these and other uses.

In his account of the bat Aldrovandus quotes the authority of one Didymus, that if the head of a bat be suspended in the gable of a dovecote, the birds will not forsake it, and Belonius (1555) quotes the same story. Perhaps the implication is that the head of the bat keeps watch over the doings of the birds as well as acting in a protective manner. This protective power seems to be implied also in Gesner's (1555) quotation of Kiranid, who says that if the figure of a bat be engraved in a rhinoceros stone (which is in the tip of a rhinoceros horn) and at its foot a sturgeon (*acus piscis*), and if underneath the stone the root of a certain herb be placed, the whole makes an effective charm for warding off demons; while if it be placed by the head of someone without his knowledge, he will not sleep. A similar power lies in the head of a bat by itself. For if you cut off the head of a live bat, tie it up in black skin, and place it by the left arm of anyone, he will not sleep until it is removed. Watchfulness by night seems again to be implied in the tradition that if a live bat is carried thrice around the house and then nailed head downward over the window it acts as a charm to ward off evil. Especially is this done, Pliny tells us, in the case of a sheepfold; for, after being carried three times around it, the poor creature is hung by the feet above the lintel as a protection. This ancient custom is still followed in Gascony and in Brittany, according to De Rennes, who mentions also that one Paul Irebure of his acquaintance never failed each year to nail a bat against his front door above the metal plate bearing the name of an insurance company, "because that keeps away misfortune!" Indeed, I was lately assured by a Dutch naturalist that to this day a bat thus cruelly impaled above the door is seen occasionally in Holland as a survival of this ancient custom. Even in England this tradition still persists, for Dawson (1925) tells that in 1922 he found a Sussex farmer nailing a bat, head downward, above the entrance of his barn!

The uncanny power ascribed to bats of seeing in the dark was believed to be transferable to human beings by making appropriate use of them. Thus old Albertus Magnus, an authority of the thirteenth century, writes in his work on *The Wonders of the World*: "If you wish to see anything submerged and deep in the night, and that it may not be more hidden from thee than in the day, and that you may read books in a dark night, — anoint your face with the blood of a bat, and that will happen which I say." The power of seeing the invisible by the aid of bats' eyes was well recognized among the Gypsies, for Leland (1891), writing of Gypsy sorcery, relates that in the Tyrol he who bears the left eye of a bat on his person may become invisible; and in Hesse it was tradition that he who wears the heart of a bat bound to his arm with red thread will always win at cards — perhaps through being more watchful than his companions. The same writer describes the manufacture of a charm against the "chagrin" that rides horses by night. It consists of some of the horse's hair, a little salt, and the blood of a bat, mixed with meal and cooked to form a little cake. With this the foot of the afflicted horse is smeared, and the empty pipkin then placed within the trunk of a high tree; at the same time an incantation is uttered, concluding with the admonition:

> Stay so long here
> Till it shall be full.

Again, perhaps, the watchfulness by night to ward off danger may be the quality transmitted by the bat's blood, or possibly one devil is set against another. Pliny affirms that if an ox be afflicted with a certain disease, a bat bound to the affected beast will relieve its suffering.

In our Halloween frolics bats and witches seem to have a natural association, and one recalls vividly the witches' incantation in *Macbeth*, where in their cave they mix a potent brew, including such ingredients as

> Eye of newt and toe of frog,
> Wool of bat and tongue of dog,

surely a rare collection, but each no doubt with its special significance. But it must have been seldom, even in the blackest days of witchcraft, that so tragic a fate befell any innocent person as that meted out to Lady Jacaume, who was publicly burned to death at Bayonne in 1332 on the evidence of her neighbors, who affirmed that "crowds of bats" harbored "around her house and walled-in garden" (De Rennes).

Bats seem to have been a favorite source of material among those who dealt in ancient magic. The blood, heart, and other parts of the creature were frequently used by witches for specific purposes, and mysterious characters were written in bats' blood by sorcerers. Pliny is authority for the statement that a clot of bat's blood surreptitiously placed under the pillow of a sleeping woman induces desire; while a bat's head dried or its heart similarly placed will drive away sleep, or, if purposely worn by anyone, will prevent him from being overcome by drowsiness.

Dawson (1925) quotes in translation an interesting bit from an ancient Greco-Egyptian papyrus, giving an infallible prescription whereby a woman may attract to herself the man she desires. "Take the eyes of a bat, while it is still alive, then let it go. Then take uncooked flour or unrefined wax and fashion a little dog, and insert the right eye of the bat into the dog's right eye, and the left likewise into the left." Manipulations are then made with a needle, the eyes are sealed in a vase, and the whole is thrown down at a crossroads. The ancient writer ends with the assurance that "if you want to bring him you shall succeed." Evidently, again, it is the watchfulness of the bat that gives the charm its value, while the dog perhaps adds faithfulness and ability to fetch "him" back. The same author tells that in a Greek papyrus in the British Museum the expression "by the blood of a black bat" is used as a conjuration.

A splendid collection of old prescriptions in which bats figure as ingredients has been brought together by Dawson (1925), already quoted, after a search through ancient medical lore. Pliny gives others and Aldrovandus has a number. The oldest known reference to the use of the bat in medicine, according to the author first mentioned, is found in the "Papyrus Ebers," which recommends that in cases of trachoma, a common eye disease of the East, "to prevent the growing of eyelashes after they have been pulled out," apply an ointment made of frankincense, lizards' blood, and bats' blood in equal parts; another consists of equal parts of bats' blood, ground potsherd, and honey. The magical power of the bat to see in the dark perhaps gives this mixture its potency, or maybe it is the depilatory effect that is to be transferred to the patient, or both. In the same papyrus a certain affection of the throat is cured by taking a cut-open bat and bandaging therewith immediately, until a cure is effected(!). A contrary result may be secured by the same ingredient, for in the "Magical Papyrus of London and Leiden" (second century A.D.) it is stated that bat's blood put in a man's eye will cause blindness. An interesting belief of a similar sort was told me by a Chinese naturalist, Dr. Liu, who says that in North China it is held that a person who kills a bat will become blind (lucky for me that I live elsewhere!).

A Coptic medical papyrus examined by Dawson, dating from the ninth to tenth century, contains 237 prescriptions of which only the 194th mentions the bat, the urine of which, it states, mixed with gall of the fish, *Cyprinus niloticus*, plus the juice of the wild rue, is used as a cure for dimness of vision. Pliny, whose authority stood unquestioned in the earlier centuries of our era, says that the blood of a bat mixed with the juice of a thistle is a remedy for serpent bites, while the gall of a bat mixed with vinegar is the antidote for the bite of a shrew (then believed to be equally noxious), and the bat's heart is a cure for the poison of ants.

The Arabic physician, Ibu al-Beithar, devotes a long chapter of his book to the many medicinal virtues of bats (Dawson, 1925). Cooked in sesame oil, the bat is an embrocation for sciatica; a decoction is good for gout and paralysis; cooked in oil of jasmine and allowed to macerate in a metal pot, it is excellent for asthma; while the gall assists childbirth. In connection with this last, it is interesting to find in India at the present day a belief that the bone from the wing of the flying fox, if bound to the ankle with hair from a black cow's tail, will ensure painless parturition. The brain of a bat, Ibu recommends further, if pounded and boiled, is sovereign for leucoma of the eyes, and if mixed with the juice of an onion will cure cataract! The same author furnishes a variation of the use of a bat in preventing doves from forsaking their cote, for instead of fastening the body in the gable of their home, he advises burying a bat's head near it. Again, an opposite effect may be produced in a similar way, for a bat's head put in a mouse hole will instantly cause the pests to leave — here perhaps a case of like curing like, the mouse-like appearance of the bat serving as a sort of homeopathy, or perhaps the watchfulness of the bat is invoked. An old Syriac book quoted by Dawson recommends the heads of young bats or swallows pounded and mixed with honey to be smeared on the eyelids to aid dim vision; or the dung of bats together with lizards' dung and other ingredients may be put to the same use — a case of kill or cure. The same work says further of the bat: "Put its head in the covering of thy head, and thou shalt never be vanquished all the days of thy life. Hang its eyes on thy person and thou shalt not be afraid of the scorpion." These virtues may explain why young Hieronymus, when he went first into battle, bore on his lance a bat, possibly for protection or perhaps as signifying his own versatility of spirit. It is worth mentioning too, in passing, that an ancient form of spear used in the Middle Ages, with a point in the shape of a trident and having the central blade longer than the lateral ones, was called a *chauve-souris*.

It may have been that the virtue of some of the strange prescriptions in which bats played a part lay in the difficulty of procuring the proper ingredients, so that, though one would fain try the remedy, the medicine was beyond the ordinary man's power to compound; or the failure of the dose might readily be excused on the ground of some inaccuracy in its preparation. Dawson describes a remarkable "bat's balsam" devised as an unguent for hypochondriacs by Mayenne (died 1655), who was physician to two French and three English kings. It contained, among other things, adders, bats, sucking whelps, earthworms, hog's grease, the marrow of a stag, and the thigh bone of an ox — a potent combination and no doubt efficacious, even if the hypochondriac merely read the label with its list of ingredients. Dr. R. James in 1752 affirmed that the flesh of a bat properly prepared was good "for a *Schirrus*, and the Gout, and the blood cures an Alopecia." Gesner (1555) gives the following recipe for a bat salve for the cure of rheumatism ("arthriticis doloribus"): take twelve bats, St. Johnswort, rancid butter, aristolochia, and castor, and boil together until it becomes an ointment. The number twelve here may signify the twelve apostles or even go back to something older. A more modern instance of the efficacy of bats in rheumatism is reported by Dr. M. W. Lyon, Jr. (1931), who, when visiting a bat cave in Indiana, learned that a few years before some local person had collected a large number of small bats at the cave (probably Myotis) and, having tried out their oil, used it to relieve rheumatism, with beneficial results. In India, too, McCann (1934) tells that the fat of flying foxes is held by the natives to be a great help in this same complaint, as well as in preventing baldness. Aldrovandus adds a number of excellent recipes to the list, collected from various sources: thus Avicenna says that to cure a tumor, take a bat's head dried and drink it with three fingers of syrup and vinegar; or, take the heads of seven fat bats, washed and treated with vinegar, in a glass. For gout Galenus advises three bats boiled in rain water, to which add an ounce of flaxseed, three raw eggs, a cup of oil, dung of an ox, an ounce of wax — mix well and apply to the afflicted part. In another recipe twelve bats boiled in rain water form an important item. A bat's brain or its blood, mixed with the juice of buckthorn and honey, is good for dim eyesight, while certain magi declared that anointing one's self with bat's blood would ward off pain for an entire year! Dried bat dung rubbed to a powder with the heart and tongue may induce hydrophobia, and Rasip is quoted (by Aldrovandus) as authority for the discovery that "he who shall eat the tongue or the heart of a bat shall flee from water and die" — hydrophobia again. But he may be cured as one would a person bitten by a mad dog, by first inducing vomiting, then giving fresh goats' milk, bezoar, and river crabs!

The virtue of bat dung was believed in by the Arabs, according to Forskål, a pupil of Linnaeus, who visited Egypt before 1775. Writing in Latin, he tells that the desert Arabs gather the substance for frequent medicinal use, taking it internally;

mixed with vinegar, it was applied externally upon tumors. It was once commonly held that the urine of a bat had septic qualities. Ancient authority has it, too, that the ashes of burned bats or of owls, if drunk with wine, will promote lactation, or if a nurse's milk has stopped, the nipples are to be bathed in a solution of the same for a like purpose. Aldrovandus, who recounts this belief, confesses, however, that he does not regard it as very efficacious; but the wings of a bat, reduced to ashes and mixed with oil, if rubbed on, are good for a fever.

In our own country few if any of these ancient cures have survived. John Lawson, however, in his *History of North Carolina* (1714), speaks of the "Bat or Rearmouse" as the same there as in England. "The Indian Children are much addicted to eat Dirt, and so are some of the Christians. But roast a Bat on a Skewer, then pull the Skin off, and make the Child that eats Dirt eat the roasted [Rearmouse], and he will never eat Dirt again. This is held an infallible Remedy" — and doubtless one that few parents would need to try twice.

The efficacy of bats when applied for removing or preventing the growth of hair is affirmed by many old writers. Either the blood of a bat or its brain, used alone or mixed with hedgehog's gall or goat's milk, formed an excellent depilatory. The growth of hair on the thighs in children, wrote the Arab physician Ibu al-Beithar, may be prevented by rubbing on bat's blood. Seager (1896) mentions a similar belief in Shakespeare's time, for the blood "anointed on the eyelids suffereth not the hair to grow again." According to Dawson (1925), in India even at the present day "some women rub the blood of the small garden bat which has well-developed ears, into the artificially dilated lobes of their own ears, so as to strengthen them. The wings of bats are highly prized as a hair wash. They are crushed and mixed with cocoanut oil and other ingredients. The mixture is kept underground in a closed vessel for three months, and then used to prevent the hair from falling out or turning gray." Thus the connection of bats with hair, either staying in or coming out, doubtless goes back to prehistory.

While little now survives of the magical uses of bats, they still serve a purpose even in modern times, namely, in the production of guano, valuable as fertilizer in some warm countries. In Cuba, Puerto Rico, and other West Indian islands, where certain limestone caves have been used by bats for centuries, tons of guano may accumulate, which, often mixed with cave earth through disintegration of the walls or through inwash during rains, forms an excellent fertilizer much sought by local agriculturalists. From some of the larger caves many tons of this accumulation have been removed in the past to renew the thin soil of these islands, so that in some places the accessible supply has been much worked out. Large deposits of guano, usually in limestone caves, have been reported from the southwestern United States (Texas and New Mexico); from Brazil and Uruguay, the Philippines, Marianas, the Federated Malay States, Borneo, India, the Transvaal, and Egypt; and from Italy, southern France, and other countries bordering on the Mediterranean, evidently occurring where conditions are suitable for the congregation of large bat populations and where the caverns are not too wet. In a detailed account of the analysis and experimental value of bat guanos of Puerto Rico, P. L. Gile and J. O. Carrero (1918) have summarized a large amount of valuable data on this subject. In general they divide the substance into three groups, according to its condition: bat manure, which is relatively fresh; decomposed guano; and phosphatic guano, although these classes are not sharply distinct. The substance if formed by the excreta of frugivorous bats is far less valuable than if it is from insectivorous species, since the nitrogen content is much less. The fresh guano is the most valuable and in some cases is collected about once a year or so, if it accumulates in sufficient quantities. The results of eleven analyses showed an average, for fresh deposits, of about 11 per cent nitrogen, 7 per cent phosphoric acid, 5 per cent of citrate-soluble phosphoric acid, about 2 per cent of potash, 3.5 per cent of sulphur trioxid, and traces of iron, alumina, lime, and magnesia. Where water enters the cave, the soluble elements are leached out and carred down to the limestone rock below, with which they react to form less soluble calcium phosphates and sulphate, while the potash and nitrates disappear with the drainage water. Bacterial decay also ensues, so that in the second stage, decomposed guano, there is a great reduction in the nitrogen content, 1 or 2 per cent, but an increase in the phosphoric acid to 10 or 20 per cent and of the citrate-soluble phosphoric acid to from 3 to 10 per cent. The third stage, phosphatic guano, represents the end result of the leaching and decomposition. It "contains practically no nitrogen and consists of the insoluble phosphates of lime, iron, or alumina, mixed with siliceous impurities," with a high phosphoric-acid content. Since different crops and different soils require different proportions of these chemicals, it is clear that not all bat guanos are equally efficacious as fertilizer for a given crop, although the fresh substance is the best for general purposes. To make the best use of such deposits, samples should be analyzed and their appropriate use determined for various crops and soils. The authors quoted report, therefore, that the value of bat guano for a particular crop may vary from 0 to $47.60 a ton (as of 1914), according to its condition, with an average value of about $7.14 a ton. A survey of the Puerto Rican caves showed as an estimate something over 16,000 tons of the substance then available.

In his interesting volume on the *Animal Life of Carlsbad Cavern*, New Mexico, Vernon Bailey has given a valuable account of the great deposits of guano originally in the outer part of the cavern. Here it was estimated that the deposit extended for a quarter of a mile and in places was a hundred feet wide, varying up to a nearly equal depth. The "guano bat," or Mexican free-tailed bat (*Tadarida mexicana*), which congregates here literally by the million during part of the year, autumn, winter, and spring, is the chief factor in producing these deposits. Between the years 1901 and 1921 this great deposit was worked commercially, with from twenty to forty men at a time shoveling it into sacks, which were hoisted out and shipped by rail to a California fertilizer company. During the period of greatest activity, for about fifteen years, this work went on from September to March; one to three carloads of guano were shipped daily, each carload weighing about forty tons. The prices realized for it were said to run from twenty to eighty dollars a ton, the older material of course being less valuable. At the present time there is little in the caves, as it accumulates slowly.

It is this same species of bat that was brought into public notice a few years ago through the attempts of Dr. C. A. R. Campbell of San Antonio, Texas, to increase their numbers by the erection of "municipal bat roosts," of stout wooden construction. He believed that the bats would not only eradicate mosquitoes and malaria, but also prove an asset by supplying guano in merchantable quantities. The experiment as it relates to malaria is elsewhere mentioned, but it was said that the guano deposits were not very large in the few cases of successful colonization. Further attempts to commercialize the idea of establishing "bat towers," with colonies of insect-eating bats, resulted in the wide advertisement of offers to erect such structures in apple-growing districts at a high cost by a western firm, which assured the prospective investor that the bats would entirely free his orchards of the codling moth. Needless to say, the rosy plan would have had very little likelihood of success, for the more northerly bats of the apple-growing areas are less highly colonial, and even though they could be induced to take up quarters in an artificial roost would probably have little effect on the general numbers of orchard pests.

The use of bat guano has been tried in parts of the East where the small swifts, Collocalia, that make the edible birds' nests, share the caves with the bats, occupying different sections, however; and it is reported that the bird guano is here preferred to that from the bats. In northern New South Wales bat guano has been used by local settlers as a fertilizer, and I once visited several caves from which large quantities had been removed. The accumulations were, however, relatively small, for most of the caves seemed to be inhabited by the bats as winter quarters during hibernation, when there is little deposit of manure.

According to T. Norris (1874), bat guano was utilized by the

Confederate States during our Civil War as a source of making niter for gunpowder, in the latter years of the struggle, when effective blockade by the North had rendered this ingredient nearly unobtainable from outside sources. The best deposits were said to be those in some large caves of northern Texas, and so valuable were they that the Confederate government detailed the larger part of a regiment to guard them. No doubt the bat that produced the deposits was the same free-tailed species, *Tadarida mexicana*, aptly termed by Bailey the "guano bat."

# CHAPTER IV

## BATS AS PETS

[A bat] . . . is no bird but a wingèd mouse; for she creeps with her wings, is without feathers, and flyeth with a kinde of skin, as bees and flies do; excepting that the Bats wing hath a farre thicker and stronger skin. And this creature thus mungrell-like, cannot look very lovely. — John Swan's *Speculum Mundi*, Cambridge, England, 1635.

IN spite of John Swan's aspersions upon the looks of a bat, these much maligned creatures make attractive and interesting pets, even though their chief interests in life seem to be food, sleep, and escape. Most of the smaller insect-eating species quickly become tame and very soon learn to eat such unaccustomed food as meal worms and to lap water drops from one's finger.

I have at various times kept the big brown bat (*Eptesicus fuscus*) for days on end in a small box on my desk. One that I caught had evidently just emerged from hibernation and appeared in the house, flying back and forth through the hallway. Eventually he came into my room, and with the door closed to prevent his escape, he soon tired and hung up on the picture-molding for rest. Here I made him prisoner by carefully approaching and placing a box over him. Bats have rather few natural enemies and perhaps for this reason show little fear. My captive soon settled in a corner of the box, clinging to its rim with his hind feet. I picked him up gently. But he was not to be molested with impunity, for instantly his jaws opened wide and his strong teeth seized my finger tip with all the fury of a tiny bulldog. With sharp squeaks and clicks he sunk his strong canines into the skin, giving convulsive bites without ever letting go. A bat of this size will easily draw blood if he strikes a place where the skin is thin, but my finger tip held. I finally got him to let go and calm down a little. Holding him in my closed fingers so that only his head protruded, I offered him a drop of water on the end of a pencil, placing it against his nose. Almost at once his thin red tongue protruded as he eagerly lapped it up. Several drops were taken in this way, for bats that hibernate in houses must get very thirsty by late winter. Insects were not easy to find at this season, so the food question at once became the next problem. But a visit to the

FIG. 7—The big brown bat (*Eptesicus fuscus*), a captive hanging up asleep. This bat is common in the United States, frequently spending the winter in city houses. Boston, Massachusetts. Two-thirds natural size.

nearest bird store provided several dozen mealworms — smooth-skinned, pale-brownish larvae of a species of beetle — a delicacy much appreciated by cage birds. So I next undertook to educate the bat's taste similarly, for doubtless in a natural state mealworms were quite unknown to my pet. I found him on my return hanging quietly by the claws of his hind feet from the edge of his box, with its improvised cover of netting. When I gently lifted this he came to life at once, opened his jaws to their fullest extent, ready to tackle any creature large or small. I next picked up a struggling mealworm in a pair of small forceps and placed one end of the creature in his open mouth. Instantly his jaws closed in a vicelike grip, his sharp canines puncturing the plump body of the mealworm as if it were a "hot-dog." His whole attitude was one of fierce resistance, with every intent to vent his fury on whatever disturbed his peace. Then, suddenly, as the tasty juice oozed into his mouth, his entire behavior changed. The tense jaw muscles relaxed, his defiant squeaks ceased, and I could sense the working of his mind as his wrath abated and he began to taste the squirming morsel with rising interest. In a few seconds all recollection of his situation seemed to have vanished, while the unfortunate mealworm, chewed over from end to end, was promptly swallowed, and my captive looked hopefully up for more. One after another he chewed down two dozen mealworms, and by now we had established friendly relations. For several days he lived in the narrow confines of his box, sleeping during the daytime; but at evening he became more alert, twitched his ears slightly when the gauze cover was lifted, and looked up expectantly for his mealworms and water. One day, however, in my absence he worked loose a corner of the netting and made his escape, as pets usually do. A long search in every cranny of the room failed to discover him, nor was there any obvious way whereby he might have gone out, except by a space under the door through which he must have crawled.

Another time a friend brought me a little brown bat (*Myotis lucifugus*) that he had found hanging behind a blind one September morning. This smaller species behaved in much the same way, at first greeting my advances with open mouth, ready to set his delicate teeth into my hand at once, but very quickly he learned to regard me merely as a source of food. Peter, as I dubbed him, was particularly fond of bluebottle flies, then easily obtained for him on the window, and would crunch down as many as I could catch, taking them daintily from my fingers, all the while uttering explosive little squeaks of resentment

FIG. 8—The little brown bat (*Myotis lucifugus*), a common species over most of temperate North America. Above, the captive hanging up asleep, natural size. Below, resting on the floor of its cage, slightly enlarged. Cambridge, Massachusetts.

at being held in my closed hand. When the bluebottles gave out, I tried him on an ordinary house fly. The first one offered he seized eagerly, as if anticipating a treat, but evidently he did not like the taste and spat it out at once. Others I offered he treated in the same way, giving each a testing bite, then rejecting it with a disgusted shake of the head and little squeaks and clicks of protest, at the same time backing way from the unpleasant object. Evidently there are flies and flies. Mealworms he found quite to his taste and would eat a number at a sitting (or, shall I say, a hanging?), chewing each one from end to end before he swallowed it. All the manipulation of his food seemed to be performed with the aid of lips and tongue. If I opened my fingers he at once would try to fly away, biting savagely when held. If he dropped an insect he never tried to recover it, but looked up to see if another were forthcoming. An unusually lively fly he would seize, then instantly turn his head under his body, holding the morsel against the tail membrane, which was turned forward to form a sort of pocket preventing its escape while he secured a new hold. This is a regular habit of bats of this type, belonging to the family Vespertilionidae. The horseshoe bat (Rhinolophus), belonging to a distinct family (the Rhinolophidae), has a much less voluminous tail membrane, and when at rest curls the tail over the back. It is said that it has a somewhat similar habit, but holds the struggling insect against the membrane of the fore part of the arm instead.

Peter became at length very tame and learned to eat a variety of strange things, even bits of angle worms, if cut up small and fed to him with forceps. If small crickets, grasshoppers, or bluebottles were put alive in his box he was instantly alert and would shuffle quickly after them, pouncing upon them and at once, having seized one in his mouth, would double his head under to hold the prey securely against the tail membrane. When resting on a flat surface he had a curious spidery appearance, supporting himself on the thumbs and tips of the wrists, his wings folded snugly at the sides, and his body raised on the hind feet. One morning I found my pet dead in his box after a month of captivity.

Another Myotis I had was even tamer and would allow me to take him from his cage and feed him mealworms one after another, while he hung from my finger by the sharp claws of his hind feet.

Bats of various species have often been kept in captivity by European naturalists, either as casual pets or for the study of their hibernation. The first to record the habit of "pouching" the prey by aid of the tail membrane was Gilbert White, who in his classic *Natural History of Selborne*, in a letter of September 9, 1767, writes:

I was much entertained last summer with a tame bat, which would take flies out of a person's hand. If you gave it any thing to eat, it brought its wings round before the mouth, hovering and hiding its head in the manner of birds of prey when they feed. The adroitness it showed in shearing off the wings of flies, which were always rejected, was worthy of observation, and pleased me much. Insects seemed to be most acceptable, though it did not refuse raw flesh when offered: so that the notion, that bats go down chimneys and gnaw men's bacon, seems no improbable story. While I amused myself with this wonderful quadruped, I saw it several times confute the vulgar opinion, that bats when down on a flat surface cannot get on the wing again, by rising with great ease from the floor. It ran, I observed, with more dispatch than I was aware of; but in a most ridiculous and grotesque manner.

In a footnote to this account in the 1837 edition by Bennett, it is added that Gilbert White's bat was probably the common pipistrelle of Europe, a very small species. Additional notes are quoted from Daniell (later published in the *Proceedings* of the Zoological Society of London), concerning other specimens of this species kept in captivity by that gentleman. He received five from Elvetham, England, and kept them for a time on a diet of flies, but writes that his

pets were so hungry as to require more time to be expended in fly-catching than I was disposed to devote to them; and I then tried to feed them with cooked meat; but this they rejected. Raw beef was, however, eaten with avidity; and an evident preference was given to those pieces which had been moistened with water.

Daniell also tried a new and easier way of feeding his pets by attaching a slice of beef to the side of the box in which they were kept, thus attracting flies for them. This, he writes, not only spared me the trouble of feeding them, but also, by attracting the flies, afforded good sport in observing the animals obtain their own food by this new kind of bat-fowling. The weather being warm, many blue-bottles were attracted by the meat; and, on one of these approaching within range of the bats' wings, it was sure to be struck down by their action, the animal itself falling at the same instant with all its membranes expanded, cowering over the devoted fly, with its head thrust under them in order to secure its prey.

This habit of partly covering the prey with the wings may be characteristic of the pipistrelle, for I did not observe it in my Myotis. Daniell's pets died one by one, the last survivor having lived only nineteen days in captivity. He records also his experiences with captive noctule bats (*Nyctalus noctula*), a much larger and stronger species. He had five of these, one only of which was a male. This last proved "exceedingly restless and savage from the first; biting the females and breaking his teeth against the wires of the cage." He survived only three days, refusing all food; while of the females, all likewise perished after two more days, except one, which he tried with various foods and found that "she evinced a decided preference for the hearts, livers, &c. of fowls," so that she was fed chiefly on these. Large flies were always rejected, though two cockchafers were partly eaten. Her appetite was at times voracious, "the quantity eaten exceeding half an ounce, although the weight of the animal was no more than ten drachms." Finally, on June 23, after five weeks in captivity, she gave birth to a single young one, but unfortunately died the same evening. The young one, however, was still alive and was kept carefully wrapped up in flannel. It would suck milk from a sponge and "by these attentions was preserved for eight days, at the end of which period it died." Its eyes were then not yet open, and it was but scantily covered with hair. This seems to be the first experiment, if only partially successful, in the care and feeding of infant bats.

Whitaker (1905) has given an interesting account of a female noctule bat which he captured from a colony in a hollow tree in England on June 28, 1905. Two days later she gave birth to a young one. He describes her as taking a position at the top of her box so as to hang across the corner, "head down with one foot on each side," then

as soon as ever the head of the baby bat protruded, it commenced to squeak lustily. The young one was quite free in about four minutes' time, and worked its way under the shoulder of its mother, and so round on to her back, where it clung quite exposed, head downward. There was no afterbirth, and the mother . . . busied herself with washing and brushing her fur all over for a long time afterwards.

After next taking a good repast of mealworms, she washed up the young one, much as a cat would wash a kitten. The mother was "particularly tame"; he had but to open the cage any time of night or day, chirrup to her, when she would prick up her ears and come shuffling down the side of the cage to the floor and on to his hand. She would take as many mealworms as he would offer her, usually bringing her baby with her. She consumed an average of seven dozen mealworms a day, or about a quarter of an ounce of food, adding an occasional moth and a few caterpillars.

When the baby bat was eleven days old it was still quite naked and the eyes were unopened. It was at about this time that the mother escaped, leaving the young one behind. Hoping to recapture his pet, the owner left the partly opened cage outdoors, with the young one inside, and prepared to sit up all night until the old one returned for her baby. About eleven o'clock, it began to get cold and called loudly, but without result. At 2 A.M., he became sleepy and went into the house to wash his eyes in cold water; but on his return he found the baby bat gone, nor did either it or its mother appear, though he continued his vigil till daybreak.

With care, even the smaller insect-eating bats will survive in captivity for a time, but usually succumb within at most a few months, as a result, perhaps, of the lack of normal exercise, food, and quiet. The longest captivity for a small species is that recorded by Kummerlöwe (1929) of a long-eared bat (*Plecotus auritus*) of Europe, which he kept for 428 days from November 26, 1925, to January 28, 1927. In another instance, a noctule bat (*Nyctalus noctula*) lived for 373 days in captivity (Mohr,

1932). In both cases mealworms formed the staple food, with other insects (moths, beetles, flies) as occasion offered. Mathis (1929) kept some of the large mouse-eared bats (*Myotis myotis*) in Germany for three months on a diet of mealworms and flies, of which at times they would consume prodigious numbers. For though they ate on an average about twenty mealworms a day, they would, if very hungry, take as many as seventy-five or eighty at a single feeding, and in one case a famished bat consumed over one hundred. The smaller Plecotus were more easily satisfied; from eight to ten mealworms at a time seemed usually to suffice (Kummerlöwe), though Dr. Erna Mohr fed as many as eighty in a single day to a captive that lived for seventy-seven days in a glass container. Some interesting notes are contributed by Dunckner (1931) concerning a Natterer's bat — a small species of Myotis — which he kept for fifty-eight days in Hamburg. He found the weight of this species to be about eleven grams, and the amount of food it required averaged over a quarter (26 per cent) of its own weight daily, though the actual amounts eaten varied from as low as 9 per cent of its weight to occasionally as much as 52 per cent. The box in which his pet lived was covered with wire gauze and had a small opening on one side through which the bat was fed with mealworms, presented one at a time by means of a pair of small forceps. The little bat quickly learned to come to the opening for its meals, but throughout its captivity never seemed willing to feed itself from a small dish of mealworms placed on the floor of its cage, though it soon learned to lap water from a similar dish when thirsty.

This particular bat was a female taken from a cave during hibernation, on March 19. After forty-five days of solitary confinement it gave birth on May 5 to a single young one, but unfortunately both parent and young were found dead on the same day. The interesting point is, however, that the development of the young had ensued through fertilization by sperm that had remained inactive in the uterus of the mother during the winter. Pairing had probably taken place in the preceding autumn. During its captivity Dunckner found that after nearly every meal his pet would hang head downward in its cage and spend several minutes or at times as much as half an hour in combing and dressing its fur with the claws of first one, then the other hind foot. Neither light nor noise seemed to disturb it while eating, drinking, or combing. Its range of vision seemed to be limited; at least, it would take no notice of struggling mealworms offered to it, if they were held out at more than about two inches from its nose.

Most interesting is Dr. Erna Mohr's account of her captive noctules (*Nyctalus noctula*). Two females were obtained near Hamburg, Germany, on March 28 from a hibernating colony in the tower of an old church. They were kept in an empty glass aquarium, covered by netting, and soon learned to like the succulent mealworms offered them. On June 21 one of these bats gave birth to a single young, which was found dead on the floor of the cage. Next day the second female gave birth to a young bat, and on the following day its twin appeared. The babies at birth were blind and nearly naked. In about two weeks, however, their eyes opened, and by another week their milk incisors were found to have come through. When the twins were a month old one of them died. The other seemed weak, as if in need of more nourishment. This Dr. Mohr succeeded in giving it by means of an improvised nursing bottle, from which it sucked full-strength cow's milk at half-hourly intervals. The result was surprising. The baby picked up at once, and on the next day took not only its milk but the squeezed-out contents of three mealworms besides! On the next day it was given the juice of six mealworms with that of twelve added on the following day. On the tenth day the little bat took the contents of sixty-two mealworms with the addition of more solid food in the shape of whole minced mealworms! This was followed by the yolks of soft-boiled eggs and then the albumen.

By the time the youngster was two months old, it would eat whole mealworms, and at three months, when nearly full grown, its appetite had so increased that it would consume nearly one hundred in the course of a day. Unlike Dunckner's pet, this intelligent bat would come to a small dish containing these delicacies and would eat about thirty at a time, in the morning, evening, or during the day. The adults ate nearly double this number. Flies they consistently refused. No doubt the diet of the young bat was not altogether suited to its needs, for it began to develop rickets. Its forearm became curved and the fingers were incapable of opening to spread its wing. When nearly a year old, it began to lose weight and finally died at the age of 373 days. Nevertheless, this is apparently the first instance in which a baby bat of the insectivorous type has been artificially reared, though even at best it never attained more than about half the weight of its parent. All three of these bats became remarkably tame and delighted to be carried about in a pocket or under the collar of their owner's coat. Dr. Mohr presents a table of the growth rate of the fingers in the young. At birth they are relatively short, but gradually elongate, especially the third and fourth, until adult proportions are reached. The feet, on the other hand, are of nearly full size soon after birth.

The problem of feeding captive bats of the insect-eating species becomes sometimes acute if their owner must provide mealworms and other insects throughout the winter or for shorter periods. Professor William H. Gates, however, has been very successful in keeping bats of several species alive and well in his laboratory in Louisiana by feeding them with a standard mixture of bread or crackers mixed with finely chopped hard-boiled egg and moistened with a small quantity of cream cheese, buttermilk, or milk. To this may be added finely chopped meat, vegetables, banana, yeast, dry malted milk, ovaltine, or even minced nuts. All this should be so mixed that it is not moist enough to be sticky, "yet at the same time not dry, the ideal condition being a moist crumbly mash." All the species of bats he kept liked banana, while cream cheese was by far the first choice of these artificial foods. It was found, too, that honey bees, killed and cut up, when added to the food seemed to increase its palatability. All foods must be in small pieces and must be given in shallow dishes, for bats cannot easily reach into a deep dish. Water must be at hand, for bats drink freely.

Professor Gates (1936) found that of half a dozen native species which he kept, most of the vespertilionids readily adapted themselves to these artificial conditions, but the free-tailed bats (*Tadarida cynocephala*) proved untamable and failed to thrive under restraint. They refused to eat, would drink little, and always resented handling.

Pet bats are really little more than captives that look upon their keepers as the source of supplies, for there is not much evidence of that affection and reciprocal understanding we look for in our dogs. Nevertheless, they lose any fear of their admirers and afford much entertainment, as Gilbert White found. Troughton (1931) gives an interesting account of a tame lobe-lipped bat (*Chalinolobus gouldi*), which lived a contented life for several weeks in the room of a house in the Blue Mountains of New South Wales. The late Lady Cullen, whose pet it was, recounts the following story of it. She supposes that when it was first brought to her, it had been disturbed during hibernation and picked up from the floor.

After soothing it [she writes] I let it go and it flew about the room, finally hanging upside down on the bricks by the mantelpiece. At first it flew away when I went near, but soon returned, and when it got used to my voice it took flies and a moth from my hand. It camped in the same place for a fortnight, eating readily from my hand, and finally allowing itself to be picked up. It soon became a great pet, showing a surprising amount of intelligence. It only recognized my hand and that of one other person, but would have nothing to do with strangers. When it was running about the floor and I put my hand down as it passed, it would first sniff at my fingers then quickly scramble into my hand, moving its head about and pushing its nose between my fingers looking for food. . . . I found it would greedily eat the small white grubs out of wood, beginning at the end opposite the head. It usually ate five, from half to an inch in length, then it would sleep from four to ten days. After eating it would lick its wings, clean its fur, and go to sleep in my hand. It no longer lived by the fireplace, but had moved to the window side of a curtain, a very cold place; it found its way there each night from where I had placed it when I went to bed. It also lapped water from a spoon. . . . All the manipulation when eating a moth and discarding the wings was done entirely by the lips and tongue, not helped by the thumbs. . . . I had a partly tamed bat when I was a girl; I never handled it but it lived in my room and always came when I called it, and fluttered close to my face when I went into my room at dusk, creating a good deal of interest.

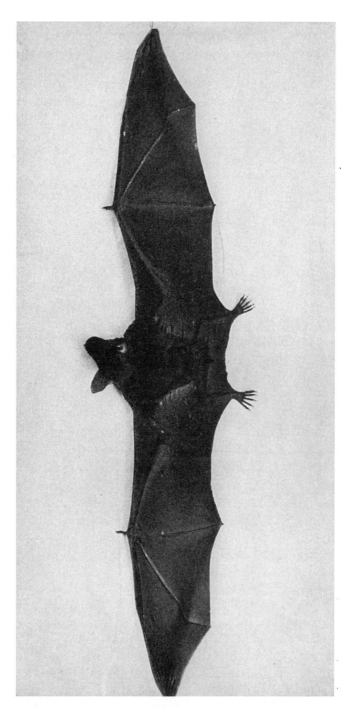

Fig. 9—A spear-nosed bat (*Phyllostomus hastatus panamensis*) from a fresh specimen spread out to show its seventeen-inch stretch of wing, the short stumpy tail, and short interfemoral membrane. Panama. Courtesy of Professor W. H. Weston, phot. This bat is one of the largest American species.

The smaller bats seldom live long in captivity, but in a wild state no doubt may reach an age of several years. The only positive data at hand relate to the common pipistrelle of eastern United States, of which four were banded by Dr. Arthur A. Allen in New York State and recaptured three years later. Some of the large fruit bats of the Old World attain a ripe old age as captives in zoological gardens. Major Stanley S. Flower (1931) reports that one lived in the London Gardens for seventeen years and two months, in this case the large Indian flying fox, *Pteropus giganteus*. The Australian species, *P. poliocephalus*, has also been kept for a shorter period there, after having survived the journey from the Antipodes. A still greater age is recorded for the smaller rousette bat, *Rousettus leachi*, of southern Africa, which in the Gizeh Zoological Gardens near Cairo, Egypt, had attained nineteen years and nine months, as noted by Major Flower, once the director of that institution. A colony of rousettes, probably again *R. leachi*, has been kept in the London Gardens for many years beginning in 1875, and they have bred there regularly. The secretary, P. L. Sclater, annually noted in his reports the birth of young in every month of the year, especially in April, May, and June. Other European zoos, as at Hamburg and elsewhere in Germany, have kept and bred fruit bats. Of one species, *Pteropus whitmeei*, of Samoa, Whitmee (1874) wrote that the natives there tame it, and it never leaves their houses; but he found that one he reared from a very youthful stage and an adult that he kept for two or three months were always very shy and rather savage.

Few attempts have been made to keep in captivity the Central and South American leaf-nosed bats, of the family Phyllostomidae. This group is of especial interest, since it includes both large and small species, some of them probably almost wholly insectivorous, while others show all the transitional stages, at least in tooth structure, from that type to a frugivorous one. Others again, the largest members of the family, are to a great extent carnivorous, perhaps because, like other larger predators, they require greater amounts of food at a time. This need has no doubt led to their preying on small birds and

mice, as well as on other and lesser species of bats. One of
these, the large spear-nosed bat (*Phyllostomus hastatus panamensis*), has been successfully maintained in a captive state by
Major Lawrence H. Dunn in Panama, while investigating certain tropical diseases. He found (1933) that the bats readily
responded to captivity and at first fed freely on ripe bananas
with an occasional bit of meat. Their strong sharp teeth are
well suited for a flesh diet, which he finally tested by trying
one of his bats with various small animals. He found that it
would kill and eat smaller bats and birds, as well as house
mice, when introduced alive into its cage, devouring them almost
completely except for the feathers of the birds, the tails of the
mice, and the feet and membranes of the bats, which were
usually rejected, as well as other less edible portions. Large
cockroaches, too, proved very acceptable. No doubt similar
food is taken in a wild state. This particular bat survived in
the narrow confines of its cage for just twenty-four weeks. It
conclusively showed its preference for a meat diet, but would
also take ripe banana when other food was unavailable.

A related genus, Vampyrus, the largest American bat, has
also proved to be a hunter, feeding in part at least upon small
rodents and birds, thus recalling similar habits in the false
vampires of India. The habits of this rather uncommon species
of our tropics have only lately become better known through
the investigations of Dr. R. L. Ditmars (1935), who found that
they were partial to the great hollow trunks of the giant ceiba
trees in the forests of Trinidad. By following this clue, he succeeded in bringing back four alive to the New York Zoological
Gardens, where for the first time living specimens have been
exhibited. These, he writes, have become very tame.

But of all the bats, the strangest in point of diet is the true
vampire of the American tropics, which feeds exclusively on the
blood of other animals. These it approaches at night when they
are quiet, either alighting directly on them or landing near by
on the ground and crawling up close enough to make a quick
gouging bite with its lancet-like incisor and canine teeth, then
licking up the blood that wells from the wound. The first suc-

cessful attempt at keeping this bat alive in captivity is recounted by Dr. Herbert C. Clark and Dr. Lawrence H. Dunn, in connection with their study of certain diseases of horses and cattle in Panama. They succeeded in keeping vampires for months on a diet of blood obtained at a local slaughterhouse and defibrinated to prevent clotting. The bats, though shy at first, eventually became accustomed to persons standing quietly near their enclosure and would feed from a small dish until their stomachs bulged. In his recent paper with A. M. Greenhall, Dr. Ditmars has recounted his own experiences in maintaining one of these bats alive at the New York Zoological Gardens, in the same way. This bat became so tame that it allowed itself to be photographed while feeding or coming toward its dish. Its gait is most peculiar for a bat, for its stands high on its hind legs with the long thumbs turned outward, supporting the fore end of the body.

CHAPTER V

BATS AS FOOD

NOTWITHSTANDING that the Mosaic law as laid down in Deuter-
onomy (xiv: 18) forbade the eating of bats by the Hebrews,
as being "unclean" birds, they are nevertheless much relished
by some of the Eastern and African peoples. For although the
lesser insectivorous species may be less palatable or too small
to offer much in the way of sustenance for adults, some even
of these find favor among the children of African natives. One
common species in particular, the little pipistrelle that hides
by day under the thatch of the low village roofs, is often sought
out by the youngsters, who go about from house to house lift-
ing up the thatch here and there to discover the sleepy morsels,
and roast and eat them as tidbits (Chapin). There is no reason,
however, why some of the larger kinds of fruit bats, whose diet
is largely fruit juices, buds, and flowers, should not be altogether
suitable for food when once the prejudice against their strange
appearance is overcome. Indeed, among many Eastern races
they have been an article of diet since ancient times. Thus
Strabo, the Greek geographer, wrote that in Borsippa, a city of
Babylon in Mesopotamia, situated in the bend of the Euphrates,
there are great multitudes of bats far larger than those known
to the Mediterranean nations, and these served the inhabitants
as food. Scaliger, a writer of the Middle Ages, tells that the
large bats which occur abundantly in the Isle of Catigan in
the South Sea are eaten by the natives, and hearty meat they
must have been if one were to believe his statement that "they
are big as eagles and taste like chickens" (Aldrovandus, 1681).

The bats eaten by the Babylonians were most likely one of
the smaller fruit-eating species, probably one of the rousettes
(Rousettus), but in India it was the larger flying fox (*Pteropus
giganteus*), a species that ranges westward to the Indian penin-

sula. Of this large bat, Tennent (1861) writes that it is killed
by the natives of Ceylon for the sake of its flesh, which, as he
was told by a gentleman who had eaten it, resembles that of
the hare. He adds that in western India the native Portuguese
of Goa eat the flying fox and pronounce it delicate and far
from disagreeable in flavor. This testimony is confirmed by
Hutton (1872), who says that "notwithstanding their strong
disagreeable odour and forbidding appearance, the Kanjars, or
gipsies, residing in the neighbourhood used to catch them and
eat them when other food was scarce or dear." Colonel Sykes
of India fame, mentions that in the Mahratta country, where it
is called *warbagool*, it is eaten by the lower class of native
Portuguese, and he himself had tried them and could testify
to their savoriness. In parts of Ceylon, writes Wroughton
(1915b), the flying foxes sometimes occur in thousands, "abso-
lutely covering the trees they are feeding on and making an
astonishing noise with their wings, as, when frightened, they
rise in black clouds in the air. They have locally an edible
value and sell for as much as 35 cents [Indian] apiece." Again,
Dodsworth (1914) mentions that in the Calcutta bird and animal market he saw several large cages filled with these great
bats, which are bought in numbers by the Chinese, who esteem
them a great delicacy. The Latin name given a related species
of the East Indies by Geoffroy was *Pteropus edulis*, in reference
to their use as food.

Elsewhere, within the range of the flying fox, of which there
are various species, it is frequently eaten by the native peoples.
The Malay natives of Borneo are not at all averse to "bat pie"
(Banks, 1931), and related large species are relished by the
natives in Java and the Philippines. When fat and in good condition, one of these bats will weigh two pounds or more. In
Samoa the *manu lagi* or "animal of the heavens," as the Samoans
call it, is frequently killed and eaten when it comes to raid the
breadfruit trees about the villages. They are taken by fixing a
prickly bush to a long bamboo pole, and by striking a bat with
this as it flies past, its wings become entangled. The people
declare that they are far preferable to fowl, a statement which,

if the Samoan fowl is anything like as well put together as some of the African ones I have eaten, I can very readily believe. In the Seychelles Islands where, curiously enough, *Pteropus edwardsii* occurs, although absent from the neighboring mainland of Africa, the Creole inhabitants esteem it a favorite food. "When skinned within a few minutes after death, and roasted the same day, the flesh, though dark, is very good" (E. P. Wright, 1868).

In parts of eastern Australia the native blacks welcome the appearance of the flying foxes, of which some three or four species make periodic visitations to certain north and east coast districts when the Port Moreton figs are ripe or other small fruits are plentiful. At such times the bats often establish large temporary roosts or "camps," perhaps in a tea-tree swamp or on an island in a stream. Formerly, at least, these great congregations of bats were eagerly sought out and the animals killed in quantities by the blacks, who would light smoke fires under the roost trees to stupefy them and then knock them down with boomerangs or other missiles. The fresh meat is a great boon to the coastal tribes, who thus eke out their slender fare and secure an acceptable change from a diet largely of fish. In a famous Australian cookbook is a recipe for the proper cooking of these animals to form a dish suitable for a white man's palate. Its author, Mrs. Lance Rawson, took the idea in part from the natives, and I am indebted to Mr. W. H. Ifould, of the Public Library of New South Wales, for a transcription of her rule. She writes:

Flying Foxes are excellent eating, though anything but agreeable creatures to touch, or indeed to have anything to do with on account of the strong unpleasant smell they have, but once get rid of the wings and skin and you will hardly know the flesh from pork. . . . I cut them up, along with an onion, and seasoned with all sorts of herbs, and stewed them for a couple of hours, then turned them into a pie dish and covered with a good paste. Curried, you would not know Flying Fox from pork, indeed the flesh when they are in season very much resembles sucking pig. I don't think they are good except in the fruit season, as when there is no fruit they live on scrub berries and leaves, which give them an unpleasant flavour. The Kanakas told me this, and I afterward proved it myself, for when there was little or no good fruit the foxes were thin and tough, indeed quite uneatable.

FIG. 10—Part of a great roost or "camp" of the gray-headed fruit bat or flying fox (*Pteropus poliocephalus*) in Queensland. The slender trees are bent with the weight of the festoons of bats. Courtesy of Mr. Otho Webb, phot.

In his description of China, published in 1738, Du Halde, writing of the animals of Shensi Province, includes "a singular species of Bats as big as Hens, which the *Chinese* prefer to the nicest Pullets," but Shensi is too far north for flying foxes, so that possibly one of the larger horseshoe bats is intended.

In Africa, where some of the lesser sizes of fruit bats occur, such as the genera Epomophorus and Rousettus, these are sometimes added to the little black boiling pots of the natives to eke out a slender fare. Arthur Loveridge recounts enlisting the help of some tribesmen in Tanganyika in procuring specimens of the latter genus. The native guide led the way for several hundred yards through dripping rain forest and at length came out at a gorge, down which tumbled a cascade with a roar that nearly drowned out their voices. Here was a cavern, low at the entrance but rising to a vaulted roof inside. Two of the men were specialists in bat catching. They asked that no lamp be lighted lest it disturb the quarry and, disappearing into the gloom, presently returned with ten of these large bats that they had fished out from crannies and cracks among the rocks of the cave walls. Asked the reason for their proficiency, they replied evasively that they wanted the skins for making caps! But this, it seemed, was a thorough falsehood, the real reason being, as one of Loveridge's men afterward informed him, that they were accustomed to hunt the creatures for food but were ashamed to admit it. Perhaps, too, there were more subtle reasons in the nature of a *tabu* that forbade their revealing the true purpose.

Rousette bats (*R. lanosus kempi*) abound in some of the large caverns on Mount Elgon, Kenya Colony, East Africa, and Granvik (1924) records that while he was there he found the nomadic forest-living natives of the Wandorobo tribe living "to a great extent on these Fruit-bats" during their occasional sojourns in the caves.

In Liberia, where the meat-hungry native will eat almost any sort of animal food, my native "boy" once begged for the bodies of four large straw-colored fruit bats (*Eidolon stramineum*), the skins of which I was preparing as specimens. They looked none too tempting as morsels, but I gladly complied with his wish. Next morning on my inquiring how they had tasted — if they were "good chop" (food) — he smiled sheepishly and replied, "Dey verra hard, sir," evidently having found them more "chewy" than he had anticipated! Perhaps they should have been cooked in some better way. At all events, bats are extensively eaten by various Negro tribes. In the native markets of Old Calabar, West Africa, A. Murray (1869) observed that the bodies of some large species of fruit bat were regularly offered for sale, all "ready trussed," and evidently a recognized form of delicacy.

The bat caves of the Akwa Yafe River, in West Africa, are said by Amaury Talbot (writing in the *Wide World Magazine*) to be recognized as the property of the Ododop people, who value them highly for their supply of vast numbers of bats, which they regard as a delicacy. What kind of bats these were does not appear, but evidently they were some small species. The caves are less than a mile from the river bank and are reached by a path through the bush, leading to a little dell at the bottom of which is the entrance. Just beyond the mouth of the cavern two underground streams join and flow away into the blackness, while within the extensive tunnels the shrill voices of the bats sound above the rush of the waters. The method of capturing them is as follows. At each known entrance of the cave, men armed with long sticks are stationed to knock down the bats that come out while the principal hunters make their way inside, accompanied by lantern-bearers and carrying triangular nets fastened at the ends of long poles. With these they sweep the roofs, enmeshing hundreds of the dusky denizens and driving others to the entrances.

Apparently the native peoples of tropical America do not make much use of bats as food, although several of the larger species, as the fruit-eating Artibeus and related types might be palatable. Yet the only report I have found of their being eaten is in an old work compiled by several authors, the *Navigatio Orientalis*, in which one of the writers tells that in the Isle of St. John (the name given by Columbus to Puerto Rico) bats were brought to the explorers, not only fit to eat but most acceptable in taste and plumpness. It is added that the hair is first removed by scalding as we do with the feathers of a fowl, and the flesh is then left all white.

After all, there may be many worse things to eat than a good "bat pie."

## CHAPTER VI

## WHERE BATS HIDE

*Lucanius Nictipotum fluvium appellari a Vespertilionibus fingit, eumque praeterlabi insulam somni, quae sola has aves procreat, et circa eum undique circumjacere sylvam cujus arbores sint papaveres, et procera, et mandragorae, in quibus illae aves sederant. — Aldrovandus, 1681.*

In his volume on ornithology old Aldrovandus in the quotation above tells of a Latin author, Lucanius, who described the river Nyctipotus (the Waters of Night), which flows past the Isle of Sleep and takes its name from the bats, its only inhabitants. On every side it is surrounded by a vast forest of tall trees like poppies and mandrakes, themselves signifying sleep and mystery, wherein the bats settle for rest. Yet perhaps the description is not altogether fanciful, but may have had its origin in some traveler's tale of a secluded refuge such as the large fruit bats often occupy for their daytime roost. A wooded island in the midst of some large stream or at no great distance offshore is often selected as a roosting place by the flying foxes (Pteropus) in the Old World tropics, where in comparative security they pass the day undisturbed. Such a river-island I have seen in eastern Australia, where numbers of the large gray-headed species had taken refuge for a short season, and again, in Liberia, a "bat island" was described to me, two days' journey from the coast up the St. Paul River, where multitudes of large bats, perhaps the hammer-headed or the straw-colored species, hung by day in the partly bare tree tops. Several writers have described the large colonies of Pteropus that inhabit by day certain small islands off the coasts of Ceylon or of Malaysia, whence the bats would set forth at nightfall for their feeding grounds on the adjacent mainland. Willey (1904) speaks of the great flights of gray crows in Ceylon that every evening pass out to Barberyn Island, a quarter of a mile from the main shore, to roost, while at the same time a stream of flying foxes, which had roosted there all day in the tops of the tall *jak* trees, flew in the opposite direction to feed during the night on the mainland. In the early morning the companies of crows and bats pass again in reverse order, the crows to forage on the land, the bats to sleep on the island.

Bats, being nocturnal creatures and, for the most part, relatively defenseless, usually hide away during the daylight hours where they may be secure from enemies and disturbance. To many species comparative darkness is then essential, but others seem to be troubled little or none by daylight. The retreats chosen are of great variety and often more or less characteristic of the particular kind of bat. So, too, are the sleeping postures and social relations, whether solitary or in groups, or even in large masses.

Among the family of fruit bats (Pteropidae) the large flying foxes (Pteropus) apparently without exception spend the day suspended from the upper branches of trees in companies, often of large size. In Australia four species are common, roosting in gatherings often acres in extent, known locally as "camps," where tall slender tea-trees or mangroves rise from some large and almost impenetrable swamp. In India the giant flying fox (*P. giganteus*) selects the upper part of some large single tree or clump of trees, often in the depths of a forest or, if undisturbed, in the close proximity of a village. Such roosts may be frequented year after year until the upper branches become quite bare, owing to the damage to young shoots and leaves as the bats alight. These roosts are well described by Tickell (1842), Tennent (1861), and McCann (1934), and may number many hundreds of individuals. There is much commotion in the early morning hours when the bats come in, with constant quarreling and bickering as newcomers attempt to alight and fight for places. Even during the hours of mid-forenoon, or occasionally at other times of day, there is more or less moving about, until one wonders if they secure any sleep at all. At length, however, most of them settle down, hanging by both legs or by one, and with heads bent against their breasts and partly covered by the voluminous wings folded across the stomach, they nap unconcernedly in the full glare of the sun, looking like so many ripe fruits. A contrast is found in the curious tube-nosed fruit bat, Nyctimene, which inclines to be solitary, hanging when at rest against a moss-covered trunk of a forest tree. It has a curious pattern of small yellow dots on the skin of the forearm and wing membranes, which may help to break up its outlines and so be of protective value when the bat is at rest. Another genus, Dobsonia, instead of having a variegated pattern with a contrasting reddish or yellow mantle as do most of the Pteropi, is uniformly dark, and the naked wing membranes meet in the middle of the back. Its roosting habits are in accordance with this type of coloring, for it frequents caves by day.

A fairly general rule seems to be that tree-living species are somewhat brighter colored or marked with reddish or orange, and may have contrasting white markings or lines on the head or the body, which to some extent break up their general outline, thus perhaps offering protection when the bats are at rest. Among the smaller fruit bats that roost in foliage, the straw-colored bat (Eidolon) has yellowish fur, and the epaulette bats of Africa are somewhat russet or tawny, the males with a conspicuous pair of white shoulder tufts, and both sexes with smaller white marks about the ever-moving ears. I once came upon a company of these in eastern Africa, hanging along the length of the midrib of a sago palm above a small stream, sheltered by the overhanging fronds. Another genus of this group, the rousette bats (Rousettus), is wholly dark sooty in coloring in its various species, all of which are cave-dwellers. The flower-feeding genus Eonycteris, of the Orient, is also cave-dwelling by day. It is a curious correlation that these genera, in which there is no need for protecting the face from sunlight, have the terminal joints of the wings folded back under the long bones of the hand, while in the Pteropi and the epaulette bats, which hang up in trees, these joints do not tuck away in this manner, but are kept extended and turned toward the center line of the chest so that the wings may cover the head and breast of the bats as they hang sleeping in the open. A favorite roosting place of the straw-colored bat is among the faded and drooping fronds at the summit of a palm, among which they cluster closely by day. At Lahej, Arabia, Percival and Dodson found many thus ensconced in groups of 16 to 50 in the highest palms of a date plantation, from which, after they were once settled, it was difficult to disturb them. In the early mornings, however, they were a considerable time in getting properly adjusted, advertising their presence with much squeaking and moving about. Many of the smaller fruit bats of this family are more or less solitary, hanging by day in dense foliage, so that they are seldom seen and hard to find, a fact which no doubt accounts in some measure for their comparative rarity in collections (Megaloglossus and Plerotes in Africa, Macroglossus and Syconycteris in the Orient).

Among the smaller bats of the suborder Microchiroptera, the family of mouse-tailed bats (Rhinopomidae), with a nearly complete second finger and long mouse-like tail, is somewhat primitive in structure, as well as in its habit of resting, often clinging by all four feet (claws and thumbs) from the ceiling of a cave, a method perhaps less advanced than in those species that hang from the hind toes alone. A common small species that frequents the pyramids of Egypt I once found in a long-deserted chamber in the interior of one of these, hanging upside down from the roof like spiders. Others, however, sought the shelter of narrow fissures in the rock at the far end of a passage, well underground. Lacking rock fissures or caves, these bats take up their abode in the crevices of buildings or old ruins. The authors above mentioned found them in Arabia occupying the towers of native villages in company with a small species of hollow-faced bat (Nycteris). In the sultan's "palace" at Lahej, the passages leading to his private apartments were haunted by hundreds of these bats, so that the deposit of their droppings made an almost unbearable stench. The roofs of the passages are built of sticks laid across from wall to wall, and the bats crawl in between these, so that it is difficult to get at them. Another family that retains certain primitive features of structure, the sheath-tailed bats (Emballonuridae), likewise shows in some species the habit of hanging by "all fours" when at rest, proving that they have not altogether lost the footlike use of the fore limb. Of these, the large species of the genus Taphozous hide in the fissures and cracks of rocks or even in rock piles, as well as in hollow trees, or less often in houses. This power gives them a ready ability to move about on a surface in any direction, so that when suddenly brought to light they will scuttle away, often running rapidly in a sidewise direction like so many crabs. Phillips (1922), writing of the black-bearded species in Ceylon, says, however, that they often hide singly or in pairs in the crowns of cocoanut palms, choosing one with dead fronds hanging down, and creeping in behind a stem or clinging to the trunk with thumbs and hind claws, rather than hanging by the hind feet alone. Blyth (1844) had a number in India that he captured in a nook between a pillar and the adjacent wall. When he put them in a box, they "clung with perfect facility to the smooth mahogany back of a cage into which they were put, hitching their claws into the minute pores of the wood and creeping upon it in a manner that was surprising." The large white-bellied species (*Taphozous mauritianus*) of Africa is described by Lang and Chapin (1917) in the Congo as not at all partial to dark places, but coming freely about the houses and preferring to cling along the outer side of brick walls just below the thatched roof. Sometimes as many as a dozen could be seen along such a wall, each more or less by itself, ready at any time of day to shift nervously sidewise or climb to the top of the wall if a person passed underneath. A second species, on the other hand, *T. sudani*, preferred the shelter of a dark rock fissure in the side of a steep hill, while a third, of a related genus, *Saccolaimus peli*, a large brown bat, characteristically selects hollow trees.

The Old World horseshoe bats of the families Rhinolophidae and Hipposideridae are for the most part cave-dwellers, but some of the species both large and small will take up residence in unused darkened rooms of houses or, as in Europe, in old castles, hanging from the roof or walls. Some are solitary, living singly or a pair together, while others are highly social, congregating in large colonies. An Indian species, *Hipposideros fulvus*, is often found in the burrows of the large crested porcupine (Wroughton, 1915), and a similar habit has been recorded by Loveridge (1923) for one of the hollow-faced bats (*Nycteris luteola*) in Tanganyika Territory, eastern Africa. He had seven brought in to him once by a boy who had captured them in an occupied burrow. Other species of this family (Nycteridae) often congregate in cavities within the trunk of hollow standing trees, but in the West African forests one of the larger species (*Nycteris arge*), of solitary habits, is partial to the tunnel-like interior of old fallen trees. Several times in Liberia I found such prostrate forest giants inhabited by a single bat of this species. Such a tree that I visited on several occasions was the regular haunt of one of these bats, but though I made various attempts to capture it, I always found it alert and ready to dash out from the dark interior before I had crawled in a dozen feet. Percival and Dodson in Arabia found a small species of the same genus frequenting village towers in company with the mouse-tailed bats. Writing of Nyasaland, Wood (in Kershaw, 1922a) says that bats of this genus are chiefly found in the hollows of large forest trees, particularly of one known as "njale," a species of Sterculia, which nearly always becomes completely hollow for the whole length of its trunk when old. He had never examined one without finding numbers of Nycteris inside, and they seem to be very common. Curiously, however, he never found them in hollow palms, though he had examined hundreds, "possibly because the latter are almost always tenanted by numbers" of other bats, particularly Scotophilus and Mops.

In the family Vespertilionidae, containing the common small bats of the north temperate region, as well as some tropical species, there is wide variation in the choice of resting places. Some are tree-dwellers, retaining perhaps a primitive habit, and in these there is sometimes bright or contrasting color, as in the red bat and the hoary bat of the Americas, with frosted reddish or buffy fur, and contrasted white shoulder spot. A related genus of the Old World, Scotomanes, is bright orange buff with irregular white markings. This type of coloring often has a protective value, giving the bat hanging quietly at rest the appearance of a withered leaf. An interesting genus of this family, Kerivoula, includes a number of species of small bats which together comprise a separate subfamily, Kerivoulinae. They are all, apparently, of rather solitary habits, most of them forest-dwelling and confined to the Old World tropics. The most beautiful is *K. picta*, the painted bat, with bright orange fur and black wings and contrasted orange areas along the fingers. It is said to hang frequently among the withered leaves of vines, simulating their appearance closely, or, as in Ceylon, it may be found among the dry hanging fronds of a plantain or among dead leaves of other kinds. Major S. S. Flower mentions obtaining one in Siam that was found "in the flower of the Calla lily." Some of the African species are dull colored, olive brown, in some mixed with shiny gray hairs simulating a tuft of moss. They live singly or in pairs in thick jungle, darting out like large moths when disturbed, to take refuge in some other thick clump of leaves.

A very remarkable habit found in some of these bats is the selection of the disused nests of birds as roosting places. This was first discovered by John Kirk in 1864, who, while examining the hanging, ball-shaped nests of a colony of weaverbirds in Zululand, South Africa, found several small bats tucked away singly or in pairs in a few of the nests. The weaver was probably the common yellow-and-black spectacled weaver (*Hyphanturgus ocularis*), which breeds in large colonies over parts of the more open country of southeastern Africa and constructs substantial globular nests well woven of strands of palm-leaf or other fibers, with an entrance hole on one side near the upper part so arranged as to be partly sheltered by the over-hang. These nests are strong enough to withstand the elements for more than one season and may be repaired by the birds for use in a later nesting period. Kirk's observation was substantiated a few years since by Mr. Austin Roberts, who found two of these little bats in a nest of this weaver, by the White Umfolosi River, in the Transvaal. Kirk described his bats as a new species, which he called *Nycticejus nidicola*, but they prove to belong to the genus *Kerivoula*, while those found by Roberts are an allied race (*Kerivoula nidicola zuluensis*). The latter writer had the further good fortune to find a similar curious roosting habit in another species of the genus, *Kerivoula lanosa lucia*, in northeastern Zululand. In this case, however, the small covered nest of a sunbird was the shelter selected. As he was examining this disused nest, a mud wasp flew out, and on opening the structure, he found it half filled with the wasp's nest. Noticing hair beneath this, he examined further and found two tiny young bats, the mother of which was discovered hiding in the upper half of the nest among its fibrous material. Here, then, are bird's-nest roosting habits in two different species of Kerivoula, each of which selects a different type of nest for its use.

These discoveries make it seem very probable that a long overlooked account by the explorer Heuglin (1877) refers to yet another species of this genus of bats, and its habit of utilizing weaverbird nests for a roost. He collected three specimens from the hanging nest of a weaver in Ethiopia and, deciding that they represented a new species, named them *Nycticejus eriophorus*, in reference to their characteristically cottony and crinkled fur. This bat has never since been taken, unless it be the same as *Kerivoula harringtoni*, described in recent years from Ethiopia.

How similar habits may develop in a parallel way is illustrated by the fact that a small species of Australian bat is known to utilize the old nests of both the white-browed and the yellow-throated scrub-wrens (*Sericornis*). Thus in one case Mr. A. F. Bassett Hull, while examining a nest of the former at Ourimbah, New South Wales, found it to contain five small bats which flew out when disturbed. On another occasion Mr. J. S. P. Ramsay in the same region disturbed several small bats from a nest of the latter bird. In neither case was the identity of the bats made out, but since *Kerivoula* is unknown from Australia, they were perhaps one of the little pipistrelles (Le Souef, Burrill, and Troughton, 1926).

Another bat with special roosting habits is the shagreened

bat, *Rhinopterus floweri*, which is found in the drier portions of eastern Africa and is peculiar in having the backs of the forearms and legs covered with little roughened raised areas, giving it a scabby look. Its special habits may account for its rarity in collections, for De Winton (1901) found it in the

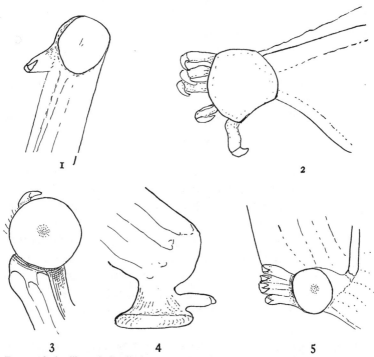

FIG. 11—Sucker-like pads for clinging to smooth surfaces. 1, pad at the wrist, and 2, pad on the sole of the foot of the bamboo bat (*Tylonycteris pachypus*) of southeastern Asia; 3, the large sucker at the wrist; 4, a side view to show its stem; 5, the smaller sessile sucker on the sole of the foot in the disk-winged bat (*Thyroptera albiventer*) of tropical South America. Enlarged.

Sudan, hiding by day "in the acacia thickets low down near the roots of the trees. At dusk it crawls up the branches and takes flight, uttering a very characteristic squeak, which it continues to make on the wing."

One of the very smallest bats is *Tylonycteris pachypus* of the East Indies and the tropical parts of India and the Malayan peninsula. Its favorite resting place by day seems to be within the hollow joint of a bamboo stem, to which access is obtained often by a mere crack in a broken culm. For such a narrow entrance this bat is well adapted, for its skull is remarkably flattened. The feet, too, have the soles modified to form a suction pad (see figure) enabling the bat to cling to a smooth surface, such as that of bamboo. A nearly similar, though less developed, suction pad is formed by the sole of the hind foot in the small brown pipistrelle of eastern Africa (*Pipistrellus nana*), whose favorite roosting place is the central rolled-up leaf of a banana plant, to the smooth sides of which this modification of the foot may help it to cling. Of course the frond soon grows larger and expands, so that the bats have to change leaves at frequent intervals. The most remarkable of such structures is found in the genus Thyroptera of tropical America, in which there is a round sucking disk with a little stem, beneath each wrist and a smaller disk on the sole of the foot. By means of these it can easily cling to a polished surface, and is at times found in the rolled fronds of bananas or in curled large leaves. Dunn records that the sucking power of a single disk was sufficient to support the entire weight of a dead specimen.

In Ceylon the small olive-brown fruit bats (*Cynopterus brachyotis ceylonensis*) show a decided preference for the talipot palm as a roost, for above all places they like to spend the day hanging in the folded umbrella-like leaves of this palm. Usually only small companies of six to a dozen live in any one palm or group of them. They hang singly or two may share a frond, suspended from the midrib by one foot with the wings wrapped about the body. The old males especially seem to be solitary, each keeping to his own tree. When talipot palms are not available, this bat may harbor in thick palmyra or arecanut palms or, rarely, in hollow trees. Phillips (1924), who made these observations, adds that in the Passara district of Uva small companies of these bats may at times be found inside the large hanging fruit clusters of the kitul palm, "having bitten off the centre 'seed strings,' to leave a hollow into which they can disappear." No other bat of the Old World is known to make a house for itself in this way. Unlike many mammals, bats make no nests either for their own shelter or for their young, although one occasionally meets with this belief. Indeed, one author (Daly, 1888) has described supposed "bats' nests" made of moss, found in a cave in Borneo, where thousands of free-tailed bats (Chaerephon) roosted; but these nests were evidently built by birds, probably by the small swifts that inhabited the cave with the bats. Nevertheless, two species of South American leaf-nosed bats (Phyllostomidae) have lately been shown to prepare a daytime shelter for themselves by biting partly through large leaves or fronds so that the terminal half bends down to form a peak, beneath which they may rest secure from sun and rain. This remarkable habit was first brought to the attention of naturalists in 1932 by Barbour, in the case of *Uroderma bilobatum*, a small fruit-eating species.

At various places about Ancon, in the Canal Zone, the large fanlike fronds of the introduced palm, Prichardia, were found cut nearly through with a line of holes across the pleated surface, causing the terminal part to bend downward at an angle, in the peak of which the bats took shelter by day. In one case as many as ten of these cut fronds were found on a single tree. The line of perforations may run nearly transversely across the blade, or it may be slightly concave or convex, or even be V-shaped, with the point at the midrib. A number of the bats were collected from these shelters, and all proved to be of the same species, the yellow-eared bat (*Uroderma bilobatum*), but the males showed a tendency to roost singly, each with a whole leaf to himself, while the females with their young clustered in small groups. The bats were easily disturbed by day, flying swiftly and unerringly to other palms with cut fronds, as if familiar with their locations and used to shifting from one to another. All attempts to watch them at work resulted in failure, but in order to gain some idea of their manner of cutting the fronds, all those so treated were removed from several palms by day, and in one case a fresh cutting was found next morning in one of the remaining fronds, evidently made during the night; a single bat was hanging beneath the sheltering blade. As Dr. Barbour remarks, this is evidently a new habit insofar as the introduced palm is concerned, but it is quite possible, as

FIG. 12—A bats' penthouse. The two fronds in the lower right-hand part of the palm have been partly cut across by the yellow-eared bat (*Uroderma bilobatum*), so that the end of the blades hangs down to form a shelter, in the peak of which the bats rest by day. Canal Zone. Courtesy of Dr. Thomas Barbour.

A

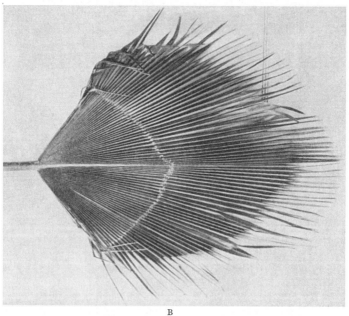

B

FIG. 13—Details of the bats' penthouse. A palm frond cut by the yellow-eared bat (*Uroderma bilobatum*), so that the terminal part hangs down to form a sheltered peak. Canal Zone. Courtesy of Dr. Thomas Barbour.

A. The frond in natural position.
B. The frond spread out to show the line of cuts made by the bats across the plaits.

he himself suggests, that these bats in other cases may habitually make use of other kinds of large leaves, and in a later note
he quotes the observation of Dr. Herbert C. Clark, who found
a young frond of a coco palm similarly cut. Goldman had previously recorded that they may be found by day hiding under
the shelter of bent palm fronds of other species, in the forest,
but if these had been cut by the bats to cause bending, he at
least had not noticed it. Coincidentally with Dr. Barbour's note
appeared one by Dr. Frank M. Chapman (1932) reporting an
almost identical habit in the case of an allied species, *Artibeus
watsoni*, a small fruit bat with two whitish stripes on each side
of the head. On Barro Colorado Island, Canal Zone, he found
the fronds of a native species of palm cut in a very similar way,
so that the end of the blade hung down to form a penthouse
shelter beneath which the bats depended, protected against
the sun and rain. Apparently there has been little previous
record of the whereabouts of these small fruit bats during daytime hours, but Van Tyne found that a very similar species in
Honduras was a forest-dweller, for although it was previously
known from very few specimens, he succeeded in obtaining a
number by stretching a bird-net across openings in forest
growth. In Panama, Goldman records obtaining a specimen of
*A. watsoni* that was hanging by day from the under side of a
banana leaf, but in this case there was apparently no attempt at
altering the shelter, perhaps because the mature banana leaf
naturally bends downward.

Except for these, I know of no other instances in which bats
make over their natural shelter for greater protection. Some
few species, however, are quick to adapt themselves to man-
made structures and readily take up their abode in houses.
Such are usually somewhat social species that form larger or
smaller colonies, occupying the interspaces between the roof or
walls and the outer sheathing of houses, and thus gaining for
themselves the name of "house bats." They usually obtain
access to their retreats through narrow cracks and hence are
often difficult to get at and not easily dislodged. In the course
of time their accumulated droppings develop a disagreeable

pungent odor, while some species, especially the free-tailed bats, by their constant scrambling and squeaking, may become a source of positive annoyance to the human occupants. In New England and in other parts of temperate North America the common little brown bat (*Myotis lucifugus*) frequently forms such colonies. These may be behind the closed blinds of some disused room or inside the walls. Occasionally a group will be found in a darkened garret, hanging behind a brick chimney or under the eaves. I have seen such a colony in the peak of a barn where narrow cracks between the roofing boards gave entrance to shallow spaces under the shingles. On hot days in summer these spaces must have become unbearably warm, for the bats in the noon hours would leave their shelter and hang from the edges of the boards inside. Their droppings and urine falling upon cars or other things below rendered their presence more or less objectionable. Formerly there was a large colony in a little red schoolhouse, long disused, at Dublin, New Hampshire, and I have known of many others similarly in buildings. These seem to be wholly deserted in late autumn, for in these northern latitudes the colonies seek caves or other shelters where they may pass the cold season in hibernation under cool but fairly equable conditions. In caves I have investigated in New England the winter temperature is about 44° F. In the southwestern United States one or two other species of this genus (*Myotis yumanensis* and *M. velifer*) occasionally occupy old disused buildings, and in India a small, delicate species, *M. muricola*, owes its Latin name to its predilection for houses. The common small Pipistrellus of the eastern United States (*P. subflavus*), as well as the European *P. pipistrellus*, frequently shelters in buildings. The former I have seen in dense clusters either in the peak of the roof of a shed or barn or in a dark corner under a porch. A small African species of the same genus, *P. stampflii*, commonly associates itself with native villages, hiding by day singly or in small sleepy groups under the loose thatch of the circular huts. In the United States the common large brown bat (*Eptesicus fuscus*) is particularly a house-frequenting species, often common in summer even in

A

B

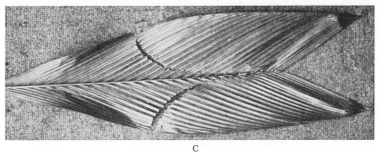

C

FIG. 14—A bat-made shelter.

A. A native palm, *Geonoma decurrens*, showing a frond on each side (about in the middle)
   cut by the leaf-nosed bat, *Artibeus watsoni*, so that the tip hangs down to form a shelter
   tent. Barro Colorado Island, Canal Zone.
B. One of the cut fronds from the side to show the manner in which the tip falls down
   to make a shelter.
C. The frond from above showing the line of cuts. Courtesy of Dr. Frank M. Chapman, phot.

the larger cities in consequence. Its habit of flying at about
the height of the third storey results often in its coming in
through open windows, causing consternation among the people
in the room. These bats seldom form large colonies but are
usually found singly, in pairs, or in small groups. At times they
even come down disused chimneys and appear in a room otherwise screened, then mysteriously evade pursuit by crawling

FIG. 15—Watson's leaf-nosed bat (*Artibeus watsoni*), a species that cuts the tips of palm
fronds to form a shelter for roosting. Barro Colorado, Panama. About natural size. Kindness of
Dr. Frank M. Chapman, phot.

under the crack of a door to escape. In the latitude of New
England this bat frequently winters in city houses or public
buildings, gaining entrance through the chimney or by the crack
of a window in late fall and remaining dormant for a longer or
shorter time. Such places are no doubt much less humid than
the caves they would naturally frequent at this season, so that
they seem to dry out as the winter advances; this may rouse
them from hibernation, for occasionally they appear in midwinter flying about unexpectedly in hallways or rooms, or even
outdoors, where often they must succumb to the cold. If caught,
they will eagerly take water offered to them a drop at a time on

the end of a finger and seem very thirsty. Dr. R. C. Murphy (1917) has described one seen on a winter's eve in New York City that flew to a partly frozen brook and lapped water at the edge of the ice. A related genus of the Old World, Scotophilus, includes at least two species, S. *kuhli* and S. *wroughtoni*, that are common as house bats in India, usually forming rather small colonies.

The mouse-tail bats (Rhinopoma) turn house-dwellers in Egypt and Arabia. A thriving colony in a covered passage of the Sultan's palace at Lahej has already been mentioned. They also seek the depths of the great pyramids, roosting by day in the dark central chamber or taking refuge in fissures of the living rock itself. Some of the species of horseshoe bats of the Old World also frequently associate with man, seeking disused rooms or lofts, where they hang from the upper parts of the walls. A few of these are colonial, while others live solitary or in pairs. Thus in Africa, *Hipposideros caffer* often lives in houses in large colonies, while of its larger woolly-looking relatives, *H. cyclotis*, I once found a single one, living apparently as the only inhabitant of an unused room in a native house of Liberia. The bats of the related family Rhinolophidae also show a few that are house bats, such as *Rhinolophus rouxi* in India and Ceylon, although, like most of the other species of the genus, it prefers caves. In the New World a few of the leaf-nosed bats of the family Phyllostomidae have become to a slight extent house-dwellers, a habit obviously taken up since occupation by Europeans. Thus, the long-tongued bat, *Glossophaga soricina*, is noted by Thomas (1888) as a common house bat in Demerara, and in Brazil it will frequent darkened rooms of abandoned buildings, hanging from the walls. In general, however, it prefers caves, as do most other species of the family, though a few are tree-dwellers. The big-eared Otopterus will sometimes hang up in a darkened room, as well as in caves or even hollow trees, and is not averse to going underground, for once in the old fort at Nassau, in the Bahama Islands, I found a small colony in the abandoned dungeon cut in limestone rock. When disturbed, they sought refuge even deeper, disappearing down the shaft of a well sunk in the floor. Another big-eared bat (*Tonatia*) of this family has been found in Ecuador, roosting in a rabbit burrow.

It is, however, among the Molossidae, the velvet-furred free-tailed bats, so common in the tropics, that the house-haunting habit is most marked. The common "guano bat" (*Tadarida mexicana*) of our Southwest often colonizes in this way, hundreds sometimes occupying the interspaces beneath roofing or behind walls of white men's houses, whence they swarm out just at sunset in a continuous stream, through some crevice that serves for entrance. In the West Indies, where local forms occur on the different groups of islands, it is common to find colonies in buildings even in the cities, and the bats have evidently found such shelters more available than caves, for it is unusual now to find them except in buildings, such as churches, warehouses, or even dwellings. Some of the species of Molossus and occasionally of Eumops, related genera, do the same, while other allied genera in Africa and India, especially Chaerephon, readily become "house bats" and often make themselves such a nuisance that something has to be done; a "battue" is held, the little creatures are smoked out, or the roof is removed, and numbers are killed. This, however, may be of little avail unless their entrance holes are afterwards completely blocked, for the remnant will return and start anew. In the tropics a common style of inexpensive construction is to make walls of brick or stone, perhaps also of wood, then adding the roof of corrugated sheets of galvanized iron. If there is an airspace between these sheets and the ceiling, the bats gain entrance under the eaves where the corrugations leave little archways at the contact with the vertical walls. Such colonies once established are often hard to break up. Sometimes the roofing sheets may be lifted and the interspace filled with thorny twigs. In one instance in the island of St. Kitts, West Indies, where repairs to the ceiling of a church revealed a colony of bats and bees, various methods were suggested for getting rid of both. In the course of sundry trials, the building was closed as tightly as possible and after the removal of metal objects was thoroughly fumigated with burning sulphur. The ventilators were then closed with strong wire mesh to keep out the bats, while beams and rafters were covered with solignum. When the recess of the ceiling, where the bats had dwelt, was opened, an accumulation of guano was found, amounting to four cartloads. A few months later word was received from the minister of the church that the effort to eradicate the bats appeared to have been successful (*Agricultural News*, Barbados). A recent circular of the U. S. Bureau of Biological Survey (Wildlife Research and Management Leaflet BS–7) recommends a simpler method of control, one that does not involve destruction of these useful insectivorous species, namely, the use of liberal amounts of naphthalene flakes, two to five pounds for colonies of ordinary size. This is sprinkled inside their retreats and is said to prove effective in driving them away, as the fumes are highly objectionable to them. If necessary, the treatment may be repeated after a week or so. On the other hand, when not in our dwellings, bats are valuable citizens whose presence is to be encouraged.

Perhaps the majority of bats are cave-dwellers. Some, like our New England species of Myotis, resort to caves chiefly in winter for hibernation, scattering for the summer into surrounding districts to take up residence in more open situations, old buildings, hollow trees, or under loose fragments of bark. But in the warmer parts of the world especially, bats live permanently in caves, hanging by day from the walls or clinging to the ceiling. Often limestone caves have small chimney-like depressions in the roof, at the top of which the bats will cluster, protected against direct light. Lacking caves, they will take advantage of deep pits, mine tunnels, or long culverts. But not every cave is suitable for bats. For most species it must be deep enough or have a chamber so situated around a bend that light does not penetrate and the bats may rest in complete darkness. Some, however, do not mind a dim light and will hang by day near the entrance or merely beneath the overhang of a large boulder, taking flight at once if too closely approached. Writing of the small horseshoe bat (*Rhinolophus hipposideros minor*) in Ireland, Coward (1907) says that, although living in caves, it may occupy different caves in summer from those occupied in winter, or may in the cold season move farther in to a deeper part of the cave, where probably the temperature is more equable than near the mouth. Other species, like the Indian false vampire (*Megaderma spasma*), may live indifferently in caves, hollow trees, or disused lofts of houses. The large fruit-eating bat of the American tropics (*Artibeus jamaicensis*), though usually a cave-dweller, will frequently spend the day hanging in the foliage of trees or beneath the crown of a palm. The fish-eating Noctilio of tropical America usually selects deep narrow fissures in rock for its daytime retreat, and the vampire (Desmodus) seems to prefer fissures inside larger caves. Some of the sheath-tailed bats, such as *Taphozous melanopogon*, also like fissures and rock crevices and, like the American vampire, are adept at scrambling sidewise, crablike, into such retreats. Carriker found in Venezuela that Micronycteris, a small leaf-nosed species with large ears, was never met with in deep tunnels, but preferred short prospect tunnels or open workings where light entered freely. They were always hanging in some little cavity in the roof just within the entrance, or clinging to roots under a small overhanging bank, and were quick to take flight at the least alarm.

The existence of caves in a region no doubt has a marked influence on the bat fauna, conditioning their very presence and especially their abundance. Caverns are dissolved out in limestone formations by rainwater or stream action, so that colonial species of bats are found in numbers in such places. The caves in Virginia, Pennsylvania, Indiana, and Kentucky offer familiar instances. In these, great numbers of bats gather from the surrounding areas for the winter, and some are inhabited also in the summer. The famous Chilibrillo Caves in Panama, the year-round home of many hundreds of bats, and similar caverns in North Borneo and Montalban in the Philippines are well known. The limestone regions of southern Europe offer shelter to several species, of which Miniopterus and Rhinolophus, as well as species of Myotis, are the chief. These bats have lived in close association in these caves for many thousands of years, and remains of fossil bats closely related to Rhinolophus have been found in early Tertiary formations of France and Germany that undoubtedly were preserved through becoming covered up by cave detritus. In the West Indies and in the southeastern part of Asia limestone caves of large size occur. Those along the Mekong River in Indo-China harbor thousands of various species. If one were to map out the limestone regions of the world, one would undoubtedly find it an excellent guide to localities for cave-haunting bats. Equally favorable caverns are also found occasionally in volcanic areas, where old lava flows have cooled on the exterior, while the molten interior has flowed on, leaving a long tunnel. Such tunnels, superimposed one on another, have been graphically described by H. L. Ward (1904) in the province of Vera Cruz, Mexico, near Jalapa. One such, to which access was obtained by a hole broken through the roof, was locally known to the inhabitants for the

great number of bats that nightly issue from this hole in the nearly level ground, and from them has received the not inappropriate name of El Infernillo, or the little hell. As far as I could ascertain no one had entered the tunnel previous to my visit. My assistant, Teran, and myself let ourselves down by a rope, which we tied to a piece of wood placed across the opening, until we reached a conical pile of rocks formed by the breaking down of the roof some 20 or 30 feet above. At this point is a sort of rotunda about 200 feet in diameter by perhaps 50 feet in height. Slanting down at a moderately steep grade is a tunnel extending only a few rods before it is choked with soil that apparently has been deposited by water entering the hole in the roof. In the opposite direction the tunnel, sloping upward, extends for an unknown distance and is of ample dimensions, perhaps 30 feet in width by the same in height, very regular in section and but slightly serpentine in direction. The temperature was decidedly hot and the atmosphere close and oppressive. For some distance a faint glimmer of light, reflected from the rotunda, furnished sufficient illumination until a change in the pitch of the tunnel shut off this supply and we were forced to light our candles. A few desultory squeaks, now near, now far away, increasing in number as we advanced, the flitting of shadowy wings and an occasional swish as one came near our ears, showed that the bats were alive to our presence.

Shading our candles, we could see a short distance ahead, and there, clinging feet uppermost to the sides of the cave, from roof almost to the floor, were bats as far as we could see. Those near by and on the lower levels, with their heads thrown up, were standing on their wrists with bodies clear of the walls, ready to let loose and fly away at a moment's warning.

By making stealthy, rapid sorties we were able to capture a number with our hands; but were more interested in noting the methodical manner in which they disposed themselves — each species in a band of some feet or yards in width; then a slight vacant space, followed by a band of another species. Hand collecting was rather slow, and time was pressing; so we tried a few shots to good effect. The roar and concussion started the bats by the myriad, and in a moment the air was filled with thousands of flying forms. Instantly our candles were blown out by the wind from their wings, and in the Stygian darkness we were continually struck severe blows in the face and body by these living missiles, the roar of whose wings mingled with their shrieks was as deafening as the passage of an express train in a railway tunnel. For a moment it seemed impossible to stand against the storm of swirling and eddying bats that in their wild career seemed to have entirely lost their usual knack of avoiding objects. Soon the roar quieted so that I could hear Teran shouting to me not over twenty feet away. He was a high-strung, nervous lad, and that moment's experience had put him on the verge of hysterics.

Four species of bats belonging to as many genera were collected here, *Mormoops megalophylla*, *Natalus stramineus*, *Chilonycteris rubiginosa*, and *Pteronotus davyi*, while in adjacent tunnels were found hundreds of *Myotis velifer*.

CHAPTER VII

# WHAT BATS LIVE BY

"Lardi crustam proposui, quam non tetegit" (I placed before it a rind of bacon, which it left untouched). With these words Johannes Hermann in his *Observationes Zoologicae* (1804) briefly described what seems to have been the first attempt to test by experiment the belief once widely held in Europe that bats are particularly fond of bacon. His negative result does not now seem so surprising, but what has since been found out concerning the food habits of these misunderstood animals is indeed far more astonishing. For we have come to know that the choice of food, whether an animal or a vegetable diet, has been among mammals a very potent factor in their evolution, if not one of its chief causes, tending to bring about changes in the structure of the teeth as well as of other parts of the body, the better to secure and utilize it.

There can be little doubt that bats were primitively insect-feeders, just as at the present day are most of the small marsupials and the varied group of small insectivores which are more immediately related to bats. It is typical of all these animals that the molar teeth are fitted for cutting up the soft bodies of insects by means of their three sharp main cusps with cutting ridges or crests connecting them, to form in the upper teeth a distinct W-pattern on the outer side of the molar. The long sharp canines are suited for seizing and firmly holding the prey, while the small intermediate teeth or premolars are usually pointed or sharp-edged for assisting in the work.

A great variety of insects are eaten by bats, for the most part, naturally, those that are active by night when bats are abroad. That this insectivorous habit was once common to the whole group is indicated by the fact that the greater number of the species now living are insect feeders, while in some of the families there are those of transitional habits, and others that have now become altogether vegetarians. The insect remains found in the stomachs and droppings of bats constitute a definite clue to the kinds eaten by them and often indicate clear preferences for different species. Usually, however, these are reduced to such minute fragments that even a microscopic examination tells little more than the orders or families to which the larger pieces belong. In many insectivorous bats, including especially the Vespertilionidae, such as the small brown Myotis, Eptesicus, and others, the tail membrane plays an important part in the capture of prey during flight. Immediately a good-sized insect is seized in the jaws, this membrane is curved downward and forward to form a sort of pouch; at the same instant the head is bent down into this net to prevent the escape of the insect, while the grip of the jaws is momentarily relaxed to give several quick bites, disabling the insect and allowing the bat then to chew it up with the sharp cusps of the molars. This action, which is carried out also when the bat is at rest, can be seen excellently in captives when fed. It was first described by the naturalist, Gilbert White, in his classic *Natural History of Selborne*.

Perhaps the first to make an accurate study of the insect food of bats was a German entomologist, Dr. Hiller (1858), who examined microscopically the droppings collected under a roosting place of some small species — perhaps Myotis or Plecotus — of Europe, and found them to consist chiefly of a mass of undigested scales of geometrid moths ("inch-worms"), which he identified as belonging to the genera Agrotis, Geometra, and Botys. He suggested that the bat in question showed a remarkably selective diet, since all these moths are members of a single family, Geometridae.

Some years ago the late Professor Clinton F. Hodge stated his belief that bats are an appreciable factor in keeping down the codling moth and mosquitoes. The moth in the larval stage bores into the core of ripening apples and so is a great orchard pest. Hodge found nine of these grubs in one minute in an orchard near his house at Worcester, Massachusetts, while in another orchard a mile away he was able to discover but four in an hour's search. The relative freedom from the pest in the latter instance he attributed to the fact that a colony of between seventy-five and a hundred bats lived in an old barn close to the orchard. Nevertheless, there may have been other factors involved, and no positive evidence was obtained, either through

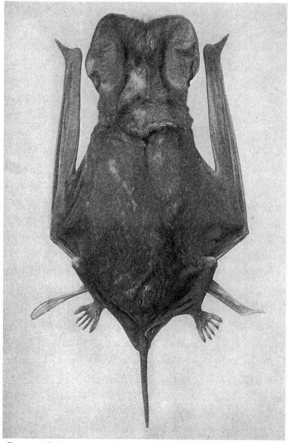

FIG. 16—California mastiff bat (*Eumops californicus*), Covina, California, the largest of the free-tailed bats in the United States. (From a fresh specimen.) Courtesy of A. Brazier Howell, phot.

direct observation or from examination of droppings, that the codling moth forms a special diet of any species of bat. Hodge's statements, however, seem to have carried authority and were widely copied, with the result that a few years ago an enterprising western firm advertised that it would erect for orchard growers at a considerable price approved "bat roosts" in order that they might thus insure their fruit against the ravages of the insect. Needless to say, the chances of a sizeable colony of bats taking up residence in such a structure are small, even though

FIG. 17—California mastiff bat (*Eumops californicus*) from beneath, showing its wide gape for insect-catching. Covina, California, from a fresh specimen. Courtesy of A. Brazier Howell, phot.

they might prove a help in this work, while the fact that apples grow best in the north-temperate climates where few species of bats with highly social habits occur, again renders such an investment a very uncertain one. In his attempts to colonize the "guano bat" (*Tadarida mexicana*) in Texas and elsewhere in the Southwest, Dr. Charles A. R. Campbell was perhaps influenced in part by Hodge's statement that bats feed largely on mosquitoes, for he goes so far as to assume that this species feeds almost exclusively on them and that these bats are therefore a most important factor in the control of malaria, a mosquito-borne disease. However, a microscopic examination of the dung of these bats, made independently by T. I. Storer (1926) and by E. A. Goldman (1926), revealed no evidence that mosquitoes were eaten. Instead, the guano obtained under the roosting places showed 90 per cent remains of moths. Scales from moths' wings are also to be identified in a figure published by Campbell, showng insect remains from a similar source, and adduced by him as proof of a mosquito diet. An African relative of the "guano bat," *Chaerephon limbatus*, abundant in Nyasaland, is said by Rodney C. Wood (in Kershaw, 1922a) to be valuable from its habit of devouring the adult moths of the cotton bollworm, of which also a large Scotophilus is fond. Another African species, the big-eared *Lavia frons*, is said, however, to feed in part on mosquitoes, for the stomach contents of specimens from the Dinka country of the upper Nile, examined by Hinton and Kershaw (1920), are said to have consisted of the remains of mosquitoes and small flies. Probably, however, it is safe to say that mosquitoes really form a negligible fraction of the diet of insectivorous bats. In Matabeleland, South Africa, Chubb (1909) mentions that the small brown species, *Eptesicus capensis*, which is common in that region, appearing just after sunset, frequents especially the vicinity of cowsheds, attracted by the abundance of insects over manure heaps.

The veteran British naturalist, Professor E. B. Poulton (1929), has published some interesting notes on the insects eaten by bats, with special reference to those supposed to be endowed with warning colors. From a study of the moth wings dropped by bats (species undetermined) in sheltered roosting places in England, he found that the "yellow-wing" (*Xanthia ferruginea*) was commonly taken, and the list includes in addition forty species of noctuids, six of geometrids, two of arctiids, and a few others. Of the common long-eared bat (*Plecotus auritus*), which seeks its prey among leafy branches, picking off many kinds of insects, he quotes an observation of Jeffrey, who watched it actually taking moths (*Plusia*) from arbutus flowers, first closing the wings and folding down the long ears before beginning to feed. Millais says that it will even alight on fresh cattle dung to devour the "red flies" found there. Another British observer, Whitaker, while examining sallows with a lantern one April night, repeatedly watched these bats alight on twigs and deliberately pick off moths from the flowers. In captivity they would seldom attack an insect at rest but were immediately attentive to the buzzing or fluttering of one held in the closed hand near the cage. The large noctule bat (*Nyctalus noctula*), Poulton writes, is particularly fond of beetles, which it catches in flight, eating the body but letting fall the hard wing covers. Millais says he has had these rejected shards drop on his face or seen them fall on the surface of a pool where noctules were feeding. They also eat moths, and a captive would even take a few caterpillars and pupae. An oil beetle offered it, however, was refused, and a small beetle with red "warning marks" was spat out at once, as was also a distasteful cinnamon moth, the bat shaking its head as if in disgust. Mealworms were a novel food to the noctule, which at first it did not understand, but after the "juice" was smeared on the bat's lips, these larvae were devoured at once. Winged ants and mayflies were taken also. Poulton tried various "procryptic" or concealingly colored moths on a little pipistrelle bat in captivity, but found that, like other bats, it disliked the magpie moth (Abraxus). Of this it first took a good bite, then spat it out, at the same time backing away to the far side of the cage, "coughing and spluttering in the most ludicrous manner" at the shabby trick. I have at various times tried the little brown bat (*Myotis lucifugus*) and the large brown bat (*Eptesicus fuscus*) with the common house fly, which at first they would seize and then reject as if distasteful, though if hungry they might eat a few without any sign of relish; large bluebottle flies filled with eggs, however, they delighted in, crunching the succulent morsels in their jaws and looking up for more. On the other hand, Poulton found that a barbastelle (*Barbastella barbastellus*) held captive in a room would pick off house flies from the ceiling and devour them in flight. Perhaps they are an acquired taste! The same bat, when offered a large cockroach, ate it but refused to take any more. Poulton further mentions a fondness for caddis flies on the part of the small *Myotis daubentoni* of Europe, a species often caught by anglers at night on artificial flies. Killington (1932), in continuation of Poulton's work, identified in the droppings of (probably) Plecotus in England, a number of neuropterous insects, including four species of Hemerobiidae (may flies) — *Hemerobius lutescens* and three kinds of Boriomyia; while Feytaud (1913) is quoted as authority for bats' taking the lace-winged fly, Chrysops, despite its disagreeable odor. This insect is of great value in checking the ravages of plant lice in the vineyards, so that in this case the bats are perhaps slightly harmful. However, it is unlikely that lace-wings form any considerable part of the diet.

One would hardly suppose that such day-flying insects as dragonflies would be much eaten by bats, but a Spanish zoologist, Codina (1912), who investigated this possibility, quotes his friend Don Emilio Tarré of Barcelona as saying that he believed bats are more dangerous enemies to them than birds. Speaking of the large dragonfly, *Anax imperator*, he adds that often on late afternoons in August he had watched one passing and repassing before the front of his house in pursuit of small insects, when suddenly a "common" bat that had appeared early flying overhead would stoop at it. But the dragonfly, instantly descending almost to the ground, would avoid its adversary, which at once rose and continued on its course. He had often called the attention of friends to this amusing spectacle. Because of their daytime activity bees and wasps must seldom come in the way of bats. However, Burt (1934) describes a curious incident that befell a little pallid bat (*Myotis californicus pallidus*) near Mormon Well, Nevada. For some reason unknown, this bat chanced to be abroad in the bright light of noonday, flying about a cement tank where some horses were watering. Presently it was seen to seize a large wasp (Pepsis) of the kind known as "tarantula hawk," that was flying about the water, and the two came to the ground together. "The bat was squeaking and biting the tarantula hawk which in turn was clinging to the bat's face and applying the stinger to the top of the bat's head. They had been fighting for three or four minutes when they were separated." What the outcome of the struggle might have been was not learned, for the wasp flew away, "but the bat was collected."

A few notes are available as to the insects taken by some of the larger bats of the southwestern United States. Huey (1925), writing of *Otopterus californicus*, a big-eared, leaf-nosed species, found under the roosting place of a colony at Potholes, California, abundant fecal remains, among which were identified wings and other parts of such large locusts as Schistocerca and Trimerotropis, together with those of moths, including sphinx moths, *Celerio lineata*, and Smerinthus, a noctuid moth (Peridroma) and a cossid, as well as wings and body of a cicada and elytra of a beetle (Melloidae). Fresh willow leaves under the roosts were believed to have been brought in by the bats, which perhaps seized insect and leaf together and then retired to the cave to complete the meal at leisure. This habit of bringing large insects to an habitual roost to eat is probably common to various species. Thus Hutton (1872) mentions a pair of big horseshoe bats, *Hipposideros armiger*, that lived in a loft near his home in India. He often saw them after a brief foray return to this shelter to eat some large insect, the wings of which were dropped to the floor. I once made a similar observation in the case of an allied species, *H. cyclops*, in Liberia, while spending the night in a disused native house. Hearing the swish of a bat's wings in the early morning as it flew past into one of the rooms, I investigated next morning and found the bat suspended from the top of the rough wall, the sole occupant of the dark chamber. The floor beneath its place of rest and several other places at the foot of the adjacent wall were littered with the large whitish wings of a big ground-living cockroach. Evidently this insect was a favorite food, and the bat must have frequented the retreat for some time.

In a recent paper on the food of the big brown bat (*Eptesicus fuscus*) Dr. W. J. Hamilton, Jr. (1933) gives the result of the analysis of 2,200 pellets of dung collected below a roost of this species in West Virginia. After soaking out the material in water, crushing and picking it apart, the identifiable remains, consisting chiefly of wing fragments, legs, and mouthparts of insects, were mounted on microscope slides for identification. Frequently, however, as many as ten pellets would be passed before a fragment even remotely identifiable could be found, indicating the thoroughness of a bat's mastication. Hamilton reports that of the insects thus determined, over one third were beetles, about one quarter were hymenopterans, one eighth flies, and the rest comprised samples of other orders. The figures given are: Coleoptera (beetles), 36.1%; Hymenoptera, 26.3%; Diptera (flies), 13.2%; Plecoptera (stone flies), 6.5%; Ephemeridae (may flies), 4.6%; Hemiptera (bugs), 3.4%; Trichoptera (caddis flies), 3.2%; Neuroptera (lace-wings), 3.2%; Mecoptera, 2.7%; Orthoptera, 0.6% — a varied diet. Of the beetles recognized, the scarabaeids, including cockchafers and May beetles, were most frequent and are injurious species, while the click beetles, the larvae of which are the "wire worms," are also destructive. On the other hand, lampyrids and histerids, the latter carrion feeders, may be regarded as useful from the human point of view. There were a few remains of water beetles (hydrophilids) also. The Hymenoptera were in part flying ants and in part ichneumons (braconids and ichneumonoids), the latter useful as parasites of injurious insects. Curiously, no remains of moths were discovered, although their characteristic wing-scales were found in the droppings of the lump-nosed bat (Corynorhinus).

While most insectivorous bats probably take their prey on the wing, some species will occasionally descend to the ground for it. This habit is well attested in the case of the pale cave bat (*Antrozous pallidus*) of the southwestern United States. The late Dr. E. W. Nelson once saw one catch a Jerusalem cricket on the ground, and Dr. R. T. Hatt found beneath the roost of a colony of this bat numerous remains of the same insect, as well as those of scorpions (*Anuroctonus phaiodactylus*), a large grasshopper (Schistocerca), and a potato beetle (*Polyphylla decimlineata*). Some interesting notes on the ground-feeding habits of this bat are supplied by Burt (1934, p. 397), from Indian Springs, Nevada. Here in early summer a ranch owner told of watching these bats "alight on the green lawn in front of their house and catch June beetles." The observation is corroborated by Burt, who observed the bats flying low over the lawn, often alighting on the ground to catch these insects. On one occasion a bat was seen "apparently struggling with something on the ground," but when closely approached, it arose and started to fly away. It was, however, brought down with a shot. When picked up, it was found to have one of the beetles in its mouth. The collector then suspended the beetle by a long thread from the branch of a tree, and directing a light upon it, presently caught another bat of the same species when it seized the bait. These bats are late flyers and were found to occupy "a feeding zone . . . much lower down than that of Pipistrellus. Their usual flight was from three to four feet above the ground, slow, and fairly straight." The big-eared African bat, Lavia, is also said at times to feed on or near the ground. Speke (Sclater and Speke, 1864) tells of routing these bats from among tall grass where they seemed to be feeding.

In the tropics at certain seasons, when the "white ants" or termites are swarming, the air is filled with myriads of these soft-bodied insects, which then are eagerly eaten by many species of bats.

Larger predatory animals of most species require food in proportionate quantities, so that the larger species of bats naturally come to seek the larger as well as smaller insects. Hutton (1872) gives an interesting account of the big horse-shoe bat, *Hipposideros armiger*, of the southeastern parts of Asia and its liking for a giant species of cicada or harvest-fly which is abundant at certain times of year in forest tracts along the foothills of the Himalayas in India, above five thousand feet. This insect frequents oak trees and, as the sun sets, pours forth a deafening and discordant song, continuing for about a quarter of an hour. At this time the bat emerges and, seemingly attracted by the sounds, wheels around the trees, scanning each branch as he slowly passes by . . . until at length, detecting the unfortunate minstrel all unconscious of its danger and drowned in its own melody, it darts suddenly into the tree, and snatching the still scream- ing insect from its perch, bears it away, still harping upon one string, and jerking out an occasional wailing note as the ruthless bat deliberately devours it on the wing.

If the bat's swoop only scares out the insect, he awaits its song again from some other tree.

Other large insectivorous bats may on occasion prey on smaller species of their own kind or upon other small verte- brates. Even the large Myotis (*M. blythii*) of India, if con- fined in a cage with smaller bats, will prey upon them, according to Hutton (1872), who further attests to the same habit in the case of the big horseshoe bat just mentioned, as well as in *Rhinolophus luctus* and even the large species of Scotophilus, a house bat in India. For this reason, probably, small caves harbor only one of these species, since it is only in the more extensive caverns that there is room for both large and small species of bats to live without interference, and in these places they spend the day in groups, each species by itself. It is thus not surprising to find that in the Old World family Mega- dermidae (false vampires) and in at least one case in the New World family of leaf-nosed bats (Phyllostomidae) carnivorous habits have been acquired. This fact seems to have first been noticed by the British naturalist Blyth in 1842 in India. One evening as he sat in a lighted room, a false vampire (*Lyro- derma lyra*) flew in. Thinking to capture it, he closed the door and was surprised to see it drop what at first he thought was its young but which, on picking it up, he found to his astonish- ment was a small pipistrelle bat with a bleeding wound behind the ear. Placing both bats in the folds of a handkerchief, he put them next morning in a cage, but no sooner did the Lyro- derma perceive the pipistrelle, when it "fastened on it with the ferocity of a tiger, again seizing it behind the ear." Then having apparently "sucked" its blood till no more flowed, it com- menced to devour the little bat, leaving nothing but the head and portions of the wings.

Others have since confirmed and extended these observations. Blyth himself (1875) reports that on successive occasions Colonel McMaster of Rangoon had two canaries killed by these bats, which must have entered the bird-cage by slipping between the wires. It is a common habit of this bat to bring its prey to the shelter of a veranda or to some other convenient place, there to devour it at leisure while hanging against the wall, letting drop the discarded fragments. Frith (quoted by Blanford) records that a number of these bats nightly frequented his porch at Mymensing, Burma, and every morning the floor beneath their feasting place was strewn with the fragments dropped. These included not only the wings of large grasshoppers and crickets, but also the hind legs of small frogs — never of toads — which in this instance appeared to constitute the bats' chief diet. On one occasion the remains of a small fish were present among the debris. Fry (1929) was able to corroborate these observations "in every respect." He writes that the bats "used to drop frogs' hind quarters, etc., on my mosquito curtain. On one occasion a mouse's head was picked up. Remains of small fish were found, though how bats catch a fish, I am not prepared to guess." Another observer, Aitken (1907), also found remains of frogs and mice dropped by these bats "in our bedrooms and verandahs" in India, and once "the headless trunk of a tame mouse which had escaped from my cage was found in the morning in the cage" of a captive bat, into whose clutches it had evidently wandered. This captive bat would also eat small birds given it, devouring first of all the head. Aitken adds that frequently this species may be seen flitting about trees after dusk, manifestly looking for birds. In Ceylon, E. E. Green (1907, 1910) mentions finding one morning on his veranda the wings of a sunbird (Cinnyris) and the remains of a small bat, evidently dropped by the Lyroderma, while on other occasions he had gathered up the wings and feathers of three or four birds each morning for several months in succession from a single room, to which the bats had gained access. The birds included such species as silver-eyes (Zosterops), sunbirds (Cinnyris), and flower-peckers chiefly.

During three years' residence at Gauripur in Assam, Primrose (1907) noticed remains of various small birds — chiefly the Indian bush chat (*Pratincola maura*) — small bats and insects on his veranda floor, and more than once had scared this bat away from dead birds he had hung up preparatory to skinning, to find that already their breasts and abdomens had been damaged. Again, Gleadow (1907), writing from Salsette, India, complains that these bats used to annoy him by catching mice about his house, "and fetching birds out of their comfortable nests at night and chewing them up in the corners of verandahs and rooms," where he had sometimes surprised them at their feasts. When small birds were fed to caged bats they would catch them with a swoop of the wings and, seizing the bird close behind the neck, would hang up and commence chewing the neck in two, first cutting off and dropping the head, then continuing to chew steadily along to the feet and tail, which were let fall. Captive individuals kept in Ceylon by W. W. A. Phillips (1922) devoured a small bat, *Pipistrellus mimus*, a dead mouse, and part of a young gerbil. He had at various times seen them at dusk flitting in and out among trees instead of hawking in the open, and observes that they are difficult to drive away from chosen daytime haunts. Although it is seldom that one may see an actual capture, McCann (1934) recounts that one evening at Poona, India, while sitting in a lighted room, he saw a small pipistrelle bat come in and begin circling around the room at full speed. Shortly after, one of the large Lyrodermas entered and began chasing the smaller bat, which in about a minute it captured, but after carrying it about for a brief time, dropped it in trying to get out the door. Soon after, however, it reëntered the room as if to retrieve its prey, but as the observer had arisen, the bat took fright and left.

In addition to its varied diet of insects, fish, frogs, birds, mice, and small bats, this species will sometimes hunt along the sides of walls and pick off the geckos or wall lizards that come out at night in search of insects. To judge from the evidence presented, the false vampire shows local differences in food preference, feeding in some places, or perhaps seasons, largely on

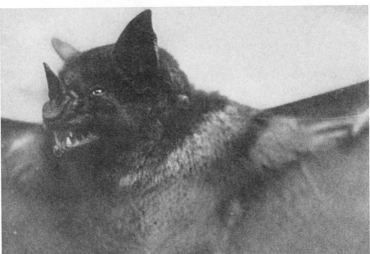

Fig. 18—The spear-nosed bat (*Phyllostomus hastatus panamensis*). A large carnivorous species of the leaf-nosed family, Phyllostomidae, found in the American tropics. Courtesy of Dr. Herbert C. Clark.

frogs or fish, or in others depending chiefly on small birds and bats, with the addition of larger insects. A large Australian bat, Macroderma, a genus closely related to Lyroderma, is said by Wood Jones (1925) to feed to a large extent on other smaller bats. He records the interesting fact that in a cave deposit in the Carrieton district of South Australia he found a number of mummified bodies of this species, the intestinal contents of which consisted entirely of masses of hair of small insectivorous bats. So far as known, Macroderma, though once common in the region, now no longer is found there, a fact which he attributes to the slow drying out of large areas of this portion of Australia. That small bats are not its only article of diet, however, seems obvious from the fact that I found in the stomach of one examined a few insect remains including a leg of a large beetle.

Among the larger South American bats, one or two at least are known to have carnivorous habits, particularly the spear-nosed bat (Phyllostomus). Hensel, in 1869, recounted an incident that came to his notice while in Brazil. A German physician and naturalist, Herr Friedrich of Blumenau,. Sta. Catharina Province, one evening observed a large bat fly in at the open window of his room, and saw it seize and kill a swallow which had a nest under construction in the room and was roosting there. Possibly this was the large Phyllostomus. To test these propensities Dr. Lawrence H. Dunn (1934) carried out some interesting experiments with a female of the large Central American race, *P. hastatus panamensis*, which he kept in captivity over five and a half months at the Gorgas Memorial Laboratory at Panama. For the first few days the bat was kept supplied with ripe banana, of which small amounts were eaten. Five days later a small dish containing five cubic centimeters of defibrinated blood was placed in the cage and by the next morning had been taken by the bat. It repeated the performance the following night, devouring in addition a piece of monkey liver and a portion of banana. On the three following days several large cockroaches were placed in the cage and were eaten — five the first night, then eight, then ten. About seven seemed to be a sufficient night's ration, those then remaining being eaten the following day. The bat was next tried on house mice, which were introduced into the cage at evening. These, too, were consumed by the bat in the course of the night. Then for twenty-five days it survived on a diet of banana alone. On succeeding days one or two mice were killed and eaten nightly. Then three small birds were disposed of in like manner.

Thinking to test its cannibalistic traits, Dr. Dunn next tried placing one or two small bats in the cage. A female long-tongued bat (*Glossophaga soricina leachii*) was admitted to the upper part of the cage, where it hung itself up, seeming to pay no particular attention to its larger fellow prisoner, hanging only six inches away; but the next morning all that remained of it was the wings and conjoined legs. Later, a Carollia (*C. perspicillata azteca*) was put in the cage and also was devoured; a second bat of this species, however, was not killed for two days. Other species of bats killed and eaten in the later course of the experiment were the small free-tailed bat (*Molossus coibensis*), a small fruit-eating species, the yellow-eared bat (*Uroderma bilobatum*), and even the little bulldog bat (*Dirias albiventer minor*). Of the last, however, the thorax and back were usually rejected, perhaps because of the powerful odor from the axillary glands, while the toothed portions of the jaws were also discarded. Apparently the usual method of procedure was to seize the prey by the neck or transfer the hold to the head, biting through the skull to cause the victim's death; then beginning at the head end, it would devour the body in a leisurely way and finally drop the posteriormost portion, though sometimes, if hungry, it would eat every bit of a mouse, even the tail. In the 168 days during which the Phyllostomus was caged, it ate 25 house mice, 13 bats, and 3 birds, as well as a considerable ration of banana.

Bats often drink, much as swallows do, skimming close to the surface of a pool or stream, now and again touching the water lightly as they take a sip in passing. It has been suggested, too, that they may pick up water beetles in this way, so that perhaps one may understand how a few species have developed the habit of catching small fish at the surface. The fact that the false vampire (Lyroderma) of the Old World tropics sometimes catches fish has already been mentioned. So far as known, however, only two New World bats are fish-eating, the large hare-lipped or mastiff bat (Noctilio) of tropical America, and a species of Pizonyx, related to the widely distributed Myotis, found along the coasts and islands of the Gulf of California. In both, though they belong to widely distinct families, the hind feet are of relatively enormous size, with long stout toes, heavily clawed, doubtless for use in gaffing their prey. Charles Kingsley in 1871, in his entertaining book, *At Last* (p. 132), seems to have been the first writer to call attention to this habit, and his observations have been amply confirmed by later writers, among them J. E. Benedict (1926), who has placed on record some notes on the subject made in 1883–84, when, as naturalist aboard the U. S. Fish Commission steamer *Albatross*, he visited the sea caves on Mona Island, Caribbean Sea, in search of the strange oil-bird, Steatornis.

In one place [he writes] the water was very smooth under the shelter of the land, and a rather large number of pelicans were flying back and forth, or sometimes resting on the surface. Now and then a pelican would plunge into the water, no doubt aiming at the schools of small fish near the surface. . . . In doing this they wounded some of the fish so that they floated to the surface dead or dying. We saw a number of them as we went on our way. Many rather large bats were flying about with the pelicans, occasionally gliding down to the surface, touching the water it seemed to me with the membrane between the legs and tail, and then ascending with a sharp turn as they touched the water. It appeared to me that they were fishing and had a community of interest with the pelicans as it were, taking the crumbs which fell from their table in the form of dead or wounded fish. I did not actually see them take a fish, but they acted as if they were doing so. If not, why were they flying with the pelicans on a bright afternoon? We could not get near enough to shoot one, and Mr. Morrison said that we could paddle to where they lived behind a rock. We soon came to a place where the ocean ground-swell broke against a cliff. Here a huge scale rested against the face of the cliff, the opening being parallel with it. Now and then a bat would go in or out. We put the canoe as close up as was safe, and fired a charge of shot at such an angle that the shot would rebound into the cleft. Out came the bats, and we shot several as they flew about. An examination of the stomachs revealed the remains of fish exclusively.

The matter has been investigated more recently by G. G. Goodwin (1928), who reviews at length the few published notes on the subject and gives the details of his own observations made in the West Indies. He found that although fish may be freely eaten, these bats often eke out their diet with a variety of insect food. Analysis of stomach contents in ten mastiff bats showed in one case 100 per cent fish, probably small species of Engraulidae; two others contained traces of fish in addition to a mole-cricket and unidentifiable mucus, bits of gravel, and vegetable matter, perhaps taken incidentally with the cricket, while the remaining seven stomachs contained insects, of which the names are given, including mole-cricket, winged ants, beetles, cockroach, stink-bugs, and a spider. He mentions their coming to freshwater pools to drink on the wing; their flight is relatively slow, and several knocked into the water swam readily with the wings submerged as oars and only the head above the surface.

Gosse (1847), writing of the habits of this species in Jamaica, tells of giving to a captive a large cockroach which it took at once and worked the masticated fragments into its cheek pouches. After a brief interval, these were returned to the mouth "by a contortion of the jaw, aided by the motion of the muscles of the pouch," and again chewed until all was swallowed. A bit of bird meat was treated in the same way, but after a second mastication was expelled.

Of the other fish-eating species, *Pizonyx vivesi*, very little is known. It was first described in 1901 by Menegaux from two specimens captured under stones heaped up by the waves on Cardonal Island, off Lower California, and was at that time referred to the genus Myotis, of which it may be regarded as an offshoot, slightly modified as to its feet for the capture of its special food. In 1904 a dead individual was picked up on the beach at Guaymas, Sonora. Miller, in 1928, suggested that it would prove to be a fish-eater, as indicated by its long, stoutly clawed feet, but although specimens were in that year secured on Isla Partida, Gulf of California, their stomachs were empty. It was not until January 1932 that the question was satisfactorily settled by Dr. W. H. Burt, who again visited the island

and secured a series of the bats by turning over loose rocks among the crevices of which they hid during the day, often sharing their retreat with a species of petrel of partly nocturnal habits. The stomachs of two bats captured just before daybreak were found to be "distended with finely chewed fish remains," which were determined by Dr. B. W. Evermann as "belonging to the sardine tribe."

The only other instance I have found of fish-eating bats, apart from the case of the false vampire, previously mentioned, is an account by J. Shortt (1863) of watching the big Indian fruit bat (*Pteropus giganteus*) at Couleeveran, India, whose activities at a small "tank" or pond in the early evening attracted his attention. The pool teemed with small fish, skipping and jumping at the surface. He described the bats as "hovering over the water and seizing with their feet the fish, with which they then made off to some tamarind-trees on the bund of the tank to devour them at their leisure, I suppose." This he observed on several subsequent occasions and even shot two or three of the bats to make certain of their identity, but unfortunately he seems to have made no examination of their stomach contents. McCann (1934) therefore very properly doubts his conclusion that the bats were fishing, but believes rather that they were instead taking a drink at the pool. The observation has never been confirmed, and certainly it would be very strange for so typical a fruit-eater as Pteropus to depart thus radically from its normal diet. For the same reason one may question the report quoted by Dobson (1873) that a colony of the smaller fruit bats (*Rousettus leschenaulti*), living near the sea at Moulmein, were seen to feed on mollusks left exposed by the ebb tide. Andersen (1912, p. 21), however, inclines to accept the statement and suggests that it would seem to "explain the occurrence of an allied species (*R. arabicus*) in so dreary a desert as the island of Kishm, Persian Gulf," where Blanford found a colony in the salt caves, a situation in which "an exclusively fruit-eating mammal could hardly exist." Nevertheless, these bats are believed often to make long flights for food, and there may have been some fruiting date palms within feeding radius. One other small bat, *Rickettia pilosa*, of southeastern Asia, has, like Noctilio and Pizonyx, disproportionately large hind feet, with wings attached halfway up on the tibia, suggesting again possible fish-catching habits, but of this no positive evidence is available.

Of all the bats, perhaps the most specialized in feeding habits are the true vampires of tropical America, which subsist solely upon the fresh blood of other mammals and of birds. They comprise, so far as known, three genera, Desmodus, Diphylla, and Diaemus, which together form a distinct family, Desmodontidae, allied to the leaf-nosed group, Phyllostomidae. The first of these genera is the best known, while the others are so rare that only a few specimens have ever been taken. The teeth of Desmodus are admirably adapted to its needs. In the upper jaw they are reduced to a single incisor, the canine, one premolar, and one molar, with in the lower jaw a second incisor and premolar besides. Of these teeth only the incisors and canines are functional, enlarged and sharp-edged for snipping out a small section of the victim's skin to make a shallow wound from which the blood is lapped up as it oozes forth. A good deal has been written of experiences with this bat, best of all an excellent summary account by Ditmars and Greenhall (1935), with photographic illustrations. As long ago as 1865 Huxley described the stomach, the cardiac end of which has become enormously elongated to form a somewhat tubular structure for holding and digesting blood. The vampire will attack cattle, mules, horses, and goats tethered or loose in the fields at night, and even domesticated fowls asleep on their roosts, to say nothing of human victims. Instances are known where it has been necessary to drive herds of cattle to some other district to avoid constant annoyance from these bats. Such a case was reported in Costa Rica by Cyril F. Underwood. In Trinidad, Caracciola (1895) found that "they seem to delight in poultry and attack their birds in the neck." He once saw "an unfortunate hen which had been bitten in the night so weak she could not stand and in nine cases out of ten the feathered victim dies."

Hensel (1869), who made observations on this bat in Brazil, near Rio, wrote that where the approaches to the horse and mule stalls were open it was frequently necessary to hang lighted lamps close by to prevent the intrusions of vampires. Sanborn (1931) also mentions the effectiveness of

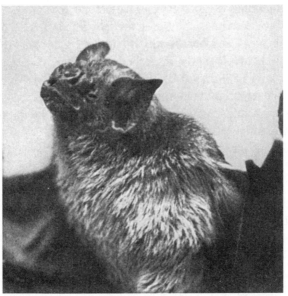

FIG. 19—The vampire bat of Central America (*Desmodus rotundus murinus*). Courtesy of Dr. Herbert C. Clark.

this method. The wound left by the vampire's bite is, according to Hensel, easily detected and very characteristic. Instead of the punchlike hole left by the canines of a small carnivore, the bat leaves a shallow and clean-cut scoop from which the blood continues to ooze for a much longer time than from a stablike wound that would soon clot over. Hensel remarks that not infrequently horses or mules that have been bitten during the night show still a little trickle of blood in the morning, running from the neck or shoulder down the foreleg to the ground. It is evidently in making these cuts that the scalpriform and sharp-edged incisors of vampires are useful. Of its habits Hensel says that he had found them usually in abundance in rock caves or occasionally in large hollow trees. If handled, they will bite with lightning-like quickness, always gouging a little slice of skin from the surface, to leave a characteristic wound; for, unlike other bats, they do not cling with the teeth. Horses and mules seem to be attacked in preference to cattle, perhaps because of their thinner skin. Hensel mentions a large cave in sandstone near St. Cruz, Brazil, in which lived a colony of some two hundred of these bats, yet a few cows and horses which pastured day and night close by were relatively little disturbed by them. Had the entire colony sought the blood of these animals it would have been impossible to keep them there. He concludes, therefore, that since horses and cattle have not been available to the vampires as food until recent times, they perhaps subsist partly by catching small mammals and birds and devouring their blood. In this cave the vampires hid during the day in cracks of the rocks at the farthest recesses, but as dusk came on they would appear from these retreats and assemble at a certain spot near the entrance to the cave, awaiting there the coming on of complete darkness. It was at this spot that they then apparently deposited their semiliquid, pitchlike dung, of which near a foot in thickness covered the floor underneath the spot.

They have an uncanny watchfulness, waiting until their intended victim is quiet or asleep, then alighting close by and walking deliberately to the feet of a horse or cow, or again landing lightly on its withers to make the incision in the skin and lap the welling blood. Human victims may sleep on, quite unaware of the unwelcome visitor, to find in the morning a slight wound in an unguarded nose or toe, with a trickle of blood flowing from it. The late Dr. William C. Farabee told me of such an experience in his own case. While traveling down the Amazon valley, he awoke one morning to find that a vampire during the night had gouged a small piece of skin from the tip of his nose and had evidently feasted while he slept, for the wound was still bleeding slightly. Leo Miller (in J. A. Allen, 1916), writing of his experiences in Colombia, tells that many such instances had come under his notice, where natives had been attacked, usually on the toe, fingertip, or nose. Each stated that he had not been awakened by the operation and that the wound had bled freely afterward. An acquaintance in British Guiana described how he had been bled repeatedly and finally decided to lie awake and kill the creature. After a while, he heard a flutter in the darkness as something struck the covers some distance from his exposed feet. He could feel the bat slowly working its way across the sheets till it reached his foot, when he suddenly struck at it, but missed. The bat fluttered about the room for some moments, then returned when all was quiet. This was repeated a number of times, and always the bat alighted some distance away and crawled toward the point of attack. In one of the intervals the watcher dosed off for a few minutes, and then awakened with a start to find that his assailant had taken advantage of his lapse of vigilance to gorge itself at his expense. Obviously the domestic animals that are so often attacked are relatively new arrivals in the bat's domain, so that previous to the coming of the white man the vampires must have devoted their attention to other species, though exactly which is still a question. No doubt, however, a number of native birds and mammals are attacked.

My friend, Mr. B. Patterson Bole, Jr., tells me that while collecting mammals in Panama he one morning found a spiny rat (Proechimys) in one of his traps that had evidently been attacked during the night by a vampire, as shown by two characteristic wounds on its neck. Burmeister calls attention to the fact that mules and horses are usually bitten in special places where the bats can easily reach the skin, especially on the withers, where the hair is rubbed off. The animals are usually attacked while asleep, but if they are not, they shake themselves or stamp to drive the bat off. Various authors agree that lighted lamps close to the stalls will prevent the vampires from troubling the animals, and occasionally bits of bright tin are hung up near the animals for the same purpose, though their effect is perhaps doubtful. Burmeister had never heard of an animal's dying from loss of blood as a result of these bats, but if repeatedly attacked it may become much weakened, especially in the cool part of the year when food is less abundant. The story that the vampire fans its victim to keep it from awakening is of course quite fabulous.

No doubt all bats were originally insect eaters, inheriting this trait directly from their hypothetical ancestors of the Order Insectivora. Hence it is easy to understand how carnivorous and finally sanguinivorous habits may have been developed in the special cases just cited. That others, however, should have evolved the habit of living on vegetable food is extremely interesting and a further proof of the great adaptability and extreme specialization of this group of mammals. Vegetarian habits are found in but two of the families, namely the leaf-nosed bats, Phyllostomidae, of the New World tropics, and the flying foxes and their allies, Pteropidae, of the warmer parts of the Old World. That this habit should be confined to groups living in the warmer parts of the globe is readily understood, for it is only in these regions that fruits or flowers are to be found at all times, as different species of trees or shrubs come successively into bearing at their appropriate seasons. Nevertheless, variation in the blossoming and fruiting times of foodplants entails a more or less nomadic life among these bats, which must seek out their provender when and where it becomes available. These two families offer a number of interesting contrasts and parallelisms in their particular adaptations for vegetable food. For whereas only certain members of the American leaf-nosed bats are vegetarians, nearly the entire group of flying foxes has this special diet (Nyctimene seems to feed in part at least on insects). In the former the habit is confined practically to three related groups or subfamilies, while the remaining members still pursue insect prey.

These three groups seem to be independent lines of evolution, derived from insect-eating ancestors with teeth like those of the other living members of the family. Thus the genus Micronycteris, found from Central America to southern Brazil, may be thought of as one of the more primitive genera of Phyllostomi-

dae, in which the number of teeth is but two less than the highest
number (36) found in any known bat, while their structure is
still that characteristic of insectivorous species, with a well-
marked W-pattern of the cusps of the upper molars. From such
a condition the three groups of fruit-eaters have departed
along two general lines. On the one hand the subfamily Stenoderminae, which includes many large and small forms, representing nineteen genera, has tended to strengthen the chewing
power of the jaws by a shortening of the facial part of the skull,
so that in such an extreme case as Ametrida the length of the
rostrum from eye to tip of snout is considerably less than half
as long as the braincase. This implies, further, that in order to
accommodate the teeth the snout is much broadened, so that
the upper tooth rows form a wide arch. In addition, the molar
teeth are adapted for crushing pulp by becoming very wide,
often with roughened surfaces to the flat crowns. In the opposite direction an independent line has been followed by two other
subfamilies. In one, the Phyllonycterinae, now confined to the
islands of the Greater Antilles, the rostrum is only moderately
lengthened and the molar teeth are of relatively small size with
their cusps low and degenerate. In the other, the Glossophaginae, found on the mainland and in the West Indies alike,
a similar line of development has gone still farther, resulting
in a long and narrow snout with correspondingly slender and
elongate teeth, while the tongue has become very narrow and
so long that it is capable of being extended far beyond the lips.
At its tip the tongue has developed numerous thread-like papillae
forming a little brush, while in some species the lower incisors
tend to be very small or even are shed entirely in the adult, or
again, as in Choeronycteris, are permanently absent, to facili-
tate the rapid movements of the tongue as it runs in and out.
For in contrast to the first group, or Stenoderminae, which are
pulp crushers, these last feed by licking out soft pulp or juices,
or are nectar-feeders, visiting large blossoms by night and reaching the nectar at the base of the corolla with the extensile tongue.
A parallel is found in the Old World Pteropidae, some of whose
members are modified in a somewhat similar way for feeding on

the nectar of flowers. In the New World bats with vegetarian habits the evolution of the teeth for this kind of diet has so modified the structure of the molars that the original sharp cusps are often much reduced and may be difficult to identify with those of their insect-eating relatives of the same family; but in the Old World Pteropidae this change has gone so far that there is little trace left of the original cusps. Instead, the teeth are simple two-cusped structures or the molars are nearly flat-crowned.

In the big-eared bat (Otopterus) of the West Indies and North America, we have a case of transitional habits, for it appears to be in part insectivorous and in part vegetarian in its diet. Writing of this bat as observed by him in Jamaica, Osburn (1865) says that on the floor of a cave below a roost of a colony, he found a heap of wings of large Orthoptera they had brought in, and saw one bat let drop the wings and legs of a large grasshopper. According to Osburn, if his identification may be accepted, they are also fond of certain berries, such as breadnut (Brosimum), roseapple (*Eugenia jambos*), and fustic (*Morus tinctoria*). In one instance he mentions, the big-eared bats came nightly to rest beneath a friend's veranda in Jamaica and made themselves a nuisance by voiding their excrement against the wall of the house. In another, a neighbor complained that they came in through the open window by night and, hanging up on the lofty curtain frame of his bed, dropped fragments of their feasts on the bedclothes and sleeper below!

Very little careful study has been made of the diet and food preferences or their seasonal variation in the American fruit-eating bats. Probably very few fruits are available at all times of the year, but bananas may be one of these, and their pulp is greedily taken by certain species, particularly by the common *Carollia perspicillata*, of Central and South America. The late Leo Miller (quoted by J. A. Allen, 1916d), while collecting on the Rio Pescador, Colombia, found this species so destructive to plantains and other fruits that they were a real nuisance to the natives. Bananas and plantains had to be cut green, for upon showing the slightest traces of ripening they were attacked by hordes of hungry bats, which would even squeeze through crevices in mud walls to get at the fruit hung inside to ripen. By placing a few ripe bananas in his room, he attracted great numbers that kept up a constant roar with their wings. "The next morning only the skins of the bananas remained." On another occasion he hung a bunch of ripe bananas covered with a netting in his room and after dark "bats began to pour through the open door and window in a steady stream, and circling round a few times, landed on the net," where many became entangled. When he brought a lighted lamp, most of them left, but others remained, continuing their frantic efforts to reach the fruit. In a short time sixty of this species were captured. So attractive is this fruit to bats that even the large carnivorous spear-nosed bats, as already mentioned, were kept for some time in captivity on a diet of banana alone by Dr. Lawrence Dunn. Possibly vegetarian habits may have first been developed through their learning to like the meaty pulp of this fruit. Possibly, too, a liking for soft fruits may have been developed through eating insects attracted to them, so that in taking the one they would chance to sample the other. What seems to be a case of this sort is recounted by Wood (in Kershaw, 1922) in a note on the large horseshoe bat (*Hipposideros commersoni marungensis*) of Nyasaland, Africa. He says that when a species of wild fig known as the mtundu-tree "ripens its fruits all along the stems of its branches, these bats come around in hundreds, like swarms of fruit-bats, land on the tree, and seize the fruits, fragments of which are scattered all around, and are often carried to other trees near by, and pieces dropped there. The natives state that they eat the fruit and call them by the same name as the true fruit-bats, i.e., 'mleme.' I wrote this to Mr. Oldfield Thomas, who replied that no Hipposideros was a fruit-eater. On examination of the figs, I found that practically every fruit was attacked by a large weevil, the larvae of which were inside the fruit. It is therefore probable that it is upon these weevil larvae that the bat is really feeding, and that they only seize the fruit to tear it apart to get the larvae. But in certain cases the fruit is often chewed into a pulp, as I have found the remains of it in this condition everywhere around the trees."

Another abundant fruit-eater in tropical America is the large leaf-nosed bat of the genus Artibeus, of which there are several species. In the West Indies I have found them to be very fond of the thin layer of pulp surrounding the small nutlike fruits of a tall palm of the genus Acrocomia; these grow in large clusters high up on the trunk below the feathery top. The bats have a habit of carrying off these nuts to a convenient resting place, there to hang up and gnaw off the pulp at leisure. In a large cave I visited in Puerto Rico many of these bats spent the day in the absolute darkness of a far chamber and had evidently been in the habit of bringing the palm nuts in with them on returning to roost. For on the ground a strange sight was disclosed by the light of a lantern, where multitudes of the nuts dropped by the bats had germinated in the damp soil of the cave floor and sent up a ghostly thicket of thin white stalks to a height of two or three feet before the shoots had died from lack of sunlight. In Trinidad the late Colonel Feilden (1889), while inspecting the Royal Botanical Garden in company with the superintendent, J. H. Hart, observed under certain trees numbers of large brown nuts, some six inches in circumference, that had been brought in and partly eaten by bats, doubtless of this genus. These must have come from a distance, for the fruits did not belong to any of the trees in the garden, nor did Hart know of any such trees in the neighborhood. On the ground beneath certain places were accumulations of seeds of various kinds brought by the same bats, which evidently resorted to favorite trees by night, where, suspended by their feet from favorite branches, they could eat their booty undisturbed. That bats may be an important factor in the dissemination of such seeds is further pointed out by this author. It would have been interesting to know what species of plants were represented and the nature of the parts eaten, whether pulp or harder parts. Osburn (1865) mentions finding kernels of breadnut (Brosimum) brought into a cave by these bats while the cave floor was strewn with the gnawed berries of the sea grape (*Cordia collococca*), fragments of unripe mangoes and of roseapple.

The small leaf-nosed bats of the subfamily Glossophaginae have further specialized in fruit eating to the extent of feeding on soft pulp or juice only, to secure which their long narrow tongues are capable of being run out an inch or more beyond the lips while the tip is provided with stiff long papillae that act as a brush to lap up the liquid. Osburn (1865) describes the actions of a captive bat of the related group Phyllonycterinae, which he calls *Phyllonycteris poeyi*, though more likely it was one of the allied genus Erophylla, of Jamaica. He presented the bat with a ripe berry of the sea grape, to which, however, it at first paid no attention until he broke it open, when immediately the bat began licking out the juice and pulp by quick movements of its long tongue. To finish the feast, the bat "brought up the wrists to the muzzle, took the berry between them, gave it two or three energetic bites, and then held the berry off," applying the long thumbs dexterously to hold it firmly, even turning the berry around with what appeared to be a reverse action of the wrists.

The long-nosed bats of the subfamily Glossophaginae, including the genera Glossophaga, Choeronycteris, and probably Lonchophylla, are to some extent, at least, nectar feeders, alighting on the corollas of large night-blooming flowers to lap up with their long tongues the honeyed liquid at the bottom of the cup. Thus, the first-named is known to come to the flowers of the calabash tree and the night-blooming cacti in Central America and Mexico. In their search for this food they appear to act as pollinators, transferring pollen from flower to flower, as described in the following chapter. Another and very rare species of this group is *Leptonycteris nivalis* of tropical America, in which the long fimbriate tongue is also adapted for flower-feeding. Dugès (1906), a Mexican naturalist, describes a specimen found in a garden at Guanajuato, the stomach of which was filled with pollen. A microscopical examination showed that this pollen was from the large white-flowered *Mal-*

*vaviscus acerifolius* that grew abundantly in the garden. The bat was picked up dead under a nest of black wasps, which had apparently stung it to death. Dugès supposes that it had been attracted by the dark liquid honey which these insects produce and in attempting to secure this had incurred the fury of the wasps.

The various bats of the flying-fox family (Pteropidae) of the Old World are, so far as certainly known, almost exclusively feeders on fruit, flower buds, pollen, and nectar, though the tube-nosed Nyctimene in one instance was found to have insect remains in the stomach. An excellent account of the habits of the common flying fox of India has been given by McCann (1934), who briefly summarizes the observations of Tennent, Tickell, and others, adding many notes of his own. He lists six species of wild fig tree (Ficus) which this bat feeds upon, and its fruit is a favorite with other species of the genus, as well as of related genera in the countries where it is found. In parts of southeastern Australia the ripening of the berry-like fruits of the Port Moreton and other figs is the signal for the arrival of three or four species of Pteropus, which, however, do not confine their attention to this tree alone but raid the plantations of fruit growers, often doing considerable damage to the fruit crops, for they come in hordes against which methods of extermination have thus far had little effect. The economic aspects of these attacks in eastern Australia have been made the subject of a special investigation by Ratcliffe (1931), who concludes, however, that on the whole the losses are really much less than supposed, even though in some cases large. The very great numbers of these bats, he finds, are in reality mainly supported by the flowering trees of the open eucalyptus type of forest, and they subsist largely on the wild figs in their season, while only a small part of the total bat population is concerned with the attacks on cultivated fruit, partly owing to the fact that the main commercial fruit-growing districts are relatively isolated and inconsiderable areas. Bananas are attacked when ripe, but since for commercial purposes the bunches are cut green, they are relatively safe; of citrus fruits, mandarin oranges are taken in preference to other kinds, but on the whole are not damaged seriously except in occasional instances; pineapples are usually immune, but in rare cases flying foxes have been known to crawl on the ground in their attempts to get at them when other food is scarce.

In certain seasons pome fruits, such as apples and pears, will be passed over when natural food is obtainable, while stone fruits such as peaches and plums are sometimes seriously damaged, though by taking precautionary measures the losses can be greatly reduced. Pawpaws when ripe are much relished by the four species of Pteropus occurring in eastern Australia, and many are damaged by bites and scratches that are not eaten. Mangoes are especially liked by these bats, as are also custard apples, but since these are picked for market before they are quite ripe, they suffer little. Hitherto no effective methods for reducing the population of fruit bats in Australia have been discovered, but Ratcliffe makes the reassuring statement that "contrary to the general belief, the flying fox is not a serious menace to the commercial fruit industry," notwithstanding that in eastern Australia its numbers "are far greater than is generally imagined."

In India the common flying fox, *Pteropus giganteus*, is described by Tickell, Tennent, McCann, and others as feeding on various ripe fruits in season, such as figs, guavas, plantains, roseapple, and mowhooa berries, but, as with the Australian species, oranges are generally avoided. Another favorite food is the flower buds of the silk-cotton tree (*Eriodendron orientale*). Some species seem to prefer flowers and flower buds. Thus the little red flying fox (*P. scapulatus*) of Australia especially delights in eucalyptus blossoms, while the large black *P. gouldi* of the same country is said to be so fond of these that its flesh becomes redolent of their pungent scent, making it impalatable to any but the natives.

In the East Indies and Oceania many of the more isolated island groups are inhabited permanently by local races of fruit bats, which must obviously have a more limited variety and amount of available fruit to draw upon, so that a study of their diet would be especially interesting in comparison with that of continental species. There are many scattered notes in the literature of the subject, of which a few may be added. Thus in July 1874 Moseley, of the famous *Challenger* expedition, found *Pteropus tonganus* at Tonga Tabu feeding on the bright red flowers of an indigenous tree; in the Samoan Islands *P. samoensis* is very fond of the breadfruit (Artocarpus), and since the trees are to be found chiefly about villages, many of the bats that come to raid the trees are killed by the natives for food. Other cultivated fruits are also attacked, such as bananas (especially the *Musa chinensis*), the hog-plum (*Spondias dulcis*), and sweet oranges, for which it has a great liking. On Christmas Island, the local *P. natalis* is said by Andrews (1900) to have become largely diurnal in habits. Near the settlement they destroy bananas and pawpaws but when wild fruits are ripe, particularly those of the "saoh" (Sideroxylon) and "gatet" (Inocarpus), comparatively few visit gardens, but keep to the forests. Two species occur on the island of Aneitum, one of which (*P. anetianus*) is said to be practically confined to the windward side, where it finds sufficient tree fruit for its needs and in season devours quantities of Vaccinium berries from low bushes which grow abundantly on the lower slopes of the hills; on the leeward side of the same island, *P. geddiei* is the common species, inhabiting thick woods near the sea, but coming in numbers about the villages with the ripening of the two annual crops of breadfruit, of which they are very destructive (Macgillivray, 1860). The natives utilize them as food, catching them sometimes in traps, made like those used in fishing — circular, flat-bottomed baskets with a hole at the top, baited with a pawpaw.

In the New Hebrides islands, where *Pteropus geddiei*, and a smaller species, *P. eotinus*, live permanently, Dr. and Mrs. J. R. Baker were able to follow the dietary around the calendar. Of the first species they write (1936):

Two favorite foods, papaw and banana, are available throughout the year. The figs of *Ficus copiosa* are also said by the natives to be eaten by the fruit-bats, and they also are probably available at all seasons. Bread-

FIG. 20—Gray-headed fruit bat or flying fox (*Pteropus poliocephalus*) of Queensland, Australia, suspended head downward, in resting posture. Note the narrow ears, the head looking forward, the free thumb, the claw on the tip of the index finger, the short and narrow interfemoral membrane with its spurlike spreader. Courtesy of Mr. Otho Webb, phot.

fruit was available from September to April, and during this period probably formed one of the main foods of the species [*P. geddiei*]. In January the natives told us that they were eating the large fruit of the "nenget" (not yet identified); in February, the flowers or fruits of the hardwood tree, *Glochidion ramiflorum*, and the almond-like kernels of *Terminalia Catappa*; in March, *T. Catappa* again, as well as guava; and in May, the pulp of the one-seeded fruit of *Dracontomelon* . . . and perhaps also the chestnut-like seeds from the huge pods of *Castanospermum australe*.

This varied diet gives a seasonal change which may be correlated with other habits. Since the bats chew these pulpy fruits and swallow almost nothing but the juices, rejecting the rest, it is not possible to tell much about the nature of the diet by examining stomach contents.

In the Mascarene Islands fruit bats have been familiar since white occupation. Buffon quotes a letter from his correspondent, de la Nux, that on Réunion, their favorite fruits are banana, guavas, and mistletoe berries, while in the southern summer, January and February, they come in numbers to feed on the flowers of certain umbellifers in the lower part of the island, often covering the ground with the blossoms torn off. In the Seychelles almost any fruit is taken, but mangoes and the "fruit de Cythère" (*Spondias cytherea*) are especial favorites.

The food habits of the smaller fruit bats of the family Pteropidae are still rather little known, but in the case of the genera Eidolon (straw-colored bat), Epomophorus and its allies (the epaulet bats), and Rousettus (the rousette bats) of Africa and southern Asia, wild figs, guavas, and bananas are generally liked. Probably the juice is the main attraction, for the seeds and fleshy pulp are usually rejected in a small pellet from the mouth after chewing and squeezing. In some places dates are eaten when they become ripe, as Percival and Dodson noticed at Lahej, Arabia, where it was necessary to enclose each bunch in a bag woven of palm fronds to protect the fruit from the straw-colored bat. This species was abundant there for only about a week in mid-August, coincident with the maturing of the date crop. It also attacks the fruit of the Borassus palm, sometimes literally eating a way into the fruit clusters (Heuglin). A curious habit attributed to this bat is that of gnawing into stems of soft wood, apparently for the sap and perhaps in lack of sufficient moisture from its usual food. At all events Thomas and Hinton (1923a) have reported that on the Gold Coast of West Africa, R. H. Bunting of the Agricultural Department discovered that a grove of Araucarias was being seriously damaged in a time of drought by some animal gnawing into the stems. He succeeded in capturing and sending to the British Museum some of these bats caught in the act. The same authors mention that the stem of a small tree, identified as either Odina or Sclerocarya, similarly gnawed, was brought to the British Museum by an expedition exploring Jebel Marra, on the southern edge of the Sahara in Darfur, and they suppose this fruit bat again to be the culprit. The allied genus, Rousettus, which occurs not only over most of Africa but eastward also to southern Asia and the East Indies, is said to be very destructive to the loquat (Eriobotrya) in South Africa, but Layard's statement that it will occasionally snap insects off flowers seems to require confirmation. In Cyprus the Mediterranean representative of the genus is reported as damaging fruit crops, particularly oranges and dates, the bunches of the latter requiring protection during the ripening season, as in Arabia, by tying them in sacks (Bate).

Some of the smaller members of the Pteropidae show an extraordinarily interesting parallelism with certain of the New World Phyllostomidae or leaf-nose bats, in having specialized on a diet of flower pollen and nectar, with the result that they have in a similar way developed long and slender tongues, with stiff rasplike papillae for lapping up this food. Most of these are contained in a special subfamily, appropriately named Macroglossinae, and comprise seven genera, most of which are confined to islands of the East Indian archipelago. One, however, Eonycteris, extends to the Malayan region, and curiously another, Megaloglossus, is found in the forest region of West Africa. All agree in the peculiar structure of the tongue and in the reduced condition of the teeth, which become much narrowed. Another interesting parallel is found in a member of the epaulet-bat group of Africa, Plerotes, of which only a few specimens are known. It seems to have independently acquired a similar long tongue, slender jaws, narrowed teeth, like the Macroglossinae, but is not closely allied to them. One would expect that it must have similar habits of feeding on pollen and nectar and, as with some other bats of like habits, that it may assist in the cross-fertilization of flowers, as described in a later chapter. Little, however, is definitely recorded of their habits. One genus, Notopteris, remarkable among fruit bats for its long free tail, is said to frequent banana plants when the flowers are in bloom and possibly feeds on them. More precise evidence is given by Bartels (1908) in the case of the genus Eonycteris, one of the larger members of the subfamily Macroglossinae. In the latter part of the year 1907 he noticed numbers of these bats coming and going about the flowers of agaves blossoming in the Botanical Garden at Buitenzorg, Java. Sometimes the bats would alight momentarily upon a blossom. The stomach of only one of the specimens he secured contained food, which proved to be an abundance of pollen. No doubt other bats of the family are to some extent flower-eaters also, as McCann indicates in the case of Cynopterus, while the abundant sweet nectar exuded by certain night-blooming trees in the tropics of the Old World is doubtless taken to some extent.

# CHAPTER VIII

## BAT FLOWERS

It has long been known that many plants are cross-fertilized through the agency of insects, which visit the flowers for the sake of the nectar exuded within the base of the corolla. Often elaborate devices have been evolved to insure the success of this method, so that an insect crawling into the flower cup for the honey must brush against the anthers on the ends of the stamens and thus carry away pollen grains, which in turn are rubbed off on the stigma of the next blossom visited. Many flowers are so constructed that only special kinds of insects can reach the honey and bring about pollination in this way. Some flowers have stamens that snap up when touched at their base, throwing the pollen over the insect, or, as in the mountain laurel, the stamens are stretched back in little pockets of the corolla, to be released like a spring when an insect sufficiently heavy bears down on the lip of the blossom. Other flowers are adapted for pollination by hummingbirds or, in the Old World tropics, by sun-birds or the small "flower-peckers." This implies a very long period of gradual adjustment between the flower and its visitors. Such flowers are usually of bright colors such as will attract the birds' attention.

It is less generally known that a few tropical plants appear to depend in part or perhaps in some cases chiefly on certain kinds of bats which visit the flowers by night in search of nectar or pollen. The Austrian botanist Professor Otto Porsch (1932) has made a special study of such "bat flowers" and in a recent contribution has summarized what is known of this interesting relation. From his paper, chiefly, the following notes are drawn. According to this author, some two dozen genera of tropical plants, mainly trees, probably owe their cross-fertilization in a greater or less degree to small species of nectar-loving bats, but this has been actually observed in about half a dozen genera only, while in the other cases it is inferred from the flower structure.

Apparently Moseley, one of the naturalists on the famous voyage of the *Challenger*, was the first to suggest bats as the pollinating agents in the case of various flowering trees. He noticed that in the Fiji, Samoa, and Caroline Islands the bright-red flowers of certain native trees formed an important item in the diet of the local races of large fruit bat (Pteropus). It is also known that the small red flying fox (*Pteropus scapulatus*) of eastern Australia is a blossom-feeder, and it may have been this species that Moseley observed at Botany Bay, New South Wales, in May, "feeding on the flowers of the gum trees" (Eucalyptus). He adds (1879, p. 291) that these bats "must probably often act as fertilizers, by carrying pollen from tree to tree, adherent to their fur." Pollination in this way by these large bats must, however, be only incidental and occasional, without special adaptation by either flower or bat. Later, W. Burck in 1892 noticed in the Botanic Garden at Buitenzorg, Java, that bats were actively visiting the flowers of *Freycinetia funicularis*, a species with long white blossoms, native to the island of Amboina, and he suggested that they were agents in pollination, although Porsch believes rather that it is a bird-adapted species. Here again, the bats were apparently one of the large species of Pteropus, pollination by which might be but incidental.

In 1897 J. H. Hart, the Keeper of the Royal Botanical Garden in Trinidad, first observed pollination by a New World species of bat. This was in the case of the *Bauhinia megalandra*, a tropical tree native to that region, that grows to a height of about thirty feet. Its long white blossoms open in the early evening — in January at about six o'clock. For half an hour or so beforehand, Hart saw small bats of apparently more than one species flying from flower to flower, and as the bat left, the blossom would fall to the ground. The next morning not a single whole blossom remained on the tree, for those that had not fallen were more or less torn and bereft of their long white petals. The bats in visiting the flower appear to alight on the projecting portion of the corolla, and seizing the erect and recurved standard, completely tear it to pieces or break it off. There is no secretion of nectar by these flowers, hence Hart supposed that the bats are attracted by the insects drawn in turn by the perfume of the flowers. In order to secure these insects the bats must enter the flower in such a way that they come into contact with the stamens and effect pollination. In a further note on this subject, Hart adds that the flowers of still another tree — the "wallaba" (*Eperua falcata*) — are visited by bats. One of these latter was captured and identified as "*Glossonycteris*" [*Anoura*] *geoffroyi*, a leaf-nosed species of the subfamily Glossophaginae, in which the tongue is very long and slender, adapted for reaching into the base of the corolla. The behavior of the bat was so similar to that of a large night moth that it was at first mistaken for one. Hart had no doubt that cross-pollination was effected by this bat.

In 1907 Hubert Winkler expressed the opinion that the African "sausage tree" (*Kigelia africana*) is probably specially adapted for cross-fertilization by bats, basing his surmise on the structural peculiarities of the large blossoms. But it remained for Fr. Heide in 1927 to confirm this by actual observation in the case of the related *Kigelia aethiopica* and another tropical tree, *Markhamia stipulata*. His observations were made in the botanic gardens at Buitenzorg, Dutch East Indies, and the species of bat identified as *Eonycteris spelaea*, one of the smaller fruit bats of the subfamily Macroglossinae, in which the muzzle is narrow and the tongue long and protrusible, with abundant rasplike papillae, pointing backward. He believed that the bats were feeding upon the pollen of the flowers, for a specimen shot in the act of visiting a blossom had only pollen on its tongue and in its stomach, but no portions of flower petals. Heide further suspected that the calabash tree (Crescentia) might similarly be pollinated by bats, but his attempts to catch one by spreading birdlime on the petals were unsuccessful.

Quite independently of Heide, a Dutch naturalist, Pijl, suggested the intervention of bats as pollinators of the sausage tree and of still another species, *Oroxylum indicum*, although actual field observations were lacking to prove it. More recently, the agency of small fruit bats as pollinators was described for a related Indian species of sausage tree, *Kigelia pinnata*, by McCann (1931). The large red blossoms of this tree open in the evening between half-past five o'clock and sunset, and by the following forenoon, if fertilization has taken place, the corolla drops to the ground, leaving only the calyx and style in place; if unfertilized, the entire flower falls away from the articulation immediately below the corolla. The latter is a deep blood-red inside and yellowish green outside. The petals are large and fleshy with many wrinkles and furrows. When open, the blossoms emit a strong and rather disagreeable odor. They have four large, erect stamens with thickened bases, which, with the long projecting pistil, fill the throat of the flower. Several glands at its base secrete an abundant clear sweetish nectar, which fills the base of the corolla and trickles out into the furrows of the lower petal when the flower is bent downward.

Unaware of Pijl's observations, the same author calls attention again to the similarly deep-red flowers of *Oroxylum indicum*, which also share the habit of opening only at night, so that it is hardly possible to secure a photograph of the tree in blossom except by flashlight. The perfume of these blossoms is said to be reminiscent of carrion. A further interesting adaptation of the sausage tree he found to be that the anthers of those flowers that open early in the evening were not yet in condition to scatter their pollen, thus excluding birds as fertilizers; but those examined later in the evening were now perfectly ripe, so that the slightest jerk caused them to drop pollen directly on the lower petal. So abundant is the nectar that in plucking a flowering branch "one literally gets a shower bath" as it trickles from the furrows of the lower petal. During the flowering season of these trees, from March to July (thus a very long one), McCann found that they were regularly visited by the small fruit bats which he identifies as *Cynopterus sphinx*, although no specimens were taken. On several occasions he saw them alighting on the blossoms and thrusting their heads deep within the corollas, hang on for a short time before flying off again, thereby bending the flower down and causing the nectar to ooze out upon the lower petal, where it is eagerly lapped up. On entering the flower, the bat must dislodge the pollen over its head and at the same time rub the projecting stigma over its neck and upper back. Both these trees, Kigelia and Oroxylum, belong to the same botanical family, Bignoniaceae.

Porsch, in his paper of 1927, makes note of the marks of the bat's thumb-claws on the corollas, and particularly gives an account of the fertilization of the flowers of two species of calabash tree (*Crescentia cujete* and *C. alata*) by bats. His

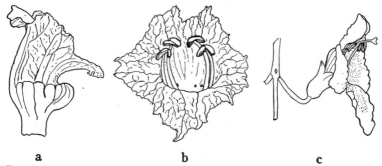

a                                   b                                   c

Fig. 21—Flowers adapted for fertilization by the agency of bats. (a) Side view and (b) front view of the blossom of the calabash tree (Crescentia) of Central America (after Porsch) three-fifths natural size; (c) side view of the flower of the sausage tree (Kigelia) of India (after McCann) about one-third natural size. Both show the landing platform, the wide corolla, the erect stamens, and the large nectary for attracting bats.

observations were made in Costa Rica, where, as elsewhere in the American tropics, these trees are frequently planted for the sake of the useful bowl-like dishes to be made from the fruits. The flowers have an unusually wide corolla, which is wrinkled and furrowed. They open only by night, but nevertheless are somewhat visited toward evening by hummingbirds, no doubt because of their abundant nectar. At about half-past five in the afternoon the flowers commence to open and reach the height of blossoming in the early hours of night while bats are active, closing again at early dawn. Like the bat flowers of the eastern tropics, they emit a strong odor which to Porsch suggested the rank smell of freshly cut kohlrabi. He gives a vivid account of two evening visits he made to one of these trees which in early May was near the end of its flowering season. In the soft coolness of the tropic night, surrounded by the myriad twinkling lights of fireflies, he took up his station close to one of the trees, allowing the beams of his oil lamp and flashlight to fall upon the branches, thus bringing several of the large blossoms into full view. Some of these had previously been examined just before sunset and were found to contain as insect visitors a few stingless bees (Trigona), a stray ant or two, and one lady-beetle. A reëxamination at about six P.M. showed that even these insects had forsaken the blossoms. A half-hour later the first bats appeared, at almost the same time on two consecutive evenings, and thereafter they were constantly seen during the next hour and a half, paying no attention to the lighted lamp near by. The bats were much more "nervous" in their actions even than hummingbirds. Darting like arrows, they would alight momentarily on a blossom, clinging to the outer part of the corolla and dipping their heads quickly within, and as quickly darting away, leaving the flower trembling on its short, elastic stem. There was none of the lacerating and destroying of the blossom, such as was noted in the case of the sausage tree (Kigelia) and in Markhamia. Apparently the bats were seeking chiefly the nectar, and with their long extensile tongue also lapped up any pollen that fell on the lower lip of the corolla. The species of bat that visited the calabash trees in such numbers proved to be the common shrewlike bat, *Glossophaga soricina*, an abundant and widespread species in tropical America. At the time when they were thus actively visiting the tree, the flowers were found to be expanded to the utmost.

In his summary note on bat flowers, Dr. Porsch (1932a) regards the following genera of plants as certainly dependent upon bats for fertilization: the sausage trees (Kigelia), Markhamia, the calabash tree (Crescentia), Amphitecna, Parmentiera, Oroxylum, the durian tree (Durio), the silk-cotton trees (Ceiba and Bombax), the baobab tree (Adansonia), Caryocar, Eperua, Vriesa, Alcantarea, Thecophyllum, and the century-plant (Agave). Several other genera are also in all probability visited by bats and pollinated by them: Calliandra, Jambosa,

Eucalyptus, Sonneratia, Barringtonia, Capparis, Crataeva, and sundry other cactus genera such as Pilocereus, the night-blooming cereus. The adaptive characters of bat flowers for this method of pollination he summarizes as follows: (1) the habit of night-blooming; (2) a strong and peculiar odor; (3) a remarkably wide and erect corolla allowing the bat to insert its head and shoulders easily; (4) the large size and depth of the flower; (5) a characteristic outer extension of the corolla. No doubt the bats are guided by their sense of smell in finding the blossoms and are attracted by the nectar. In the flower-feeding fruit bats the olfactory lobes of the brain are well developed and Moller (1932) has shown that in Glossophaga these organs are far better developed than in insectivorous species.

While the flower-visiting habit is certainly known in Glossophaga and perhaps Anoura among American bats, it is highly probable that other genera of the same subfamily (Glossophaginae) are honey-seekers also and play a part in cross-fertilization of the night-blooming plants. Of such would be probably Choeronycteris, Hylonycteris, and Leptonycteris, as well as the close relative of the last, Lichonycteris, which, like one of the species of Glossophaga, has lost the lower incisors in correlation with its method of feeding by means of its long extensile tongue. In all these genera the muzzle is slender, the nose-leaf small, and the tongue long and narrow. Their teeth are but little modified from an insectivorous type, although small, and with a tendency to reduce or lose the lower incisors to give the tongue free play. The nectar-feeding bats of the Old World tropics, so far as made out, are also comprised within a single subfamily, the Macroglossinae, paralleling somewhat in their structure the Glossophaginae, though belonging to a separate suborder, of the fruit-bat group. They are small species, though one, Eonycteris, is nearly double the bulk of Glossophaga. Macroglossus and Syconycteris are smaller, among the smallest of the Pteropidae. That all these bats as well as the flowers they fertilize are tropical is readily understood when one considers that a bat of flower-seeking habits must find food of this type available over a considerable part of the year. The long flowering season of many tropical species, extending sometimes over several months, is therefore an important factor, as well as the fact that the season is different in various flowers, so that their times of blooming overlap and thus afford a continuous supply.

# CHAPTER IX

# WINGS IN THE DARK

The Wings of a Batt are wonderful strange, consisting of one intire Skin, webb'd together like the Feet of a Water-Fowl; the Claws or Hooks on the tops of the Wings this Creature makes use of, to hang by to any thing it is minded. — Albin, 1740.

BATS are the only mammals that have attained the power of flight, but what they were like before they were true fliers, we can only conjecture. For the very earliest bats of which we possess adequate knowledge, beautifully preserved as fossils in certain Eocene deposits of Europe, had wings of excellent development, proving that already in early Tertiary times, some fifty million years ago, they had gained mastery over the air. Indeed, so far as we can tell from the scanty evidence at hand, they have changed relatively little in essential details of structure up to the present day.

Probably the ancestors of bats were small tree-living shrew-like creatures that first learned to extend their leaps from bough to bough by flattening themselves out so as to spread the skin along the sides of the body for greater support in the air. Gradually in this way a wide membrane developed along the sides (the plagiopatagium) very much as we see at the present time in several types of forest-living marsupials of Australia, or in the flying squirrels of our northern woods. The next step was probably the addition of another sail by the extension of the skin to form a membrane from the heel to the base of the tail. This finally extended to the very tip and was given additional support by the tail itself, which acted as a sort of spar. Such a membrane (called the uropatagium) is present in the majority of living bats as well as in the curious "flying lemur" or colugo of oriental forests, and is developed to a less extent in some of the "flying opossums" and in the scaly-tailed squirrels of African forests, some of which are as small as mice, some as large as a gray squirrel, with broad side membranes. The colugo also indicates a further step, in the growth of an additional membrane (the propatagium) from the front of the upper arm to the side of the neck, but most important of all, the long slender fingers of its hand are all connected by a webbing that extends all the way to the base of the claws, forming a hand membrane (the chiropatagium). Although the "flying lemurs" progressed no further in the development of flight, they indicate what may have been a somewhat intermediate stage in that direction, from which a batlike type could have been evolved through the further lengthening of the fingers and the membrane they support. In the colugo the thumb is included in the hand membrane, but in bats it is largely free and remains short, while the propatagium is less extended. For this and various other reasons of an anatomical nature, the colugos must be regarded as a separate and divergent line only remotely related to the bats.

If the ancestral bats passed through stages somewhat like these and attained the power of propelling themselves by the hand membranes, while the side and tail membranes gave them support in the air, their further evolution must have had to do mainly with the perfection of details, which nevertheless involved many slight changes and adjustments to the new way of life. It is one of the remarkable things about these animals that among the many living species we see a wide variety in the degree of these changes, so that it is often possible to trace many of the steps. Miller (1907) has pointed out that the upper-arm bone (humerus) varies in its development in different groups of bats. In the poorer fliers the head of the bone has a simple articulation with the cavity of the shoulder blade, but in the bats that have the greatest power of flight, such as the Vespertilionidae and the free-tailed bats of the family Molossidae, two small supplementary heads are developed, of which the outer (the trochiter) is large and forms a secondary articulation by means of a distinct facet against the shoulder blade. In the latter family also the fifth finger is short, producing a long narrow wing, comparable to that of swifts among birds, and these birds may often be seen at sunset flying with molossid bats in the tropics, the two having a nearly similar speed. Revilliod (1916) believes that in its earlier types the wing of bats had the upper arm but little shorter than the forearm, and the third finger only slightly longer than the latter, the fourth and fifth fingers a little shorter still, but the fourth the shortest. It would thus perhaps resemble the wing of young modern bats, before the full development is attained.

The ancestors of present-day bats must have had separate and well-developed radius and ulna in the forearm, while the thumb and fingers must have had the typical number of joints characteristic of most mammals, that is, two joints in the thumb and three in each of the other fingers. The metacarpals or bones forming the back of the hand were probably relatively shorter. This condition has been considerably altered. For the metacarpals are much lengthened in modern bats and the finger joints reduced or otherwise modified. In the active work of flying most of the labor is taken by the radius or inner bone of the forearm, with the result that it has increased in size. The outer bone or ulna, however, has degenerated, until, as in the fruit bats, it has become a mere thread, losing its outer end altogether while the basal end remains to form a loose elbow joint. In all other bats the slender ulna unites with the radius a short distance beyond its base.

The thumb is always separate from the rest of the wing and helps, when the animal is crawling, to hook the body along by the aid of its terminal claw. In the dainty little South American bats of the family Furipteridae, however, the thumb is much shortened and its claw quite gone, a condition unique in the entire group. The meaning of this is unknown. A still more remarkable condition is found in the disk-winged bats of South and Central America, in which the thumb is likewise small, but has developed a large round sucker with a short stem and a similar but smaller disk on the sole of the hind foot. By means of these suckers, the disk-winged bats (Thyropteridae) can rest upside down on a perfectly smooth surface. Indeed, one of their favorite roosting places is inside the long narrow tube formed by an unrolled banana frond, to the shiny surface of which they cling by the aid of these unique structures. Somewhat similar but sessile adhesive disks are present in a curious little bat, Myzopoda, found only in the island of Madagascar on the other side of the world. This remarkable species forms a family by itself, but is probably most nearly related to the disk-winged bats. Still a third genus, Tylonycteris, the little bamboo bat of the East, has adhesive pads on wrist and foot (see Figure 11). It lives by day inside the hollow joints of bamboo, entering through narrow cracks.

Of the four fingers of the hand, the first or index finger is the only one to retain three small phalanges or joints and a terminal claw, but this condition is found only in the fruit bats (Pteropidae) of the Old World, and even in a few genera of these, such as the long-tailed Notopteris and the flower-feeding Eonycteris, the claw is missing. In all the other bats, constituting the suborder Microchiroptera, the index finger has lost its claw and terminal joint. In the mouse-tailed bats (Rhinopoma), however, the two basal joints or phalanges are still present, and this is regarded as one of the primitive traits of this group. Other families, such as the leaf-nosed bats (Phyllostomidae) and the vespertilionid bats (Vespertilionidae), retain one basal joint only. In most others, as in the horseshoe bats and the hollow-faced bats, even this has been lost, and the long metacarpal alone remains, lying close against the third metacarpal to stiffen the fore edge of the wing. The third digit of the hand is always the longest. Its three phalanges are present and bony in the leaf-nosed bats, as well as in their relatives, the vampires, and in the disk-winged bats (Thyropteridae) and their distant relatives of Madagascar, the Myzopodidae; but in most other families the third or terminal joint has more or less degenerated and become cartilaginous, as it always is in the fourth and fifth fingers.

When at rest or hanging up, the wings are folded so that the long metacarpal bones close like the spokes of an umbrella, but there is a certain amount of variation in the method of folding the terminal joints, characteristic of different groups.

With many of the fruit bats the terminal joints are kept nearly straight, and the metacarpals slightly spread, so that the wings are folded over the entire front of the chest, while the head and chin rest against the breast. In this way these bats sleep by day with their heads concealed under the wings. Among some of the horseshoe bats (Rhinolophus) a nearly similar method is seen (Figure 22), but the forearms are in addition slightly raised and nearly touch over the middle of the back, so that the bats are almost completely shrouded in their ample wing membranes while sleeping. The terminal joints of the third and fourth fingers are folded back against the inner side of the wing. This method of covering the head with the wings is perhaps helpful in keeping out the light and weather in tree-roosting bats (as many of the fruit-eating species are), but the horseshoe bats are mainly cave-dwellers. It is perhaps a primitive habit as well, for the more specialized bats do not bend the head forward upon the breast. Instead, it hangs straight downward, and when the bat is aroused it can be raised slightly. A curious method of folding the wing is found in the sheath-tailed bats, in all of which the basal phalanx of the long third finger is bent back upon the *upper* surface of the wing, while the terminal one is extended behind. This folding also involves the last joint of the fourth finger, which is similarly turned back upon itself against the upper surface. In most bats these joints are merely turned under against the lower surface, with the terminal joint of the long third finger directed forward, as in the Vespertilionidae. But in the free-tailed bats (Molossidae) the condition somewhat resembles that in the sheath-tails, with the basal phalanx of the third finger turned forward, then the terminal one turned back. When thus bent, these joints lie against the inner instead of the outer surface of the wing.

The loss of fur from the wing membranes doubtless is an adaptation to reduce the drag or resistance of the air in flight. Hair is usually reduced also on the tail membrane, although a few bats, such as the red and the hoary bats of America, have abundant fur on their upper surfaces, notwithstanding that they are among the best flying species. The nakedness of the mem-

FIG. 22—Horseshoe bats (*Rhinolophus hipposideros*) in a typical sleeping posture, hibernating in a German cave. Courtesy of Ernst Krause, phot.

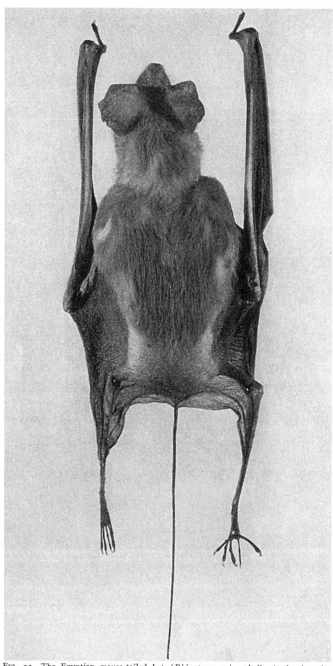

FIG. 23—The Egyptian mouse-tailed bat (*Rhinopoma microphyllum*) showing the long slender tail, the very narrow tail membrane at its base, the slender hind feet, and the naked lower back, beneath the skin of which is an accumulation of fat. The specimen, from one of the Pyramids of Egypt, is in the Museum of Comparative Zoölogy; enlarged one quarter.

branes also makes more effective a peculiar development of the nerve endings in the skin as delicate organs of touch. This has been carefully studied in but few bats, first perhaps by a German, Schöbl (1871), in the common serotine bat (*Eptesicus serotinus*) of Europe. He found that the nerves in the wing membranes end either as threads in a network below the outer layer of the skin, or in a characteristic terminal structure projecting like a small cone of microscopic size. These cones are associated with a short hair and were regarded by Schöbl as being delicate organs of touch, while the deeper network he suggested may be for perception of temperature or pain.

In most bats the wing membranes extend along the sides of the body, and the fur ends at the point where they begin. In one genus of fruit bats, Dobsonia, a curious development is found: the membranes come off not from the sides but from the very center of the back along the line of the spine, so that as they are naked, the entire back of the bat is devoid of hair. Still more strange, an exact parallel is found in the naked-backed bat, Pteronotus, a much smaller, insectivorous species in the American tropics. Why the wings should be so voluminous is not evident, though there is possibly an advantage in making an air pocket on their under surface, which would act like the under side of an umbrella in a gust of wind, to give support.

The largest bats of all are found in the family Pteropidae or flying foxes, of which the Javanese species, *Pteropus vampyrus*, attains a maximum size with a forearm of as much as 220 mm. in length, giving a spread of wings of some fifty inches. It is about equaled by the great black flying fox of the Philippine Islands, belonging to the related genus Acerodon. But these are giants of their tribe, for most of the species are small, some, such as the tiny bamboo bat (Tylonycteris) or certain members of the genus Pipistrellus, hardly exceeding 27 mm. in length of forearm and, when curled up, appearing no bigger than the end of one's thumb.

The tail and its membrane (the uropatagium) vary greatly in different species of bats. In the most primitive state the tail was probably long and wholly free and the membrane absent. A next stage would be the development of a narrow flange from the heel bone (or calcaneum) to the base of the tail, a condition which among living bats is found in the fruit bat, Notopteris, an old-fashioned genus, still surviving in the Fiji Islands, the New Hebrides, and New Caledonia, of the East Indian archipelago. In the other fruit bats the tail is either very short or absent altogether. Apart from these bats (which retain various ancient traits and form the suborder Megachiroptera), a like condition is found again in the most primitive genus of the other suborder (Microchiroptera), namely in the little mouse-tailed bats (Rhinopoma) of Egypt and India, except that the slender tail is longer in proportion. A tail almost wholly free from the membrane is thus probably a stage still preserved in the course of the complete development of this additional sail. The velvet-furred free-tailed bats of the family Molossidae mostly agree in showing a slight advance in the development of this membrane, which is carried out about halfway to the tip of the tail. In most of the other families of bats the tail remains long and either extends as a support out to the margin of the tail membrane or, as in the sheath-tailed family (Emballonuridae), projects about halfway out on its upper surface.

Very remarkable, however, is the variation shown in the leaf-nosed bats of South America (of the family Phyllostomidae), for here we find all stages from those genera (as Lonchorhina and Macrophyllum) in which the tail is long and has a membrane extending quite to its tip, to those like Sturnira, in which the tail has disappeared and even the membrane has become narrowed to a mere ridge along the inner side of the leg to the short calcaneum. A few of these stages are shown in the accompanying figures (Figures 24, 25). Thus in Anthorhina and Micronycteris the tail has shrunk to about half the length of the membrane, which is spread in part by the very long and stout calcanea from the ankle, while the reduced tail still gives some added support. These bats are, probably, chiefly insectivorous in their diet, as shown in part by their teeth,

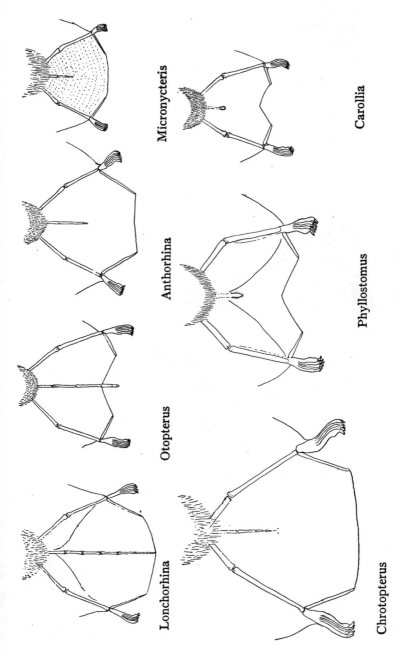

FIG. 24—Tail membrane of leaf-nosed bats.

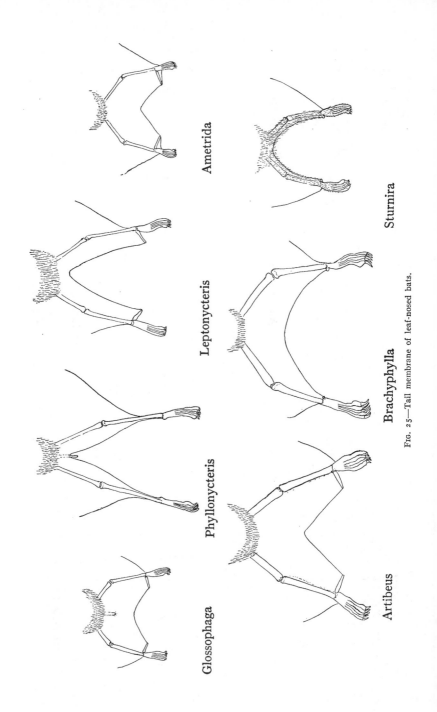

Ametrida

Sturnira

Leptonycteris

Brachyphylla

Phyllonycteris

Artibeus

Glossophaga

Fig. 25—Tail membrane of leaf-nosed bats.

which still retain the primitive knifelike cusps in the molars. Chrotopterus, a large bat, is nearly similar, but instead of living on insects, is in all probability largely carnivorous. Phyllostomus and Carollia are in about the same stage in tail reduction but differ in having the very tip of the tail projecting from the upper surface of the membrane. These two genera are in part, at least, fruit eaters. Turning to the subfamily Glossophaginae, which subsist on fruit juices and the nectar and pollen of flowers, for which they are fitted by their long protrusible tongues, the tail is very short in Glossophaga, and its membrane is reduced in the middle, while the calcanea which spread it are short. This process is carried still further in Phyllonycteris and Leptonycteris, but in different ways, for the former, though retaining a stump of a tail, has lost the calcanea and the membrane is very narrow, while the latter has lost the tail and shortened the calcanea which still serve to extend a narrowed membrane. The four genera, Ametrida, Artibeus, Brachyphylla, and Sturnira are all essentially fruit-eating, and show stages in the reduction of the membrane to practically nothing. All have lost the tail, and the calcanea have become shortened in the two latter to mere nodules. The explanation probably is that in those bats of this family that capture living prey the tail membrane is used as a sort of landing-net, to be thrown forward when an insect is caught, so that the prey may be held against it and prevented from escaping, while, as first described by Gilbert White in his *Natural History of Selborne*, a fresh hold is secured. The frugivorous bats have no need for such a net, as their food is largely or wholly inert and more easily handled. Thus it seems probable that the leaf-nosed bats of this family were at first insectivorous with long tails, complete tail membranes, and well-developed calcanea for spreaders, but some of them took up a frugivorous diet and gradually lost these parts, although in different ways among the various genera. On the other hand, the Old World fruit bats (Pteropidae) may have acquired their vegetarian habits very early in the history of the group before a tail membrane was developed, so that in most of the living species the tail, if present at all, has shrunk to a small remnant free from the membrane, which remains, as perhaps it primitively was, a mere flange. The history of the tail and its membrane in diverse genera of bats is thus an interesting and complex one, probably correlated with their different food preferences and method of feeding. We are still in great need of more details about the nature of the food taken by a majority of bats and their means of securing it.

### FLIGHT OF BATS

Bats have acquired many other peculiarities adapting them for flight in addition to their supporting membranes and the changes in the arm and hand to form a wing. Their short necks, heavy chest muscles, tapering abdomens, slender hind legs with reversed knee joints, and the soft fluffy fur that fills in irregularities of form, as well as the absence of fur from the wings, all help to make flying possible and to reduce the resistance to the air. The manner of flight differs widely in the different species. The fruit bats with their clumsy bodies and ample wings are steady fliers capable of fairly rapid and often long-sustained flight in their journeys to and from favorite feeding grounds. Among these the flying foxes are the largest of bats, the largest of all being the great *Pteropus vampyrus* of Malaysia and the East Indies, with a spread of about four feet. One may hear the measured *swish, swish,* of their wings as they come in the early evening to hang up in some well-laden fig tree to feed on the fruit. They look as big as night herons as they pass in the moonlight. At the opposite extreme are the free-tailed bats of the tropics, perhaps the swiftest fliers of them all. Their wings, like those of the more rapidly flying birds, are relatively long and narrow and their wingbeats swift. I have often seen the early risers among them flying high above the buildings of the town with a speed and movement so much like that of the swifts that at first glance it is sometimes difficult to tell which is bat and which is bird, as the two career about overhead at sunset. The bats, however, in the pursuit of insects now and again vary their course with sudden short dives and

Fig. 26—Gray-headed fruit bat or flying fox (*Pteropus poliocephalus*). Queensland, Australia. Courtesy of Otho Webb, phot.

Fig. 27—Large fruit bats or flying foxes (*Pteropus natalis*) in free flight; Christmas Island, Indian Ocean. Courtesy of M. W. F. Tweedie, phot.

turns, checking and darting irregularly in a way that birds seem unable to do. Some of the large insect-eating bats, such as the big sheath-tails (Saccolaimus) of Africa and India, love wide spaces, as dusk approaches flying swiftly with strong vigorous sweeps of the wings several gunshots above ground, now and then swooping down near the earth, then rising lightly again. Many of the smaller bats have relatively short, broad wings and exhibit a very different type of flight: some, like the little pipistrelles, remind one of large moths or butterflies, as with short, quick strokes they flutter irregularly about; others again, such as the small brown bats (Myotis), are faster and more erratic, diving, turning, and dodging, now popping into view against a sunset glow, now vanishing in the shadows. To the bat collector these offer the most difficult mark for shooting, especially among trees. Some, such as the horseshoe bats or the big-eared Plecotus, hunt among leafy twigs or come fearlessly into open houses, and with slow, hovering flight, search the ceilings and peaks near the roof to pick off resting insects. These bats, particularly the horseshoe group, are thus able to pass in and out of narrow spaces with ease. Tomes, an English naturalist, recounts that one of the lesser horseshoe bats, when confined in a room, searched everywhere for an exit, flying into every part of the room, behind and under the furniture, even under a bookcase standing against a wall, where there were scarcely three inches between it and the floor. Finally, the bat examined some book shelves in a recess of the room and darted in and out of the space left where one of the books had been removed, without appearing to touch anything with its wing tips. Such actions disclose a control over the direction and speed of flight found in few other types of bats.

The only investigator to analyze the flight of bats by means of motion pictures is Dr. Max Eisentraut (1936), who has lately succeeded in making films of several smaller species in Germany, by confining the bats in a room where the camera could be directed at them within narrow bounds. The larger noctule bat, however, was unable to make the necessary sustained flight in close quarters, since its speed and size require greater space for maneuvering. In general he describes the wing motions as much like those of birds, with the stroke downward and forward, the recovery upward and backward in a slightly differing course. Progress in direct flight follows a slightly wavy course, owing to the lift of the down stroke and the drop during the up stroke, but to the eye the bat seems to be traveling on a level course in ordinary rowing type of flight. In hovering, which certain bats such as the long-eared and horseshoe bats are capable of doing, the body is held nearly perpendicularly while the same stroke is used, so that the bat is really flying upward with just sufficient exertion to overcome the down pull of gravity. Bats can glide for short distances, but have not acquired the ability to soar on outspread wings as hawks or other large birds do. Doubtless their bodies are too light to have much stability if this were attempted, while again, there would be no need for soaring since flight in bats is for active hunting or to travel from one feeding place to another, or to the roost. Steering is done by the wings, which may be partly furled or given a stronger stroke on one side or the other. The tail seems to have little or no share in guiding the direction of flight, a fact of course obvious in those bats that have very short tails or none at all. Yet, as seen in some of the photographs of bats with well-developed tail membranes, the drag of the air pressure, when the tail is curled forward toward the belly, must tend to turn the body down somewhat. Dr. Eisentraut shows in a set of motion-picture figures how a large mouse-eared bat takes off from its position hanging on a perch. Instead of letting go and opening the wings as it drops, it first opens its wings and with a quick stroke or two raises the body and then lets go. In this bat the film shows that about eleven or twelve wing beats are made a second, and in this time the bat travels about fourteen feet. In the lesser horseshoe bat the number of strokes per second is higher, about sixteen to eighteen.

### SENSES OF BATS

"Blind as a bat," the saying is, but like most old adages, it falls far short of the truth. For the eyes of bats, though small, are none the less well developed and look bright and shining on close inspection. When examined microscopically, they show most of the elements usually present in the retina of other mammals. A large brown bat I once studied revealed unusually thick supporting fibers, known as Müller's fibers. Kolmer (1926) and, earlier, Fritsch have studied the finer structure of the bat's eye. The former compares his results in the investigation of sixteen genera of fruit bats (Megachiroptera) with those made on an equal number of Microchiroptera. He finds very marked and important differences between these two groups, for while the eyes of the latter are apparently like those of most mammals in general structure of the retina, those of the fruit bats are unlike any known type of eye. They differ in having curious and extremely small finger-like projections of the inner coat of the eyeball that penetrate the outer layers of the retina; each of these tapering fingers encloses a small artery that abruptly ends in a capillary. Thus the receptive surface upon which light falls consists of twenty to thirty thousand of these little finger-like cones, and these bear the so-called rods, which perceive light and are minute rectangular cells. By thus increasing the surface for rods, a great many more can be fitted in than in an ordinary eye in which the retina is like the inner surface of a hollow ball. The meaning of this is unknown. Day-living animals usually have, in alternation with the rods, a large number of cells called cones, in which are minute grains that are affected by light and are believed to be the cause of color perception. In many or most animals active at dusk or by night these are lacking, and Kolmer says that the fruit bats also are without them. Hence they probably do not see colors as we do, which is not surprising, for at night very little color can be seen. Probably in general bats are color-blind, yet they see well, and if, as occasionally happens, they are abroad by day, they seem to show no sign of being dazzled even in bright sunlight, but fly accurately about in their drab world. With many night-living animals the eyes are relatively large in order to gather all the available light for seeing in the dark, but the smaller bats show nothing of the sort. Indeed, their eyes are relatively much smaller than in mice of about the same size. On the other hand, they are larger and better developed than in moles and shrews, in which these organs are degenerate.

The question then arises, how are bats able to live in dark places and to secure their insect prey by night without constantly dashing into obstacles in their flight? For apparently there must be some other guiding sense than sight. The answer is still in doubt, although many attempts have been made to find the solution. As long ago as 1794, Spallanzani, an Italian, experimented with bats deprived of their sight to see if they could successfully avoid silk threads hung in the room. He satisfied himself that they could, when blinded, still make their way in and out among the threads without touching them. His conclusion that they were guided by some special sense is still widely quoted; but in later years these experiments have been repeated with greater care, for example by Rollinat and Trouessart (1900) in France and by Hahn (1908) in America. Hahn used thin black wires instead of threads, suspending a line of them from the rafters of the experiment room at distances averaging about eleven inches apart. These made it easier to detect whether or not a bat flew against a wire in passing, for it would give out a sound when struck. He first tried normal uninjured bats, mostly a species of small Myotis, liberating them one at a time in the room and watching their actions carefully. They would usually fly rapidly about at first, then, as they began to tire, would alight frequently on the walls or objects. Each time the bat approached close to the wires or passed through or appeared to dodge, it was counted as a trial. In over 2,000 trials with 47 of the small Myotis he recorded about 25 per cent of hits. He then tried 12 of the same animals deprived of sight by having their eyes covered with an opaque mixture of lamp black and glue, and found that in 600 trials

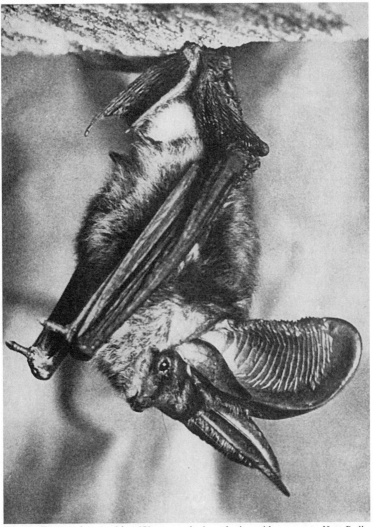

Fig. 28—European long-eared bat (*Plecotus auritus*) awakening, with ears erect. Near Berlin, Germany. Enlarged. Courtesy of Ernst Krause, phot.

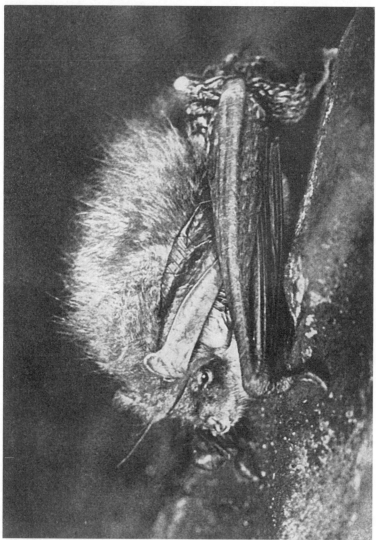

FIG. 29—A European long-eared bat (*Plecotus auritus*) at rest, showing the long ears and the long narrow tragus folded back under the forearm. Near Berlin, Germany. Enlarged. Courtesy of Ernst Krause, phot.

the percentage of hits was nearly 22, or even better than when the eyes were not covered. Evidently, then, the bats depended little on sight in avoiding the wires. In a second set of experiments he amputated the delicate ears and tragus, with about the same result, as if the bats did not depend on these large membranes to warn them by reflecting sound waves. Rollinat and Trouessart had already reached similar conclusions.

Hahn then tried a third series of experiments, this time closing the ear orifice by stopping it with a small plug of plaster of Paris, which he allowed to harden before liberating the animals. At once the percentage of hits increased, averaging about 66 per cent. Evidently the internal ear, with its acute sense of hearing, is a main factor, not only in helping bats to avoid obstacles, but also in aiding them to hear the hum of a passing insect. No doubt it is the echo of vibrations set in motion by air currents that they really perceive. Finally, to test the possibility that the sensitive nerve endings in the membranes are helpful in detecting such vibrations, he carried out a fourth set of experiments, in which the bats used were given a coating of vaseline. In this case, although the percentage of hits was large, about 36 to 40 per cent, he noticed that the bats were more labored in their flight, perhaps as a mechanical result of being covered with the sticky substance, so that the result of eliminating the nerve endings is not conclusive. Hahn concludes that Spallanzani was probably mistaken in supposing that bats always avoid obstacles in their path of flight. It is quite probable, however, that different species vary greatly in their quickness of perception, and Hahn found that even individual bats of the same species differ in this respect, depending no doubt on a variety of circumstances. For example, many of the American leaf-nosed bats have become fruit eaters and are proportionally heavier-bodied than their insectivorous relatives, with the result that they are less agile and perhaps duller in their perceptions. An illustration of this is given by Van Tyne (1933), who describes catching bats in Guatemala by stretching a fine-meshed trammel net across an opening in the forest. In the course of a month over forty bats were taken, of which one was a vampire and the rest included four species of fruit-eating bats, chiefly Artibeus. No insectivorous species were caught. Probably the latter hunt largely by ear and are quick to take note of minute echoes set up by air waves reflected from objects or from moving insects in their flight. In this the inner ear is doubtless of first importance, while the enlarged ears and tragus often must aid in gathering sound. An account of the internal ear, well illustrated, was published by Staněk in 1933.

Bats in a closed room almost invariably explore every corner and usually find the cracks under doors, in the sides of the room, or under the roof. They frequently escape by squeezing through openings that one would think too small for their bodies. When they find these, Hahn comments, their "manner often indicates that they are attracted to an opening from a distance of several feet when the air currents are the apparent stimulus." I have occasionally noticed the same thing. Once a large brown bat which I had loosed in a room, after flying back and forth a number of times, suddenly came opposite a door through which a perceptible draft was blowing. He instantly turned to follow it up and escaped.

Many of the families of smaller bats (Microchiroptera) have conspicuous nose leaves or membranous outgrowths from the muzzle or lips. These vary in their details in different genera or even among closely allied species. Thus the horseshoe bats, as the name implies, have a wide, thin, horseshoe-shaped leaf covering the muzzle and passing into an erect portion near the level of the eyes. There may be a few specially lengthened hairs arising from this, which are doubtless tactile organs. The false vampire (Megaderma) has a large oval leaf standing erect at the tip of the nose, while the South American leaf-nosed bats (Phyllostomidae) exhibit a variety of such structures, most of them of more or less lance-shaped form. In addition, a few of them have lappets on the lips or, more often, a series of small, rounded warts. Others again have small wattles on the sides of the face. On the whole, these seem to be most developed in the insect-eating species, and less so in those that have become fruit eaters, so that their use may be for better perception in

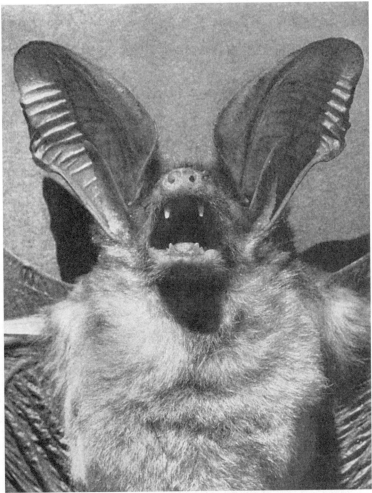

FIG. 30—The pallid cave bat (*Antrozous pallidus*) of western United States, showing the enlarged ears and long tragus. Twice natural size. Courtesy of Wharton Huber, phot.

A

Fig. 31—A. Enlarged head of the California mastiff bat (*Eumops californicus*), showing the overhanging upper lip, the small eye, and the ear with its stiff central keel. Courtesy of A. Brazier Howell, phot.

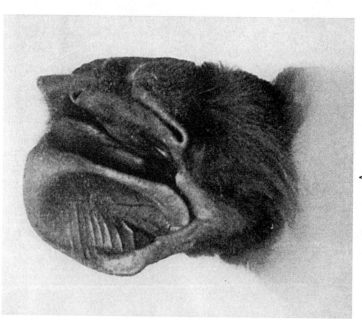

B

Fig. 31—B. Enlarged head of the western red bat (*Lasiurus borealis teliotis*), with short, rounded ears and a prominent erect tragus or leaflike expansion at the ear opening. Courtesy of A. Brazier Howell, phot.

some way not yet clearly understood. Possibly they may act as receptors for air vibrations set up by passing insects or reflected from near-by objects. At all events, Sir Hiram Maxim, acting on the assumption that these membranes do behave in this way, invented a device for detecting obstacles in a ship's path at night or in a fog by sending out vibrations of a low tone from the ship's prow and recording the echo by delicate membranes on board. In this way essentially has been developed the modern method of making deep soundings by recording the time required for the echo to reach the observer from the ocean bottom. Although bats with relatively smaller ears seem to get on as well as those with enormous ears and long tragi, it does not follow that these membranes are not helpful in hearing minute sounds.

So far as is known, there is but one bat, the large horseshoe bat, *Hipposideros armatus*, of the Oriental region, in which the nose leaves differ conspicuously in the two sexes. This was first pointed out by Dobson (1878) and later by Osgood (1932). They are much larger and differently shaped in adult males than in the females and hence may have some significance of a sexual nature, as in finding the females, though this is wholly conjectural. It is worth mentioning, however, that in late summer, as in August, which is probably the mating season, the males develop a very strong odor not noticeable in the opposite sex (Hinton and Lindsay, 1926).

Bats have an excellent place-memory. Eisentraut has shown that the same bat will return in successive autumns to the same part of the identical cave to hibernate, and there is evidence that bats can return to these caves from a long distance after a summer's absence. Experiments with captive bats carried out by Hahn (1908), as well as observations on free individuals, prove that they quickly learn the location of exit holes or of feeding corners in a cage and can return to their chosen haunts from a considerable distance. Dr. Charles Campbell (1925) claims to have marked a number of "guano bats" with white paint and liberated them by day at a distance of thirty miles from the home cave and found that they returned to it in about 58 minutes! Some experiments made recently by my friend, Mr. Donald Griffin, in carrying little brown bats (*Myotis lucifugus*) a number of miles out to sea from their roosting place in an old building, had a similar result, for he later recovered at least one of them, marked with a numbered band. This homing instinct is believed to be owing to a well-developed kinesthetic sense or, as we say of ourselves, "a bump of locality," whereby we subconsciously keep aware of our location through the effect of motions made, or associate certain places with the proper movements requisite to reach them, as when in a dark room already familiar, we go at once to the desired objective even though the path involve various turns.

We do not yet know how far the sense of smell may be useful to bats in finding their regular haunts or in discovering their own kind, or even in locating their food. They are usually provided with scent glands which give forth a strong musky odor that is easily detected even by ourselves. In roosts where many bats regularly gather this odor, as well as that from their droppings, is often perceptible from a considerable distance and very likely is an aid to the animals in finding their chosen haunts on the return from a night's excursions. In the same way it may attract bats of the same species to join other colonies. An extreme instance is perhaps that related by Cott (1926) of the fish-eating bat (Noctilio). He found several colonies living in hollow trees on Marajó Island near the mouth of the Amazon River. He writes that they "possess a peculiarly powerful and unpleasant smell, which is so strong that the presence of the bats may be discovered and their exact whereabouts determined by it alone. Frequently, when riding over the *campo*, I have detected the smell at a distance of more than 100 yards from the nearest part of the copse which they occupied." Positive evidence that bats living in one colony may change residence and join another at a considerable distance is perhaps still lacking, but the known fluctuations in the populations of certain colonies observed by various persons are indicative of more or less shifting.

Scent glands are present in some of our common bats, such as Eptesicus, the big brown, in the form of swellings along the upper lip, while Pipistrellus has in addition a rounded wartlike gland in the midline of the upper throat. The strong musky odor is apparently emitted under excitement, for often on first catching one of these bats it is not noticeable; shortly, however, as he struggles to escape, it becomes quite obvious. In some bats there is a large gland in the center of the forehead, as in some of the Old World horseshoe bats of the genus Rhinolophus. Others develop a large pouchlike gland in the middle of the lower throat, as in Cheiromeles and Eumops, members of the Molossidae or free-tailed family, and in Taphozous, the tomb bat of the Emballonuridae or sheath-tailed group. This, however, may vary in its development among related species or even in the two sexes of the same species. Thus it is absent in both sexes of some species of Taphozous, while in others it is large in the male and very small or absent in the female, facts which point to its use as of value in attracting or stimulating the females at the breeding season especially. In the California mastiff bat (*Eumops californicus*) A. B. Howell (1920) finds it present in the males, but easily overlooked except at such times, for it shrinks until it appears as a "tiny dent" only. When, however, the males are sexually active, as in late March, the gland swells to a small doughnut-shaped mass 14 millimeters in diameter and 4 deep, with a correspondingly enlarged opening through which the strong-scented secretion is poured. In addition to these glands on the head and throat, a few bats have glands situated in the membranes. Thus, a species of pipistrelle (*Pipistrellus lophurus*) from Tenasserim, is described as having in the males a patch of glandular hairs at the base of the tail, marking the presence of glands in the membrane, an unusual condition.

Still more remarkable, however, are the South American sac-winged bats, members of the sheath-tailed family, in which a large pouchlike gland is present in the membrane that extends from the fore shoulder to the wrist. In one genus, Saccopteryx, this opens near the elbow and forearm on the upper side of the membrane and is much more conspicuous in the males. It can be opened widely by the action of a small muscular strand, but ordinarily the mouth is closely pursed together. In preserved specimens this gland is often very conspicuous when everted, as it is whitish inside and contrasts with the dark membrane. A related genus, Peropteryx, has a similar sac, except that it is situated farther forward near the front edge of the forearm membrane. In another genus, Pizonyx, a fish-eating bat of the Vespertilionidae, a curious glandular mass has been described by Miller, situated in the membrane between the forearm and the fifth finger of the wing. It is about of the size and shape of an oat, and is absent in the only male at hand, though well developed in three females, an unusual reversal of the situation commonly found.

While the value of these scent glands is not always clear, it seems very probable that in many cases they are active at the breeding period and that their odor is helpful in attracting the opposite sex through indicating the breeding condition. The scent may be of use in locating the daytime retreat, or it may even be repellent to certain enemies. We do not know; nevertheless the presence of scent glands implies a well-developed sense of smell in order to detect their odor. It is certain that this power is of use in the case of fruit-eating bats, to enable them to find food, for it is well known that in the South American tropics a bunch of ripe bananas hung in a room will quickly attract numbers of certain species as Carollia. In another chapter I have quoted the experience of the late Leo Miller who secured a large series of specimens in this way, and it seems clear too that the flower-feeding bats are attracted by the strong odor of certain blossoms.

The skeleton of bats shows many adaptations to their peculiar mode of life. In flying birds the two great breast muscles of either side furnish the motive power for the wings — an outer one that pulls the wing downward and forward, and an inner one that raises it upward and back. The latter has a tendon passing through an opening at the shoulder joint like a rope through a pulley to the yardarm of a mast, so that a downward pull raises the sail. In bats there is no such pulley arrangement. Instead, the wing is raised by the muscles of the shoulder, as in ourselves. In birds the breast muscles are very large, so that a deep bony keel is formed on the center of the breastbone between the masses of opposite sides to give a solid wall for their attachment. In bats these muscles are less bulky, but yet sizeable enough to require a similar though smaller keel. The breastbone (or sternum) consists of three sections: the foremost (or presternum) is wide, affording a strong union with the collarbone or clavicle of each side and with the end of the first rib; while from its under surface arises a short vertical keel separating the breast muscles of opposite sides. The second section (or mesosternum) consists of a series of short bony pieces which in most mammals are separate, one to each of the anterior pairs of ribs, but in bats these unite to form a single rodlike bone with a keel that varies in development from a slight ridge to a distinct bony plate. Finally, the terminal part (or xiphisternum) is a short tapering section, which may be distinct in the fruit bats (Pteropidae) but in other groups usually fuses with the middle portion in adults and may bear a continuation of the shallow keel. Additional strength is given to the shoulder by the fusion of the presternum to the first rib (in Megadermidae) or, in addition (Rhinolophidae), by the fusion of the first rib to the two vertebrae with which it articulates, that is, the last neck vertebra and the first of the rib-bearing series. This is carried still farther in the horseshoe bats of the family Hipposideridae, by the fusion of the first two ribs and their vertebrae, thus making a solid ring of bone. The need for this remarkable strengthening in these small bats, as Miller (1907) points out, is not evident, for the largest bats of all, the great flying foxes, do not show it, thus, in correlation with their other more primitive characters, retaining a more simple condition.

The hind limbs of bats are no less modified than the fore. All the digits have been shortened, and the terminal claw is much curved, so that the toes form five hooks of practically equal length which together act as a grapple whereby the animal hangs itself up to rest. The knees do not bend forward as in most mammals, but outward, or the entire leg may be extended straight back. When hanging up, the Vespertilionid bats, such as our common North American species, cling by both feet with the knees bent slightly out at an angle (as seen in Figure 7), but in some other groups, such as the fruit bats and the horseshoe bats (Figures 20, 22), the knees are not bent at all. The bat suspends itself with the legs straightened out above it. In this position it will sometimes let go one foot and hang by a single hind leg like an animated pear. It will also, if approached, pivot on this leg slightly, turning to see the source of the disturbance. The horseshoe bats are very clever when alighting on a ceiling-like roof, in quickly turning the feet upward and securing a foothold on a horizontal surface above; others, however, are less skillful, and first alight upon a wall, head up, but instantly reverse their position to hang head downward. In most bats the fibula or outer bone of the shank is imperfect at its upper end, where it becomes cartilaginous, while the heel bone (calcaneum) is frequently very long and slender, forming a supporting rod along the basal edge of the tail membrane.

In their internal anatomy there are some interesting correlations between the diet and the structure of the stomach. This organ in insectivorous bats is small and simple, of a flask shape, convex at the left or cardiac side, much as in the human stomach on a smaller scale (seen in the figures from below and hence on the right side). This is the primitive form, but in some bats it has become much altered. Thus, in the fruit bats (Pteropidae), as well as in the fruit-eating members of the leaf-nosed bats (Phyllostomidae) of tropical America, the cardiac portion has become much enlarged, for apparently a diet of fruit pulp and juices requires more bulk and longer digestion to provide the requisite amount of nourishment. Here, then, is an interesting case of parallel development, resulting from similar feeding habits in these two unrelated groups of bats. Some of the Pteropidae, as Eonycteris of the East Indies, feed largely on nectar and probably pollen as well, and these show

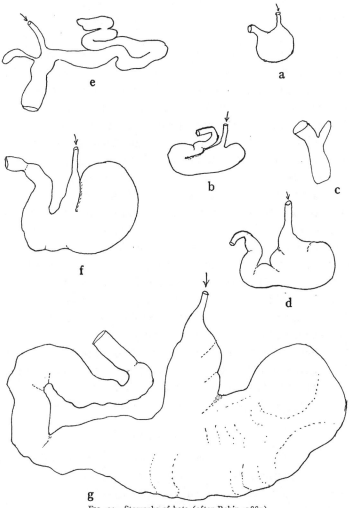

FIG. 32—Stomachs of bats (after Robin, 1881).
A. An insectivorous sheath-tailed bat, *Emballonura nigrescens,* × 2.
B. A nectar-feeding fruit bat, *Eonycteris spelaea,* natural size.
C. Portion of the intestine, showing the appendix, of the false vampire, *Megaderma spasma.*
D. An American fruit-eating bat of the leaf-nosed family, *Carollia perspicillata.* × 2.
E. The tubular stomach of a vampire bat, *Desmodus rotundus,* for blood-feeding, natural size.
F. The hammer-headed bat, *Hypsignathus monstrosus,* of Africa, a fruit-eating species, natural size.
G. The Indian flying fox, *Pteropus giganteus,* a fruit bat, natural size.

a slightly different form of stomach, in which the cardiac side of the organ is enlarged and somewhat hemispherical, while the opposite side is lengthened and tubular. The most remarkable stomach of all is that of the vampire bats (Desmodus), which feed on blood. In them the cardiac end of the stomach is drawn out into a long tube, which becomes folded upon itself in order to pack away in the body cavity. When feeding, the bats lap the blood which flows from a wound they make in the skin of their victim, and they may continue their meal for twenty minutes or more at a time, if undisturbed, until their bellies become distended with the repast. Such a modification of the stomach might easily have been derived from the type seen in some of the fruit-eating bats in which the cardiac end is already enlarged, so that one might suppose that the vampires were first fruit-juice eaters and later learned to puncture the skins of animals to secure their juices. Some of these types of stomach are here shown in outline drawings adapted from the work by Robin (1881) on the comparative anatomy of bats.

Thomas Huxley in 1865 was the first to describe the peculiar formation of the stomach in vampire bats. The intestine in most bats is simple and usually lacks an appendix or coecum. A very small one is present, however, in a few species; thus, the false vampire (Megaderma) has a minute appendix about one sixteenth of an inch long, as first described by Cantor in 1846.

### KINDS OF BATS

In the present state of our knowledge it is not possible to give even an approximate count of the total number of species and races of bats. Nor will this be possible until much further study of group after group has been made to determine what are distinct species, what are races of these, and how many of the named forms are really valid. Miller (1907) writes that "it seems highly probable that the total number of recognized bats will eventually exceed 2,000 named forms," an estimate which will have to suffice for the present. Probably the total number of genera, at least of those now living, will not be greatly increased in the future. Miller, again, lists "at least

173," and in the thirty years that have since elapsed, a few others have been described, some of which were previously unknown, while others result from subdividing some of the older genera into smaller groups. These additions and changes bring the total up to slightly over 200 genera, distributed among seventeen families. Of these seventeen major groups, five consist of a single genus each, indicating a great age and a persistance to modern times. Four other families comprise two, three, or four genera each; two others consist of about thirteen; while the three largest families make up the majority, namely, the Old World Pteropidae or fruit bats with some thirty-seven genera, the American leaf-nosed bats with about fifty-six, and the widespread simple-nosed bats of the family Vespertilionidae with about forty-five genera. Of these large families, only the first has been adequately reviewed. It includes according to Andersen (1912) no less than 186 species and 228 races or slightly variant local forms.

# CHAPTER X

# COLOR IN BATS

Tori naki sato no komori (Like a bat in a village where there are no birds). — Japanese proverb.

WHILE bats may lack the brilliant and varied colors of some birds and insects, many of them are nevertheless very beautiful in an unobtrusive way. Delicate tints and shades of brown are frequent, deepening in some to sooty or blackish, or in others brightening to warm russet, chestnut, or even orange. Pattern, too, may develop to enhance the effect by the contrast of differently colored areas. Dull coloring goes with life in the dark, for at night when bats are active, or by day when they are at rest in caves or hollows, colors are little obvious and in most species probably play an unimportant part in their lives. With others, however, the case is different, especially if they sleep by day hanging in the foliage of trees or against the bark.

Color in bats is owing to the presence of minute granules of pigment. Under a magnification of seven hundred diameters, Andersen (1917) found these granules in an Indian bat (Rhinolophus) arranged in lengthwise rows, so as to produce a striated appearance. These granules appear to be of two chief sorts, a dark blackish brown and a reddish, but it seems likely from what little we know at present that the first may become transformed into reddish through oxidation. Blackish coloring probably results from the presence of dark pigment grains, either alone or in greater abundance than the reddish; while paler shades perhaps result from fewer numbers of the granules, a condition described among rodents, in which colors have been more carefully studied, as "dilution." Red pigment, when present alone, probably produces chestnut and other varying shades of that type or, when in lesser amounts, the orange and yellow tints of some bats. Combinations of both sorts of pigment probably give the different shades of brown. One has

but to glance at a series of specimens to realize the wide range
of coloring that may result from these simple factors.

Even cave-dwelling bats, in which colors might seem a negligible matter, show a great variety of tint according to the
species. A few are really black, such as some of the glossy
mastiff bats (Molossus) of the American tropics, and a large
Chinese species, *Ia io*, a vespertilionid. More are dull gray,
like our "guano bat" of the Southwest, or brown in varying
tints, like many of the small species of Myotis or the big brown
bats (*Eptesicus fuscus*).

Depth of coloring is partly a matter of climate. A good
illustration of this is the little brown bat (*Myotis lucifugus*),
a species which ranges over nearly the whole of North America
from tree limit in the north to Mexico in the south. In eastern
and northern parts of this area it is a brassy brown, but in the
drier country of our far Southwest it becomes beautifully pale,
almost whitish or buffy, like a number of other desert animals;
again, passing into the saturate and humid climate of the northwest coast it becomes very dark and sooty in appearance. Toward the tropics, with moist atmosphere and heat, colors tend
to become dark also, but rich and bright in tone, instead of
dull and sooty. Intermediate tints are found in transitional
areas. In the dry deserts of southwestern United States, a few
species agree in becoming extremely pale, such as the cave bat
(*Antrozous pallidus*) and the pygmy canyon bat (*Pipistrellus
hesperus*), the latter, however, with contrastingly black membranes. There is something about arid climate that reduces
the amount of dark pigment produced in many animals, quite
apart from any consideration of concealing coloration, and this
effect may in some species of bats extend to the skin of the
membranes as well. Again, pigmentation is limited by other
factors not so clear. Thus, Kuhl's bat (*Pipistrellus kuhli*) of
Europe and Africa has usually a white edging to its otherwise
more or less dark wings, especially in the dry regions, and
white wing edges are found occasionally in the little brown
bats of the drier regions of Arizona and southeastern California.
In a few species the wings are paler than the body, as in a small

West African Eptesicus (*E. tenuipinnis*), which has all its membranes white, but the body brownish, although it inhabits the moist forested country of Liberia and the Gold Coast. The white wings give it a ghostly appearance as it flits past in the early twilight. Some of the pipistrelles of East Africa and western Asia are white-winged also. I once saw a number of white-winged pipistrelles flitting about over the water in the shelter of a patch of reeds on a river in Kenya Colony, East Africa, their pale forms making a vivid contrast with one or two dark brown individuals of another species, active at the same time. The bats of this genus are very early fliers and often make a first appearance before the sun has set.

In most mammals, including the majority of bats, the fur is dark or slaty at the base, with the paler or brighter tints at the exposed tips of the hairs. This is readily seen on parting the fur by blowing it gently. But there are numerous exceptions. Some of the horseshoe bats, such as *Hipposideros caffer*, which ranges throughout Africa, have the concealed bases of the fur white and only the tips brown. The short-furred "guano bat" of our Southwest shows the same thing. In other species an even tint prevails all the way to the base of the hairs. Why this should be we do not know, but such contradictions are frequent in Nature. Tints of yellow are not uncommon among bats, with occasionally an almost complete loss of blackish, as in some of the horseshoe bats of the Old World or in the dainty long-legged bats (Chilonatalus) of the West Indies. That these adult colors have been evolved from more somber hues is evident from the fact that the youngish animals are considerably darker. Rarely are the young paler than the adult, but this is true of one of the species of spear-nosed bat (Phyllostomus) of South America.

A curious anomaly in coloration is the ghost bat (Diclidurus) of the American tropics, one of the sheath-tailed family. About the size of the common big brown bat of North America, it looks wholly pure white, fur, wings, and membranes, a beautiful if spectral creature. The fur, however, if parted, shows slaty gray at the extreme base. So far as is known, this bat is a cave dweller by day. Another white bat is a rare species, *Ectophylla alba*, of the leaf-nosed family of South America. Of what avail the white livery may be, or whether in the darkness the coloring is a matter of indifference, is at present wholly unknown.

But if the colors of cave bats are dull and uniform on the whole, those of tree-living species are often varied and beautiful or develop contrasting patterns. Familiar examples are the American red bat (*Lasiurus borealis*) and the hoary bat (*L. cinereus*). The latter is large, over thirteen inches in spread of wings, its fur much mixed with bright buffy and frosted with white-tipped hairs, as its name implies. The membranes share in bright coloring, the black-rimmed ears contrasting with the buffy neck and the dark wings varied with areas of bright orange along the fingers. No doubt this contrasted style of coloring breaks up any effect of solidity, while the frosted appearance causes it to blend with gray or lichened bark when it rests by day clinging to a tree trunk, or disguises it as a faded leaf when hanging amongst foliage. The red bat, with a pronounced russet and dusted appearance, is similarly protected. In his "Journals" Thoreau recounts coming upon a red bat hanging suspended from a frond of the Interrupted Fern, just above the brown fruiting portions. So well did its rusty brown coloring simulate the woolly substance of the fern that he at first mistook it for a large cocoon or a big moth, and aptly describes the fur as resembling the plush of a ripe cattail head. Others have also told of mistaking this dainty creature for a withered leaf hanging from a branch by day.

The red bat is remarkable, if not almost unique, among bats in that the sexes are contrastingly different in color. For while the fur of the female is dull in its buffy and pale chestnut, much frosted with a minute peppering of white-tipped hairs, the male is much brighter, almost orange red. Both have a sharply defined triangular spot of white at the base of the wing, and as a further unusual trait the whole upper surface of the tail membrane is thickly furred. This last peculiarity may add to the concealing value of the color pattern and at the same time recall a primitive condition when all the membranes were furry. An Indian bat, Harpiocephalus, much resembles a female red bat in its dull chestnut color and also has a furry tail membrane, so that we may infer that it, too, is tree-living. Little is known of its habits, however. Another Indian species, but of a different genus (*Myotis formosus*), is beautifully colored with orange fur and orange markings along the fingers of the wings, contrasting in a startling manner with the black of the other parts of the membranes. Of its choice of resting places, little is recorded, though one observer found a specimen hanging by day in tall jungle grass. A larger species of similar coloring occurs in Africa, and is probably a tree dweller. Sexual dichromatism occurs not only in the red bat but is found also in the large fish-eating hare-lipped bat (Noctilio) of the American tropics. In this species the adult males become a brilliant orange rufous, slightly darker on the back than on the lower side, while the females are a dull shade of dark brown to drab above, paling to buffy or whitish below. Another case is that of the small fruit bats of the genus Cynopterus of the oriental tropics, in which the adult males acquire bright reddish shoulders, while the females remain olive brown.

One of the most beautiful of bats is another oriental species, the painted bat (*Kerivoula picta*). Of dainty and delicate form, its fluffy fur is a brilliant orange rufous, with orange-colored areas along the fingers contrasting sharply with the otherwise black membranes. It rests by day among vines and leafy growths, where it might easily pass as a russet leaf. One was once found in Siam sleeping inside the flower of a calla lily. The other members of this genus are duller-colored. They are forest-dwellers in part, hanging by day in the shelter of vegetation; some have their fur much frosted with white, which doubtless helps to render them less conspicuous against the bark or among twigs and leaves. In the open thorn-bush country of eastern Africa lives another shade-haunting species, the great-eared bat (*Lavia frons*). For its daytime roost it usually chooses the shelter of a thick bush overgrown with a canopy of vines, where it hangs up singly or sometimes in pairs. But

FIG. 33—The hoary bat (*Lasiurus cinereus*), the largest species of northeastern North America, living by day in trees. A sketch from life of a specimen taken at Concord, Massachusetts, October 21, 1916. J. Henry Blake, del.

it is at all times alert, ready to fly out and seek other shelter if too closely approached. Its pearl-gray fur, becoming yellowish on the lower back, blends perhaps with the tone of the vegetation, but its bright orange-yellow wings give it a very birdlike appearance as it darts away to fresh cover. In its handsome coloring its differs sharply from other members of its family, the Megadermidae, which are dull-colored cave haunters, so that again we have a correlation between bright colors and tree haunts.

Among the fruit bats the large flying foxes (Pteropus) that hang by day in companies among the treetops have developed a very characteristic pattern of color. Usually the back is blackish or with a slight sprinkling of paler hairs, but the head, neck, and shoulders are contrastingly yellowish or golden, or rufous, varying with the species. This coloring forms a mantle, sharply defined where it meets the black, and often extends to the lower surfaces. Since these bats hang by day without attempt at concealment, the pattern seems to have little significance for protection. Most of the smaller members of the family are more uniform in color, dull brown or olive brown, shading into reddish at the shoulders in some, and are less given to roosting in open view, but hang along the under side of a palm frond or beneath a leafy crown.

Pattern produced by contrasting small areas of white is found in many bats that roost in trees. Such markings, as Abbott Thayer first demonstrated, may be of concealing value, not so much by the resemblances they may produce as by the contrasts they make. For white marks, passing at casual glance for high lights, tend to break up the definite outlines of a familiar form, so that the object is not recognized for what it really is. In this category may fall the white facial stripes of the leaf-nosed bats, Artibeus and Uroderma, the former of partly tree-roosting habits, the latter sheltering under large overhanging leaves. Related genera, as Vampyrops and Chiroderma, of tropical America, have in addition a white line down the middle of the back, contrasting with their otherwise uniformly dull brownish coloring. Both these are probably tree-dwellers, though little is known of their habits. Contrasting streaks or small patches of white are found in other tree bats, such as the soft-colored Glauconycteris of Africa, with a whitish line along the sides or on each shoulder. One species, the

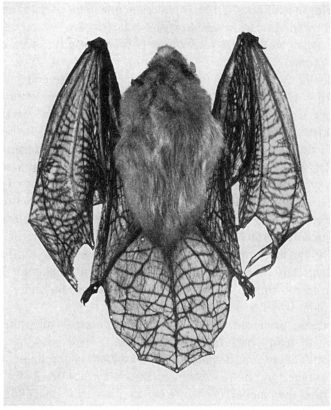

Fig. 34—The butterfly bat (*Glauconycteris variegata papilio*), of the Cameroons, West Africa, in which the veining of the membranes is outlined in darker color, giving it a resemblance to a skeletonized leaf. From a specimen in the Museum of Comparative Zoölogy, natural size.

butterfly bat (*Glauconycteris v. papilio*), is remarkable for the network of dark lines following the veining of its otherwise pale membranes, a device which may have protective value by causing a resemblance to a skeletonized leaf.

Another genus, the harlequin bat (Scotomanes) of south-eastern Asia, shows an almost startling effect through the contrasting presence of a white spinal stripe with other white markings on a brilliant rufous ground. Swinhoe writes of seeing a cluster of these bats hanging among the leaves of a forest tree in Formosa and of mistaking them at first for some large fruit. A remarkable long-eared bat, Euderma, of the southwestern United States, as yet known from a bare half-dozen specimens, is unusual in its black livery with a large white splotch on each shoulder and another at the root of the tail, producing a "death's head" appearance, as Dr. J. Grinnell (1910) has aptly re-

FIG. 35—The black and white bat (*Euderma maculatum*) in which the contrasting spots of white on the black body form a "death's head" pattern; from a preserved specimen. A species of the southwestern United States of which about half a dozen individuals are known. Courtesy of Dr. and Mrs. Joseph Grinnell.

marked. So startling a pattern may have a protective value, but the habits of the species are almost unknown. Indeed, in all these cases it may be unsafe to assume that the bats are better concealed through these markings, for their true significance may be something altogether different.

An interesting pattern that really does seem to have value through protective resemblance is that seen in the tube-nosed fruit bats of the genus Nyctimene, found from Celebes to Timor, New Guinea, and the Solomon Islands. There is usually a dark-brown spinal stripe, and the wings and forearms are sprinkled with round yellow dots contrasting with the dark skin, perhaps simulating the background of irregular markings and lichens of the tree trunks against which the bat hangs solitarily by day.

In their book, *Concealing Coloration in the Animal Kingdom*, the Thayers point out that most bats do not show "obliterative shading," that gradation of coloring from darker on the back to paler or white on the lower surface whereby in many land animals and birds concealment of the motionless form is helped through counteraction of the shadow on the lower side. This is perhaps owing to the fact that bats hang up by the hind feet when at rest and even when active do not usually frequent lighted places. Nevertheless, in most species the under side is slightly the paler, and there are some in which the entire lower surface is contrastingly white, or others in which the chest may be dark but the abdomen paler, even white at the base of the tail, in direct contrast to what one might expect. Evidently some other explanation than that presumed for terrestrial animals must be worked out.

There is another type of coloring in bats which may be owing to purely physiological causes and have no obvious relation to the habits or requirements of the animal. This results from either an accentuation of one or another color factor, or its absence altogether. Thus, if the blackish element predominates, the coloring becomes abnormally blackish, a condition known as melanism; if the red becomes the prevailing tint, erythrism results; if no pigment is formed, we have a condition of albinism. Both albinism and melanism are rare in bats. A white bat occurs perhaps once in many thousand. Complete albinism includes even the dark coat of the retina, so that the eyes look pink. I have seen one or two case of albinism in the red bat, and the Museum of Comparative Zoology has a beautiful pure white specimen of the little mastiff bat (*Molossus tropido-rhynchus*) of Cuba, taken at the same time with a number of normally dark individuals from a colony. A pure white pipistrelle is preserved in the British Museum, and similar albinos are reported for a horseshoe bat and for a brown bat (*Eptesicus capensis*) in museums of South Africa. In an account of the vast numbers of free-tailed bats (*Chaerephon plicatus*) that nightly swarm forth from a great cave in North Borneo, Pryer (1884) writes that among the many thousands that streamed

away at dusk he saw three albinos. These were well known
to the native Malays, who spoke of them as the Rajah, his son,
and wife. But whether it was in every case the same three or
others related to them is another matter. It is well known that
albinism, when it once appears, may be inherited either by
direct interbreeding of albino animals or indirectly by cross-
breeding with normally colored individuals. In the second case
the offspring are all colored like the normal parent, but interbreeding these young produces in the second generation an
average of 25 per cent of albinos; or if one of them is bred back
to the albino, 50 per cent of each type results. In a large population, however, the chances are small that the proper combination of parents will take place necessary to give rise to albino
young.

Melanism, or the production of abnormally black individuals
through complete or partial disappearance of the red element
in the color combination, is perhaps even rarer than albinism,
the complete loss of pigmentation. A possible case, however,
is that of Ensleven's bat (*Lasiurus ensleveni*), a supposed
species or race of southern Brazil and Uruguay. This bat is
in most respects like the form of red bat found in the same
region, but is blackish instead of red. Some three specimens
only are known. Melanism has also been reported in the
common pipistrelle of eastern United States (F. L. Osgood,
1936). When once established, this condition may become a
dominant character in heredity and eventually pervade a whole
population, so that a black race results. Among others, familiar
instances are the black fox squirrel of the southern United
States, a race of black gophers on the Pacific coast, the black
honey creeper of St. Vincent in the West Indies. Among bats,
a parallel case is found in some of the flying foxes (Pteropus)
which, on certain islands of the East Indies, have evolved
black races such as *P. natalis* of Christmas Island or *P. modi-
glianii* of Engano Island, and several others. Often in these cases
some trace of the yellowish mantle may be detected, as a
reminiscence of what was probably a well-developed pattern,
now lost through having been bred out in the course of ages.

On islands with a limited area and a limited population, such a result no doubt is more easily brought about than on a larger continental land mass.

Finally, a more interesting problem is presented by certain bats that develop alternative color phases, so that in one and the same species, or even in the same colony, some are brown of a certain shade, while others are reddish, with sometimes intermediate individuals. Once more the underlying causes are doubtless physiological, yet not altogether clear. The only species in which this has been carefully studied is the rufous horseshoe bat (*Rhinolophus rouxi*), a common species in India. Andersen (1917) found that when about fully grown the bats of the year undergo an autumnal molt like the adults. The new coat is dark brown above, mouse gray beneath. Very soon most of the individuals begin to change to brighter tints from auburn to orange rufous or even "xanthine-orange," so that by spring many of the colony are extremely brilliant in coloring. A second molt takes place probably in May or June, when again the mouse-brown fur replaces the old coat, and this in turn changes to the brilliant tints of rufous. The interesting thing is that many individuals remain dull-colored without changing to the brighter colors. Andersen believes that the change of color is owing to the oxidation of the brown pigment, which implies a chemical change in the pigment granules of the hairs, but as yet we have no clue as to why some bats change and others do not. Nevertheless, there is some evidence that climatic conditions may have an influence. At any rate, we find in a number of tropical species of bats two color phases, one of some shade of brown or blackish, the other of a much clearer reddish or rufous. The reddish phase is usually the rarer, but in some it is the more usual and might conceivably become the sole coloring in the adult. Thus, in tropical America a small blackish-brown species of Myotis (*M. nigricans*), which is common from Paraguay to Mexico, occurs rarely with the fur dull reddish brown except at the base of the hairs, where it may be slaty. Such an individual was once described as a distinct species, but the presence of a number so colored, among a colony of the blackish type, shows that this is but a color phase.

Occasional red individuals turn up also in a related South American species, *Myotis ruber*. In a house-living bat, *Scotophilus castaneus*, of Java, the red phase is particularly bright, a deep brilliant rufous, slightly paler below. Dull olive-brown individuals occur in the same colonies with the bright ones. Among the American leaf-nosed bats a similar thing is found. An abundant small species, the short-tailed bat, *Carollia perspicillata*, found from Mexico to southern Brazil, is usually of a dull drab brown with whitish bases to the fur, but one or two in a series of fifty from Central America are clear pale orange. The same thing happens in some other members of this family. Thus the three species of spear-nosed bats (Phyllostomus) in central Brazil and the Panama region, though usually dark smoky brown, show a small proportion of clear dull-russet individuals in the proportion of about one in a dozen or fifteen, while the small Micronycteris, with disproportionately large ears and ordinarily of a dull fawn color with white bases to the hairs, has lately been found to have in one species (*M. minuta*) from the Amazon region a brilliant orange-rufous phase of great beauty. In a series of ten of these, all but one or two were of this color in slightly varying degrees of intensity, the others, however, more nearly the usual brownish or fawn. On the opposite side of the globe, an Australian horseshoe bat, *Rhinolophus megaphyllus*, found in the eastern part of the continent, is usually a drab color in the temperate parts of its range, but in the tropical portion, as in northern Queensland, it exhibits a brilliant orange phase, with individuals of intermediate tints in the same colony. Similar rufous and dull-brown phases occur in the hare-lipped bats (Noctilio and Dirias) of the American tropics, and rufous or black individuals of the free-tailed genus Molossus are well known in the same regions. Even the vampire bat, Desmodus, has a grayer and a browner type of coloring. From these facts the conclusion seems warranted that the hot moist atmosphere of the tropics favors the development of more brilliant orange and rufous phases in bats, either through causing oxidation of pigments or in some other way not yet understood.  In a few tropical bats the brighter condition has become the dominant one, as in the East African horseshoe bat, *Hipposideros ruber*, in which the duller brown phase is less common than the red, or in the small reddish or rufous *Myotis bocagei*, in which no brown phase is known. Possibly, then, we have in such cases some of the steps toward the attainment of a more evolved condition in the color of the fur.

# CHAPTER XI

# BATS' TEETH AND THEIR MEANING

'Tis a secret must be locked within the teeth.
— *Measure for Measure*, iii: 2.

PERHAPS because of the prominent ears of bats, they are in the minds of most people wingèd mice. But this is far from the truth. Their real relationship is nearer to the insectivores (Order Insectivora), which include the moles, shrews, and their allies, one of the most ancient and primitive groups of placental mammals, that forms a sort of starting point for the evolution of modern types, now so diverse. In mammals there is usually a close correspondence between the nature of the food and the structure of the teeth, so that if the latter are examined it is possible to tell with much assurance the general nature of the diet. This close adaptation, however, has come about only as the result of slow adjustment over millions of years from a generalized type, such as we still see surviving in the opossum and some other marsupials, or in the moles and shrews, with some changes, the details of which often throw much light on the relationships of the species. For this and other reasons the tooth structure of mammals becomes of great importance as an aid to their classification.

As to the number of teeth, the greatest number present in the insectivores is forty-four, or eleven on each side in either jaw. In the more generalized forms these consist of three incisors above and below on each side, followed by a long bladelike canine for puncturing and holding the prey; then come four premolars which usually increase in size from first to fourth; and, finally, three molars of larger size and slightly different form, which are chiefly concerned with crushing the food or cutting it up. In most mammals the first three of these groups are preceded by milk teeth, which are shed early in the life of the individual and replaced by the permanent teeth, but the molars have no such forerunners. In the bats the obvious distinction in form between these four groups of teeth is usually clear, but no bats, living or fossil, are known to have the full number of forty-four. For the upper incisors are at most two instead of three on each side, and the premolars never exceed three in each jaw, so that the greatest number of teeth known in bats is thirty-eight. These are written as a formula, in which $i$ stands for incisor, $c$ for canine, $pm$ for premolar, and $m$ for molar, as follows:

$$i\ \frac{2}{3}\ \ c\ \frac{1}{1}\ \ pm\ \frac{3}{3}\ \ m\ \frac{3}{3}\ =\ 38;$$

or the formula may be written in a different way, giving each tooth its serial number in the set, thus:

$$i\ \frac{023}{123}\ \ c\ \frac{1}{1}\ \ pm\ \frac{0234}{0234}\ \ m\ \frac{123}{123}\ =\ 38.$$

The latter formula shows also which of the original forty-four teeth have been lost, by the presence of a cipher in their place; but to determine this is not always easy and requires much comparative study. In different genera of bats the tooth formula varies considerably and is characteristic of particular groups.

Specialization has taken place in two directions: first, in the reduction of the number of teeth, and second, in the modification of the teeth themselves for the better performance of the work required of them. Reduction in the number usually accompanies a shortening of the muzzle and so of the tooth row itself, in order that greater biting power may be exerted at the tip of the jaws by bringing them nearer the jaw muscles. This is just the opposite of the trend in insectivores, in which the muzzle tends to lengthen and the first pair of incisors enlarges like a pair of tongs. In insect-eating bats the long canines seize and pierce the prey, which is then reduced to minute fragments by the sharp-edged premolars and by the bladelike crests that connect the cusps of the molars. These latter perform the chief work of cutting up the food and are placed farthest back under the muscle masses of the jaw, where the greatest power can be applied. On the other hand, those bats that live upon fruit (such as the fruit bats, Pteropidae, or many of the leaf-nosed bats, Phyllostomidae) need crushing as well as cutting teeth, and we find that they have attained this end by widening these teeth and lowering their cusps to make a somewhat flattened surface. One group in each of the two families has, however, taken a different trend in diet and has become nectar-feeding, with the result that the jaws are much lengthened and narrowed, the teeth are reduced in size, and the tongue is very long and slender, capable of being protruded far beyond the lips for reaching into the corollas of flowers and lapping up the honey. The details of these changes and the tooth formulae character-istic of the different genera of bats have been set forth by Miller (1907) and are extremely interesting from an evolu-tionary point of view. It will suffice, however, to mention a few of the more important points.

No bat is known to have the full number of three incisors on each side of the upper jaw. These small teeth are carried by the premaxillary bone and may be two, or one; or, as in some of the Megadermidae, none at all, and even the small pre-maxillary bones themselves may be missing. In the lower jaw, however, the full three are often present, but in some groups may be reduced in number in a similar way. In the upper jaw, according to Miller, it is probably the innermost of the three that is permanently lost, since the premaxillary is usually re-duced on that side, frequently leaving a space in the middle where the bones fail to meet, as in the family Vespertilionidae. Again, the two upper incisors bite against the two outer ones of the lower jaw as if the two sets corresponded. When but a single upper incisor is present, it is apparently the middle one of the original three, while the outermost one is lost. This is indi-cated by the fact that in genera with two upper incisors the outer one is usually the smaller and the more reduced in details of form. In the lower jaw, on the other hand, the outermost incisor is often the first to disappear. Of the two that then re-main, the inner one seems to be in the fruit bats (Pteropidae) the next to degenerate, for it is often the smaller, owing perhaps to the action of the long tongue, so that in those with but a single lower incisor on either side (such as Dobsonia, or Notopteris) it is number two that remains. Among other bats (the Microchiroptera), however, the reduction seems regularly to take place from the outermost to the innermost, so that in the few genera with only one lower incisor on each side it is number one that persists. This is seen in certain free-tailed bats (family Molossidae), where, owing to progressive narrowing of the chin, the lower incisors become smaller and show in re-

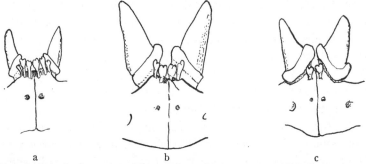

a                    b                    c

FIG. 36—Reduction in number of lower incisors with increase in size and function of the cingulum cusp of the canine. a, Mexican free-tailed bat (*Tadarida mexicana*); b, Osborn's free-tailed bat (*Mops osborni*); c, Bonda free-tailed bat (*Molossus bondae*). Enlarged seven times.

lated genera steps in the process of reduction. Thus in the American species of velvet-furred "guano bats" (Tadarida) all three lower incisors are present, but the outermost one is very small. In the related Mops and Chaerephon of the Old World the next stage is seen, in which only the two middle incisors are left, while in another, Molossops, in which two are also present, the outer one is the smaller. Finally, in Molossus, the mastiff bats of the American tropics, the latter tooth, too, has gone, leaving but one on each side, which apparently corresponds to the innermost or number one of the original three. In these genera the reduction in the lower incisors is correlated with the increasing size of the canine and its inner cingulum cusp (as seen in the accompanying figure), so that in the latter stages the cusp seems to take over the function of the small incisors beneath it.

Of the premolar teeth, immediately following the canines, no bat is known with more than three, hence one of the original four has long ago been eliminated. It is generally believed that the missing tooth is number one of the four, and this view is upheld by Miller (1907); but Thomas (1908) contends that it is the second or number two. The determination is made more difficult by the fact that in bats there are usually but two milk premolars, so that it is uncertain to which of the permanent set these correspond. Probably, however, they represent numbers three and four.

Miller lists ten genera of bats in which thirty-eight teeth are present. These include four of the family Vespertilionidae and four of the Natalidae, as well as two genera somewhat allied to the latter, Thyroptera and Myzopoda, each representing a family by itself. In all these there are three premolars in both upper and lower jaws. Other genera, including most of the fruit bats, retain three premolars either in both jaws or in the lower one, while the other sets of teeth are reduced. Where only two premolars are present in the upper jaw these are apparently numbers three and four in the fruit-eating bats of the families Pteropidae and Phyllostomidae, and in the Natalid bats and their allies, the Furipteridae and Thyropteridae, whereas in most of the insect-eating bats of the other families the premolars are numbers two and four. In the lower jaw the middle one of the three premolars is the first to become reduced in all the smaller bats (Microchiroptera), whereas in the fruit bats (Megachiroptera) the opposite is the case, for invariably the first one is the smallest and the second one the largest. These two groups undoubtedly represent divergent lines of evolution. In the next stage one would expect the reduced tooth to disappear entirely, and this is true in many of the Microchiroptera, but all three teeth are present in the fruit bats, none of which is known to have lost the first lower premolar.

The molar teeth begin to show reduction at the hinder end of the series. The last one in either or both jaws may become smaller and in related forms be missing altogether. The most highly specialized condition of all is found in the vampire bat, in which there is left but one incisor, the canine, one premolar, and one molar in the upper jaw, with one additional incisor and premolar in the lower. Yet even here the premolar and molar teeth are so small as to be functionless, for the incisors and

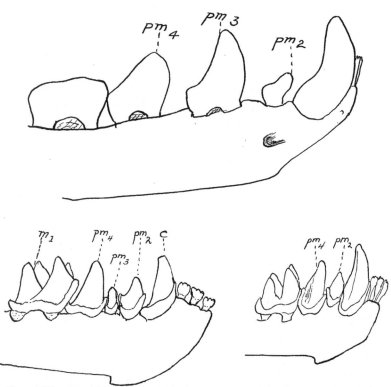

Fig. 37—Divergent evolution of the premolars. Upper figure: in Cynopterus the middle premolar (pm₃) is largest, while the anteriormost (pm₂) is most reduced; lower left, in Myotis, the middle premolar is the one most reduced, and in Eptesicus (lower right) is lost altogether. Enlarged.

canines suffice for piercing the skin of the victim. Here, then, the teeth are reduced to a minimum both in number and in function.

The living species of bats present a wide variety in the structure of the teeth themselves. Among the smaller insect-eating bats the upper incisors may be merely slender points (Molossus), or there may be a secondary cusp on the hinder side (Coelops). The lower ones are often more complex, with in the Vespertilionidae and some other families three minute divisions. In the hollow-faced bats (Nycteridae) the upper incisors may show a similar structure, with the crown divided into three or, in some, into two short cusps. The use of these, it has been suggested, is to act as a comb to aid in dressing and cleaning the fur, an occupation in which bats spend considerable time and care. In the South American leaf-nosed bats the incisors are usually rather compressed, with more chisel-like shape, often notched at the free border. No doubt these assist in cutting the skin of fruits on the pulp and juices of which they feed. This has been carried to an extreme in the vampire bats, in which the incisors are like keen-edged scalpels and much enlarged. The canine teeth of bats invariably retain much of their primitive condition, being long and pointed in both jaws, and exceeding the other teeth in height. They vary, however, in details of form and in some bats may even develop a strong shoulder or a secondary cusp at the back edge. The lower canine always closes in front of the upper, sometimes with its point fitting into a space between the upper canine and the outer incisor. Sometimes this space is lacking, but the tip of the lower canine fits into a hollow on the hinder or the outer side of the upper incisor. The premolar teeth are usually sharp-edged and are in form somewhat like a short broad canine. Rarely are they as large as the latter, but their crowns with the cutting edges help in a similar way to slice up the food.

In the insect-eating species the molars resemble those of the moles and shrews of the order Insectivora and afford clear evidence of relationship between the two groups. In the upper jaw the first two are usually much alike and consist of two high outer cusps, the paracone in front and the metacone back of it, with a third, the protocone, internal to the first. Often there is a fourth smaller one, the hypocone, behind the protocone, making thus four in all, arranged more or less in opposite pairs. Each of the outer cones has two sharp ridges or commissures extending to the outer edge of the tooth, the four ridges together forming a distinct W-shaped pattern in which the two lower points of the W are formed by paracone and metacone respectively, while the three upper points form shorter projections or styles, named from front to back, parastyle, mesostyle, and metastyle. The lower molars are shaped somewhat differently, with five cusps, of which the three in front are higher and together form a triangle or trigon, while the two others are lower, side by side, and constitute the heel of the tooth. These sharp cusps and ridges of the opposing teeth act as scissors to cut up the insect food into such minute fragments that it is often difficult to find in the stomach contents bits large enough to identify.

In the fruit-eating bats this typical and primitive condition is considerably altered, first, by the loss of the styles, so that the two outer main cusps of the upper molars come at the external edge of the tooth. Then the cones become shorter, while at the same time the inner part of the tooth becomes broader, adapting it more and more for crushing fruit pulp. Various stages in this process are beautifully shown in the South American leaf-nosed bats, Phyllostomidae, many of whose members have taken up a fruit diet, while in the Old World Pteropidae, which are all fruit and blossom feeders, it reaches its culmination in the broadly oval flat-crowned molars.

While many bats have lost the last molar, numbers one and two are present in all except two genera of vampires, Desmodus and Diaemus, in which only one remains as a vestige in the upper as well as in the lower jaw, and in Nyctimene, a fruit bat, in which there is one in the upper but two in the lower jaw. The loss of these teeth can be traced in the early stages in some genera, in which number three molar becomes smaller, then loses its last commissure, the final angle of the W. Then the tooth becomes further reduced, consisting of hardly more than a V. In the genus Artibeus, fruit-eating members of the Phyllostomidae, it is present but very small in *A. planirostris* but in the allied species *A. jamaicensis* is completely absent. Such stages doubtless represent the evolutionary course whereby the loss of these teeth has gradually come about. The interesting thing is that the process is a slow one and has proceeded at varying rates in different allied groups.

The milk teeth in young bats are very interesting because of their remarkable specialization. For while in most mam-

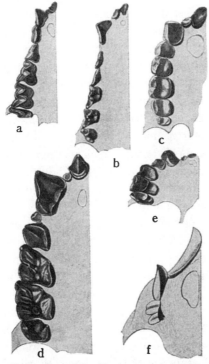

FIG. 38—Evolution of the upper teeth with change of food habits in the leaf-nosed bats (Phyllostomidae) and the vampire bat (Desmodontidae). (a) Crowns of the upper teeth in an insectivorous species (Micronycteris), showing the primitive W-shaped pattern of the cusps in the molars; (b) the same in the long-tongued bat (Glossophaga), but with the crowns much narrowed and the W-pattern distorted; (c) the same in a fruit-eating species (Sturnira), in which the W-pattern has largely been lost and the inner part of the molars broadened for crushing; (d) the tooth row of a larger fruit-eating species (Brachyphylla), with the complete loss of the W-pattern in the molars, with added ridging and broadening of the molars and last premolar; (e) the same of another fruit-eater (Centurio), showing additional broadening of all the cheek teeth, together with shortening and widening of the entire palate, and loss of the last molar; (f) crown view of the upper tooth row in a vampire (Desmodus), in which the functional teeth are but two, a bladelike incisor and canine for puncturing the victim's skin, while only one premolar and one molar remain, both small and degenerate. (After G. S. Miller, Jr., reproduced by courtesy of the U. S. National Museum.)

mals they bear a general resemblance to the teeth of the second or permanent set, in bats they are very different. The largest number known is twenty-two, consisting of two upper and three lower incisors, an upper and a lower canine, and two upper and two lower premolars on each side, as expressed by the formula:

$$dp \frac{2}{3} \quad dc \frac{1}{1} \quad dpm \frac{2}{2} = 22$$

(*d* indicating deciduous). All these teeth are shed at an early age and are replaced by the corresponding teeth of the second set, which push them out in rising from the gums. Curiously, this formula is characteristic of most bats, so far as is known, without regard to the amount of reduction in number of the adult teeth, with the exception, however, of the fruit bats (Pteropidae), the American leaf-nosed bats (Phyllostomidae), and the vampire bats (Desmodontidae), in which the outer lower milk incisor seems to be lacking, leaving but two on each side instead of three (Miller, 1907). This condition corresponds in general with that in the adults of these families, in which the number of lower incisors is also reduced, usually to two or one on each side.

The form of the teeth is peculiar. In such bats as the common brown species, Myotis and Eptesicus of the Vespertilionidae, they are perhaps less altered from their original state, for, as shown by Spillman (1927), both upper and lower milk incisors have the crowns distinctly though minutely three-cusped. This resemblance to the permanent incisors may indicate a more primitive, less altered state than in some of the leaf-nosed bats, in which they are two-cusped. The simplest condition of all occurs in the fruit bats (Pteropidae), in which the milk incisors are short straight spicules. By some this is regarded as the primitive and more ancestral condition, but it seems likely to be the more modified and specialized. The milk teeth of bats are often hooklike, with their tips turned in toward the mouth. For it is generally believed that their function is to help the young in clinging to the fur of the mother as she flies about with them when they are still very small. So firm is their hold that it sometimes requires a considerable pull to detach a baby bat clinging in this way. Thus these hooklike teeth partly make up for the loss of clinging power in the fore limbs, which have been modified to form wings.

In most young bats these milk teeth are shed in a relatively short time, for they cease to be useful when the babies are too large to be carried by the mother in flight. They therefore take no part in securing and chewing food. A further peculiarity is seen in the horseshoe bats (Rhinolophus), in which the milk teeth are resorbed before birth and so never function at all, as pointed out by Leche. Why this should be is not apparent, but it suggests that the young are for some reason in less need of their assistance.

Evidence that the peculiar form of the milk teeth in bats is really a derived and adaptive trait, is fortunately supplied by one of the oldest known fossil bats, Archaeonycteris of the upper Eocene of Germany. Of this species Revilliod (1917a) has described a jaw which showed a milk premolar in place, with the permanent premolar coming in beneath it. The former, instead of being a slender hooklike tooth, shows a crown very similar to that of a tooth of the second set, of larger size and with more or less of a cutting edge, a condition such as one might expect to find in the older ancestral bats, and one resembling that in the insectivores from which the bats have been derived.

# CHAPTER XII

## AN ANCIENT LINEAGE

The sorriest bat which cowers through noontide
While other birds are jocund, has one time
When moon and stars are blinded, and the prime
Of earth is his to claim, nor find a peer.
— Robert Browning: *Sordello*.

IN tracing out the evolution of animals, three main lines of approach are open: first, that of comparative anatomy, whereby characters common to a group and therefore relatively primitive may be ascertained; second, that of embryology, which may indicate earlier stages quickly passed through in the growing individual; and third, that of paleontology, whereby the fossil remains of more ancient forms may be directly compared with those of their relatives still surviving. Of these three methods the last obviously gives the most nearly accurate picture of the forms of long ago and offers a means of estimating how far their modern descendants have diverged from them. Unfortunately, however, the preservation of these ancient creatures as fossils is a matter of such rare occurrence that, of the millions of individuals which must have lived and died in past ages, only the merest fraction may chance to be preserved. That any of these should now come to light to be cherished and studied, rests again on an infinitely small chance.

For the conditions favoring the preservation of fossils are relatively rare. They imply, among other things, that the animal once dead should fall in such a spot that its bones are protected against destruction by soon becoming covered with earth or silt (as when it falls into a shallow stream or pool), and that this covering should remain undisturbed and gradually harden, while the bones themselves eventually become mineralized. Owing to destructive action of the elements, the older such remains become, the fewer are their chances of longer survival. The little that we know of fossil bats is chiefly based on fragments that probably were preserved in cave deposits. Some, no doubt, are of bats that died natural deaths in these retreats and, falling to the ground, in time became covered by cave earth washing in after rains or disintegrating from the roof and walls of the cave. Caverns are often formed by the dissolving out of limestone rock by rain or surface water. These not only form shelters for many kinds of bats but also are used by owls as daytime retreats, so that the remains of bats eaten by these birds are often cast up in pellets by them and accumulate on the floor of the cave beneath habitual roosts, where under favorable conditions they may be covered over and preserved. Such deposits are well known in the limestone caves of the West Indies, often forming solid masses more or less permeated and cemented together by infiltrating lime, forming a hard "breccia." More rarely, the dead animal falls into sluggish water or a shallow pool and, sinking to the bottom, is before long completely covered by fine silt. If undisturbed, the silty deposit may eventually harden into rock such as shale, and the enclosed animal thus may remain preserved whole or nearly so. Fossils of this kind are sometimes discovered by splitting the thin layers of the shale, revealing most beautifully even the outlines of the softer parts. Probably of such a nature are the wonderfully preserved fossil bats of the "Braunkohle" of Messel, in Darmstadt, Germany, the age of which is approximately fifty million years. Forest-dwelling bats that roost by day among trees or in hollow trunks would stand infinitely less chance of being thus preserved and for untold ages must have lived and perished, leaving no telltale bones for the Age of Man to discover. It seems very likely that what we do know of fossil bats is derived chiefly from what were originally cavern deposits, so that they may be thought of as representing a minute sample merely of the cave-haunting species of long ago. Perhaps, too, the more primitive kinds were in those days tree livers, so that the likelihood of discovering their remains is even more remote.

### A TIME SCALE

In reviewing what we know of the bats of the past, some sort of time scale is needed in order to picture more readily their age and order of succession. From a study of fossil-bearing rocks geologists have made out four great periods during which living creatures have left their traces. These are: the Primary, or oldest, during which plants, invertebrates, and fishes are the forms mainly represented; the Secondary, often called the Age of Reptiles, since this group seems then to have flourished exceedingly and to have given rise to two branches of warm-blooded vertebrates, the birds and the mammals; the Tertiary, or Age of Mammals, in which this group became the dominant type; and finally, the Quaternary, or Age of Man, from the beginning of the last Ice Age to the present time. Probably even by the close of the Secondary, both birds and mammals had evolved a long way, so that with the opening of the Tertiary practically all the modern orders were already established or foreshadowed, together with others that later died out. The last Ice Age represents the beginning of the Quaternary in which we now live.

Many attempts have been made to determine the length of time that these ages and their subdivisions represent. The most recent and probably the most nearly accurate is that of Barrell, in 1917, who based his calculations on the known rate at which certain radioactive minerals were found to break down into other simpler types. By comparing samples of rock from various strata, some notion of their age was reached, enabling him to work out a tentative time scale. This at least gives an idea of the vast lengths of time involved and the relative duration of the different periods. The following table, based on this work, shows that the length of the Tertiary epoch alone represents a time of approximately sixty million years, while the last period of the Cretaceous, in the preceding Secondary time, was nearly as long. Mammals appear to have been derived from reptile-like ancestors beginning probably in the

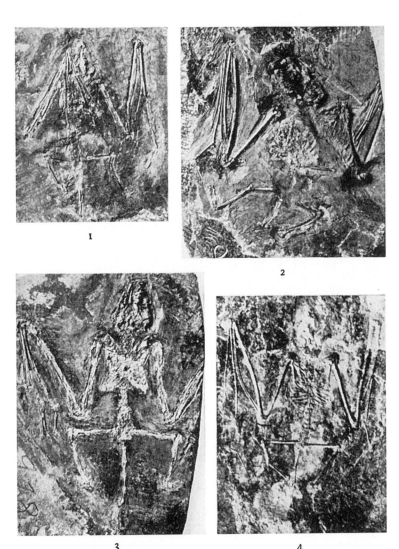

1

2

3

4

FIG. 39—The oldest known fossil bats, from early Eocene deposits of Messel, near Darmstadt, Germany, about fifty million years old. About three-quarters natural size. After Revilliod, 1917a.

1 and 4. Palaeochiropteryx tupaiodon.
2. Palaeochiropteryx spiegeli.
3. Archaeonycteris trigonodon.

Jurassic period, so that their course of evolution has covered approximately 180 million years.

| EPOCH | DURATION IN MILLIONS OF YEARS | TOTAL ELAPSED TIME IN MILLIONS OF YEARS |
|---|---|---|
| QUATERNARY PERIOD (Age of Man) | | |
| Holocene or Recent | 1.5–.5 | 1.5– 0.5 |
| Pleistocene or Ice Age | 1–1.5 | 2.5– 2.0 |
| TERTIARY PERIOD (Age of Mammals) | | |
| Pliocene | 6–7.5 | 8.5– 9.5 |
| Miocene | 12–14 | 20.5– 23.5 |
| Oligocene | about 16 | 36.5– 39.5 |
| Eocene (including Paleocene) | 20–26 | 56.5– 65.5 |
| SECONDARY PERIOD (Age of Reptiles) | | |
| Cretaceous | 40–50 | 96.5–115.5 |
| Comanche | 24–35 | 120.5–150.5 |
| Jurassic | 35–45 | 155.5–195.5 |
| Triassic | about 45 | 200.5–240.5 |

### THE ORIGIN OF BATS

The oldest known fossil remains of bats date from early Eocene times and prove that as long ago as the record shows they were even then "perfectly good" bats. As a distinct order of mammals they have so continued through the intervening sixty million years to the present day with little essential change. Of their previous history the record is still an absolute blank, yet there can be little doubt that they represent an offshoot of the primitive order of Insectivora, which they resemble in many particulars of tooth structure and in the discoidal form of the placenta. The Insectivora include on the one hand the moles, shrews, and hedgehogs, with a number of other more or less distantly related types, and on the other hand the tree shrews of eastern Asia and the elephant shrews of Africa. The tree shrews differ from other members of the order in being partly arboreal in habits, retaining with this presumably ancient mode of living a number of primitive points of structure, such as a complete bony orbit and five well-developed toes on each foot. They have even been regarded, doubtless correctly, as a sort of living fossil, foreshadowing the evolutionary course of the lemur-ape-human lines of divergence. As placental mammals, the tree shrews show also nearly the maximum number of teeth characteristic of this division, namely, two upper and three lower incisors, an upper and a lower canine, three premolars and three molars in both jaws, a number equaled but not exceeded by many bats. This may be expressed as a formula, using the initial letters of the different groups of teeth, as

$$i \frac{2}{3} \quad c \frac{1}{1} \quad pm \frac{3}{3} \quad m \frac{3}{3} \; = \; 38.$$

This formula is derived from a 44-toothed condition by the suppression of an upper incisor and an upper and a lower premolar on each side. The missing teeth, according to Thomas and Knud Andersen, are the outermost or third upper incisor and the second of the original four premolars.

It is probably safe to assume that the pre-Tertiary ancestors of bats were small shrewlike mammals living in forests and having long tails, five toes on each foot, and at least thirty-eight teeth, of which the molars showed the primitive W-shaped pattern of cusps such as are seen in many of the modern members of both groups; they also must have had deciduous and discoidal placentas. The transition from this tree-climbing ancestor to the flying bat may be easily pictured through analogy with certain forest-living mammals of the present day. An active life in trees not only requires the ability to travel along the branches but frequently necessitates crossing from one tree to the next. Most squirrels or monkeys do this by taking flying leaps, catching the twigs of adjacent branches, and hurrying on. This again implies a sense of balance and an ability to judge distances and avoid mistakes. The next step is some means of prolonging the leap, of covering more ground more quickly and thus developing greater efficiency in competition with other species. This problem has been partly solved by many mammals and along independent lines, through the development of a parachute-like membrane from the loose skin at the sides, which is spread by the outstretched limbs and allows the animal to volplane from one tree to another. Our flying squirrels are familiar examples, and a similar device is found in the giant flying squirrels of the East, the curious spiny-tailed squirrels of Africa, and in at least three genera of Australian forest-living marsupials ranging in size from Acrobates (about as large as a mouse) to Petauroides (about as big as a kitten). This side membrane (or plagiopatagium) is primarily a source of support in gliding through the air, and since it develops only in tree-living types of animals, the ancestors of bats must also have been tree livers of small size, that gained through this development the power of extending their leap.

The next step must have been the gradual elongation of the fingers of the hand, carrying the extended skin with them to form a webbing, and thus making a true wing. A stage of this sort is shown in the living species of flying lemur (Galeopterus) of the Far East and the Philippines, in which the lateral membrane is present, as well as another (the uropatagium) connecting the tail and the hind legs and a smaller one (the propatagium) from the sides of the neck to the forearm. Most interesting of all, however, the hands of this extraordinary animal are somewhat lengthened and webbed 'way to the ends of the claws, which are sharp and curved for climbing. The long, slender limb bones serve to spread all this sail, but as yet there is no true flight or propulsion in the air. However, the flying lemur, although almost a bat in some respects and with teeth that definitely ally it to the Insectivora, must be regarded as a separate offshoot or line from that basic order, for the hand web (or chiropatagium) includes the thumb as well as the four other fingers of the hand, whereas in bats the thumbs, or at least the terminal joints, are free.

We are therefore justified in assuming that the ancestors of bats first were arboreal shrewlike species, which later developed side membranes for parachuting, then in most cases a membrane from the tail to the foot, and finally one from the sides of the lower neck to the forearm. This was followed by a lengthening of the fingers and the extension of a membrane between them. There must have been a stage succeeding, where the fingers became longer and more slender, the third and fourth longest of all and capable of being fluttered with a downward stroke to maintain the animal in the air a little longer or send it a little farther on. One may imagine that once the fluttering movement began, the wing would rapidly develop so as to enable a weak flight, for the intermediate condition of having the fingers too long for comfortable climbing and yet too short for flight must have been of doubtful advantage. At some such stage as this the great group of bats or Chiroptera (meaning hand-winged) must have had its origin. And evidently Nature's experiment was a success, as shown by the abundance of species and the various lines of evolutionary progress seen among them at the present day. All this evolution must have taken place in the days preceding the Tertiary Period; at the same time a reduction in the number of teeth from the primitive forty-four and a shortening of the long snout of the insectivore had been attained, for no bat yet known, even the earliest Tertiary fossil, has three upper incisors or all four of the premolar teeth in either jaw.

### FOSSIL BATS

What is believed by its describer, the late Dr. W. D. Matthew, to be the very earliest-known fragment of a bat was named by him in 1917 *Zanycteris paleocenus*. The generic name means "very much of a bat," but the fragment, consisting of only a portion of the upper jaw, leaves one far from satisfied. It is of minute size and was obtained from the lowest true Eocene or the upper Palaeocene of the Wasatch beds near Ignacio, Colorado. Of the teeth, the incisors are quite lacking, but the canine is long and unusually slender for a bat. Following it is a space or diastema, succeeded by three premolar and three molar teeth. No other known insectivorous bat has a toothless interval between the canine and the premolars, but instead the tendency is to reduce this space by shortening the maxillary bone and thus crowding the premolars together, with the resulting loss of some of them. The angular outline of the posterior molars is more like that of many Insectivora than of bats. All things considered, this tantalizing fragment seems to the writer (with due deference to Dr. Matthew's opinion) quite as likely to be an insectivore (a view lately confirmed by Dr. G. G. Simpson).

By way of happy contrast, some of the most excellently preserved Tertiary bat remains are also those next in age, and constitute the very oldest bats of which we have really definite knowledge. These comprise a number of remarkably well-preserved fossils from the middle Eocene (Lutetian) of Messel, near Darmstadt, Germany. They have been most carefully studied and described by Revilliod (1917a). Of no less than thirty-eight specimens, eighteen showed nearly the entire dentition, and several are so nearly intact in thin layers of slate that the bones of the skeleton can be fairly well made out and measured. They include, however, but three or four species belonging to two genera, previously undescribed. These are named Palaeochiropteryx and Archaeonycteris (meaning "ancient hand-wing" and "ancient bat," respectively), the former represented by two species, a smaller (*P. tupaiodon*) and a slightly larger (*P. spiegeli*); the latter by at least one species (*A. trigonodon*). Of Palaeochiropteryx the complete dentition is known, namely two upper and three lower incisors, the canines, and three each of premolars and molars in each jaw above and below, making 38 teeth in all, a formula found in at least three living families. To one of these, the straw-colored bats (Natalidae), the teeth show further resemblance in that the first premolar is likewise the smallest and single-rooted, the second and third successively larger, with two and three roots respectively. The premolars and molars in both jaws all stand in the line of the tooth row, showing no tendency to crowding out. The third lower premolar, however, is notable for having a very distinct second inner cone (metaconid), usually absent in modern bats. The dentition, therefore, is not much more primitive than in many bats still living, such as those of the genus Myotis. The spinal column is preserved in one of the fossils and shows that only one of the vertebrae is united with the hip (ilium). The tails are imperfect in all, but evidently were fairly long.

Remains of Eocene bats have also been found in the Geisel valley, near Halle a.S., Germany. Here, in the so-called "brown coal" deposits, which are only a little less ancient than those of Messel, have been found extremely well-preserved remains of bats which Florian Heller (1935) has lately described as a distinct genus and species, *Cecilonycteris prisca*. Like Palaeo-chiropteryx of Messel, its last lower premolar shows a well-developed metaconid or inner cusp, and a heel or talon, but in other respects the two do not seem very closely related. It is uncertain whether this structure of the fourth lower premolar is an ancient or a progressive one, but perhaps the former. The first specimens obtained were completely destroyed by the contraction of the material in which they were imbedded, when it was dried out, but later, by infiltrating with paraffin and cellulose, the others were saved. So excellent is their state of preservation that the teeth and minute bones and even the outline of the wing membranes are traceable. There are thirty-eight teeth in all, the same number as in the living Myotis and a few other modern bats, and the lower premolars increase regularly in size from front to back, as in the modern long-legged bats (Natalidae) of Central America. The radius or inner bone of the forearm is proportionally shorter than in most living species, but the delicate ulna unites with it about halfway of its length, as in all modern types except the fruit bats (Pteropidae). The wing membrane included the legs and the entire tail.

Primitive traits among these oldest known bats are: in the skull, relatively unreduced number of teeth and the lack of crowding in the upper tooth row; in the wing, the relative shortness of the forearm as compared with the upper arm (humerus), and the low outer projection (trochiter) at the head of the humerus, which in some modern bats increases in size to give a double articulation for the upper arm.

Archaeonycteris was an extraordinary bat in that its milk

teeth retained the original unmodified state of the insectivores. In the adult the tooth formula is reduced as compared with Palaeochiropteryx, with but two instead of three premolars in the lower jaw. The upper dentition, however, is unknown. The cusps of the lower premolars and molars are even more distinct, those of the heel or talon of the latter more like those of primitive insectivores, with the outer obviously higher than the inner, though not so large or so nearly equaling the main anterior cusps as in modern bats. Most remarkable is the fact that one specimen shows a lower milk tooth being replaced by the permanent premolar below it. This milk tooth resembles a true molar in form, with two roots, and in this differs from the one-rooted permanent tooth and departs from the condition known in any other bat, for in at least the living species the milk teeth are simple hooklike structures for clinging to the fur of the mother. This retention of a primitive type of milk tooth is thus an interesting and important point of likeness to the insectivores whence the bats have been derived, while the molar teeth show a corresponding resemblance to those of the tupaia or tree shrew. As in Palaeochiropteryx, the upper arm is relatively short in comparison with the forearm, and in both the ulna unites with the radius near the middle as in some living bats, though in others (such as the flying foxes) the ulna is free and almost threadlike terminally. Revilliod regards these two genera as so different from all other known bats as to merit the rank of separate families, neither of them, however, ancestral to any modern group.

Obviously, then, these early Eocene bats had already progressed far along the lines characteristic of the order, though showing in many respects less advance than most modern forms over the primitive conditions. Their teeth were slightly more like those of insectivores and the milk teeth lacked the highly specialized form found in the living bats. Evidently, however, we must seek still farther back in antiquity for the hypothetical stage with three upper incisors and four premolars, while the presumably older condition, showing the beginnings of wing development through the lengthening of the fingers of the hand, is even farther back in the pre-Tertiary times.

It would be interesting to know something of the habits of these ancient bats and to learn by what chance their tiny skeletons have survived these millions of years. One might conjecture that the three species of Messel were associated in life just as now we may find two or even three species of Myotis and Miniopterus living in the same cavern, or hibernating together. The bat with milk teeth indicates a young of the year that perhaps had fallen to the floor of the cave and perished. Perhaps, too, there was a sluggish stream or a temporary pool in their retreat, into which these specimens fell and were soon after covered by a deposit of fine silt and so preserved.

Although Cope, in 1880, described a supposed fossil bat — "*Vesperugo anemophilus*" — from the Eocene formation of Wind River, Wyoming, the specimen was never figured and is now lost, so that its true identity is still uncertain. In Europe, however, other Eocene bats have been discovered at Egerkingen and Mormont, Switzerland, and at Montmartre and Célas, France. From the first two localities Revilliod has announced three extinct genera — Pseudorhinolophus and Paleunycteris from Egerkingen and the remarkable Paradoxonycteris from Mormont — while from the two French sites the remains are so fragmentary as to be indeterminable beyond the fact that they are insectivorous bats. This author, to whom we owe our knowledge of the bats in question, does not attempt to place Paleunycteris in any of the known families of bats, although Paradoxonycteris (if indeed it is surely a bat) should perhaps be given that distinction. On the other hand, Pseudorhinolophus is the earliest known member of the horseshoe bat family (Rhinolophidae), a group which seems to have flourished in the early Tertiary days and is still abundant in the warmer parts of the Old World from the British Isles to Japan and southward to Africa and Australia. More interesting still, however, is his discovery of what appears to be a true Rhinolophus from the "Ludien" formation of Mormont, the dominant genus of this same family at the present day. But of all the localities that have furnished remains of fossil bats, the richest and most famous is that of the so-called phosphorites of Quercy, in France. The deposits here are of slightly later age, either late Eocene or early Oligocene (perhaps partaking of both), and are believed to have been originally laid down in limestone caverns, the roofs of which in the course of time fell in, so that after having furnished for unknown years a place of refuge for cave-dwelling bats, they later formed a pitfall for many other larger mammals. The locality is now destroyed through human settlement, but its fauna was fortunately rescued and brilliantly studied by Filhol and others.

A recent review of the abundant remains of bats by Revilliod (1917, 1920, 1922) reveals many interesting things. The genus Pseudorhinolophus, found in the earlier deposits of Egerkingen by this author and at Mormont by Pictet, is here represented again by the same species (*P. morleti*) still persisting, as well as by four other species. This must have been an abundant genus in those days and persisted probably into middle Miocene times if Revilliod's identification of the *Rhinolophus collongensis* of Depéret, as a member of this genus, be correct. The related genera, Palaeophyllophora and Paraphyllophora are both represented at Quercy, the former by two species, the latter by one, with in addition two species believed to represent the modern horseshoe bat genus, Rhinolophus (*R. priscus* and *R. pumilio*). The Quercy deposits also yielded the first known fossils of the family Megadermidae, the big-eared bats (sometimes called false vampires), still represented in the tropics of the Old World by such genera as Lavia of Africa and Megaderma of southern Asia, but here known from three species of the genus Necromantis. These were large bats, hardly smaller than the Australian Macroderma, and combined sundry primitive traits with others of high specialization. Thus there were three small upper premolars, of which the middle one was the smallest, the nasal bones were present in nearly normal development instead of absent as in modern megaderms, and the reduction of the premaxilla was apparently only partial, with probably a remnant of the ascending branch, while in the modern genera the entire premaxillary has disappeared. On the other hand, the lower molars are specialized in the height of their anterior cutting cusps, while the lower canines are enlarged at the expense of the incisors, so that their roots are nearly in contact and the incisors have apparently disappeared. In modern megaderms the upper premolars are reduced from the original four to two or one, but in Necromantis, Revilliod interprets the alveoli as indicating three, of which the middle one is smallest, so that not only is the genus more primitive than any of those now living in respect to the number of these teeth, but also it confirms the view that in the reduction of the lower premolars the third of the original four disappears before the second and fourth.

In a later age a similar large species lived in France, where at Grive-St. Alban fragments of a skull and an entire humerus have been found in deposits of middle Miocene age. This bat, originally named as a small fruit bat, *"Cynonycteris" gaillardi* Trouessart, has so far progressed beyond the Oligocene stage that it has lost the small middle premolar in the lower jaw and is therefore believed by Gaillard to be worthy of a distinct new generic name, Miomegaderma. The large braincase of Necromantis is mentioned by Revilliod as a progressive character and may indicate high intelligence coupled perhaps with carnivorous habits, as in the modern Megaderma, which actively hunts for prey in the form of small birds and bats, mice, frogs, and night-living lizards. Its presence in France in the Miocene times may further indicate a warmer climate then than now, for the members of this family at the present age seem to prefer tropical climes.

At least three other of the modern families of bats occur among the fossil remains at Quercy, namely: the sheath-tailed family, Emballonuridae, with four species of the extinct genus Vespertiliavus (including *V. bourguignati* of Filhol and three others described by Revilliod); the family Vespertilionidae, a progressive group represented by a single member of the otherwise unknown genus Nycterobius (*N. grandis*); and finally, the family of free-tailed bats, Molossidae, of which an unmistakable end of a humerus with the characteristic long outer process or trochiter beside the head was found. In addition to this interesting assemblage, there are two species of Paleunycteris, differing from the two found in the earlier, Eocene deposits of Egerkingen. This genus is unknown from later deposits, and even the family it represents is uncertain. Thus we have in all no less than twenty-one species of bats described from the Quercy remains, referable to at least nine genera. Should some other deposit of a later age and equally rich in bat remains ever be discovered, it would give us a wonderfully illuminating view of the cave-haunting species of other days and shed additional light on the evolution of this group. Unfortunately, however, the species known from later formations are few and the remains in most cases lamentably imperfect. The excellent tabular view given by Revilliod (1922) shows that, so far as present evidence goes, Pseudorhinolophus survived into middle Miocene times (one species), as did also its relative Paraphyllophora, as indicated by the fragments named *P. lugdunensis* (from the "Vindobonien"). The living genus Rhinolophus is represented in deposits of later Oligocene times (*R. sp.?* of the Stampian; *R. lemanensis* of late Aquitanian) as well as of middle Miocene (*R. delphinensis*), and its species are still numerous in the tropical parts of the Old World. Another extinct genus of this family is known from a single specimen, *Palaeonycteris robustus* from the later Oligocene of St. Gérand de Puy, France.

The earliest-known fruit bat or Megachiropteran dates from the Stampian beds of Oligocene Age, a fairly well-preserved fossil, showing various parts of the skeleton. It was found at Monteviale, Italy, and has been named *Archaeopteropus transiens*. Its hand is characterized by the relatively long second finger, with claw, and by the fifth digit's having three instead of but two joints or phalanges. The hard matrix has prevented a study of the teeth, but it is said that they appear to be sharp-cusped, more like those of an insect-eating bat than like those of modern fruit bats; so that it forms a sort of missing link connecting these two groups.

The palaeontologist Schlosser has named from the early Oligocene of the Egyptian Fayûm some fragments of a bat which he regards as representing the South American leaf-nosed family, Phyllostomidae, namely *Provampyrus orientalis*. It seems very doubtful, however, if this allocation is correct, and the specimens require more careful review.

While, as one might expect, bats of the more primitive families Rhinolophidae, Megadermidae, and Emballonuridae, are commonest in the Eocene deposits, especially as represented at Quercy, those of the more modernized Vespertilionidae and Molossidae are correspondingly few. Thus at Quercy the genus Nycterobius (*N. gracilis*), otherwise unknown, is the only vespertilionid yet found. In the Stampian and Aquitanian deposits (middle and late Oligocene) and in the Vindobonien (middle Miocene) a number of jaws and other fragments have been discovered, all of which are regarded as representing the modern genus Myotis, with three upper and three lower premolars. At least four species are known from fossils in these two periods. Their presence indicates that Myotis was probably even then common and widespread, just as today it is numerous in species and individuals in both Old and New Worlds. A somewhat closely allied bat, *Samonycteris majori*, known from a single well-preserved skull from the Isle of Samos, recalls Kerivoula, a funnel-eared bat of the Vespertilionidae. Its age is late Miocene. Of the free-tailed bats (Molossidae), the genus Nyctinomus (*N. stehlini*) is first definitely recorded from late Oligocene beds at Pyrmont and St. Gérand le Puy, France, while a second species, *N. helveticus*, comes from the middle Miocene of Anwil, Switzerland. This is at present a widespread genus in the tropics and subtropics.

Very few bats are known from deposits of late Tertiary Age. Revilliod lists none from the Pliocene, but in 1930 Kormos, in a review of the preglacial fauna of Somlyoe Mountain, in Hungary, near Püspökfürdö, listed five genera, all of which are still found in that country: Myotis (*oxygnathus* group), Barbastella, Plecotus, Vespertilio, and Eptesicus. Two of these he regards as new species, giving them new names, but no description, namely, *Eptesicus praeglacialis* and *Plecotus crassidens*. These and other associated fossil mammals he finds contemporaneous with the so-called "Cromerian" fauna of the British Isles, dating from the middle stage of the Upper Pliocene.

Much interest has been aroused by the finding of abundant cave deposits near Peking (Peiping), China, which in their fossils carry the record back into Pleistocene and late Pliocene times, and include a new fossil man (Sinanthropus) of primitive type. The small mammals have lately been reported on by Young (1934) and include remains of several species of bats. Among these he has identified abundant fragments of the genus Myotis but fails to identify them with any of the species now living in North China. Jaws of a species of the ancient genus Rhinolophus are, however, believed to represent an extinct species slightly different from those at present known to be living, and are given a new name, *R. pleistocaenicus*. Still other jaws are doubtfully referred to the tropical genus Hesperoptenus as a new and very large species, *H. giganteus*, but there can be little question that they do not represent this genus at all and probably are instead an *Eptesicus*, not very different from the living serotine bat, or even identical with the species still common in that region. In recent years two genera have been described from the Pliocene of the United States. The first of these, described in 1930 by Dr. E. R. Hall, as *Mystipterus vespertilio*, is a jaw fragment retaining the last lower molar, found in a Lower Pliocene or Upper Miocene deposit in Esmerelda County, Nevada. Although regarded by Hall as belonging to the family Vespertilionidae, and possibly related to the Old World genus Miniopterus, any estimate of relationship on such a basis is admittedly provisional. More satisfactory is a fragment comprising the rostrum and palate described by Stirton (1931) from the late Pliocene of San Pedro Valley, California. The specimen is placed in the family Vespertilionidae and given the name *Simonycteris stocki* in reference to the shortened rostrum, in which it somewhat resembles the red bat and the brown bat. There are two upper incisors, a single premolar, and three molars.

The known remains of Pleistocene bats are again fewer than might have been expected. Wettstein has described as new species certain fragments found in interglacial deposits in Dragon's Cave, near Mixnitz, Austria, referring them to the living genera still found in that country, namely, Barbastella (*B. schadleri*), Myotis (*M. mixnitzensis*), and Plecotus (*P. abeli*). Similarly, in the United States the bat remains described as *Corynorhinus alleganiensis* from Cumberland Cave, Maryland, and *Eptesicus fuscus grandis* from the Conard fissure, Arkansas, are not very different from their present-day relatives of the same genera living in these same regions. On the other hand, some interest attaches to a mandible of a bat obtained with other early Pleistocene fossils at Melbourne, Florida, that appears to represent a large free-tailed bat allied to Molossus but differing in the details of the teeth. This I have described as *Molossides floridanus*. The Pleistocene, as others have pointed out, was a time doubtless of extinction rather than of active evolution, when probably many surviving genera of bats died out without leaving much trace.

Investigation of cave deposits in the Greater Antilles of recent years has brought to light many interesting remains of bats, not only of species still living in those islands and confined to them but also a few skulls of species not hitherto found alive. These deposits in most cases are probably of no great age, dating from the present back to late Pleistocene times. Since the discovery and occupation of the West Indies by white men, great changes have taken place in the local faunas, so that many species have now become scarce or even extinct that were then doubtless common. It may be that the extreme rarity of certain Antillean species of bats on these islands, as for example the genera Phyllops, Ariteus, and others, indicates approaching extinction as a result partly of changed conditions, such as clearing and burning of forest growth with the accompanying destruction of food and shelter.

In Puerto Rico the exhaustive investigations of the cave fauna by H. E. Anthony (1918) have resulted in the interesting discovery of three bats of fruit-eating genera (*Monophyllus frater, Stenoderma rufum,* and *Phyllonycteris major*) which seem now to be extinct. All three belong to relict West Indian genera, unknown on the American mainland. The first is a larger edition of a species (*Phyllonycteris portoricensis*) still locally common on the island; the second was first made known in 1813 from a single specimen in the Paris Museum, without locality, no second specimen of which had ever been found. But Anthony's discovery of numerous remains in the deposits at Cathedral Cave, Morovis, indicates that it is a West Indian species, probably now extinct, doubtless living on Puerto Rico over a century ago; the third is especially interesting because it is a Puerto Rican representative of a genus otherwise known only from Cuba and, like so many other Antillean species, indicates a former more intimate connection between the faunas of these islands. Of the numerous other bats which are represented by fossil remains from these cave deposits, living colonies still survive in the caves. It is noteworthy that the three extinct species are fruit eaters, while the insectivorous species, so far as is known, persist, implying a possible connection with forest destruction.

## FAMILIES AND GENERA OF FOSSIL BATS

### MEGACHIROPTERA

|  |  | |
|---|---|---|
| Pteropidae | | |
| Archaeopteropus transiens | Oligocene | Probably an insectivore |

### MICROCHIROPTERA

|  |  | |
|---|---|---|
| Family | | |
| Zanycteris paleocenus | Eocene | |
| Archaeonycteridae | | |
| Archaeonycteris | Eocene (Messel) | Two species |
| Palaeochiropterygidae | | |
| Palaeochiropteryx | Eocene (Messel) | Two species |
| Cecilionycteris | Eocene (Geisel valley) | One species |
| Rhinolophidae (sensu lato) | | |
| Pseudorhinolophus | Eocene to Oligocene (Europe) | Seven species |
| Palaeophyllophora | Oligocene to ? Middle Miocene (Europe) | Four species |
| Palaeonycteris | Late Oligocene (Europe) | One species |
| Rhinolophus | Middle Eocene to Recent (Eurasia) | Several species |
| Megadermidae | | |
| Necromantis | Late Eocene or Early Oligocene to mid-Miocene | Three species |

| | | |
|---|---|---|
| Emballonuridae | | |
| Vespertiliavus | Late Eocene or Early Oligocene (Europe) | Four species |
| Vespertilionidae | | |
| Nycterobius | Late Eocene or Early Oligocene (Europe) | One species |
| Myotis | Oligocene to Recent | Four or more |
| Samonycteris | Late Miocene (Europe) | One species |
| Simonycteris | Pliocene (Arizona) | One species |
| Mystipterus | Pliocene (Nevada) | One species |
| Genera incognita | Oligocene, Miocene (Europe) | Several species |
| Molossidae | | |
| Nyctinomus (s.l.) | Oligocene to Recent | Two species |
| Molossides | Pleistocene (Florida) | One species |
| Incertae sedis | | |
| Paleunycteris | Eocene to Oligocene (Europe) | Four species |
| Paradoxonycteris | Eocene (Europe) | One species |
| Various species described as "Vespertilio" | Eocene to Oligocene (Europe) | |

# CHAPTER XIII

# THE GEOGRAPHIC DISTRIBUTION OF BATS

In their geographic distribution bats offer many interesting points, some of them difficult to explain. Why, for example, are the fruit bats confined to the Old World? Why are the leaf-nosed bats confined to the American tropics? How may we explain the fact that the disk-winged bats of tropical America find a close relative in the sucker-footed bat of Madagascar? What does it mean that several genera in the West Indies are unknown on the neighboring continents? These are but a few of the puzzles that their present distribution affords.

Three chief factors determine these matters: first, the means whereby bats may go from place to place; second, the history of the land areas they inhabit; and third, their individual preferences in respect to climate, food, and other conditions of life. These three factors govern the distribution not only of bats, but of other animals and of plants as well, so that often we find a whole series of both whose presence is limited by similar causes, forming a loose association characteristic of certain areas. Thus temperate Eurasia and North America show many similarities in their characteristic fauna, so that the name Holarctic Region is used to cover both together; on the other hand, their differences afford a basis for distinguishing the Old World area as the Palaearctic Region, and that of the New World as the Nearctic Region. Further, the warmer parts of the New World present many peculiar and characteristic species, so that the term Neotropical Region is applied to Central and South America. In the Old World, for the same reason, the continent of Africa south of the Sahara is spoken of as the Ethiopian Region, and the eastern portion of the Asiatic tropics as the Oriental Region. Finally, Australia and New Guinea together form another division, the Australasian Region, with its characteristic fauna and flora. Nevertheless, the problem is not so simple as this convenient division seems to imply, for the boundaries are seldom sharply defined, scarcely any two species have exactly the same distribution, and there are exceptions to every rule. Let us explore the subject in more detail.

Bats, like birds and insects, have the power of flight so that they can extend their wanderings from place to place far more readily that terrestrial species are able to do. For this reason it is sometimes argued that their distribution must be less limited than that of the more earthbound creatures. Yet this is only to a slight extent true; for, excepting the migratory species, most bats remain closely confined to particular regions and in general show no tendency to extend their bounds. Hence local races may develop in portions of the general range. Species inhabiting groups of islands tend to remain there and in time develop small characteristic differences from their nearest relatives, which may themselves develop along their own lines. Thus, races or eventually species may arise through isolation. Again, in the case of a widespread species, whose general range may cover a large part of a continent, the differing conditions of climate, acting uniformly on the populations of different areas, may eventually bring about slight but obvious variations correlated with such areas. Thus, in deserts bats may develop very pale whitish races; in cool moist areas their colors darken and become dull or smoky; in warm moist regions their tints are richer and brighter; while in parts with intermediate conditions, the colors are transitional. Proportions of size may also vary from one area to another. Thus, races or, in time, species may arise through climatic or geographic variation.

Through its influence on plant distribution climate also limits the food and shelter available for animals. Fruit-eating bats must seek out areas where their special food is found in sustaining quantities. Those that rest by day among trees are again limited by the presence or absence of tree growth. Cave-dwelling bats are only abundant where suitable caverns exist, such as in limestone regions, so that the geology of the area may become an important factor in their distribution. Because of these various necessities bats, as well as more terrestrial mammals, tend to remain where the best conditions are found. They do not usually go off across unknown seas in search of new territory, though in rare instances they may be carried or blown far out of their usual area; but such waifs must usually die, without starting new colonies. Extension of the range must come as a slow and gradual process, following along lands where food and shelter are obtainable, into new and likewise favorable regions. Any subsequent break in this land connection must isolate the colonies at both ends. This is probably the usual explanation of the occurrence of continental faunas on islands, such as on Java, Borneo, or Madagascar. On the other hand, it is likely that the bat population of some of the islands of the East Indian archipelago has been derived from over-water arrivals from neighboring islands, though this is doubtless an uncommon occurrence.

The latest classification of bats (by Miller, 1907) divides them into two major groups: the Megachiroptera, which comprises but a single family, the Pteropidae; and the Microchiroptera, containing the remaining families, sixteen in number, the greater part of which are of insectivorous species or are bats with some particular diet, such as fruit or blood. These seventeen families may be sorted according to their distribution over the main land masses of the earth into three groups: (1) those confined to the continents and islands of the Old World, eight in all; (2) those confined to the New World, six; and (3) those which occur in both Old and New Worlds, of which there are three only. These may be grouped in tabular form as follows:

FAMILIES CONFINED TO OLD WORLD

| | |
|---|---|
| Pteropidae (fruit bats) | Hipposideridae (horseshoe bats) |
| Megadermidae (false vampires) | Nycteridae (hollow-faced bats) |
| Rhinopomidae (mouse-tailed bats) | Mystacopidae (short-tailed bats) |
| Rhinolophidae (horseshoe bats) | Myzopodidae (sucker-footed bats) |

CONFINED TO NEW WORLD

Noctilionidae (hare-lipped bats)      Desmodontidae (vampire bats)
Natalidae (long-legged bats)         Phyllostomidae (leaf-nosed bats)
Furipteridae (smoky bats)            Thyropteridae (disk-winged bats)

COMMON TO BOTH HEMISPHERES

Emballonuridae (sheath-tailed bats)      Molossidae (free-tailed bats)
Vespertilionidae (vespertilionid bats)

Of the eight families in the first group, two are represented at the present day by but a single species each. These are the short-tailed bat, Mystacops, constituting the family Mystacopidae, of New Zealand; and the sucker-footed bat, Myzopoda, of Madagascar, forming the sole member of the family Myzopodidae. They may be looked upon as the last ends of ancient lines, once more wide-ranging but now dying out and preserved only on these island refuges. Indeed, it is believed that Mystacops has already nearly gone, for with the clearing of New Zealand forests the hollow trees in which it lived have been largely destroyed, leaving it shelterless. Of Myzopoda very little is known, and there are few specimens in existence. The remaining six families are chiefly tropical and subtropical in distribution. The Pteropidae or fruit bats, which retain many primitive, together with highly specialized traits, still flourish in the Old World. The largest are the flying foxes (Pteropus), of which there are a number of species, centering in the East Indies and ranging eastward to Australia and the Pacific islands as far as the Samoa group. One species occurs as far north as the Japanese archipelago, while to the westward the genus occurs on the mainland as far as the Indian peninsula. It is absent from the mainland of Africa but, strangely, occurs in the islands of the Malasgay group and on the small island of Pemba, over four hundred miles from the latter and only some forty miles from the African coast. The four species of these islands are related to those of the Malayan region rather than to those of India and Ceylon, so that their occurrence here is difficult to account for. Did they arrive as wind-blown waifs from the east, or did they populate these islands from the African mainland in ancient times and then become extinct there? At the present time their place on the continent of Africa is taken by various other genera of the family, mostly of small species. Thus the rousette bats (Rousettus) are found from Cyprus in the eastern Mediterranean southward over Africa and eastward across India to the Philippines, New Guinea, and the Solomon Islands. The epaulet bats (Epomops and Epomophorus) are characteristic of Africa south of the Sahara. Most of the genera of this family — at least twenty out of the thirty or so known — occur only in various islands of the East Indian archipelago, such as Borneo, Celebes, the Philippines, and New Guinea, and appear to be wholly absent from the mainland of Asia. We may suppose that these again represent remnants of a once more widespread group, now isolated in these protected spots. In Africa south of the Sahara only eight genera of fruit bats are found, most of them rather closely related to the epaulet bats. One of these, however, Megaloglossus, is of special interest, for it represents in the West African forests the subfamily Megaloglossinae, of flower-feeding habits, with peculiarly narrow skull, degenerate teeth, and long extensile tongue, while the other seven genera of the subfamily occur in southeastern India and in the East Indian archipelago. It is thus one of various species of animals now isolated in the West African forest and separated by thousands of miles from their close relatives in the forest regions of south-eastern Asia. Probably at some remote and moister period, this forest was more or less continuous, but by gradual encroachment of the desert areas of central Asia its continuity was long ago broken, so that now we find related species still surviving at its opposite ends. This division may have taken place in mid-Tertiary times, so that many of these related forms have since had time to become now widely different. An example of this is perhaps the close relationship of the small flat-headed bat, Mimetillus of West Africa, to its representative in the East, Tylonycteris, both with the similar habit of crawling into cracks of bamboo stems. The brush-tailed porcupine of West and Central Africa is closely like that of Malaysia, while among birds, the bat-eating hawk, Machaerhamphus, has a similar distribution, and many other cases might be cited.

Among the Microchiroptera the most primitive stock is perhaps to be found in the mouse-tailed bats, Rhinopomidae, with but a single genus comprising three well-marked species. Their distribution is subtropical to tropical, from Egypt across India to Burma and Sumatra, but they avoid forests and are found in the drier parts of these regions. The hollow-faced bats, Nycteridae, afford additional confirmation of the view that a continuous forest once extended from the Congo to the Malay region. For although only a single genus, Nycteris, is known, several species large and small inhabit the forests of central Africa, with a few others that extend out into the thinly wooded and even arid parts of eastern Africa as far as the upper Nile valley. To the eastward the family is absent until we come to the Malay peninsula, Java and Timor, where again it turns up. Lönnberg has suggested that Nycteris is essentially a forest-loving type but in eastern Africa has spread out from this environment into the "steppe" regions of scattered tree growth surrounding the forest, so that distinct species have developed there. Perhaps another view is possible, namely, that the species now found in this drier or savanna area are merely the modified descendants of species that lived there when the country was more thickly forested. In that case they would have evolved with the changing environment rather than have invaded new areas from a forest source.

A peculiar family is the Megadermidae, big-eared bats including the false vampires of India and Ceylon. It is a tropical group. Of its five genera, Lavia with its orange-yellow wings is a common and characteristic bat of thorn-bush country in tropical Africa, while its close ally, Cardioderma, is East African. Of the three other genera, Megaderma and Lyroderma are the vampires of India eastward to Malaysia, while the former extends as far as the Philippines. The third genus, Macroderma, is a large bat of Australia.

The horseshoe bats are assigned by Miller (1907) to two families: the Rhinolophidae, containing the single genus Rhinolophus; and the Hipposideridae, with the genus Hipposideros and a half dozen other genera of fewer species. These are diversified groups, comprising many species. They are found chiefly in the tropics, including Africa and the areas eastward to India, South China, and the East Indies; but a few species of Rhinolophus have invaded more temperate latitudes to the northward — two in England and others in Japan. One rare genus of Hipposideridae, Coelops, found in the oriental region, has a counterpart or close relative in another rare genus, Cloeotis, of East Africa.

Six families of bats are confined to the New World. All are tropical in distribution or penetrate but a short distance into the subtropics. Of these, the Noctilionidae or hare-lipped bats, which include the fish-eating Noctilio and its smaller relative, Dirias, occur mainly in northern South America and Central America, although the former occurs in the West Indies as well. The largest and most varied of the New World families comprises the leaf-nosed bats, Phyllostomidae, most of which have an erect, fleshy leaf, shaped like a spearhead, growing from the tip of the nose, very different from the nose leaves of the horseshoe bats. These bats seem rather strictly limited in distribution to warm latitudes, for of the fifty or more genera known, only three or four reach the extreme southwestern borders of the United States in Arizona and southern California. A number of genera occur in the West Indies, but are absent on the opposite shores of Florida, despite its close proximity, with the exception of an occasional waif such as the record of Artibeus made a number of years ago from Key West. The American vampire bats, forming the family Desmodontidae, comprise three genera only, of which the best known is Desmodus, ranging from southern Brazil to southern Mexico. They are probably derived from the leaf-nosed Phyllostomidae and are altogether tropical.

Of a more restricted distribution is the family of long-legged bats, Natalidae, with four closely related genera. The species are all small and delicately formed. Three of the genera are confined to islands of the West Indies and the Caribbean Sea —

Chilonatalus in Cuba, Jamaica, the Bahamas, and Old Providence; Nyctiellus in Cuba and the southern Bahamas; Phodotes in the island of Curaçao off Venezuela. The fourth genus — Natalus — a yellowish type of bat, occurs in some of the West Indies, as well as on the mainland as far north as central Mexico. There is thus a certain parallelism with the distribution of the Old World fruit bats, some genera of which are now found only on islands of the East Indies, while others occur on the mainland as well. Probably in both cases the island genera are but remnants of groups with a once wider area of dispersal. Two genera, Furipterus and Amorphochilus, are grouped by Miller in a related family, the Furipteridae or smoky bats. They are from tropical South America and should perhaps be thought of as distant mainland cousins of the Natalidae, while the disk-winged bats, again wholly tropical in South and Central America, may represent a collateral line of evolution, with a near affinity perhaps to the Madagascan Myzopodidae.

Of the three families common to both hemispheres, two — the sheath-tailed bats (Emballonuridae) and the free-tailed bats (Molossidae) — are of tropical and subtropical occurrence, so that their members are now widely separated on opposite sides of the globe; while the third family, the vespertilionid bats (Vespertilionidae), which includes most of the familiar species of Europe and North America, is the only one that is truly cosmopolitan, with a wide variety of genera and species in both temperate and tropical regions. The bats of this family, while they have developed a complex shoulder joint, show nevertheless a simple condition in other parts. The tail is long and contained in the interfemoral membrane, there are no outgrowths on the muzzle, and the teeth in some genera, such as Myotis and Kerivoula, are little reduced in number. Indeed, Myotis, the most primitive genus, is at the same time the most cosmopolitan of all, for in various species it is found in the northern parts of both hemispheres to the limit of tree growth from Norway to Kamchatka, and from Alaska to Labrador. In the New World the common little brown bat (*Myotis lucifugus*) occurs over all North America, while closely allied forms range through the tropics to southern Chile and Argentina. In the Old World it is represented, for example, by Daubenton's bat (*Myotis daubentonii*), which occurs all the way from western Europe across northern Asia to the coast of the Pacific Ocean with little change. Other species of Myotis, large and small, range over Europe and parts of temperate Asia and North Africa; others again are found as far south as the Cape of Good Hope, and others still live in India and Ceylon, while one, *Myotis adversus*, extends from Malaysia and the East Indies to Australia. In point of time this genus is an ancient one, for fossil forms are known from the Eocene and Oligocene deposits of France. Of all bat genera, Myotis is thus the most widespread both in time and in space. Two others of the same family are almost equally cosmopolitan: Pipistrellus, the pipistrelles, which include some of the smallest bats, and Eptesicus, the genus to which belong our common big brown bat (*E. fuscus*) and its close relative the serotine bat (*E. serotinus*) of Europe. Both genera prefer warmer climates than Myotis, hence do not extend so far to the north and south. Pipistrellus ranges eastward to New Guinea, Australia, and the Solomon Islands, while Eptesicus extends almost as far. Such wide-ranging genera evidently have still a considerable latitude in their adaptability to varying climate. On the other hand, of the forty-one genera of Vespertilionidae recognized by Miller, no others are common to both hemispheres, but twenty-seven are confined to the warmer parts of the Old, and eleven to the New World. A possible exception, however, is Nycticeius, small brownish bats of which two species are found in America. One of these is the twilight bat (*Nycticeius humeralis*) of the southeastern United States, the other a closely allied form in Cuba, but both are so nearly related to the genus Scotoecus of eastern and central Africa that they might all be as well included in a single genus.

There are many interesting correspondences between bats of the warmer parts of the two hemispheres. Thus the long-eared bat (*Plecotus auritus*) of Eurasia and northern Africa is not distantly related to the lump-nosed bat (Corynorhinus) of the southern United States (from Virginia to the Pacific coast), while a second large-eared genus, Histiotus of South America, is perhaps a near relative of the East African Laephotis. On the other hand, the family of sheath-tailed bats, Emballonuridae, is confined in the New World to the tropical regions of Central and South America, with nine distinct genera, including the ghost bat (Diclidurus) and the sac-winged bats (Saccopteryx and Peropteryx), while in the Old World tropics there are but three genera ranging from Africa to the Pacific islands, of which none is very close to the American members of the family.

The third family common to both eastern and western hemispheres, the free-tailed bats or Molossidae, is again altogether tropical. Of the dozen or more genera now known, Tadarida, to which our "guano bat" belongs, is regarded as exclusively American, though nearly allied to Nyctinomus of the Old World (southern Europe to China). Four other genera (Molossops, Eumops, Promops, Molossus) are wholly American, while six others (Platymops, Myopterus, Chaerephon, Mops, Cheiromeles, and Xiphonycteris) are as distinctly Old World in distribution. Curiously, however, a single genus and a relatively uncommon one at that, Mormopterus, is found in both hemispheres. It is known from the mainland of southeastern Africa and the islands of Madagascar, Mauritius, and Bourbon in the Old World, but elsewhere only in Cuba and Peru.

All this is very puzzling to account for; nor are bats the only animals that show corresponding anomalies. For example, among the Insectivora, the Madagascan hedgehog, Setiger, finds its nearest living relative in the solenodon of Cuba and Santo Domingo. Various theories have been advanced to account for these things, such as the former presence of land bridges, whereby the ancestors of these species might have reached the remote areas in which we now find them; or, more recently still, the Wegener hypothesis has been invoked, that the New World split from the Old and gradually drifted away, bearing with it the related forms now so widely sundered. But land bridges would afford opportunity for an exchange of faunas between two areas, while Wegener's splitting of an original land mass, if it be a tenable theory at all, must have taken place too long ago to have affected the modern fauna.

A more attractive view is put forward by Matthew (1915) in his illuminating essay on climate and evolution. He regards the main land masses of the globe as relatively stable, at least during Tertiary times, with, however, minor fluctuations of level that undoubtedly connected the northern parts of Asia and northwestern America more than once at periods not geologically very remote. Probably, too, in early Tertiary days, that is, forty to sixty million years ago, similar connections and breaks took place, when Europe and northeastern North America may have been joined for considerable periods, tending to a.community of faunas at those times. A warmer climate then prevailed in northern latitudes, as shown for example by the presence of fossil palms in Greenland. Such conditions would have made it possible for bats and other animals or plants requiring a warm climate to advance far to the north and thus avail themselves of these land connections to extend gradually from the Old World to the New. The gradual change to cooler and drier conditions in the north, culminating in the last glacial epoch, would then have forced these new arrivals to retreat slowly southward from higher latitudes, following their optimum climate, until at length their descendants would be, as we now find them, isolated from their Old World relatives in the tropics of opposite sides of the globe. Such a course at a very ancient period, perhaps in early Tertiary times, may have enabled the sheath-tailed and the free-tailed bats to reach the tropical areas of the New World. Since then, no doubt, many of these pioneer types have died out while others have continued to evolve, so that now the living genera are mainly unlike their relatives of opposite hemispheres. A few, perhaps more conservative, have changed but little, so that we find isolated remnants of closely allied species now widely sundered, such, for example, as the species of Mormopterus in East Africa and Cuba.

The history of the land masses and of their changes of climate, did we know them more fully, would probably give a complete explanation of various anomalies of present distribution. Yet many problems remain unsolved. Why did the fruit bats, in many respects an ancient and primitive group, remain in the eastern hemisphere? Or if they did reach the New World, why did they die out? Are not the disk-winged bats of South America and the sucker-footed bat of Madagascar the last remnants of a group once more widely spread, whose ancestral types became separated, in the manner explained, on opposite sides of the earth? Matthew shows that the fossil record of other and better-known groups clearly points to the Old World as a chief center of early mammalian evolution, from which the New World was populated. Isolation in the western hemisphere later was followed by further evolution among these arrivals. Subsequent land connections in the north in late Tertiary time no doubt account for the presence of various closely related species as we now find them in northern Eurasia and North America.

The effect of isolation is especially interesting in the case of island faunas. Many land masses now separated as islands were doubtless in more ancient times connected with the near-by continents from which, in part at least, their fauna was thus derived. Through their very isolation they are now kept free from invasion by newer or more aggressive arrivals evolving on the continents, and thus occupy sanctuaries where competition is less severe. Familiar examples are Borneo, Madagascar, and Australia. The first was doubtless connected with the Asiatic mainland at a recent geological period, so that its present fauna is not widely different from that of the near-by Malay peninsula. Madagascar was probably separated much longer ago from Africa, perhaps in early Tertiary, while Australia's isolation must have been nearly complete from even earlier times. Thus, we still find on Madagascar and its smaller island neighbors fruit bats representing four groups of Pteropus, all related to Malaysian but not to Indian forms, and a species of sheath-tailed bat of the genus Emballonura, now similarly eastern and no longer found in Africa or India; again, the free-tailed bat, Mormopterus, related to species of the African mainland and known also from Cuba and Peru; and finally, the sucker-footed bat, Myzopoda, the only genus peculiar to Madagascar, which forms a family by itself, though with a counterpart or close relative in the disk-winged bats of Central and South America.

The bat fauna of Australia one might expect to include ancient and primitive species comparable to the archaic egg-laying duckbills and the abundant marsupials, which with other primitive animals and plants have probably been isolated here during most of the Tertiary period's sixty million years. But curiously, Australia's bat fauna is a modernized one. About twenty genera are known, nearly all of which are found or may be expected in the neighboring large island of New Guinea or have a still wider distribution among near-by island groups; a few of the genera occur on the mainland of Asia. Thus, of the four genera of fruit bats (Pteropidae), Dobsonia, the bare-backed fruit bat, though unknown from Asia, occurs on various island groups from Celebes and the Moluccas to the Solomon Islands; Syconycteris, a long-tongued nectar-feeding bat, is found in Queensland, as well as in New Guinea and the Bismarck archipelago, and is not distantly related to another genus, Macroglossus, which ranges from New Guinea and the Solomon Islands westward to the Malay peninsula; the curious tube-nosed fruit bat, Nyctimene, extends over much the same island groups; while Pteropus, the flying fox, with five Australian species, has numerous representatives on the islands of the East Indian archipelago and on the mainland as far west as the Indian peninsula. Of the sheath-tailed bats (Emballonuridae) the genera Taphozous and Saccolaimus both occur in Australia and are represented among the islands and on the mainland as far west as India and Africa. The horseshoe bats, constituting the two families Rhinolophidae and Hipposideridae, though widespread in the warmer parts of the Old World, are poorly represented in Australia, the former by a single, somewhat primitive species, the latter by several species of Hipposideros and a second genus, Rhinonycteris, the golden bat, a rare and specialized species, with the upper premolars reduced to one on each side and with an extra cusp to the canine. The only Australian representative of the great-eared bats (Megadermidae) is Macroderma, related to the Indian false vampire, Megaderma, but even more specialized in its larger size and more modified teeth. Of the simple-nosed bats (Vespertilionidae) some nine genera are now known from Australia, of which three, Myotis, Pipistrellus, and Eptesicus, are cosmopolitan; two, Miniopterus and Scoteinus, are represented on the mainland of Asia, and in Africa as well; while two others, Glischropus and Phoniscus, are known from some of the larger islands of the East Indian archipelago. Only two genera, Chalinolobus, the groove-lipped bats, and Nyctophilus, long-eared bats, are peculiar to the Australian region, but the latter is found from Timor to the Fiji Islands and is related to the cave bat, Antrozous, of the southwestern United States, while the Chalinolobus is also represented in New Zealand. Finally, the free-tailed bats, Molossidae, are known in Australia from some three or four species of Nyctinomus and Chaerephon, related to wide-ranging types of the eastern tropics. Doubtless this rather small bat fauna consists of much more recent arrivals in Australia than the ancient marsupials, duckbills, and spiny anteaters. It may have reached the island continent by way of New Guinea and islands intermediate to the East Indies, perhaps in late Tertiary times, when land connections existed between some of them, particularly between New Guinea and northern Queensland.

The bat fauna of our West Indies is especially interesting in comparison with that of the neighboring mainland. There is some evidence that the larger islands, Cuba, Puerto Rico, Hispaniola, and Jamaica, were at one time united to form a single land mass, "Antillea," while other islands of the group, particularly the Lesser Antilles, may be of separate volcanic origin. Whether this ancient Antillea was formerly united with the American mainland or not, it is true that a surprising number of its bats do not now occur on the near-by continents. Such are the long-tongued bats of the genera Erophylla, Phyllonycteris, and Monophyllus (of the Phyllostomidae); the dainty little Nyctiellus (known from Cuba and the Bahamas); and the allied genera of long-legged bats, Chilonatalus and Phodotes (both of the family Natalidae), as well as certain genera of fruit-eating Phyllostomidae, such as Phyllops, Ariteus, Ardops, Brachyphylla, and probably Stenoderma. That all these genera are now quite unknown from the neighboring continents is proof enough of the effectiveness of their isolation as safeguarding them from invasion and crowding out by competition with other more successful types. Nevertheless, there are in these same islands various other genera which are represented by nearly identical forms on the adjacent mainland. Of such are the big-eared Otopterus, the fruit-eating Sturnira and Artibeus, all members of the Phyllostomidae, while three species of leaf-lipped bats, Chilonycteris, of the same family, occur in Cuba and two others on the mainland of Central America. Whether these now isolated genera and species reached the West Indies by following along former land connections from Central or South America, or whether they came first as wind-blown waifs or otherwise, is still a matter of controversy; but one finds it hard to believe that so many could have crossed wide stretches of sea to have effected colonization. The prevailing trade winds set toward the mainland, so that their presence in Florida or Central America would seem much more likely. Indeed, there is a single instance of both Artibeus and Eumops for Florida, waifs, probably, from Cuba; yet these strong-flying species have no permanent foothold on the peninsula.

The vespertilionid bats of the West Indies offer other interesting points. Thus, except for *Myotis nigricans*, the blackish bat, in the southern Lesser Antilles (Dominica and Grenada), no member of this nearly cosmopolitan genus is known from the islands. The brown bat, Eptesicus, occurs, however, with several local island races in the Greater Antilles, as well as a red bat, Lasiurus, allied to the seminole bat of Florida, while the presence of the twilight bat (Nycticeius) in Cuba and in southeastern

United States points to a limited community of species at some remote time. These three genera may be relatively later arrivals than the leaf-nosed bats mentioned, but how they first colonized these islands is still a puzzle. The red bat is a swift and strong flier and may have come across open sea, for we find related species both in the Hawaiian Islands and in the Galapagos group in the Pacific Ocean. Moreover, in the former group, a second species, closely related to the hoary bat of North America, is also present. Both these types are strong-flying species, with resident races in the American tropics, though in most of North America both red and hoary bats are migratory, often crossing wide stretches of sea and appearing at such an isolated spot as the Bermuda Islands while on passage. Yet that they have succeeded in becoming established in the Hawaiian Islands, over twenty-five hundred miles from the nearest mainland, is indeed an astonishing fact. No other bats are known from these islands, although a parallel is seen in the Western golden plover which winters there, coming from northwestern North America. The nearest approach from the Old World side is made by the sheath-tailed bat, *Emballonura semicaudata*, which reaches the Fiji and Samoan Islands. New Zealand offers another extreme case of isolation, for two species of bats occur here, one, the short-tailed bat, Mystacops, which constitutes a special family, and the other, a member of the genus Chalinolobus, known elsewhere only from Australia. The fact that the former is found nowhere else in the world today indicates that it must have reached these islands long ago, perhaps, like the Chalinolobus from Australia, over twelve hundred miles distant.

From this discussion it is clear that most bats are essentially warm-country mammals whose home at the present era is mainly the tropics and probably has always been so. The eastern continents, forming the main land areas, have doubtless been their chief center of evolution, for we find even at the present day more diverse types, whether as dominant or as dying-out families, in the Old World than in the New. The fact that members of both the sheath-tailed family, Emballonu-

ridae, and the free-tailed family, Molossidae, are found isolated from each other as distinct genera in the tropics of
opposite sides of the globe must mean that these and probably
other ancient groups invaded the New World from the Old
at an early time, when warmer climates and appropriate land
connections farther northward made this possible, with rare
instances perhaps of population by wind-blown waifs. Many
species, particularly of the "simple-nosed" family, Vespertili-

Fig. 40—The short-tailed bat (*Mystacops tuberculatus*) of New Zealand, from the Tararna
Range. From a dead specimen. This bat, confined to New Zealand, is a relic of some
once more widely distributed group. It forms a family, Mystacopidae, by itself. Two-thirds
natural size. E. Bruce Levy, phot.

onidae, have become adapted to temperate climates, so that
they have been enabled to take advantage of such a land connection as must again have existed in the north at the close
of the Tertiary, permitting an exchange of faunas between
western North America and northeastern Asia. The result is
that at the present time the northern parts of these two continents have a number of species with close allies on opposite
sides of the Pacific. The American leaf-nosed bats (Phyllostomidae) show an especially surprising variety of genera, with
all degrees in change of structure between insect-eating and
frugivorous types, from the latter of which may have developed
the blood-feeding vampires. The ancestors of these bats must

have reached America so long ago that the original stock has died out elsewhere, though in the western tropics it flourished.

This implies opportunity to develop unhindered, an opportunity which may have been provided by the cutting off of South America in early Tertiary times, so that for many millions of years it remained isolated. Here developed many peculiar groups of mammals whose ancestors had reached this area and were similarly cut off. Many of them evolved at length gigantic forms such as the huge ground sloths and toxodonts, the remains of which are found in the later formations of the Argentine pampas. There were no true Carnivora, no Insectivora, while the hoofed mammals were represented by a few peculiar types likewise evolved from earlier ancestors. This continued until near the end of Tertiary time, when the present Isthmus of Panama arose, once more connecting the two continents and allowing an interchange of faunas by way of the bridge so formed. In this way the great ground sloths, the tanklike glyptodonts, and armadillos, as well as leaf-nosed bats, invaded Central America as far as the southern United States, while at the same time modernized carnivores, ungulates, and even elephants entered South America from the north. An array of other creatures also crossed the isthmus from both sides, some of them later dying out, while others survived. At the present time, of some forty-five continental genera of leaf-nosed and vampire bats, at least twenty-seven are known from Central America as well as from South America, their probable source. The delicately formed long-legged bats (Natalidae) and their distant relatives now constituting the families Furipteridae (smoky bats) and Thyropteridae (disk-winged bats) were probably also isolated in South America during Tertiary time, but they seem to have been less successful and are now but a remnant. All these little bats retain the primitive number of thirty-eight teeth except the smoky bats, in which one of the three upper premolars has been eliminated. No less than three of the four genera of long-legged bats are West Indian and are no longer found on the mainland, while the two genera of smoky bats are rare and people opposite parts of the continent

— Furipterus in Brazil, Amorphochilus in Peru, with but a single species each. The disk-winged bats seem to have fared better, for two or three species are found from Ecuador to Brazil, extending into Central America, while their apparent relationship to the sucker-footed bat (Myzopoda) of Madagascar is probably further evidence of a common ancestry at a very ancient period.

As to the now cosmopolitan family of simple-nosed bats, Vespertilionidae, it seems likely that few if any of them reached South America until the more recent land connection of late Tertiary times, perhaps in the Pliocene, made such an invasion possible. Most of the South American species of this family belong to genera that are common also to North America, such as Myotis, Eptesicus, Pipistrellus, Lasiurus, and Dasypterus. Two other allied genera, Rhogeëssa and Baeodon, are very small brownish bats of which the former is known from Mexico to northern South America and the latter from Mexico only. Two genera, Histiotus and Tomopeas, are the only ones of the family peculiar to the South American continent. The former includes a few species much resembling the cosmopolitan Eptesicus, or brown bats, but has very long delicate ears. Whether it, too, may be regarded as a recent invader with other Vespertilionidae is uncertain; Miller (1907) points out its close resemblance to an East African genus, Laephotis, of which but a single species is known. But whether this likeness means close relationship or parallel development cannot be said with certainty. The genus Tomopeas, on the other hand, is perhaps in a different case. It is known from a single small species discovered in Peru and is placed by Miller in a special subfamily, since it combines "in a very remarkable manner the characters of the Vespertilionidae and Molossidae" (the free-tailed bats). It has the delicate form and the long tail wholly included in the membrane as in the former, and the peculiar ear structure and the fusion of the last cervical with the first thoracic vertebra rather characteristic of the latter. It may thus be thought of as a very ancient and ancestral type, partly bridging the gap between the two families. Its rarity and restricted

FIG. 41—The Bahama long-legged bat (*Chilonatalus tumidifrons*), a member of the family Natalidae. Distinctive of this family are the ample wings, long, slender legs, short thumbs, and long tail extending to the edge of the membrane. From a specimen in the Museum of Comparative Zoölogy, enlarged one quarter.

distribution suggest that it is now dying out, a last remnant of an early invasion, perhaps the same one that brought the ancestral leaf-nosed and long-legged bats.

All these are interesting speculations, advanced only as guesses in an attempt to explain the distribution of bats as we find them at the present time, after many millions of years of dispersal and evolution of which we are almost wholly ignorant.

# CHAPTER XIV

# SOCIAL HABITS OF BATS

THE social habits of bats differ widely even among closely related species within a single genus. Some are highly colonial, living throughout the year (particularly in the warmer countries) in great companies, and this habit may obtain, as in the flying foxes (Pteropus), among practically all the species of the genus. Others again are solitary, and this is especially true of some tree- or forest-living bats. The colonial habits of some of the large flying foxes have long been known and have been briefly described by several authors. Tickell (1842), Tennent (1863), and McCann (1934) have written of the Indian species, *Pteropus giganteus*, giving an interesting picture of the colony by day. The bats frequently select for a permanent roost some large tree quite in the center of a native village or at no great distance from its outskirts, gathering regularly in its top for their daytime sleep. Such trees may be in constant use for generations, but why the bats so often prefer the neighborhood of human activity is not clear. Possibly there is greater security than in more remote places, or it may even be, as I imagine is the case with great colonies of certain weaver-finches, that their social instincts find a certain satisfaction in the mere proximity of other communities where there is a constant stir of something going on.

The sociability of these, and some other bats as well, finds expression in a peculiar way, for although they seem desirous of companionship, hanging often in great multitudes in the selected treetops, there is also a negative factor which leads each member of the group to keep his fellows at arm's length, a sort of isolation in the crowd. The return of the bats to their roost in the early morning after an all-night foray is a lively scene. The first arrivals, after circling the roosting tree a few times, alight among the top branches and suspend themselves by the hind feet. Each newcomer does the same, endeavoring to alight on a suitable twig, possibly a favored one — and is met by threatening attitudes and screeches as he attempts to settle. With the arrival of more and more members of the colony, the din and confusion become astonishing as the bickering and contention for place go on. No doubt the end result is a certain

FIG. 42—Australian flying foxes (*Pteropus poliocephalus*); part of a large "camp" at roost near Belltrees, New South Wales. Courtesy of F. Ramsay, phot.

spacing of the roosting bats, so that they shall not be too close together. This allows each individual to rest undisturbed by the movements of its neighbor and obviates any quarreling over the food they may bring in with them. It also ensures each sufficient space to "take off" when leaving the roost in the evening. The late comers have to face the entire multitude that has already come in, and it is usually well on to mid-forenoon before all have quieted down and, with heads shielded by the wings folded over the chest, have settled for the daytime doze.

The waking-up process is usually less disorderly. As the short twilight of the tropics gathers, the colony begins to stir: the bats awaken, go through more or less cleaning of their

fur and membranes, accompanied by a certain amount of un-
mannerly screeching and threatening at their neighbors, then,
as darkness falls, they move silently off by ones, twos, or small
parties to their feeding grounds. There is thus much independ-
ence of the individual with at the same time a general companionship during resting hours. Yet, as McCann writes, even
in the hottest part of the day there is more or less movement
and readjustment of position; sometimes many, if not the
whole colony, "will be found fanning themselves with one
wing or the other. Much time is also spent in scratching [preen-
ing] until one really wonders how much rest these animals
really get." From much observation this author concludes that
"certain parties meet and have particular beats when feeding,"
implying a certain cohesion of smaller groups within the colony.
This, however, would be a difficult matter to substantiate.

Instances are recorded where flying foxes that roost regularly
in companies on offshore islands pass over to the neighboring
mainland in more or less of a body before scattering to feed,
so that there is a slight extension of their community life beyond the sleeping period. Thus Ferrar (1934) tells of a large
colony of Pteropus that regularly spent the daytime hours in
a roost on the uninhabited South Sentinel Island, seventeen
miles northwest of Little Andaman Island, in the eastern Indian Ocean. Daily, as soon as the sun sets, "out come the great
bats and disappear over the anchorage in a long-drawn-out
procession into the darkening east," headed for their feeding
grounds on the larger land mass, while at nearly the same time
a similar flight of pied imperial pigeons, going in the opposite
direction, streams to the same little isle for the night's roost.
Both must have "a good sense of direction, for South Sentinel
is a poor land mark even by day." A similar Box and Cox
relation is recorded by Willey (1904) of the large *Pteropus
giganteus* of Ceylon and the gray crows, both of which resort
to a small island, Barberyn Island, to roost. At evening the
crows are seen flying in immense numbers to rest in the trees
of the island while a procession of these large bats passes in
the opposite direction for a night's foray on the Ceylon main-

land. The islet is almost uninhabited and is covered by a plantation of coconut trees from the midribs of whose fronds the bats hang during the day, appearing shortly before sunrise, singly at first, then in companies of twenty-five or more, until a continuous stream is formed. They fly on an average somewhat higher than the crows, coming in the opposite direction, morning and evening.

In British North Borneo there are large caves in which nest thousands of the small swifts (Collocalia) that make the so-called "edible birds' nests." During the daylight hours these caves are the roosting place of multitudes of bats, chiefly one of the free-tailed species (*Chaerephon plicatus*) which emerge in clouds toward sunset, just as the swifts are gathering in the same caverns for the night. Since the birds' nests are of commercial importance, these reciprocal relations have attracted the attention of local observers, who believe that the bats, clustering on the walls of the caves, occupy a certain amount of space that the swifts might utilize for their nests, if they were in undisputed possession. Doubtless, however, the competition in all these cases is not severe, but must be materially lessened by the reciprocal habits of the bats and the birds.

Many instances could be given of bats that show great differences in the colonial habit, even among related species, and this is true for most of the several families. Thus, among the Megachiroptera the great part of the genera and species are colonial, some, like the flying foxes, conspicuously so. A few, however, live chiefly a solitary existence. Thus, the fruit-bat genus, Nyctimene, with its peculiarly mottled coloration and speckled wings, appears to be solitary, the few known specimens, as far as the record shows, having been taken hanging alone on tree trunks or from branches, a habit for which their broken coloration is particularly suitable. The smaller flower-feeding species, such as Syconycteris, appear to have similar habits. When we turn to the Microchiroptera, we find among the horseshoe bats wide variation in the gregarious trait. Some are habitually solitary in disposition, such as the large Chinese *Rhinolophus lanosus*, a dark, woolly-haired bat of which single individuals or at most a pair only have been found inhabiting a cavern. In Ceylon, W. W. A. Phillips (1924) found *Rhinolophus beddomei sobrinus* living solitary or in pairs in heavy jungle, while *Rhinolophus rouxi* is a cave dweller, consorting in large colonies. Similarly, in the related family Hipposideridae he found *Hipposideros speoris* highly colonial, gathering in caves or disused buildings in great clusters, often of several hundreds of individuals, while *H. brachyotus* occurs usually in small family parties of an adult male and female and a single young, or the old male may be by himself.

Among the hollow-faced bats (family Nycteridae) such a contrast is found in the African species, for while most of them, like *Nycteris revoili, N. hispida, N. damarensis*, are usually found in colonies inhabiting hollow trees, the large *Nycteris grandis*, as I met with it in the forests of Liberia, seems to be usually solitary, a single one being the only tenant of some huge hollow log, fallen tree, or shallow cavern. Of the New World Noctilionidae, the few known species are colonial, living in rock fissures or hollow trees. In the related family Emballonuridae or sheath-tailed bats, though some — like the Emballonura of the East Indies — occur in considerable colonies, others, like the sac-winged bats (Saccopteryx) or the snub-nosed bats (Rhynchiscus), are usually in smaller groups, three or four to a dozen; and a few, like the white bat (Diclidurus), although cave-dwelling, are, so far as is known, solitary. Instances of a like sort could be multiplied among the leaf-nosed bats of tropical America (family Phyllostomidae), many of which are gregarious, even the common Artibeus, which is in part a tree dweller, as well as the long-tongued Glossophaga, and Carollia, one of the commonest of the group; while others again are seldom found more than one or two at a time, such as the tree-living genus Ardops, confined to the West Indies. The Vespertilionidae include such colonial species as the little brown bat, *Myotis lucifugus*, so common over temperate North America, as well as others of the same genus (*M. yumanensis, M. velifer, M. grisescens, M. thysanodes*); some, however, are by contrast seldom found in more than small companies or singly, such as *M. keenii* and the long-legged bat, *M. volans*, of the West. A few, notably Leib's bat (*M. subulatus leibi*), are so unsocial that even in hibernation the individuals are found tucked away, each by itself in a cranny of a cave.

The tree-living red bat (*Lasiurus borealis*) and hoary bat (*L. cinereus*), wide-ranging in the Americas, hang up singly among the foliage of trees, rarely more than one at a time being found. The funnel-eared bats (subfamily Kerivoulinae of the Old World tropics) again show diversity of habits among members of the same genus; for the beautiful little orange-and-black *Kerivoula picta* is solitary, resting by day in a cluster of leaves or even in an open flower, while others of the genus — such as *K. hardwickei* of Asia — are usually found in small groups of less than half a dozen. The gregarious habit is highly developed in the free-tailed bats, Molossidae, most of which live in colonies, taking up their residence in caves and hollow trees or often in buildings. Colonies numbering thousands or even millions of individuals of the "guano bat" (*Tadarida mexicana*) have been reported from southwestern United States and Mexico (see V. Bailey, 1928), while various other genera such as Molossus and Eumops in the New World and Chaerephon in the Old World are equally gregarious — indeed, it seems that few of this family are solitary in habits, though perhaps this is true of *Nyctinomus taeniotis*, a large species of southern Europe, and *Tadarida femorosacca*, which is known from a few single specimens from localities in the southwestern United States.

Of the evening outpouring of the guano bats from the Carlsbad Caverns in New Mexico, both Bailey (1928) and Allison (1937) have given vivid accounts. The latter writes that in late summer and early fall they emerge in such numbers from the cave opening that they form a dense black stream visible two miles away. The column of bats was approximately cylindrical and about twenty feet in diameter. The exit occupied less than twenty minutes, so that by rough methods of calculation it was estimated that slightly under nine millions of bats had passed!

While species of the same family or even of the same genus thus show great extremes in their degree of sociability, it is frequently true that, of the Microchiroptera that hang by day among foliage, most are solitary or nearly so, and this habit is to some extent associated with contrasting pattern of color. Those that prefer caverns or hollow trees are to a greater extent social. Of course in all these matters there are exceptions. Probably the former type of life is the more primitive and among the Megachiroptera or fruit bats is general, while the latter is the more advanced. This is brought about in part by the common need for shelter, since suitable caves or hollows are relatively few, as well perhaps as by a progressive tolerance and mutual desire for company.

*Group associations* of bats are not easily studied, for a method of marking individuals must be devised in order to follow their behavior. Already, however, some investigation has been made that indicates a certain cohesion among the individuals of a given group. No doubt the best method of marking is by means of the small aluminum bands, each with a number and address, such as are now widely used in the study of bird movements. Apparently the first to make observations by this means was Dr. Arthur A. Allen of Cornell University, Ithaca, New York. In June of 1916 he was called to see a group of small pipistrelles (*Pipistrellus subflavus*) hanging in a tight cluster from the ceiling of a shaded porch at Fall Creek Gorge, New York. He was informed that the previous year the bats had been in the same spot, whence efforts to drive them away with hose and broom had been only temporarily successful. The entire cluster was captured in a net and proved to consist of four adult females, each with large embryos. After a small numbered band had been pinched on the tibia of each bat, they were carried a short distance and subsequently released and forgotten, for the house was not occupied during the two succeeding summers. Three years later, in June 1919, word was received that the bats were again in their accustomed place. A small boy had unfortunately shot them all down, and they proved to be again four females, three with the same numbered bands placed on them in

1916, while the fourth, though unbanded, was surmised by Dr. Allen to have been perhaps the fourth of the original quartet, which had, however, succeeded in removing the band. Here then was a group of three if not four females that for at least four seasons had maintained close companionship during the breeding time. A later year the same naturalist banded a group of sixteen females from a similar cluster and found that, with their young born in early July, they regularly roosted by day in the same spot till about the end of August, although the number of the young (which were not banded) seemed to have then greatly decreased. It is to be hoped that further notes on this group will be published.

Later, A. Brazier Howell and Luther Little (1924) banded three large brown bats (Eptesicus) at Covina, California, on July 20, 1921, releasing them at Pasadena, twenty miles distant. In June 1923 two of the trio were recaptured at the same roost, again indicating a certain cohesion or at least an attachment for a given locality. E. L. Poole (1932) and Donald Griffin (1934) have made similar experiments with the little brown bat (*Myotis lucifugus*) in Pennsylvania and Massachusetts, respectively, and report the return of some of their marked individuals which had been released at distances from the colony varying up to twenty-seven miles. Poole also obtained similar results with two other species, *Myotis keenii septentrionalis*, and the eastern pipistrelle (*Pipistrellus subflavus*), which were recaptured at their home caves after having been released eighteen miles distant. Campbell has recounted his experiment on this homing ability in the Mexican free-tailed bat (*Tadarida mexicana*), multitudes of which inhabited a large cave near San Antonio, Texas. A number of individuals marked with white paint were carried thirty miles away and then released. They returned to their cave at once by an almost direct line.

Such observations definitely prove that these colonial species have a strong disposition to return to favored haunts and can return from a considerable distance just as birds are known to do, a faculty which Watson has called "distant orientation";

furthermore, they tend to continue associations with others of their kind, even to the extent that small groups may keep together for a longer or shorter time. A similar habit is no doubt true of many if not most colonial species, but this lacks as yet such definite proof. Thus, Miss Guthrie (1933) adduces evidence to show that there are definite group movements among some of the bats hibernating in Missouri caves, although the extent of these fluctuations in numbers is not easy to determine. Again, Dr. Walter Granger tells me that while stationed for the winter near Wanhsien in eastern Szechwan, China, he frequently visited a cave in which a number of bats were in hibernation. In successive visits he entirely eliminated the colony of large horseshoe bats (*Hipposideros armiger*) gathered there. On again visiting the place two years later, he found no others, a fact which implied that this colony had regularly used the cave to the exclusion of others of the species.

Probably similar groups of associates occur in a little sheath-tailed bat of tropical America, *Rhynchiscus naso*. This is a delicately formed species with mixed gray and brown fur which on the forearms forms little tufts in characteristic fashion. Its distinctive habit is to roost by day in small companies, one bat clinging just above another by all four feet along the under side of a small dead tree overhanging water. Here they so much resemble the bark in tint that they would readily be overlooked, while in addition the slanting tree trunk affords protection from above and from the landward side. My friend Dr. James B. Rorer sends me the photograph here reproduced of a string of these little bats thus ensconced, taken from a canoe on the Caroni River, Trinidad. If closely approached, the whole company takes wing together and flies to some other similar retreat farther on. Observations of a like nature have been reported by M. A. Carriker and by Leo Miller (J. A. Allen, 1911, 1916d). Carriker writes that on the Rio Yuruan in Venezuela he has found them clinging flat to old stubs and limbs rising out of the water at an oblique angle; sometimes a half dozen or so would be flushed from one stub. In the course of his journey in Brazil with the late Colonel Roosevelt, Miller

Fig. 43—A company of small proboscis bats (*Rhynchiscus naso*) clinging along the under side of a stem of the Bactris Palm, overhanging water. Caroni River, Trinidad. James Birch Rorer, phot.

found them in considerable numbers along rivers or in swamps in the same kind of situation. He writes: "There may be from two to fifteen or more in a colony of both sexes. One may approach quietly in a canoe to within a few yards when they will suddenly take wing and dart swiftly away among the dense vegetation. Usually they do not fly far and often come back to the same tree they left, but they invariably light on the far side and remain concealed." The same thing was noticed in Guatemala by Murie (1935), where along the upper Belize River he found a number of such groups, ranging in number from six to thirty individuals, clinging on the under side of the sloping trunks and root buttresses of large trees growing at the water's edge. In the course of thirty miles no less than twenty of these little parties were seen, and doubtless many others escaped observation. When frightened, the entire group would fly off together, alighting on some near-by tree in a similar position. Both sexes were found in the same group, and at the time when the observations were made (March 10–20) a large proportion of the females carried embryos. It would be interesting to know more of the constitution and habits of such separate companies. The interesting points are that the group acts more or less as a unit, and that, as if by common agreement, the individuals move on to some other spot, perhaps well known to all of them.

### INTERSPECIFIC RELATIONS

Even bats that live in groups together differ greatly according to species in their proximity relations with others of their kind or of other species. With some it is usual to associate closely together while at rest during the day. Thus, the common pipistrelle (*Pipistrellus subflavus*) of the eastern United States, which often frequents buildings during the summer season, usually associates in clusters so dense that the members of the group are in intimate contact with one another. A photograph of such a group gathered in the peak of a roof is shown in Dr. Arthur A. Allen's paper (1922). The whitish-haired species (*P. hesperus*) of the southwestern United States, however, seems to be much less social and rests by day in narrow crevices of cliffs or among rocks. Many tree-living species of Microchiroptera are solitary or live in pairs such as the American red bat and hoary bat, which are nearly always found alone. Swinhoe (1870a), however, once made an interesting observation in the island of Formosa on the beautiful rufous-and-white-marked *Scotomanes rufoniger*, a tree-living species. In early July 1865, while walking through a grove of trees, he noticed close to a bunch of flowers among some big leaves a cluster which he at first took to be fruit or gall nuts, but on closer examination he discovered that the supposed galls were really the heads of bats, of which there proved to be about ten of both sexes, including a female with a young one at her breast, all hanging from the stem of a leaf in a compact cluster, partly concealed by the foliage. Some species of cave-dwelling bats will hang in close masses from the vault of their retreat, such as some members of the genus Tadarida, or they may be found packed away in crevices under hollow roofs so tightly that they lie more or less on or over one another and seem even to enjoy this close contact. I once had a number of the small Haitian Molossus, a related genus, brought to me alive from a large colony. When placed in a bag of netting, they all gradually worked their way upward to the top of the bag as it hung and finally quieted down in a close-packed mass, a position which seemed satisfactory to them notwithstanding the tropical heat.

With other bats there is often a more definite spacing, each bat hanging slightly apart from its neighbors. This was the case with a large colony of "pig-nosed bats" (*Erophylla planifrons*) I once observed in the Bahama Islands. On nearing the large dome-shaped cavern in which they lived and to which they gained access through a circular opening about a yard high, I could hear a continual squeaking and commotion going on even though it was mid-forenoon, when they should have quieted for the day. A flashlight directed through the opening of their cave disclosed a large colony of several hundred individuals covering the limestone walls, but all separated from one another by a greater or less distance, so that none of them were in contact. Perhaps their bickering cries were incident to the adjustment and proper spacing of the individuals as each fought off its neighbors to a respectful distance. Many hung by both hind feet, while others, as if more settled to rest, depended by a single leg. A flashlight photograph showing a number of what were doubtless the same species was published some years ago by the late William Lyman Underwood and shows these positions excellently. Many such contrasts of habit could be adduced, but as a final instance may be mentioned the quarreling and sparring for space and position previously described in the case of the Indian flying fox, while in a related genus (Rousettus) of smaller fruit bats the habit of the species as noticed in Arabia by Yerbury is to hang in a dense cluster. Sometimes the nature of the shelter selected for the daytime rest may determine the spacing, as in the case of a group of epaulet bats (Epomophorus) I once saw in Kenya Colony, East Africa, that were hanging, young and old, along the midrib of a shaded frond of the sago palm, separated by the distance apart of the pinnules.

It is not uncommon for several species of bats to live in the same cave or hollow tree, but in these cases it is usual to find each kind in a separate part of the cave by itself, so that all seem to get on happily together without interference. In southern Europe a common association is that of the small *Myotis capaccinii* in the same caves with the long-fingered bat, *Miniopterus schreibersii*, and a similar association was reported in a cave near Peiping, North China, in which a collector secured specimens of a larger Myotis (*M. pequinius*) and the eastern representative of the Miniopterus. These relations seem to bespeak a more or less amicable relationship among the associated forms, or at least a tolerance between species of about the same size and strength. With some of the larger species, however, their caves seem to be seldom shared by smaller and weaker kinds. This was noticed as long ago as 1817 by the German naturalist Kuhl, who wrote of the large *Myotis myotis* of Europe that when disturbed it will bite ferociously, and in captivity (under unnatural conditions, to be sure) will, if aroused, bite its neighbors and young indiscriminately. Indeed, he writes, one never finds this species associated with any other, apparently because the smaller kinds fear its vicious jaws. For similar reasons, no doubt, the eastern vampire, Mega-derma, is usually found to be the sole occupant of the caves or other retreats in which it spends the day. Thus, Wroughton (1915b) quotes the observations of C. A. Crump, a collector of much experience in India, who had "never found any other species associating with it." As elsewhere mentioned, this bat will catch and devour other smaller bats. Exceptionally, how-ever, Prater (1914) found a colony in India, inhabiting the darkest and innermost part of a cave, near the entrance of which lived a colony of Otomops, a bat large enough probably to be safe from attack by the voracious vampires.

An English naturalist, Hutton (1872), who made many in-teresting observations on bats in India, tried the experiment of confining some of these larger and more powerful species with smaller kinds of bats and found a similar state of affairs. For when the large horseshoe bats, *Rhinolophus luctus* and *Hippo-sideros armiger*, the Indian house bat (*Scotophilus temminckii*), or the large Indian Myotis (*M. blythi*) were kept in cages with small species, the larger animals would prey upon their weaker brethren. Hence it is, he concludes, that in small caves only one of these species is found occupying it; while in large and extensive caverns, several species may be present, but each in a different part by itself. Of course, in free life there is probably relatively little interference with the smaller by the larger spe-cies, for the unnaturally close confinement in a cage not only calls forth the aggressive nature of the large bats, but also makes it impossible for the small ones to escape. Even though the species living in a single cave are mutually tolerant, it is usual to find each in a group by itself, except during hiberna-tion, when sometimes several species may be found closely asso-ciated. This is often, however, merely the result of situation preference, as where in the dungeon of old Fort Charlotte, in the Bahama Islands, we once found a small colony of brown bats (Eptesicus) clustered at the top of a cone-shaped cavity in the ceiling, while a group of big-eared bats (Otopterus), consisting of adult females and their nearly full-grown young, hung from the open dome of a separate chamber and when disturbed took refuge down a well, a favorite resort. It is clear from these few instances that bats of different species differ greatly, not only in their temperaments and in their bearing toward others of their kind, but also in their tolerance of association with others of the same or more powerful species.

A curious incident I once noticed in the Bahamas was perhaps a case of intolerance between species of differing temperaments. On investigating a small cavern the entrance of which was a well-like opening in limestone rock, I found its sole occupants to be a colony of Chilonatalus, a delicate and beautiful little bat, with long slender legs and fur of a yellowish hue. On visiting the same cave a fortnight later, I was surprised to find that the long-legged bats had wholly deserted it, and instead it was now tenanted by a number of the same Erophylla, whose quarrelsome behavior has just been mentioned, and which possibly had made their presence too much for the smaller species.

*Hibernation* in bats is generally more or less of a social relation, often bringing together for their winter sleep hundreds of individuals which in summer may be scattered over a wide territory or live in smaller groups here and there outside the caves where they pass the winter. In company with friends I once visited a cave in Brandon, Vermont, in late January, when the winter snow lay deep on the ground outside. Here we examined a hibernating mass of small bats which must have numbered several hundred individuals. The greater part were a small brownish species, *Myotis sodalis*, but with them were many *M. lucifugus*, and a few *M. subulatus leibii*, *M. keenii septentrionalis*, *Pipistrellus subflavus*, and *Eptesicus fuscus*. These differed somewhat in their associational habit, the first-named hanging in a dense mass covering part of the cavern roof from which they all hung. One could thrust the fingers of the hand gently into this mass and feel the warmth of their bodies within it, while exteriorly their projecting heads and shoulders were chilly and moisture-bedewed, for the air inside was very damp. The *Myotis lucifugus* were apparently mixed in with these; at least they were not distinguished until the catch was more carefully examined by light of day. The few specimens of *M. s. leibii* were again in a characteristic situation, for instead of hanging by the hind feet, they were tucked away singly or rarely two together, in small depressions or crannies of the rock, lying down flat on their stomachs as if the very small and weak feet were insufficient to sustain them during hibernation. The temperature of the cave was that of the normal "ground temperature" at this latitude, about 44° to 46° F., although outside the thermometer stood well below zero.

Guthrie (1934) has reported that in the caves in Missouri where numbers of these Myotis winter, *M. sodalis* showed a distinct tendency to gather in dense masses, while *M. lucifugus* seemed to hang in a more scattered fashion. The advantage of the close order would seem to be that torpor would be less deep, since the greater warmth generated by the multitude of little bodies is shared by them, whereas if they hang up in more scattered fashion the mutual warmth is less available. Perhaps this may partly account for the fact observed by Guthrie, that *M. sodalis* is given to considerably more moving about than is *M. lucifugus*, for in late winter during frequent examination of the caves she found that the former species varied considerably in the numbers present on successive visits, evidently awaking and perhaps changing station or even migrating in entire groups, while the latter stayed in the caves till April with little or no evidence that they were on the move.

### SEGREGATION OF THE SEXES

With some mammals, when the female is about to give birth to her young she no longer tolerates the presence of the male but drives him from the nest, or, in case of herd animals, the females go off by themselves to have their young and afterward return to the herd. A very interesting modification of this habit among many species of colonial bats is the segregation of the sexes at the season when the young are due. At this time the female bats in some species gather together in companies by themselves to bring forth their young undisturbed, while the males either congregate in separate groups elsewhere or scatter more widely during the summer season. This habit seems first to have been recorded by the German naturalist Kuhl, in 1817, in a rare publication on the bats of his native country. In his general account he mentions the belief then prevalent among naturalists that bats live in mated pairs together, but he denies the truth of this supposition, pointing out that in a large colony the numbers of each sex are not equal. He further remarks that when the females become heavy with young they desert the males and seek some common shelter for bringing forth. He presumes that this habit is true of all bats, although specifically mentioning it in but one, Bechstein's bat (*Myotis bechsteini*), of which the largest colony he ever found consisted of thirteen females.

A decade later, Kuhl's fellow countryman C. L. Brehm (1827) independently made similar observations, of which he gives more particular details. He found that the common long-eared bats (*Plecotus auritus*) segregate by sexes to a certain extent at breeding time, but that in Bechstein's bat and the noctule bat (*Nyctalus noctula*) this behavior is very striking. He writes that the breeding season of these two is in early May, when the males can be seen actively in pursuit of the females, but that when the latter have become pregnant they live apart from the males. He tells of examining a large spruce tree that had been felled on June 9, which was found to have three cavities, two occupied by Bechstein's bat and the other by a group of noctules. One of the groups of the former consisted of twenty-two females, seventeen with large embryos, the other five with very small ones. Of recent years these observations have been much extended, and a similar segregation has been found to take place in many social species of different families of bats. Thus, in notes given me on the species *Scotophilus castaneus consobrinus*, of the island of Hainan, China, Mr. Clifford Pope found that eighteen specimens taken in April from a colony in a palm tree were all females. The group contained about a hundred others, which probably were of the same sex, though none was examined. Six weeks later, in early June, the same palm tree held a colony of several hundred, which sought shelter among the dead hanging leaves. A large number of these bats were killed, mostly adult females with suckling young, indicating that this was a maternal society. Evidence that segregation of the sexes takes place in *Pipistrellus subflavus* and *Myotis lucifugus* of the eastern United States has been adduced by Dr. Arthur A. Allen and confirmed by other observers, while W. W. A. Phillips asserts that in Ceylon the little *Pipistrellus mimus* does the same, the females with their young at certain seasons living by themselves in a group, while at other times the males are found with the colony. Other species of the genus give evidence of the same habit, but on the other hand *P. ceylonicus* is said to be found in small colonies of four or five to a dozen the year round, usually of both sexes, while the breeding season is apparently not a very well-defined one. Instances of the habit could be greatly multiplied. Thus, in the mouse-tailed bats, family Rhinopomidae, Lindsay records that of fifty taken in the Punjab, India, forty-two were females, while the sex of the others was unrecorded, but evidently the group represented (in June) a large female colony. In the family Megadermidae the false vampire (*Megaderma spasma*) of India is colonial, and W. W. A. Phillips, writing of the Ceylon race, says that these colonies live together the year round with the young which are born in May. Males seem always more numerous than the females. On the other hand, the related genus Lyroderma seems to show just the opposite tendency, for Wroughton (1914, 1915b), after much experience of collecting in India, found them invariably congregating in large numbers in caves, hollow trees, and disused wells, but the sexes usually kept apart. Of one large colony living in the roof of a dak bungalow, he collected forty-two specimens, all of which were females except seven immature males, probably the offspring of some of them. Phillips (1922) mentions a colony in Ceylon which seemed to be "mostly males." The horseshoe bats, family Rhinolophidae, of the warmer parts of the Old World, have already been mentioned as illustrating within a single genus varying degrees of sociability. Phillips (1923), writing of *R. rouxi* in Ceylon, says it is one of the most common of the cave-haunting species of that island and that both sexes apparently live together in the caves the year round, the females bearing their young in April and May. On the other hand, the Australian species, *R. megaphyllus*, appears to have the segregating habit well developed. At all events, I visited a large cavern at Kempsey, in northern New South Wales, in late December (there corresponding to our July), and in company with a friend found it inhabited by a large colony of this species. We collected a good series and examined many others, finding that all the adults we took were females, while the greater number were immatures of both sexes, their offspring already well able to fly.

During the summer while the females of some colonial species are thus dwelling apart, to bring forth and nurture their young, the males, if not keeping to separate roosts by themselves, may perhaps scatter out over a wider extent of country than the females and maintain a more or less solitary existence. Definite evidence of this is naturally difficult to obtain but is perhaps indicated by the fact that of the four species of bats that I shot, in July 1915, while encamped at timber line (about 11,000 feet altitude) on Mt. Whitney, California, all the individuals were males. These included three species of Myotis (*M. yumanensis sociabilis, M. lucifugus carissima, M. volans interior*) and an Eptesicus. Of the last, females were taken at the base of the mountain. It seems probable that these males were invaders from lower levels during the summer, seeking the abundant insect life then present, while the females were at this season engaged in the care of their young at the lower levels. A similar observation was made by Mrs. H. W. Grinnell (1918), who believes that the males of the species first named "forage singly at higher levels" in summer, for they cannot winter at these altitudes. The same author writes of the western red bat (*Lasiurus borealis teleotis*) in California that a study of the dates of capture leads to the inference "that the sexes separate during the summer months, the females remaining in the Lower Sonoran zone, while the males migrate into the Upper Sonoran and Transition zones." In this area, where the effects of altitudinal differences are rather sharply marked, such a habit is more readily observable than in areas of less contrast.

In other species the segregation of the sexes is incomplete or less marked. Thus, as I have elsewhere recorded, a large colony of free-tailed bats (*Tadarida mexicana*) that lived under a roof in Bevino, New Mexico, was investigated on the eighth of June by Wharton Huber, who found that, of about seventy specimens collected, nearly a quarter were adult males and the remainder adult females, each of which contained a single large fetus, indicating a uniform time of breeding. In another group of twelve taken at Las Cruces, on June 2, all were females, and likewise pregnant. Like other species of this family, the Molossidae, these bats are highly colonial and possibly find it less easy to discover suitable quarters for segregation, although this may perhaps occur in some degree within the same retreat at the breeding season. Thus, Osburn (1865), writing of the Jamaican Molossus, relates that when he felled a large tree from which these bats had been seen to issue, it broke in fragments, and two clusters of bats were found in the ruins, numbering from 150 to 200 individuals. Those in the upper cavity were all males, while those in the lower were mostly females with a very few males. At the time — May 30 — several of the former were found to be carrying large fetuses already.

Very little is known about whether or not the sexes in the fruit bats definitely live apart during the season while the females are having their young, but probably this habit obtains in at least some of them. The only careful study of this matter, however, seems to be that carried on in the New Hebrides by Dr. J. R. Baker and his wife (1936), especially concerning the large native species there, *Pteropus geddiei*. They write:

The social habits vary with the season of the year. Both sexes congregate together in large "camps" during the daytime from about September to about January. These are often in large Casuarina trees near the shore. When the females become pregnant, about February, they leave these camps and it becomes difficult for a time to obtain female specimens. . . . Later in the year, about June, when pregnancy is far advanced, the females may be found in inland camps which contain few or no males. At this season the males have given up their social life and live separately, and it is now difficult to obtain males.

Andrews (1900) found an apparently similar state of affairs with the fruit bats of Christmas Island, while Ratcliffe, writing of the Australian flying foxes, mentions that although the great "camps" of bats apparently do not break up in the same way, the females tend to group by themselves within the congregation during the time they are with young.

## INDIVIDUAL TERRITORY

There is a little evidence that among at least certain bats something resembling the territory proprietorship occurs, such as is well known in birds. This may be more particularly true in the case of tropical species, where stable conditions make for greater permanence of habits and tend perhaps to greater localization of an individual's range. At all events, W. W. A. Phillips (1924), who has given much attention to the habits of small mammals in Ceylon, is confident that this is true of *Hesperoptenus tickellii*, a small species having the wing membranes black marked with white. He has observed that, night after night, what seems to be the same individual will be found hawking about for insects over a definite course and will guard this "beat" by chasing off other individuals of the same species, except at seasons when food is abundant in the shape of swarms of flying termites. At times a single pair may share such a circumscribed area or "territory." Evidence that the same individual becomes accustomed to hunting over the same grounds is that, if such a bat be shot, the territory remains for a time unoccupied. Thus, H. L. Jameson (1909) mentions shooting a long-fingered bat. *Miniopterus natalensis*, in the Transvaal, which was one of two that were seen regularly every

evening just before dark, hawking up and down a row of eucalyptus trees, at a height of about forty feet. They were presumed to be a mated pair.

No doubt many species develop considerable regularity in
their habits, living for a longer or shorter period in the same
haunts and hunting over the same area, even resting for a
time in an accustomed place. In the lower Himalayas of India,
Hutton (1872) observed a pair of large horseshoe bats (*Hipposideros armiger*) that lived by day in a loft to which an open
trapdoor gave them access. They would leave this retreat
every evening about dusk and with slow deliberate flight would
hawk about near the house, never going far and returning every
now and then to the loft to rest. Evidently this was for the time
at least an established habit of life. It is well known that
some of the European and North American bats of the larger
species, at least, after hunting in the first part of the evening,
rest for a while before making a new flight. Of the large brown
bat (*Eptesicus fuscus*) which is common in eastern Massachusetts, I once knew of a pair that regularly for part of the summer
would hang up in a particular corner of a piazza roof at about
two hours or less after sunset to rest for a space, disappearing
later in the night. Habits of such regularity indicate a tendency to the establishment of routine and of occupational associations essential to the development of the "territory" instinct.
In her study of California bats, Mrs. H. W. Grinnell (1918)
spent much time observing the long-legged bat (*Myotis volans*).
She writes that "one flyway, which was used every evening,
I was inclined to believe was the route of a single individual."

PARENTAL RELATIONS

The parental relations toward the young appear to be in bats
of a primitive type. The male parent is not known to show
any active interest in his offspring; on the contrary, as we
have just seen, the males of many species, perhaps of most, live
separately from the females at the season when the young are
born, but it is not altogether clear which sex forsakes the common abode or whether both seek new quarters in those species

where complete segregation takes place. Nor is it known whether or not the same male may pair with more than one female in a season, though with some species there is reason to suppose that a single pair remains together for a time at least. In other cases, as in the *Myotis* described by Dr. Guthrie, there seems to be little doubt that several inseminations of a single female may take place, possibly by more than one male.

After the young are born, they are usually carried about by the mother, to whose breasts and fur they cling; in this the specialized and backwardly hooked milk teeth probably assist the claws very much. But their weight soon becomes too great to make flying easy for the mother, so that when a few days old they are left behind, clinging by their hind feet to the wall of their cave or, in the case of tree-living bats, to the bark of the tree, leaving the mother free to go off for her evening flight in search of food. Among cave-dwelling species there is undoubtedly a high mortality of the young at this stage, for once the baby loses its hold and falls to the ground it is probably abandoned in most cases. Thus Mohr (1933) writes that the proprietor of Indian Cave in Tennessee, where a large num-, ber of *Myotis grisescens* bred, had found it necessary to clean up "young bats 'by the shovelful' " that had dropped to the floor of the cave in the latter half of June. These young had presumably either dropped from their mothers or had fallen from the ceiling when left by the old bats, for they are not carried about by this species to any great extent. Possibly, too, the frequent presence of visitors had been a source of disturbance, and the young had fallen when the mothers had flown at the appearance of lights.

Campbell (1925, p. 72) states that in Texas, where he made observations on a large colony of free-tailed bats (*Tadarida mexicana*), many young were found to have fallen helpless to the floor of the cavern, when the "mothers . . . would dart down after them and pick them up." It seems unlikely, however, that the old ones really rescued their young, though doubtless they flew down near them. Miller relates an instance of

such parental interest, which he observed while making excavations for fossils in a cave in Haiti. A large colony disturbed by the workmen took refuge in small holes in the cave
roof, where they remained hidden. On one occasion a half-
grown young, unable to fly, fell from one of these cavities to
the ground, where it lay, helpless, uttering "chirping, bird-like
cries. Immediately the air was filled with dozens of plunging
and rising adult bats behaving in the manner of a flock of terns
hovering over a wounded companion. Not one of them actually
touched the young animal, and the confusion soon subsided, the
adults retiring again to their holes." These actions might be
interpreted as showing solicitude for the young, whose shrill
cries indicated its distress. It is interesting, however, that the
adults were apparently unable to help it. Other instances are
on record of bats coming at the cries of stricken members of
their species, as if in part from curiosity, though possibly these
actions are really a manifestation of the same feelings that
were roused by the cries of the young. Thus, Guthrie (1933,
p. 7) mentions an instance of an adult nursing female of
*Myotis grisescens* that was shot down outside a cave in Boone
County, Missouri. When picked up, it gave vent to the usual
cries bats make when disturbed, whereupon "several dozen
bats swooped from all directions and flew close to but did not
touch" the shooter. "This response was repeatedly demonstrated since the flying bats dispersed as soon as the cries
ceased. Their return was practically instantaneous when the
cries were again induced."

A very similar habit has been reported by W. W. A. Phillips
(1924) for the long-armed sheath-tailed bat (*Taphozous longimanus*) and its relative the pouched sheath-tailed species (*Saccolaimus saccolaimus*) in Ceylon. "When wounded and lying on
the ground," he observes, both species utter "a shrill piercing
squeak which not only attracts others of its own kind" but numbers of the other as well. They "come swooping down out of the
darkening sky with a rush of wings, to dash past within a foot or
two of the ground and ascend again into the blue sky." This reaction is possibly to be connected with that of solicitude for the

fallen young, though it is unknown whether both males and females share it or whether it is shown by the latter only. The author just quoted recounts two instances in Ceylon in which a young bat too small to fly was brought to him in the daytime, and at evening an adult *Pipistrellus mimus* came into the room, suckled the baby bat, and flew off with it clinging to her, as if evincing a feeling of solicitude for her offspring, which, we may conclude, it must have been. Possibly she was led to her young by some sound it made, though on this point the author makes no comment. He mentions another case, however, where a female horseshoe bat (*Hipposideros brachyotus* of Ceylon) returned again and again to her young that had been captured, in response to its sharp twitter. An incident often quoted as indicating the solicitude of a mother bat for her young was published by Godman many years ago (in his *American Natural History*, 1: 50, 1826), who had it from his friend Titian Peale of Philadelphia. He writes:

These creatures are not deficient in those affections, which, in other animals, are supposed to denote much sensibility, and always excite the sympathies of mankind. . . . In June 1823, the son of Mr. Gillespie, keeper of the city square, caught a young bat (*Vespertilio Nov-Eboracensis*, L.) which he took home with him. Three hours afterwards, in the evening, as he was conveying it to the Museum in his hand, while passing near the place where it was caught, the mother made her appearance, followed the boy for two squares, flying around him, and finally alighted on his breast, such was her anxiety to save her offspring. Both were brought to the Museum, the young one firmly adhering to its mother's teat. This faithful creature lived two days in the Museum, and then died of injuries received from her captor. The young one, being but half grown, was still too young to take care of itself, and died shortly after.

## VOICE

The voice is usually regarded as a means of communication, at least insofar as it may express the state of mind of one individual and thus affect the actions of another. In the roosting flying foxes, as well as in the bickering colony of Erophylla previously described, the sharp sounds emitted have perhaps a threat value and may therefore play a part in bringing about a proper spacing of the animals while they are at rest. The yellow-haired fruit bat (*Eidolon stramineum*) is another voluble species. Yerbury (Yerbury and Thomas, 1895) makes note that at Aden, Arabia, they were plentiful in the sultan's garden, where they frequented the tops of the tallest palms in large ball-like clusters, but they are not easy to see and would pass unnoticed were it not that they keep up an incessant chatter, the purpose of which in this case is not obvious, unless it merely expresses restlessness or discomfort. The rousette bats (*Rousettus aegyptiacus*) of the eastern Mediterranean region have a similar habit. They appear very restless and noisy even in the daytime and when undisturbed. From a resting cluster one or two individuals frequently detach themselves from the mass, and fly squeaking from one to another group (Bate, 1904).

Most bats when attacked or unexpectedly handled will utter a quick succession of guttural squeaks, as if in irritation rather than fear. Often at the same time they seize one's finger in their teeth, clinging on bulldog-like, as they sink them deeper into the skin with convulsive movements of the jaws. In general, however, most species do not seem to make special use of the voice. An outstanding exception to this is found among some of the African fruit bats, such as the species of *Epomophorus* or epaulet bats, which at frequent intervals, as they fly about the branches of trees searching for small fruits, give vent to a soft querulous note. In the large hammer-headed bat (*Hypsignathus monstrosus*) of the Congo region the voice is remarkably developed. The vocal organs of this species, as well as those of Epomophorus, have been examined by Dobson (1881), and more recently Lang and Chapin (1917) have figured and described the arrangement in the former. The bats of this group differ from other kinds in the great development of the larynx and lateral pouches or "pharyngeal sacs," which seem to have a definite relation to the voice. In the hammer-headed bat the larynx reaches its greatest size, attaining nearly a third the volume of the entire body cavity. Lang and Chapin remark that "in no other mammal is everything so entirely subordinated to the organs of voice," with "a pair of air-sacs inflated at will and a tremendous enlargement of the larynx and vocal cords." Since this apparatus is peculiar to the males, they argue that "the sound produced can hardly have any other purpose than to attract the females," although Dobson earlier supposed that the pouches and other muscles of the pharynx were developments to enable the sucking of fruit juices to better advantage. The two authors quoted show that the larynx in this bat is so large that it

actually fills the greater part of the thoracic cavity, crowding the heart and lungs back and sideways until the posterior end of the cricoid cartilage is practically in contact with the diaphragm. The trachea is wide, but folded upward on the posterior side of the larynx. This extreme development of the larynx is simply the result of the enlargements of its usual elements, . . . which have undergone extensive ossification.

While encamped on the Ituri River, northeastern Congo, these observers had an excellent chance to watch these big bats:

Every evening, shortly after sunset — about 6.15, to be exact — some thirty of them would be seen crossing the stream to the south bank, not in a flock but singly, in straggling fashion. Entering the trees on the far shore, they would start at once to call. Each individual gave a loud *pwŏk!* or *kwŏk!*, repeated at short intervals, say of 1/3 to 1/2 of a second, though occasionally several notes would be emitted in very rapid succession. This noise would continue without serious interruption till 10 or 11 o'clock, to be taken up again at intervals later on, but ceasing entirely by half an hour before daylight. We never saw them recross the river. During this performance their utter lack of fear was amazing. Neither talking, rapping on the trees, lighting a lantern, nor even firing a gun could induce them to cease their calling. Their chorus made us think of a pondful of noisy American wood-frogs, greatly magnified and transported to the treetops. At this particular spot only adult males assembled, as was shown by the nine specimens shot as they crossed the river; . . . just before they began to cross the stream, every evening, we could hear the whole chorus far back in the forest, where they evidently spent the day with their females and young. An overcast sky would delay their arrival 10 or 15 minutes, and rain would practically silence them. . . . The old males alone call in this loud fashion.

This remarkable chorus was heard nightly throughout February and March, but its precise meaning was not determined. The gathering of the males at this time seems independent of feeding habits or the attraction of food, but on the other hand the observers found no indication that the sounds affected the behavior of the females. Its communal nature, however, is interesting and evidently has some significance. In the smaller epaulet bats, in which the larynx and pharyngeal sacs are much less developed, the sounds produced by the males are apparently given while feeding or flying from tree to tree. Lang and Chapin (1917, p. 500) describe the note as a "short, tirelessly reiterated whistle," sounding like *kŭrnk!* or *kyŭrnk!*, with a whistled effect, almost musical at a distance, often repeated at intervals of about a second for many minutes without a break. Contrary to the habit of the hammer-headed bat, these epaulet bats (*Epomops franqueti*) are not gregarious and, if closely approached, fly away or become silent. The sound is a characteristic one of the region, for "throughout the year in the neighborhood of almost every village in the Ituri region, and far beyond the forest area, wherever there are propitious wooded places, its vocal efforts ring intermittently through the stillness of the night — practically from sunset to sunrise." Since the voice is largely helpful as indicative of location, it may be that its constant use by the males apprises each of the presence of another male, and thus helps in spacing the individuals, but this can hardly be the case in the hammer-headed bat, where apparently the calling males come together to a particular place for their choruses. Nor is it as yet obvious what effect, if any, the notes may have upon the actions of the females. Altogether, the sounds produced by these African fruit bats appear to be without parallel elsewhere in the group.

# CHAPTER XV

# BREEDING HABITS AND YOUNG OF BATS

As yet only a beginning has been made in the study of the breeding habits of bats, particularly as to the early stages of ovulation, fertilization, and embryonic development. In Europe various French and German investigators have given attention to a few of the native species only, while in America, Hartman and Cuyler (1927), Guthrie (1933), and Hamlett (1934a) seem to be the only ones to have done extensive work on these first phases of development. When more species have been studied, wide variation will probably be found between different groups, in the times of mating, duration of the mating season, and the relation of hibernation to ovulation and fertilization. An excellent summary of our present knowledge is given by Hartman (1933). He points out that the long-fingered bat (Miniopterus), studied in Europe by Courrier (1927), may be primitive in apparently having a very limited breeding season, which takes place in late summer and early autumn. At this season ripe ova are produced by the female, and copulation occurs as with other bats of the northern temperate regions. The important point is that the ova are fertilized at once and pregnancy ensues, continuing all winter; the young are born in spring.

In contrast, the other species of central Europe, although they mate in the autumn and possibly are sexually active in spring too, nevertheless retain the sperm from the male until the following spring, when, on coming out of hibernation, ovulation takes place and the ova start development. In Miniopterus the sexual activity of the male lasts from about July to October, while during the remaining nine months of the year there is no sperm production, and the testes remain in an inactive "resting" condition. By midsummer, after the young are grown and weaned, the female is again ready for mating. This condition in bats differs from that in rodents, in which mating may take place immediately after the young have been born. It should be remembered that Miniopterus is essentially a bat of tropical and subtropical distribution, so that in the south of Europe it is really on the northward borders of its natural range and should not be expected to resemble in breeding habits the various other vespertilionid bats of central Europe that spend the winter in more or less profound hibernation. It seems normal for the bats of the north-temperate zone in both hemispheres to mate in the autumn before they enter their places of hibernation. This adaptation to the cold northern winter and its period of prolonged inactivity results in a second adaptation, namely, that in these species the spermatozoa remain stored in the uterus of the female over winter as mucous masses full of living sperms. In the meanwhile the testes of the male shrink as sperm production ceases, although quantities may be stored in the enlarged "tail" of the epididymis.

We have already seen how in the winter the bodily activities of hibernating bats are reduced to a very minimum, so that it is not surprising that this state extends to the reproductive cells as well. Only a few European bats have been carefully followed through this period. They include the common pipistrelle (*Pipistrellus pipistrellus*), the serotine bat (*Eptesicus serotinus*), the large mouse-eared bat (*Myotis myotis*) — often referred to by earlier writers as *Vespertilio murinus*, a very different species — and the long-eared bat (*Plecotus auritus*), all members of the Vespertilionidae, in all of which the process seems to be essentially the same. During the winter in these hibernating species the egg follicle in the ovary slowly enlarges, while the vagina becomes filled by a plug formed from the mucous secretion of its walls. When spring arrives and the bats again come into regular activity, this plug is cast, ovulation takes place, and the egg starts down the oviduct, into which meanwhile the spermatozoa have made their way, and thus fertilization is effected by means of the stored sperm. Some naturalists have questioned the ability of the spermatozoa to remain alive within the body of the female all winter in this way and have suggested instead that mating again takes place in the spring when the bats come out from hibernation. Possibly both of these methods of fertilization take place, for it seems very likely that the immature individuals do not breed, at least in their first autumn. In support of the first method there is a good deal of evidence. Thus, Nakano (1928) found that in the Japanese pipistrelle (*Pipistrellus abramus*) the stored spermatozoa remain immotile within the female so long as they rest embedded in the mucous mass, and Redenz (1929), working with the long-eared bat, found that these cells would become motile with the dilution of the mass in salt solution. The sperms when thus liberated remain active at room temperature for sixteen to twenty hours and then die.

Some recent experiments of Herlant (1934) with serotine bats in Belgium are of interest here. Since it is known that injection of pituitary extract or of placenta extract can bring about a premature exclusion of the ovum from its follicle (as proved by Zondek, 1933), he made such injections with both these substances and succeeded in producing premature ovulation, with fertilization and early development, for the first time certainly recorded in mammals. Of various experiments of which the details appear, he found that a bat taken in hibernation December 12 and given a daily injection of pituitary extract already showed ovulation after four days. Again, repeating this for seven days with bats taken in hibernation on January 20, he found that on dissection the ovum had been given off and was already located in the horn of the uterus, with several cell divisions already taken place. The vitelline membrane was gone, and the embryo was in process of implantation in the uterine wall. Similar results were obtained, using placenta extracts instead. Evidently the spermatozoa become active and penetrate to the upper part of the uterine horn and produce fertilization two months ahead of the normal time in spring. Like results were obtained by Herlant with the larger horseshoe bat (*Rhinolophus ferrum-equinum*). In this bat, a member of a very different family (Rhinolophidae), several of which range far enough into the northern hemisphere to have developed the habit of hibernation, it is said that the spermatozoa are stored, not in the uterus of the female, but in a sort of pocket on the ventral surface of the vagina. Rollinat and Trouessart (1900) found that the male testes remain in an active condition throughout the winter, but they doubt if mating continues at that season. Nevertheless, this is a possibility, for in a large part of its range this bat does not hibernate very deeply, and most of the related species are characteristic of warmer countries of the Old World. The same authors believe that a single female may mate several times in succession, for often the mass of sperm accumulated in the vagina is greater than would be expected from a single mating and forms a "firmly coagulated" plug within the vagina.

The important contributions of Dr. Mary J. Guthrie (1933a) to this subject concern four species of Myotis (*M. lucifugus, M. grisescens, M. sodalis, M. keenii septentrionalis*) in addition to the eastern pipistrelle and the big brown bat (*Eptesicus fuscus*), from caves in Missouri, where they hibernate. Definite proof was found that mating had already taken place during autumn. Males examined in November, early in the hibernating period, contained considerable amounts of sperm in the lower part of the reproductive tract. Later in the winter a number of females were removed from the cave to the laboratory, when, after having been artificially revived, they were found to have shortly given off ova. This author concludes that there is much evidence that the males also become sexually active at this season and that they may then mate with the females and produce fertilization, but apparently the certain proof that might have been obtained by isolating the females throughout the winter was not secured. The recent review of Eisentraut (1936) covering the work of European investigators seems to establish, however, that in the north-temperate parts of the world bats regularly mate in the autumn, but that the males may remain until spring capable of fertilizing the females, which insures that all the latter may reproduce. The longer period during which the males are sexually active may also be necessary in order that females born the previous summer, and not mature that autumn, shall be assured reproduction.

With bats of warmer climates there is no doubt that quite different habits obtain, but as yet very little is known in a definite way. For the family of velvet-furred, free-tailed bats (Molossidae) Hartman and Cuyler (1927) have established the very interesting fact that the "guano bat" of southwestern United States has a very limited breeding period, which takes place in March. They collected specimens of this bat (*Tadarida mexicana*) in every month of the year in Texas and carefully examined the reproductive organs. Yet they found that "there are no spermatozoa in the uterus of the female nor the testis or genital tract of the male," nor does ovulation take place, except during that period. This is partly a house bat and seems to undergo a very limited kind of hibernation, which is understandable, for it belongs to an essentially tropical group, of which a few species reach the subtropical parts of southern United States. This definite mating season results in bringing about reproduction at nearly the same time in all the individuals. For example, of the female bats collected from a colony under a roof at Las Cruces, New Mexico, on June 8, every one contained a fetus, of which some were nearly ready for birth, most were large, while a few were smaller. About a quarter of the 67 specimens taken were males.

Of the South American leaf-nosed bats (Phyllostomidae) almost nothing is known of the early stages in development. However, since all the species live in the warmer parts of America and are not under the necessity of hibernating, there is no reason to expect a storage of sperm in the uterus of the female. This seems to be borne out by the work of Dr. G. W. D. Hamlett (1935), who found, on examination of a series of the long-tongued bat (*Glossophaga soricina*) in Matto Grosso, Brazil, that the mature, non-pregnant females taken between November 23 and December 4 had not yet ovulated, nor was there any trace of sperm, while in others taken at the same time many contained small embryos varying in size from cleavage stages up to a length of 15 mm. Dr. Hamlett concludes that in this region Glossophaga breeds late in the spring, shortly before the rainy season, with a variation in individual cases of between two and three weeks, as shown by the different sizes of the embryos. He thinks also that the failure to find sperm in any of the non-pregnant females indicates that ovulation succeeds mating promptly, without a long resting period between. The same is probably true also for the Old World fruit bats. There is some evidence that certain of the tropical bats may have more than one breeding season. For example, in a series of the common short-tailed bat, *Carollia perspicillata*, of the Amazon Valley, five taken on August 24, evidently from a breeding colony, contained two embryos apiece, while of ten females taken in the same area on January 24, five held a single embryo each, and four were not pregnant. These specimens, collected for the Museum of Comparative Zoology, may indicate that the young of the previous season come into breeding some six months later and have their first offspring a single young instead of twins. Or perhaps there is some other explanation. As elsewhere mentioned, the fruit bat, *Rousettus collaris*, may have no well-marked breeding season, for those kept in the zoological gardens of London have produced young in every month of the year, although it must be added that here they are not living under natural conditions.

Nevertheless, it is likely that in the fruit bats (Pteropidae) generally, there is a definitely limited breeding season, notwithstanding that these dwellers in tropical regions live under fairly even conditions of temperature the year around. The only careful study of this matter, however, is that by Dr. and Mrs. John R. Baker (1936). During two different years spent at the New Hebrides Islands, about latitude 15° south of the equator, they followed the habits of the larger flying fox, *Pteropus geddiei*, through each period. They found that in spite of the almost unvarying temperature of these tropic isles, where the average remained at 29.9° Centigrade from December to March, these bats copulate during February and March, and in by far the majority of cases the females give birth to their single young in August or September, with a few early and later dates. Breeding therefore begins in a time of year corresponding to the northern spring, although in the New Hebrides there is nothing to distinguish that season from other times of year, nor is there a marked rainy season. The period of gestation for the females is evidently about six months, but it is probably less in some of the smaller species of this family.

While studying the fruit bats at the New Hebrides, Dr. Baker also had an opportunity to extend his observations to the local species of long-fingered bat, *Miniopterus australis*, a close relative of the European bat of the same genus, *M. schreibersii*, which earlier in the chapter was shown to be exceptional in that both copulation and ovulation take place in autumn and the embryo develops very slowly during winter. These bats are essentially tropical, for several species are found in the warmer parts of the Old World, from South China to Australia and India, all of Africa, and north to southern Europe. It is only in the cooler margins of the range that they undergo "hibernation," so that they may be expected to retain the original tropical habit of copulation, followed at once by the development of the embryo. By examining specimens throughout the year from a large colony that lived in a cave in the coral rock of the New Hebrides, Baker and Bird (1936) found that in early September females held very small embryos about a millimeter long. These continued to grow regularly in size and were ready for birth in the second half of December, requiring thus approximately 110 days for their development. In the males the sexual cycle is as clearly marked. For the testes are fully functional, with abundance of sperms chiefly in July, August, and September, while at other times of the year they contain less or few, or from March to June none at all. Evidently copulation must take place in late August and September, after which the development of the embryo ensues at once. In this the tropical species of the genus quite agree with their relatives of southern Europe; but whereas the former show no delay in the course of embryonic growth, the latter, because of their partial hibernation, show a corresponding tardiness in the slow development of the embryo during the winter.

These facts give a clue to the process of adaptation to the

winter season in more northern bats which, on the whole, agree in an autumnal copulation, but the sperms are stored during the period of hibernation and do not give fertilization until spring, when the ova of the female are given off. The remarkable point in the case of the long-fingered bats of the New Hebrides is that the breeding time (August and September) corresponds to the southern spring instead of autumn, although in a climate so equable as there obtains, it can hardly be said to have a spring and autumn. One must look to some other factor than temperature as a control for this marked and regular periodicity of the time of breeding; possibly it is a result of an internal rhythm or perhaps it is owing to some unrecognized environmental condition. That it depends on differences in amount of sunlight acting on the body, as may be the case in the fruit bats that hang by day in open trees, seems to be precluded by the cave-haunting habits of these insectivorous long-fingered bats. As yet, however, we are still ignorant of the real reason.

### BIRTH

The birth of young bats has seldom been described. Perhaps the very first account is that of the French naturalist, Pierre Bélon, in his *Ornithologie*, published in 1555. He tells of his visit to a cave in Crete that was inhabited by a multitude of bats, which, as his party entered, flew about them in such numbers as nearly to extinguish the torches they carried. The females which he examined were all pregnant, and, wishing to study their anatomy, he collected some twenty specimens alive, some of which later gave birth to their young. His account (translated) sets forth the bare facts that bats make no nest for the reception of the young, but when giving birth to her young the mother instead suspends herself by the feet and the hooklets at the wrist, and in this reversed position receives the young one on to her breast, where she suckles it like any terrestrial mammal. Bélon found that at the end of a day or two she would hang the young one up by its own "hooklets," while she went forth in search of food. Of the process of birth itself he says that the mother frees the young from the enveloping membranes with her teeth and cuts the umbilical cord. He believes that the eating of the afterbirth serves to nourish the mother during the first few days until she can leave the young one behind while she hunts. It is not clear what species of bat Bélon observed in Crete, but possibly it was one of the horseshoe bats. His account accords fairly well with those of more modern naturalists and testifies to the keenness of his observation.

The birth of the young in bats was again very briefly described in 1817 by the German naturalist Kuhl, for one of the common species of his country. He says that when about to bring forth, the female hangs herself by the thumb-claws and hind feet, and in this position bends her tail with its membrane forward over the stomach, so as to form with the side membranes a perfect receiving apron for the young. When the young one comes forth, the mother severs the umbilical cord with her teeth and then licks the baby carefully all over with her tongue.

A more detailed account is that given by Dr. G. Daniell (1835), who observed the process in a noctule bat (*Nyctalus noctula*) which he had in captivity in England. On June 23 the bat seemed uneasy for an hour or so, when presently, reversing her usual hanging position, she

attached herself by her anterior limbs to a cross wire of the cage, stretching her hind legs to their utmost extent, curving the tail upwards, and expanding the membrane . . . to form a perfect nest-like cavity for the reception of the young. In a few moments the snout of the young one made its appearance, and in about five minutes the whole of its head was protruded. The female then struggled considerably until the extremities of the radii had passed, after which the young one by means of a lateral motion of its fore limbs relieved itself. It was born on its back, perfectly destitute of hair and blind; and was attached by an umbilical cord of about two inches in length. The female then licked it clean, turning it over . . . and afterwards resuming her usual position, and placing the young in the membrane of her wing, proceeded to gnaw off the umbilical cord and eat the placenta

— time occupied, seventeen minutes.

Daniell's observation that the young one was born head

first, the normal way in most mammals, is at variance with that of most other writers on the subject. Thus the classic account by Rollinat and Trouessart (1896) of the breeding habits of the large European mouse-eared bat (*Myotis myotis*, called by them *Vespertilio murinus*) describes parturition as taking about one half an hour. The first part of the young one to appear was its left knee, then the body appeared and was nearly free in twenty minutes more, and completely excluded in another ten minutes. The young in this case is born feet first and is received, as in other species described, into the apron formed by the membranes of the mother as she hangs upside down from all four feet; or she may cling upright from the wires of the cage. These authors found that the female pulls out the placenta, which is eaten, and meanwhile the young one attaches itself to a teat. The eyes of the baby bat do not open for five to nine days, and it is not until the thirteenth day that it hangs itself up beside its mother.

Some further interesting observations on the birth of young in a small brown Myotis (*M. austroriparius*) common in Florida were published by H. B. Sherman (1930). He secured over two dozen pregnant females from an old building at Gainesville in early May. Some of these were taken to the laboratory and placed in improvised cages for more careful study. Contrary to the usual rule in this genus, two young were produced by most of these females instead of but a single one. The details of the process were carefully watched in three cases. In the first, both twins were born dead and dropped to the floor of the cage, although the placenta was eaten by the mother. In the two other cases the young appeared tail end first, enclosed in the amniotic membrane, its ventral side toward that of its mother. "When about a quarter born, the amnion was torn by the teeth of the mother and a minute later the offspring popped out into the curled up interfemoral membrane." Four hours later the young were still attached by their umbilical cords, which were then seized by the mother, the placenta pulled out and eaten, together with all but about a quarter of an inch of the cord. In the third instance the amnion was already ruptured and was not torn by the teeth of the mother when the young one appeared. The elbow of one of the young now first came in view, but it was not until about three hours later that its hind quarters were extruded, followed in about twenty-five minutes more by the head, leaving one wing within the body of the parent. This was gently pulled out with forceps by the observer. After a brief rest, hanging head down in the usual position, the mother again assumed her basket-like posture, hanging back down, from all four feet, when the second young began to appear and came forth in due course. The unusual delay in the process was doubtless caused by the weakened condition of the mother after two days in captivity, during which she refused food or water. The eyes of these little bats opened in about a week.

The only account of parturition in a leaf-nosed bat seems to be that of Henry A. Blake (1885), who described his exploration of a large cave in the Bahama Islands, in which, as he estimated, a colony of nearly a thousand individuals was hanging. A single discharge of his gun brought down a number of females, one of which, apparently unhurt, was brought home and placed in a wire-screened box, in the top of which it hung. These bats were probably the common *Erophylla planifrons*, a long-tongued species that lives partly on fruit juices. At noon of the third day the birth of the young one began. The bat had been as usual hanging suspended by the claws of one hind foot, with the other bent forward at right angles. The observer presently noted that regular labor paroxysms of four to five seconds' duration now took place at intervals of about two minutes. The bat now hung by both hind legs and bent its body back or forward as if in much pain. At 12.20 o'clock, the left hind leg of the young bat protruded, doubled forward at "the second joint" (knee). The mother hung most of the time by one foot, using the other to scrape from time to time the membranous sac in which the young one was enclosed or to scratch herself as a relief from the tension. Finally, she scraped the sac till it broke, when the protruded leg straightened out and grasped the mother's wing. She then hung by her right leg, bent the left one forward till the leg of the young hooked on to it, then, by gently raising this leg, she seemed to draw the young one up. At 12.30 the second leg was free, and at once both legs grasped the mother. In another five minutes the young bat was completely excluded, with the back of its head to the front. The mother licked it for half an hour, then began to bite at the umbilical cord, resting at times as if exhausted. At three o'clock the young one was still attached but appeared to be suckling. At ten in the evening the placenta had come away and was being eaten by the mother, who let nothing fall. The young one, unfortunately, died the next day. This case is especially interesting, however, since it indicates that in the leaf-nosed bats (Phyllostomidae) the mother may hang suspended from one foot during the process, and use the other foot to assist the birth of the little one, instead of hanging spider-like from all four feet. The presentation of the young feet first is apparently normal in the few species of bats in which the conditions have been accurately observed and is unique among mammals. But this may vary, if the observations of Daniell are correct, for he distinctly noticed the appearance of the head first of all. As facts accumulate it will be interesting to compare the birth processes in different families or even genera of bats, for undoubtedly various deviations from these accounts will be found.

### NUMBER OF YOUNG

With the majority of bats a single young one is the usual number at a birth. Probably, too, twins may rarely occur in those species that usually have but one baby at a time. In the genus Myotis, including a large number of species occurring in both hemispheres, most of the North American species as well as the European usually have a single young, but the observations of Sherman, just quoted, show that the Florida species, *M. austroriparius*, regularly has two. I have found no record of any fruit bat (Pteropidae) having more than a single young one, and one is the usual number apparently among the free-tailed bats (Molossidae), the hollow-faced bats

(Nycteridae), probably in the horseshoe bats (Rhinolophidae), and doubtless other groups. On the other hand, twins are usual in a number of bats. Those of the genera Pipistrellus and Scotophilus seem regularly to have two babies; and Dr. Francis Harper (1927) has shown that the related genus Nycticeius (as represented by *N. humeralis* of the southeastern United States) also has regularly two young at a time. The same author (1929) reports that a big brown bat (*Eptesicus fuscus*) which he secured on April 2 in Georgia contained four embryos, of

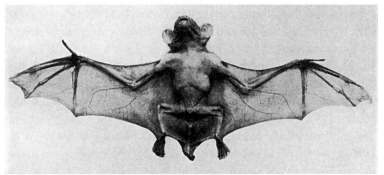

Fig. 44—A young red bat (*Lasiurus borealis*), Grinnell, Iowa; to show the outward bend of the knees, the several membranes, the relatively short fingers and large feet at this age, seen from below and about natural size. Miss Cornelia Clarke, phot.

two-millimeter length, two in the right and two in the left horn of the uterus. Ordinarily this bat has but a single young one at a time, although twins may occasionally be born. In the case of the four embryos found by Dr. Harper, as in a few similar instances, it is likely that only one would have lived to mature, and the others would, at a slightly later stage, become resorbed by the walls of the uterus.

There is some evidence also that the number of young may vary geographically even in the same species. Thus Barrett-Hamilton writes that in England the common little pipistrelle (*Pipistrellus pipistrellus*) has but a single young one, but on the Continent, in middle and southern Europe, two are frequent if not usual. Again, he says that in the British Isles the noctule bat (*Nyctalus noctula*) is not known to have more than one young at a birth, whereas continental naturalists find two as the usual number. What these facts may signify can only be guessed at present.

So far as our information goes, the only bat known to have more than two young at a birth is the American red bat. This was first reported in 1875 by Dr. Burt G. Wilder, who wrote that in the collection of the Peabody Academy of Sciences at Salem (now the Peabody Museum) were two female red bats (*Lasiurus borealis*) each with three young. Since then other cases have come to light, some of which have been summarized by Lyon (1903) and by H. L. Ward (1905). From these it appears that although one or at times two young occur, at least five cases are known in which three young were found with one mother, and three in which there were four young. This is correlated with the larger number of mammae in this genus, four. Through the courtesy of the late Miss C. Clarke of Grinnell, Iowa, I am able to reproduce here one of her photographs showing another instance of three young born to one of these pretty bats. This species is found with local variation in southern South America, and it is interesting to know that Thomas (1902), in describing as a local subspecies the red bat of Cordova, Argentina, mentions that the collector found the female had four young with her. The hoary bat (*Lasiurus cinereus*), a larger member of this same genus, may be expected to have as many as four young, since four mammae are present, but I have found no record of this number, the few cases at hand being of two young each. The allied genus Dasypterus might also be expected to have four or fewer, but this yellowish bat is rare in the warmer parts of America, the only record of young that I have found being of two, in the case of *D. xanthinus* of Sinaloa, Mexico (J. A. Allen, 1906).

Little is known about the time of gestation in bats. Probably in many of the smaller species of the northern hemisphere it is in the neighborhood of three months. At least, they become active in April, when the ova may be supposed to start development, and young are not born until late in June. No doubt the time will be found to vary in different species or from family to family. In his interesting account of bringing back alive to

FIG. 45—Red bat (*Lasiurus borealis*) with her three young, asleep by day. Grinnell, Iowa. Courtesy of Miss Cornelia Clarke, phot.

New York a vampire bat (Desmodus), Ditmars tells of the birth of its single young after at least three months of isolation, a rather long time compared to the three weeks requisite for the development of the young in the house mouse.

The early stages in the development of the embryo of bats have been only slightly studied, mostly by European investigators in the common species there available, of the family Vespertilionidae. Very recently, however, Dr. G. W. D. Hamlett (1934) has made some interesting observations on the early stages in a South American leaf-nosed bat, *Glossophaga soricina*, and in a molossid, *Molossus crassicaudatus*, which show that there may be wide variation in the method of implantation of the egg and in the structure of the placenta. In the Vespertilionidae, so far as is yet known, the egg at first lies upon the mucous membrane of the uterus without sinking deeply in, a common condition in the Carnivora and seen also in the classic laboratory mammal, the rabbit. In this family, as well as in the horseshoe bats (Rhinolophidae) and in some at least of the fruit bats (Pteropidae), the placenta or vascular mass whereby the developing young is nourished from the blood system of the mother is described as discoidal in shape, as it is in man. In Glossophaga, however, as a representative of the Phyllostomidae, the egg sinks deeply into the wall of the uterus, a method of implantation different from that of all other known bats, as well as of all other mammals in which this phase of development is known, except the anthropoid (ape and human) group. The significance of this fact must await further and more extended study. In some of the fruit bats (genus Rousettus) and in the free-tailed bats (family Molossidae) the placenta, instead of being discoidal, is diffuse, covering the surface of the trophoblast.

Dr. Hamlett finds that there are differences in the formation of the amnion, a membrane enveloping the growing embryo and enclosing a sac filled with fluid as a cushion for the developing young. In the Vespertilionidae, Rhinolophidae, and Molossidae the embryonal shield, the amnion cavity, and the primitive amnion arise through a splitting of the embryonic mass in a very early stage. The covering of the primitive amnion later degenerates, and the true amnion is formed by the upgrowth of folds at the borders of the embryonal shield. In contrast, in the Pteropidae and the Phyllostomidae, the primitive amnion does not break down, but persists and forms the true amnion. It would be valuable to compare these conditions with those in the Insectivora to see which are inheritances from ancestral types and which are later developments. The very early stages in the development of Molossus have been studied by Sansom (1932), who finds that the process in general agrees with that in other Microchiroptera.

# CHAPTER XVI

# MIGRATIONS OF BATS

As long ago as 1769 Gilbert White (*Natural History of Selborne*) suggested that the apparently brief and periodic appearance of the large noctule bat (*Nyctalus noctula*) in his part of England might be explained as a migratory habit. Later observers have shown, however, that it is resident in Great Britain throughout the year, but during the season, when cockchafers are abundant in early summer, it may appear locally in greater numbers for a few weeks. There is thus perhaps a slight shifting of the population in summer in search for this attractive food, but no real migration in the usual sense. Both the specimens that White eventually succeeded in procuring were males, and there is some evidence from other sources that this sex, while the females are busy with the care of their offspring, is given to wandering somewhat farther afield.

In the northern countries of the world the insects on which bats depend for food die off at the approach of the cold season or hide away for the winter's inactivity, so that the bats of these areas must perforce do the same or move to warmer latitudes. And this is exactly what takes place. Curiously, these two courses of action are correlated with the roosting habits. Thus, the species that frequent caves or similar dark shelters such as hollow trees for the most part retire during the autumn to caverns sufficiently deep to maintain at all times a temperature above the freezing point. Usually, as in New England and other parts of the eastern United States, such retreats are relatively few and far apart, except in limestone regions, where often there may be extensive caves and underground passages. It must be, therefore, that the many individuals gathering in them for hibernation are drawn from over a wide radius, implying migrations of a somewhat local nature. For example, in certain caves of central Vermont, as on Mt. Eolus and near

Brandon, in which no bats are to be found during visits in midsummer, there are large numbers in winter, which evidently disperse over the surrounding country with the return of the warm season.

A few species, however, that habitually hang up by day among leaves or against the trunks of trees or even under loose flakes of bark, seem averse to entering caverns, and it is among such that migration takes place comparable to the regular north and south migrations of birds, in spring and fall. So far as is at present made out, only three bats of eastern North America have this habit. These are the red bat (*Lasiurus borealis*), the larger hoary bat (*L. cinereus*), and the silver-haired bat (*Lasionycteris noctivagans*). The first two are notable for having long, narrow wings that give them strong powers of flight; the fur is of various shades of chestnut and buff, beautifully "frosted" with minute white tips, so that, as they rest among foliage or against the bole of a tree, they might easily pass for a withered leaf or a bit of lichened bark. The silver-haired bats seem to be more often found in hollows of trees or under flakes of bark, and are black, silvered with a mixture of white hairs. This last type of coloration is found in various other northern bats, such as the Old World barbastelle (*Barbastella barbastellus*), the dusky pipistrelle (*Pipistrellus pulveratus*), and the parti-colored bat (*Vespertilio murinus*), natives of Europe and Asia. Although they may be to some degree tree-dwellers, it is not known whether they have similar migratory habits.

The first to suspect the hoary bat of being a migrant was the Reverend James H. Linsley, an observant naturalist of a past generation, who resided at Stratford, Connecticut. In an important paper on local mammals, published in 1842, he mentions the capture of one of these bats in December of the year previous, "under circumstances which induced the belief that this bat migrates southerly in winter." Whatever these circumstances were, he does not divulge; but it remained for Dr. C. Hart Merriam (1888), more than forty years later, to advance more definite evidence. In this much-quoted paper

Merriam summarizes various records indicating that the hoary bat is known to summer in the northern United States and Canada, and in the autumn appears on the Atlantic seaboard to the southward, while the winter records available are from the southeastern states. Much additional data have since been acquired and confirm Merriam's conclusion. In an important paper published in 1897, G. S. Miller, Jr., details observations made at Highland Light, near the tip of Cape Cod, Massachusetts. This isolated point is largely an area of sand dunes with a scattered growth of stunted trees, affording conditions unfavorable for tree bats in summer, and is separated by the waters of Massachusetts Bay from the eastern coast line of New England. Yet numbers of hoary, red, and silver-haired bats were seen and shot here from August 21 to mid-September in 1890 and 1891, indicating a considerable movement of these species coastwise in late summer. Although after the latter date no others were seen at this point, hoary bats nevertheless continue their southward migration through New England and the Lake District during October and even into November. The very late record of Linsley — December — still stands as about the latest date, marking the close of the southward flight for this area, though there is a December date for Ann Arbor, Michigan. The hoary bat is an occasional visitor in autumn at the Bermuda Islands, some 666 miles southeast of New York, as attested by both Jones and Hurdis. How far south it extends this flight is not certainly known, but there are specimens from South Carolina in mid-January, from Montgomery (Georgia) in late January, Sterling (Georgia) in March, and Gainesville (Florida) in late February. These states are perhaps the general wintering area in the east. In the western part of North America no such definite seasonal movement has as yet been made out, for the analysis of records is complicated by the fact that the species apparently remains throughout the summer in the mountains of our Southwest. There is, however, strong ground for believing that late August specimens from Las Cruces, New Mexico, and late October individuals at Brownsville, southern Texas, are arrivals from the north. Almost nothing is definitely known about a return flight in the spring, but that must be presumed.

The migratory movements of the red bat in eastern North America closely parallel those of its relative, the hoary bat. Miller found it common at Highland Light from the latter third of August on till mid-September in 1890 and 1891. The migration is perhaps at its height at this season and probably ends slightly before that of the hoary. The migrating bats occasionally pass in numbers for a few days, as if some common impulse impelled those inhabiting a considerable area to move away southward, but since both these species are rather solitary in habits, they seldom congregate in more than small scattered groups. These migrations appear to involve the red bats all over its eastern range at least, from New England to the Great Lakes and somewhat beyond. Thus Saunders (1930) writes that when on September 9, 1929, he was gathering up several hundreds of birds that had been killed against the lighthouse at Long Point, Lake Erie, he was surprised to find three red bats among them. The next disastrous night for birds was the following September 24–25, when the light-keeper gathered up with these one hoary and a silver-haired bat. At other times a few were seen also. The last is a species of somewhat weaker flight than the two others, and its movements are less well known. Merriam (1888) was the first to adduce evidence of its migration southward. He reported that "a few small, dark-colored bats" were said by the keeper to visit Mt. Desert Rock lighthouse, twenty miles south-southeast of Mt. Desert, Maine, and fifteen miles from the nearest land, in both spring and fall. "Several" procured by the keeper about October 1, 1885, proved to be of this species, and a few years later Miller (1897a) found them at Highland Light, Cape Cod, during September and October.

All three species are occasionally found at sea far from the nearest land, as if they had wandered far or been blown to sea in the course of their passage south along the east coast. Like the two other species, this bat occurs now and again in Bermuda. A number of these waifs have been reported from time to

Fig. 46—The red bat (*Lasiurus borealis*), a migratory species of North America. Roused from sleep, the bat has spread its wings slightly. Taken at Grinnell, Iowa. Courtesy of Miss Cornelia Clarke, phot.

time, giving a slight indication of the frequency with which they must cross stretches of sea. Thus, there is a record of a red bat taken twenty miles off the Delaware Capes in 1843, and another captured off Cashe's Ledge, in the Gulf of Maine. Norton (1930) recounts that one flew aboard a fishing schooner, August 17, 1929, near the eastern end of Georges Bank, and alighting on the mainsail, was readily captured. This was about 240 miles east of Cape Cod and about 130 miles south of Cape Sable, Nova Scotia. Other interesting records of offshore migrants could be multiplied. Of the silver-haired bat, Murphy and Nichols (1913) remark that during September, when the species is migrating, "they may be seen on the beaches of the Long Island Sound, jerking along in the wind against the red evening sky." Murphy relates how on the early morning of September 6, 1907, before daybreak, while lying offshore in a small boat several miles from Sandy Hook, he saw a number of small bats struggling towards the Staten Island shore on the wings of an easterly wind and has little doubt that they were silver-hairs. An interesting note by Haagner (1921) tells that while three days out from Philadelphia, whither he was bringing some live animals for the Philadelphia zoo, he found a red bat in the morning hanging beneath the giraffe's deck stall. The distance from shore is not given but must have been several hundred miles.

Undoubtedly, larger numbers regularly follow along the coast at some distance from land, for Thomas (1921) records that the British Museum has a red bat and two silver-haired bats from a company of about a hundred which caught up with and settled upon a ship when some twenty miles off the coast of North Carolina on September 3, 1920. I have a note of a similar occurrence, in which a large number of bats appeared on and about a steamship during the night in the first week of September 1902, some ten miles off the Delaware River. The next morning some of them were captured on the deck, and the following night there was a smaller visitation, much to the dismay of the crew, who thought that they were being attacked, as the tired little creatures alighted on or about them. Although my efforts to learn the species of bat were unsuccessful, there is little doubt that they were either red or silver-haired bats, probably both.

The evidence just summarized indicates that the three species in question perform more or less regular annual migrations, but although they seem usually to pass in a rather scattered and straggling manner, they may at times associate in groups consisting of one or all three species. Yet it has rarely fallen to the lot of any naturalist to witness in detail one of these flights. The first account of such a migration by day seems to be the brief statement by the late Dr. Edgar A. Mearns (1898) in his notes on the fauna of the Hudson Highlands, to the effect that during the latter part of October and the first week of November he had seen great flights of the red bat "during the whole day." These seemed to be predominantly of one or the other sex on different days, for of several taken on two days all were males, while on two other days only females were captured. The same observer had seen a diurnal flight of hoary bats at Fort Snelling, Minnesota. Another fortunate naturalist is A. H. Howell (1908), who has recorded notes on a daytime flight of bats "of at least three sizes," possibly an association of all the three species mentioned. This was at Washington, D. C., on the morning of September 28, 1907, a mild cloudy morning with a light northeast wind. About 9 A.M. several bats appeared flying high overhead and presently several more. During the next hour over one hundred bats were noted, all flying in a leisurely manner in one direction, southwest — with the wind. They were not in flocks, but flew singly, usually only four or five in sight at one time. In contrast to their usual erratic manner of flight, their progress was very steady, "consisting chiefly of a sailing or drifting motion with occasional short flappings of the wings," and at a height of between 150 to 450 feet above the earth. A few were perhaps considerably higher. Most of them, as seen through a field glass, seemed about the size of a red bat, but no positive identification was possible. Such diurnal migrations, as Howell rightly believes, must be exceptional or they would have been more often noticed. No doubt migration is usually carried on by night and, perhaps under favorable circumstances of wind and weather, is continued into the daylight hours.

The dates of the migrating bats indicate that the autumnal movement is carried out in a leisurely manner from mid-August into November in the Northeast, but is apparently at its height in early September. Perhaps, too, there are late mass movements, following the apparent lull in mid-September, depending on the coming of the frosts. No other species of North America are certainly known to migrate in this way. Further, it is significant as evidence of their power of sustained flight that both the hoary and the red bat are represented by very similar races in the Hawaiian Islands, suggesting that these two types have alone been able to reach those oceanic islands from overseas, and implying the successful crossing of the 2,500 miles or more of open water separating them from the American mainland. The help of sailing ships in making this passage is hardly possible, for, as a result of long isolation, both bats are now somewhat different from their mainland representatives. "Representative forms" of both are also found in South America, and at least the red bat is known from the Galapagos Islands (*Lasiurus bauri*). It is still unknown whether the races of the hoary and the red bats of southern South America (Argentina) migrate northward at the approach of the southern winter, but such a habit might be expected.

Turning now to the Old World, we find that certain of the fruit bats or flying foxes make fairly regular mass migrations in search of ripening fruit, following the fruit season southward from subtropical haunts. Most of these bats are highly social in habits, assembling by day often in vast numbers in favorite roosting places. A study of their movements has recently been undertaken by Ratcliffe (1932) in eastern Australia, where at times very considerable damage is done to fruit crops by three large species of the eastern genus, Pteropus, namely the gray-headed (*P. poliocephalus*), the Gouldian (*P. gouldi*), and the spectacled bat (*P. conspicillatus*); while a fourth slightly smaller species, the red flying fox (*P. scapula-*

*tus*), is found to be chiefly a flower eater. Of these four the Gouldian and spectacled bats remain throughout the year chiefly in the subtropics of northern Australia, but the gray-headed is found slightly farther to the south, its range overlapping that of the other larger species, and extending from central Queensland into more temperate climes. The range of the red species extends farther westward in northern Australia and on the east reaches to central New South Wales or farther.

Ratcliffe found that the gray-headed bat carries out very regular seasonal migrations, moving southward in the (southern) spring from Queensland and northern New South Wales. These are mass movements, involving large sections of the bat population, which pass from one regularly tenanted roosting place or "camp" to another on their progress toward the extreme southern parts of eastern Australia. The bats seem to follow the coastal districts and may begin to move in early October, when they appear in northern New South Wales. Farther to the south, they arrive in the Hunter River valley and the Sydney area about the middle or end of November and reach the extreme southeast coasts in latitude 37° south by December. Nevertheless there is much irregularity of movements of a rather puzzling nature. It seems as if "the instinct for southerly migration is not uniform throughout the species," for a few individuals may occur at all times of the year even in the southern part of the range. Yet, on the whole, the migration is a general and regular one. "Certain camps in New South Wales are known to have been occupied for some 50 years, and it is said that local men can prophesy to within a week the date" of their departure. The smaller red flying fox is less regular in its migrations, for these are conditioned largely by the somewhat uncertain flowering of eucalyptus and other trees on the blossoms of which they feed, while the movements of the gray-headed species are determined more by the ripening season of small fruits, especially the wild figs, which form a large part of its natural food. The two species, nevertheless, are often found in association, and while the red "fox" is less common in the extreme southeast, it often frequents the same "camps" with the gray-headed.

A rather similar type of migration has been made out for at least one species of the small African fruit bats of the genus Epomophorus, the males of which have conspicuous white shoulder tufts or epaulets. According to Jameson (1909), Wahlberg's epaulet bat (*E. wahlbergi*) appears in large numbers at Taaween, in the Zoutpansberg district of South Africa, during the southern summer, attracted by the ripening crop of guavas, on which it proceeds to feast. At other seasons of the year it seems to be largely absent, perhaps withdrawing toward the tropical parts of the continent. With the great increase in fruit growing in South Africa, the depredations of these bats threaten to become of some economic importance, so that, as in Australia, attempts have been made to kill them by using poisoned fruit as bait. Curiously, however, they seem to be very resistant to strychnine, for experiments made by Kex-Blake (1931) showed that although they ate the poisoned pulp of passion fruits, no dead bats could be found afterward.

There is no doubt that other African fruit bats perform local migrations, but very little is definitely known of their extent and season. Probably, however, these are largely conditioned by the ripening of certain fruits and tree flowers, as well as by the incidence of the heavy rains. Dr. James P. Chapin (in J. A. Allen, Lang, and Chapin, 1917) has recorded some interesting notes on the yellow fruit bat (*Eidolon helvum*) made in the course of a year's sojourn in the region about Avakubi, eastern Belgian Congo, from August 1913 to September of the year following. At first none were seen, but during the last three weeks of September hundreds appeared nearly every evening flying over toward the southwest. The flight then ceased, and no more were seen till the following May, when for six or seven weeks numbers were seen regularly passing in a southwesterly direction. They seemed also to be well established in the district during June. But in July the migratory flights were resumed, so that by August all had left the region. Chapin adds that in the Aruwimi River certain small islands near Panga are famous as the roosting grounds of this bat at certain seasons. They are said to come always at low water in February and March, when they are killed in quantities by the natives for food. Although there is as yet little evidence to show where these bats come from or whither they are pro- ceeding, yet there can be little doubt that these are mass move- ments from one locality to another within the tropical parts of Africa, owing to a search for food, its failure in some districts at certain times of the year forcing them to move to other places. Or possibly the coming of the rains makes some districts unsuitable, for during a visit to Liberia in the rainy season from July to November I made constant search and regularly watched for bats in the early evenings, but saw remarkably few in areas where they should be common.

It is well known that in these parts of Africa certain species of birds that feed chiefly on flying insects migrate elsewhere during the seasons of heavy periodic rains, for insects are beaten down by the rains or adjust their hatching season to escape them, and the birds at such times must seek their food else- where. It seems quite possible that bats may feel the same necessity and that there may be some shifting of population during the rainy seasons, in the case of species that do not make regular latitudinal migrations. Perhaps such a movement was that described by Dr. Frank M. Chapman (1892), who, in writing of the common free-tailed bat (Tadarida) at Trinidad, Cuba, relates that on March 17 "thousands of these bats were seen flying to the westward. On no other occasion were they seen in anything like the same numbers."

There is very little evidence that any of the smaller Old World species of bats perform such definite migrations as the red and the hoary bats of North America with the coming of the cold season. Nevertheless, there can be no doubt that a few northern bats of Europe and Asia undergo a limited migra- tion or at least make short local flights to winter quarters from the surrounding areas. Formosov (1927) believes that at least three Russian species, the common pipistrelle (*Pipistrellus pipistrellus*), the frosted bat (*Vespertilio murinus*), and the noctule (*Nyctalus noctula*), are migratory, but this may imply merely a withdrawal to hibernating places such as caverns at a distance from their usual summer areas. Such movements are described by Hugues (1913) in the case of several species in France. Near the mouth of the Rhône and the Hérault, he found Schreibers' long-fingered bat (*Miniopterus schreibersii*) entering caves in October by hundreds, apparently coming in from elsewhere, perhaps the immediately surrounding region. Their numbers diminish in the succeeding two months, until by late December none is to be found, nor do they reappear in the caverns until the end of March, becoming abundant again in April. The greater horseshoe bat (*Rhinolophus ferrum-equinum*) does exactly the same thing. The lesser horseshoe bats (*R. hipposideros*) in the same locality seek the caves in October for hibernation, but most of them disappear by January, only a few wintering, and the same is true of the small Myotis (*M. capaccinii*) and the white-edged bat (*Pipistrellus kuhli*). Of the frosted bat (*Vespertilio murinus*), several thousands spend the summer in the old ramparts of Aigues-Mortes, but abandon them in autumn, some of the species being then found in local caverns, although all leave in the coldest months.

One cannot but suppose that the caverns here are unsuitable for the winter's sleep and are abandoned by the end of the year for less open retreats, where perhaps the temperature remains more constant. Evidently, however, there is more or less local movement and adjustment as the winter comes on, but perhaps less of a true north-south migration such as birds perform. There is very little to indicate the extent of these movements, but if they were very extensive, it seems likely that a seasonal recurrence of some of the European bats would by now have been noticed in northern Africa.

Recently Count von Finckenstein and H. Schaeffer (1934) recorded an interesting observation they made at Ullersdorf in Oberlausitz of a diurnal bat migration — or such it seemed to be — on a fine warm afternoon, September 25, 1933, with a light south-southeast wind and an overcast sky, temperature 17° C. At about 4 P.M. they first noticed the bats, numbers of which were flying more or less associated with two species of swallows. Both bats and swallows were in general passing due south, feeding as they went, in a leisurely sort of way. In the first quarter of an hour one hundred bats were counted and at least as many swallows, their course in general following the river valley toward the deep pass through the Königshainer Mountains. They were flying against the light breeze, hawking for insects as they passed, while now and then some would dart down over a pool of the river to skim its surface. Unfortunately, the species of bat could not be determined with certainty, but they appeared to be dark below, with broad ears, and with a span a little greater than that of a swallow. Presently a pair of small falcons appeared, and the observers saw them repeatedly try to catch a bat, but the bats would adroitly dodge the attack, until presently one of the hawks was successful and repaired with his prey to the top of a low oak; they failed, however, in their efforts to induce the falcon to drop the bat. After about an hour and a half of observation it began to be dusk. The bats were apparently still continuing their flight, though the swallows had gone. The observers judged that at least five hundred bats had passed on their southward flight and thought it probable that the species was the barbastelle (Barbastella), a bat that in part at least frequents hollow trees and would be likely to leave them on the approach of colder weather. In color this is a dark frosted brown, recalling the silver-haired bat of North America, which has similar habits.

An earlier observation was reported by Stadler (1922), with the addition of some interesting notes by O. Hepp, of Neuendorf-am-Main, Germany, who in 1890 on the afternoon of a fine autumn day observed, as in the previous case, several hundred swallows passing on migration from east to west, at a height of from sixty to seventy meters. Among them were a number ("viele") of bats whose species he was unable to determine. Another observer, Geyr von Schweppenburg (1923), mentions seeing two bats which he took to be noctules (*Nyctalus noctula*), at half-past one in the afternoon of October 13, 1910, flying westward at the same time that some migrating finches were passing. He refers to a similar note of Altum's. Finally, positive evidence of the long-suspected migration of the noctule has lately been obtained by Eisentraut (1935a), who has carried on extensive experiments in marking bats in Germany with individual numbered bands. In the winter of 1934–35 his collaborator, Dr. W. Meise, banded six hundred noctules taken during their hibernation in a cave near Dresden. These were then allowed to continue their sleep undisturbed. In the following summer three of these individuals were recovered, one from Peine near Hanover, a second from Susk in Poland, and a third from Kaupiai, Tverai district, Lithuania, this last at a distance of 750 kilometers (nearly 468 miles) in a straight line, northeast of its winter quarters. So far, this is the outstanding case of a marked bat's being retaken at a considerable distance from the place where it spent the winter and abundantly confirms the statement of Formosov (1927) that the species is migratory in Russia.

# CHAPTER XVII

# HIBERNATION OF BATS

TWENTY below zero! I could scarce believe it was that cold as I rolled from under a pile of quilts into the dry clear air of a January morning in Vermont. The Green Hills were white under two feet of snow, reflecting the thin winter sunshine. One would as soon have looked for bats at the North Pole! Nevertheless, fortified by a hot breakfast and warm garments, my two companions and I were soon setting forth to investigate a cave in Chittenden County where bats were said to hibernate. An eight-mile drive in the face of a biting wind brought us at length to an isolated farm among the hills, from which we made our way on foot across a field of unbroken snow, to the top of a small hill crowned with bare maples. "This is the place," announced our leader, and sure enough, just ahead was an opening in the snow from which arose a thin vapor, indicating a cavern beneath. The entrance was partly snowed over, but the warmer air from within had kept this ventilating shaft open. We quickly cleared away the drifted snow and, throwing aside outer clothing, prepared to descend through an opening in the ground between some rocks, where there was just room enough to squeeze one's body through.

Half sliding, half crawling, one at a time we went feet first down a slippery, burrow-like passage, past a projecting boulder where we had to turn sidewise to get through, and presently found ourselves in a large underground chamber, where we could stand erect and look about. Our electric flashlights showed a vaulted roof of living rock, some ten feet or more high, with nearly dry side walls of limestone, shutting down about us on all sides, giving an oppressive feeling as if they were about to fall in. The floor on which we stood sloped gently away in front and was wet with the inwash of mud. I produced a thermometer and watched the mercury climb to

42° F.; we were below the frost line! As our eyes became accustomed to the dim light, we made out a few bats hanging singly from the roof, their long fur beaded with moisture, giving them a silvery appearance, while beyond in an angle of the sloping roof, some four or five feet from the floor, were two solid masses of bats, hanging in the silence of a deep sleep. We examined these carefully. The smaller mass consisted of about three hundred and the larger we carefully estimated to contain nearly a thousand individuals, of which the greater part later proved to be the cluster bat (*Myotis sodalis*), a small chestnut-brown species. Our lights held close under them revealed a strange appearance of hundreds of tiny heads and little pinkish faces forming the under surface of the group, as they hung closely packed side by side. They felt cool to the touch, but one's fingers thrust into the mass disclosed a warmth from their bodies.

By this time our lights and the disturbance incident to handling them, even though slightly, started waking them up. This was accompanied at first by a curious soft chippering in unison, sounding like *putta-putta-putta* made with lips. One or two taken in the hand squeaked a few times and bit sleepily at a finger. Soon many were flying about the cavern, or settling in new places on the ceiling, while others disappeared through a low passage to another part of the cave. Here was a smaller and cooler chamber with a cool air current from it to the first chamber. One little cluster of bats consisted of six males; a neighboring group of fifteen was made up of six males and nine females, so that there was no definite segregation of the sexes, while a series of twenty-four picked at random was almost equally divided between the two. Further search later showed no less than six species of bats wintering in this cave. By far the greater number of them were the cluster bats, with scattering individuals of two related and closely similar species, the little brown bat (*Myotis lucifugus*), with yellowish belly and browner back, and the longer-eared *M. keenii septentrionalis*. These may have been associated with the cluster bats more closely than we could determine in the dim light. With these were a few of the big brown bat (*Eptesicus fuscus*), a relative of the European serotine bat.

We next examined more carefully the smaller pockets and crevices of the rocky walls and presently discovered to our delight a fourth and much rarer species of Myotis, showing the yellowish fur and deep black face and ears of the least brown bat (*M. subulatus leibii*). These last were evidently of solitary habits, tucked away one or rarely two together, apart from the main groups, lying belly down in a narrow chink or crevice instead of being suspended by the hind feet. Perhaps their very much smaller and more delicate feet may be cor-related with this habit. A few bats hung here and there separately from the walls, their fur glistening in the light of the lamps, with little beads of condensed moisture. Some of these proved to be the eastern pipistrelle (*Pipistrellus subflavus*), again a rather unsocial species. Here, then, were no less than six species of three genera gathered in from the neighboring region for the winter. The difference in their habits and liking for company was a noticeable characteristic. Writing of what was evidently the same species of cluster bat, Blatchley records that in Indiana he found them associating closely together for hibernation in the same way, and in one place counted 401 individuals hanging in a space one foot wide by one and seven-tenths feet long. As a summer visit to these caves showed them to be untenanted by bats, they evidently are used only for wintering.

Although, unfortunately, it was not possible to keep the wintering bats under observation during their dormant period, this has been done by Hahn (1908) in Indiana. Some of his notes made in caves at Mitchell, Indiana, bring out several interesting points. The place was an underground tunnel in limestone, with a stream flowing in it, whereby the caverns had been dissolved out. The roof had broken through in two places, making large openings. Temperature records were kept for two years in the main chamber and showed a remarkable uniformity, varying from about 51° F. in January to 57° in September. The air was always near the saturation

FIG. 47—Investigating a bat cave in Vermont; many bats were hibernating in crevices and recesses here. Courtesy of George L. Kirk, phot.

FIG. 48—A group of cluster bats (*Myotis sodalis*) in hibernation. Nickwacket Cave, Chittenden County, Vermont. George L. Kirk, phot.

point here. During the summer the bats are absent but begin to come in by early November. In the winter of 1906–07 at least five hundred bats were hibernating here, representing five species, of which the most abundant was probably the cluster bat (*Myotis sodalis*). Two other species of Myotis (*M. keenii septentrionalis*, a long-eared species, and *M. velifer*, a larger one), as well as *Pipistrellus subflavus* and the long-eared bat (Corynorhinus), were among the species wintering here. This cave at a more southern latitude (about 37° north), was much warmer than the one I visited in central Vermont, which may account for the apparently greater activity of its inmates. By carefully marking the spots where individual bats hung dormant, Hahn found that they frequently awoke during the winter months and changed about. Thus, of eighteen bats kept under observation from November 19 to December 3, fourteen had moved within a week, and not one remained in the same spot for two weeks. Later in the winter, however, an exceptional bat stayed in one spot from February 4 to 27. The pipistrelles seemed less active and averaged about two weeks in a given spot, while one remained stationary for forty-four days. In general those that come in during the autumn are fat and well nourished and soon settle down for a prolonged period of lethargy. As the winter advances, the stored fat is drawn upon, and as the bats become thinner their active periods become more frequent. Those seen in clusters now are usually awake and chattering. In late winter and early spring they often fly to the mouth of the cave and may even hang up for further sleep near the entrance. There is thus a constant testing of the conditions at the entrance, until in April or May the outer temperature permits them to leave their retreat for the summer's activity. Since these species pass the summer daylight hours in sleep and hibernate for the greater part of the cold season, Hahn concludes that they must spend nearly five-sixths of their life hanging head downward in the dark!

Further studies of cave bats in southern Minnesota by Swanson and Evans (1936) confirm Hahn's observations. Here the prevailing species was the big brown bat (*Eptesicus fuscus*), with smaller numbers of Pipistrellus and two species of Myotis (*M. lucifugus* and the longer-eared *M. keenii septentrionalis*). Visits to the cave in January, February, and March showed fluctuations in the numbers of bats to be counted. They were readily disturbed and evidently changed about from time to time. Individuals varied greatly in the degree of torpidity, some awakening much more quickly than others when examined and flying with little provocation, while others required as much as three quarters of an hour to come back to consciousness, even when taken out into daylight. The cave temperature in this case varied during the winter from 42° to 45° F. The big brown bat is the one common in the middle of even our large cities of eastern United States and frequently enters houses, perhaps coming down chimneys or through ventilators, to spend the winter tucked away in an attic or an unoccupied room. These individuals wake up from time to time, usually after early January, and may appear some evening flying about corridors or rooms as if searching for an entrance. Occasionally they make their way outside and, becoming chilled, drop to the ground or eventually perish, if the weather is wintry.

An interesting experiment with a big brown bat is related by Dr. Alexander Wetmore (1936). In early December, at Washington, D. C., as he let down an awning over his office window, one of these bats was dislodged from the folds and lay sprawling on the window sill, partly numb with the cold. Constructing a small wooden box, with a double layer of woollen blanket tacked on the inside, he hung the bat in this, upside down, within the folds of blanket. The box was then fastened to the sill and a thermometer placed in it, in such a way that the bulb rested beside the section of blanket containing the bat, while the graduated stem projected from the box where it could be read. A second thermometer fastened close by gave the external air temperature. While the box was not shaded from the afternoon sun, it was exposed to the sweep of west and northwest winds. Here it remained unopened until March 16. By this time these bats have already begun to fly in the latitude of Washington. The box was therefore taken inside and the lid carefully lifted. The bat was found alive and awake, although it had crawled outside the blanket fold, where it had been placed the previous December. Carefully replacing the lid, Dr. Wetmore returned the box to the window sill for four more days, when, on opening it once more, the bat was found resting in a semitorpid state beneath a bit of the blanket on the floor of its prison. The box was left open, and at about half-past five that afternoon the bat was found to have flown; nor did it return. The range of outdoor temperature during the winter of its confinement was much the same as that within the box, varying from 9.6° C. in December to as low as −14° in January (that is, from about 49° F. to about 7 above zero!). Of course, being enwrapped in the woollen blanket and sheltered from wind, the bat was able to conserve heat, which allowed it to withstand these lower temperatures, yet the experiment shows a great resistance to cold.

This interesting habit of hibernation or practical suspension of bodily activity for the cold season is not common to all bats, but occurs chiefly in those members of the family Vespertilionidae that range into the north-temperate zone. These include, therefore, species in the northern hemisphere belonging to the genera Myotis, Pipistrellus, Nyctalus, Eptesicus, Barbastella, Miniopterus, Plecotus, Corynorhinus, and perhaps some others. Probably some of the bats in the more southern parts of the southern hemisphere hibernate, but no evidence bearing on this point is known to me. The horseshoe bats of the Old World family Rhinolophidae, though mostly confined to the tropics, are represented in central Europe and as far north as the British Isles by a larger and a smaller species. Of these at least the latter is known to hibernate regularly, while of the former, the observations of Coward in England seem to indicate that although they spend the winter in caves, their sleep is not very deep. This may have been correlated with the comparatively warm temperature of the caves, 50–52° F., for when visited they were quick to awaken and fly, while frequent observations showed that they moved about at intervals or even went outside in warm spells to feed. A third family, the Molossidae, or free-tailed bats, may probably be included among the hibernators. This group is represented in the tropics of both the Old and the New World, and a few of the species extend to the southern boundaries of the temperate zone. It seems likely that these last undergo hibernation for a shorter or longer time at least. Thus, Vernon Bailey, writing of the "guano bat" of the southwestern United States, says that great numbers resort to the Carlsbad Caverns to winter. He did not arrive, however, until March 11, when a few of the bats were already active, leaving their cavern on warm evenings; but a series of cold nights following kept them in for a week or more, although a few would be found flying about inside the extensive underground chambers, from which they refused to go into the colder air outside. He found the temperature near the floor of the cave to be usually 55° F., and it was said to vary but little throughout the year. A number of the bats were captured for further observation, and he found that when the temperature fell to 50° they became torpid at night, stiff and unconscious, with a body temperature the same as that of the air. If gradually warmed to 60°, they became active, awakening slowly with slight movements of the stiff wings and legs.

Another and larger species of this same family, *Eumops californicus*, the California mastiff bat, is a northern member of the genus, the other members of which are confined to tropical America, including some of the larger West Indian islands. Its habits have been studied by A. B. Howell (1920) in San Bernardino County and a few other localities in southern California. He finds that they become torpid for short periods in winter, though even in late November a colony under observation was still active. One he kept in captivity remained dormant from November 5 to December 13, appearing so inert that it showed no sign of life until he moved its wings. Yet in mid-February, when there was a skim of ice every night, one roosted in an improvised shelter for only three nights. He speaks of often seeing them vibrate their wings while hanging up, doubtless a reaction for increasing the body temperature. Writing of this species and the Mexican free-tailed bat in California, Mrs. H. W. Grinnell has found both active at various times in winter, with no sign of hibernation. Instead, however, she adduces evidence that they seek more sheltered situations at this season and thus may be absent from places occupied in summer. Both these writers find that there may be short periods of cold days during which the bats remain fasting in their retreats, even though they do not seem to undergo the deep lethargy of hibernating species.

It will be interesting to review briefly the investigations of various writers regarding the condition of the bats themselves when in this deep lethargy of hibernation. It comes on gradually with the cooling of the air in late autumn and in general does not take place until the temperature outdoors fails to rise above 50 to 54° F. The caves in which bats hibernate may, as we have seen, in midwinter show a more or less constant temperature that seldom falls below 42°. The hibernating bats themselves cool so that the temperature of their bodies falls from as high as about 104° when they are active (Barkow, 1846), to the temperature of the caves in which they rest. Swanson and Evans made many careful tests, using an accurate thermometer, as well as the more precise method of the electric thermocouple, which makes it possible to test quickly a very small point of the surface without disturbing the torpid bat. Thus, on February 12, when the outside temperature fell to 35°, one cave containing pipistrelles showed 45°, while another, in which the big brown bats were hibernating, stood at 42°. A thermometer thrust among a group of the latter registered 98° F. after the bats had been slightly disturbed, indicating that a certain amount of heat was developed in the group. When, however, they were thoroughly dormant, with the cave temperature at 44°, the thermocouple applied to both the surface of the back and just inside the mouth of a bat showed exactly the same degree of heat, 44°. Others were placed in a cabinet that maintained a constant temperature of 45°, and by means of an ingenious device their temperatures were taken at the same points without having to open the cabinet, with the result that both on the surface of the body and within the mouth the bats showed exactly 45°! The temperature of this chamber was now gradually lowered until it stood at 27.6° F. or about 4° below freezing point, but now it was found that the temperature of the bats did not go so low, remaining from 1.5 to 4° F. above that of the surrounding air in the chamber, but even then it was only a fraction of a degree above 29°. Below this the apparatus did not permit of cooling, but the authors believe that the bats would have died if further cooled. In this they were doubtless correct, for the same experiments have been performed in Europe.

A Russian physiologist, using the noctule bat (*Nyctalus noctula*), the long-eared bat (Plecotus), and the little Daubenton's bat (*Myotis daubentonii*), procured near Moscow in June, subjected them to lowering temperature and found that lethargy was induced as usual. By further cooling he eventually lowered the body temperatures to within 7° F. of the freezing point (39° F.) and found that they would revive. But if their bodily heat went as low as about 30° F. (−1.2° C.) ice crystals formed in the thin membranes of the wings. Even then the bats revived, but if ice crystals began to form, with further cooling, in the fluids of the lungs and heart, the tissue of these organs was destroyed and the bats died within about twenty minutes. The English physiologists Burbank and Young (1934) and the German naturalist Eisentraut (1934) almost simultaneously published the results of investigations independently carried on along these same lines. They are remarkably in accord, although the work of the former pair was carried on chiefly in the laboratory, while Eisentraut's was mainly on cave bats near Berlin in their natural places of hibernation.

All three agree that the hibernation of bats is merely a deeper sleep induced by lowered temperature and that bats have little power of controlling the heat of the body, but, like cold-blooded vertebrates, take their temperature when at rest from that of the surrounding medium. Even in summer this holds true, for in their regular daily sleep the body quickly cools to nearly or quite the room temperature. This is aided by the great expanse of naked membrane of the wings and elsewhere, in which the blood comes close to the surface. Normally, in the latitude of Berlin, Eisentraut found that bats of several species begin to enter the caves in the latter part of November, the little pipistrelles first, with some variation according to the season, whether

FIG. 49—Three Daubenton's bats (*Myotis daubentonii*) in deep hibernation in a cave near Berlin, Germany. The moisture of the cave has covered the bats with dewdrops. Slightly enlarged. Courtesy of Ernst Krause, phot.

colder or warmer than average. Of ten species he found wintering, only the horseshoe bat (*Rhinolophus ferrum-equinum*) lives in the caves the year around, but in winter it seeks deeper levels below the frost line. When normally active in summer bats may show a body temperature as high as 104° F. (40° C.) or even a degree or two higher (to 105.7° F., according to Burbank and Young). When they commence hibernation, as in ordinary sleep, this soon falls as the bat becomes inactive, and soon the temperature is that of the surrounding air. The critical temperature at which the usual nightly activity is suspended and deeper lethargy commences is from about 46° to 50° F. (8° to 10° C.), according to Eisentraut. This accords well with observations of my own, that big brown bats begin to appear about Boston in spring evenings when the outside temperature is near 54°. Below this critical threshold ordinary sleep passes uninterruptedly into deeper lethargy and finally into complete torpidity, with the rate of respiration so low that it is hardly perceptible, and the respiratory movements so reduced that one may wait sometimes several minutes without seeing a sign of life. Swanson and Evans found that in a hibernating big brown bat breathing was irregular and there were long periods when motion completely stopped, lasting from three to eight minutes, with an average of only 4.6 respirations in half an hour. These resting periods would be followed by intervals when for about three minutes or less there might be from 23 to 48 breathings a minute. When gradually awakened, this rate rose to 200 a minute before the bat was able to fly. As to the duration of this lethargy, Eisentraut found, as did the American observers quoted, that a short waking period may not be infrequent in captive individuals kept in cool chambers, though often it may be only a few hours before the bat relapses again into its hibernating state. During this period it may fly about and feed a little if cave insects or spiders are available. Especially, will it drink, since the thinness of the membranes allows considerable evaporation of moisture and the bats wake up thirsty. For this reason, too, they prefer a cave with a moist atmosphere, though different species may vary somewhat in preferring very moist or drier situations. Thus, Barbastella seems to like the drier parts of caves, while the large *Myotis myotis* and its smaller relative *M. daubentonii* hibernate in such damp places that their fur may be beaded with drops of dew.

Hibernation in bats has attracted the notice of European naturalists for more than a century, and many careful studies have been made of its causes and the changes it induces in the

FIG. 50—Sound asleep for the winter; a group of about sixty mouse-eared bats (*Myotis myotis*) hibernating in a cave near Berlin, Germany. Courtesy of Ernst Krause, phot.

body. Thus, Winiwarter (1926) found in hibernating bats in Europe that the mucous lining of the larynx and windpipe becomes thickened, so that less air is admitted in breathing, and the supply of oxygen is thereby reduced automatically. Delsaux (1887) has reviewed at length the observations of older writers on the subject and recounts his own experiments undertaken to determine the conditions under which the reduced activities of the body continue. As early as 1808 Saissy noted the reduced breathing and stated that a hibernating bat could live for more than an hour in an atmosphere devoid of oxygen. Delsaux worked with the long-eared Plecotus and the larger *Myotis myotis* from the grottoes of Maestricht and found them very sensitive to mechanical stimulation, quickly awakening when touched. He observed the lowered rate of respiration and the rapid rise of temperature with awakening. He found that if a hibernating bat was deprived of oxygen, it soon fell to the ground. Later, Rulot (1901) made some interesting studies of bats in hibernation from the same caves. He found that at the end of the hibernating period bats had lost about a third of their original weight, while the water content increased in proportion from 1.499 per cent of the weight in early February to 3.145 per cent by April 23. The proportion of fat is much greater in November at the beginning of hibernation, when he found it was 19.4 per cent of the total weight. It gradually decreased to about 15 per cent by mid-February, to 10 per cent in mid-March, and by the end of hibernation on April 23 was only a trifle over 5 per cent of total weight. The amount of glycogen contained in the body he tested, but found only very small amounts, which diminished slowly from November to March. He concludes that the amount of this substance is too little to be of much importance as reserve food, but the consumption of stored fat and albumen is greater and is much more in late winter or early autumn than it is when the bat first enters upon its hibernation. Further studies on the gases given out or taken in during hibernation have been made by several authors. After careful experiments, Hari (1909) concludes that the exhalation of carbon-dioxide gas and the intake of oxygen are a little over one per cent of the amounts shown when the bat is in normal activity.

Merzbacher (1903) has distinguished four stages in the normal awakening from deep hibernation. The first is the condition of rigidity shown in deep lethargy, with almost no response to handling. The second stage is marked by the beginnings of slight motion, especially observable if the bat is lying on its back, when it will slowly extend first one leg and then the other, as if endeavoring to find a foothold from which it may hang in the normal resting position. This is the so-called "hanging reflex," which will take place even though the fore part of the brain has been removed, and hence is owing to entrance into activity of the medulla oblongata. As the bat passes into the third stage, the forebrain begins to function, there is a more active response and the uttering of slight characteristic sounds, until finally, with the fourth stage, the bat is fully awake and flies away. These stages, however, are not very sharply marked, and the transition from one to the other is uninterrupted. Every variation in increasing activity is accompanied by a gradual rise of temperature of the body to the final active state.

While carrying on their study of hibernating bats in England, Burbank and Young (1934) also made interesting notes on some large fruit bats, Pteropus, in captivity. This tropical species does not, of course, go into a hibernating state, but they found that it maintains a nearly constant body temperature of 33° to 37° C. (91° to 98° F.). If the air temperature becomes cool, these big bats, instead of becoming dormant, maintain their bodily warmth by continual activity, crawling about and shivering, and so by muscular movements producing heat through the chemical processes involved.

Thus, while the small bats of northern regions retain a very primitive, almost reptile-like, condition in their lack of any mechanism whereby the nervous system reacts to maintain a nearly even temperature, they nevertheless can survive cold climates by withdrawing locally into sheltered places for the winter and sleeping away the frigid season in a state so inactive that very little energy or food is required. Eisentraut also points out that this ready response to cool conditions may serve them even in summer, when a series of chilly, rainy days reduces the activity of insects on which they feed. For at such times they may hang up for several days on end and, with lowered temperature and reduced bodily processes, undergo a long fast with little discomfort.

# CHAPTER XVIII

# THE ENEMIES OF BATS

BATS have few enemies. Even the large flying foxes (Pteropus) that hang in companies by day from the exposed tops of trees, where they must be very conspicuous, appear nevertheless to live in comparative security. Other smaller kinds for the most part hide away in the daytime and are active at dusk or by night, thus escaping most of the predators. In the tropics a few of the larger bats prey to some extent upon their smaller relations, as already mentioned under food habits. These are chiefly the false vampire (*Lyroderma lyra*) of India and its relative (Macroderma) of Australia, and the large spear-nosed bats (Phyllostomus and Vampyrus) of the American tropics. Otherwise, there are no mammals that regularly make bats an article of their diet. Once in a while, to be sure, the house cat may bring in one that it has chanced upon, fluttering on or near the ground, but it seems not to like the musky scent and usually leaves it uneaten. A few other carnivorous mammals pick up a bat now and then, sometimes adding it to their slender fare. Thus, Sperry (1933) has recorded finding fragments of two silver-haired bats (*Lasionycteris noctivagans*) in the stomach of a skunk killed in January in the Pisgah National Forest, North Carolina; the skunk had also eaten insects and centipedes. The same author on another occasion found the remains of a red bat (*Lasiurus borealis*), together with those of various insects and a mole, in the stomach of a Virginia opossum in the same forest. Probably in both these cases the bats had become chilled and were picked up incidentally during nightly prowlings, for it must be exceptional for these mammals to secure a bat.

Of predatory birds, owls and hawks occasionally eat bats and in a few cases depend largely on them. The scent is evidently not a deterrent, since birds have little power of smell.

One would expect that owls, being like bats of nocturnal habits, would frequently catch and eat them, and probably a few species do. Yet in Dr. A. K. Fisher's work on the food of hawks and owls in the United States, in the preparation of which he examined nearly 2,700 stomachs of these birds, he lists but a single case in which bat remains were found, namely in the stomach of a great horned owl, from Virginia, taken October 23, 1888. This bird had eaten a silver-haired bat in addition to a cottontail rabbit, spider, and katydid! Yet probably bats are more often taken than this record indicates. Within the city limits of Cambridge, Massachusetts, a few screech owls still haunt the cavities of old trees or seek refuge in recesses of the old buildings. In such places they must now and then come upon the big brown bat (*Eptesicus fuscus*) that frequents our eastern cities in summer and winters in the houses, for on more than one occasion I have found bones and skulls of this bat mingled with feathers and bones of house sparrows or the bones of house mice in the owls' regurgitated pellets. In the marshes near San Diego, California, L. M. Huey (1926) found skulls of the western red bat (*Lasiurus borealis teliotis*) and of the whitish *Pipistrellus hesperus* in pellets probably cast up by the short-eared owl, while in Illinois, Cahn and Kemp (1930) in similar pellets of the long-eared owl found remains of two hoary bats (*Lasiurus cinereus*) and three twilight bats (*Nycticeius humeralis*), the latter a rather uncommon species for that state, where it reaches nearly its northernmost limit. As these authors suggest, it seems hardly possible that the bats were caught on the wing, yet in India, McCann (1933) reports a brown hawk owl (*Ninox scutulata*) pursuing and capturing a pipistrelle, which, to be sure, is a rather weak-flying species.

Probably the barn owl (Tyto) more frequently than other owls takes toll of bats. This may be because, like many bats, it is a cave frequenter or passes the day in hollow trees, as various bats do, and so more often comes upon them. This owl, in one or another race, is found over most of the temperate and tropical parts of the world and has a varied diet, chiefly of small rodents, with the occasional addition of birds and insects or other items. Bats are not infrequently found in the stomachs or the regurgitated pellets of these owls. Unexpectedly, perhaps, the rousettes, species of smaller fruit bats, are sometimes taken, for Bonhote (1910) writes that when at certain seasons of the year the Egyptian species (*Rousettus aegyptiacus*) comes in numbers to feed on the ripening fruit of fig trees in the Zoological Gardens at Giza, the barn owls get a great many. The larger fruit bats, Pteropus, are perhaps too powerful to be easily killed, even by these owls.

In an interesting account of a year's food of the Australian barn owl (*Tyto alba delicatula*), Lea (1922), writing from Adelaide, South Australia, gives a list of the animals identified among 730 pellets of this species collected under its roosting place. This number is based on the fact that an average of two such pellets is cast up daily. He found that most of the remains were those of the introduced rats, mice, sparrows, and starlings, but among miscellaneous items were the remains of seven bats of unidentified species. In the West Indies barn owls are found taking refuge by day in limestone caves, which in some places offer shelter also to numbers of bats. The owls prey readily on this plentiful food supply. The regurgitated pellets of owls, containing skulls and bones of bats and other animals, collect beneath their cavern roosts and in time, by infiltration of limy water, become more or less covered or may be partly mixed with cave earth and so preserved. These accumulations may occasionally form really considerable deposits, affording a knowledge of the bat fauna of the place in former times. Thus, G. S. Miller (1918) records finding in owl pellets from Haiti skulls representing five species of bats, including the genera Brachyphylla, Ardops, Artibeus, and Erophylla, of which two proved to be new local races. Similarly, Dr. F. M. Chapman found skulls of *Phyllonycteris poeyi*, a rare species, in barn owl pellets from Trinidad, Cuba. Probably the owls catch the bats as they hang at rest in the caves. The list of species that occasionally eat bats will doubtless be increased with further observation.

By contrast with owls, hawks are nearly all diurnal, hunting by day, so that they seldom have occasion to catch bats. Yet now and then a bat, chancing to be abroad in the daylight hours, may find itself pursued by a hawk. Thus, Percival and Dodson, while investigating a cave in Lahej, Arabia, found in it a large colony of the small fruit bats, *Rousettus amplexicaudatus*, numbers of which flew out into the daylight when disturbed; presently a thud would be heard as a bat was knocked to the ground by a stooping falcon. Some years ago my friend Dr. John B. May told me of seeing a sparrowhawk (*Falco sparverius*) unsuccessfully pursue a red bat (*Lasiurus borealis*) that happened to be abroad in the late afternoon, but the bat's swift and irregular flight saved its life. In Germany, von Finckenstein and Schaeffer (1934) recount observations made at Ullersdorf, in Oberlausitz, on a daytime migration of bats and swallows. At one time a pair of falcons appeared and made repeated stoops at passing bats, usually without success, although eventually one of them was seen on a low oak tree holding what appeared to be one of the bats. Another writer, Payn (1933), reports that in Suffolk, England, on several evenings he saw a kestrel at dusk pursuing bats in and out among the trees. Finally, returning with a gun, he saw the same thing again and shot the bird. In its stomach were the remains of a field mouse, as well as part of the body and wing of a small bat, apparently the rather slow-flying pipistrelle, which comes out while it is still light. This case is particularly interesting as showing how a falcon might develop the habit of frequently pursuing bats, especially those that fly in the early dusk. Exactly such a habit seems to have become a part of the usual behavior of the little white-throated falcon (*Falco albigularis*) of the American tropics, where the bat supply is fairly plentiful. This hawk subsists chiefly on grasshoppers and small birds but has learned to become somewhat crepuscular, continuing its daytime activities into the early dusk, and feeding in part on bats which it captures by direct pursuit. One author mentions seeing it pursue a large moth in the early evening. Probably its attacks on bats are limited to a few species that begin to fly while there is still some light, such as the free-tailed bats of the genera Molossus and Tadarida.

It may have been one of these hawks that so impressed the old missionary, Ligon, in Barbados. In his history of that island, published in 1673, he writes of birds seen there: "And for Hawkes, I never saw but two, and those the merriest stirrers that ever I saw fly; and one of them was in an evening just at Sun setting, which is the time the Bats rise, and soare to a good hight; and at a downcome, this *Barbary* Faulcon took one of them and carried it away." Writing of this same hawk, Murie (1935) reports that the stomach of a bird shot on Mountain Pine Ridge, Guatemala, held remains of a *Molossus aztecus*, a free-tailed bat, while Peters (1929) tells of another taken at Lancetilla, Honduras, whose crop contained skin, flesh, and parts of the skull of a bat, while the stomach held bones, hair, and partly digested flesh of other bats. He suggests that there may have been some ready source of supply, such as a roosting colony, which was visited by the bird, for at nine o'clock in the forenoon, when the specimen was killed, the flesh of the bats had hardly begun to digest. Little seems to be recorded of this bird, but it is interesting that, unlike many falcons which strike down their prey, then return to retrieve it, it seizes its quarry in mid-air, perhaps to avoid losing it in the dim light. This is then possibly a special adaptation of hunting habits to this special prey.

A still more remarkable case is that of the bat falcon of the Old World tropics, which has become specially adapted for feeding on bats. In its typical form this small hawk, known as *Machaerhamphus alcinus*, is found in the tropical forested country from eastern India to New Guinea, and is represented by a related race, *anderssoni*, in Africa from Liberia and the Cameroons to Madagascar and Natal. It haunts the forested banks of rivers and the edges of openings and is chiefly nocturnal in its habits, appearing at dusk and remaining active into the hours of darkness. It has especially large eyes for a hawk, the better to utilize the failing twilight, and its bill is short, delicate, and sharply hooked. The mouth is unusually wide, reminding one of the nightjars, for like them it seizes its prey on the wing. It is rather a rare species and because of its night-feeding habits is seldom seen.

The best account of it is that by Dr. J. P. Chapin (1932), who secured specimens in the Congo. Of his eleven birds two had the stomach empty, but the remaining nine showed eleven bats, one palm swift, six bank swallows, and five other small birds. Insects are said also to form part of the diet, but in those noted by Chapin, bats constitute full 50 per cent. This naturalist recounts that once on the Dungu River he shot one in the gathering darkness and found to his surprise that its crop and stomach held four bats, representing four species, three of which were later described as new from his collections! Two of these were free-tailed bats of the family Molossidae, swift-flying species, so that the bird's feat is the more notable. On another occasion he watched a hawk, having missed in its pursuit of a small pratincole, "making a round of about seventy-five yards in diameter," circling low over the water as if searching for small bats, which often fly close to the surface. This action was seen on two successive nights, but the stomach of the bird, which he finally shot, was empty. Another specimen, taken near the riverside village of Bombwa, contained two bats and a small bird. Their prey seems usually to be swallowed whole, on the wing, an action for which the very wide gape of the bird is admirably adapted. Chapin concludes that since the bats are not torn apart before eating, but show deep wounds, they are probably caught in the bird's talons, which are long and sharp-pointed.

Another interesting account of this bird and its habits in British North Borneo is given by H. Pryer (1884), who observed its hunting methods in the vicinity of a great cave, inhabited by vast numbers of a free-tailed bat, *Chaerephon plicatus*, as well as by multitudes of the small swift that makes the edible birds' nests. The entrance most used by the bats is a great circular chasm going sheer down into the earth. Shortly before sunset, in late March, "columns" of the bats began to appear, rising above the edge of the opening, wheeling around a high tree on the opposite side from the observer. At intervals of a few minutes a large flight would break away and, after rising high in the air, would disappear in the distance. He counted nineteen such companies going off in this way, and they continued in an uninterrupted stream until darkness settled down. Among this vast multitude were three albino bats, called by the Malays, who knew the cave well, "the rajah, his son, and wife." Just before sundown, a pair of the brahminy kites, ever present in the eastern tropics, appeared and, "taking their station over the Bat-chasm, would every now and then clumsily swoop down into the thick of the bats, generally securing a victim every time." Both these marauders he shot. In contrast to the kites were the "business-like" actions of several of the bat falcons. They would single out and pursue a bat, catching and swallowing it on the wing. Just before dawn he observed the return of the bats, which literally rained into the chasm for nearly two hours, appearing as small specks, then flashing perpendicularly down with great rapidity to disappear in the darkness of the pit below. The bat falcons were also on hand at this time, and in addition to the bats they also took toll of the swifts now just emerging for their daytime flight. In his *Birds of British India* Stuart Baker speaks of this hawk as seldom seen, though not uncommon in the Malay peninsula. It usually appears about six o'clock in the evening, haunting well-wooded country in the vicinity of limestone cliffs, in the numerous caves of which vast numbers of bats harbor. In Siam the late Dr. W. L. Abbott once found four specimens of a small bat, *Myotis muricola*, in the stomach of one of these hawks (Miller, 1898, p. 331), adding another species to the list of bats preyed upon.

No doubt bat caves such as the one described are well known to the hawks in the vicinity and are regularly visited by them. A graphic account is given by A. R. S. Anderson (1925) of a gathering of predatory birds about a bat cave in Burma, some twenty-six miles above Moulmein, on the Salween River. The entrance to the cave is about twelve feet in height and nearly twice that distance above the stream, in the base of an isolated limestone hill. Thousands of the common free-tailed bat (*Chærephon plicatus*) inhabit the cave by day and at sunset issue in "a dense stream which slowly becomes more and more closely packed, gradually thinning again, until in about twenty minutes all have emerged." At sunset he saw a pair of falcons leave their perch on trees near the summit of the hill and begin to fly back and forth near the cave, as if waiting for the fun to begin. Presently they were joined by brahminy kites, common kites, and jungle crows, until eventually a company of sixty to a hundred birds had gathered in expectation and were wheeling about near the opening of the cavern. "When the great rush occurs, the falcons, kites and crows enter the stream of bats and flying along in, and with it, and striking right and left, seize as many bats as they require." The bats in this outpouring often collide with one another and fall into the river below, whereupon they paddle themselves ashore with their wings, only to fall prey to an expectant crow.

Bats probably have few enemies among the reptile tribe. Phillips in Ceylon suggests that the large lizard, Varanus, may occasionally capture a few roosting in hollow trees, for it is an active climber. That a few species of snakes are bat-catchers, however, seems unexpected, yet this is the case. In the southern United States some of the long slender colubrid snakes included under the popular name of "Chicken Snake" sometimes frequent the retreats of roosting bats and prey upon them regularly. Dr. Charles A. R. Campbell (1925), in his book on the question of bats versus mosquitoes, tells that once while observing bats in an old barn in Texas he killed one of these snakes that had swallowed fourteen bats (species not mentioned), a large order! Another instance is supplied by C. W. Hibbard (1934), who, while exploring Dancer's Cave in Kansas, came upon a "rat snake" (*Elaphe laeta*) in one of the smaller chambers that had recently swallowed one of the large fringed Myotis (*M. velifer incautus*). Three days later another snake of the same species, "apparently in search of bats," was discovered in a crevice in the roof of a cave in Comanche County.

A friend once told me of killing a black snake in Pennsylvania that had a small bat in its stomach, and in another instance supplied me by Mr. B. Patterson Bole a snake killed in California had caught one of the large pale cave bats (*Antrozous pallidus*), common in parts of the Southwest, and had in its stomach the remains of another, perhaps of the same species. This bat will frequently alight on the ground to capture beetles and at such times no doubt may fall prey to a waiting snake, for some are largely nocturnal in habits. Silver (1928) reports a still more interesting case that came to his notice while investigating a colony of big brown bats (*Eptesicus fuscus*) that lived inside the boxed-in eaves of an attic in Maryland. On removing the boards, he found a 38-inch pilot black snake (*Elaphe obsoleta*) that had taken up its abode in the midst of the bats and was apparently making regular meals of them. Further search disclosed four cast snake skins in the compartment, indicating that the marauder had occupied this retreat for a considerable time and grown large on its diet.

Probably tree-living bats are seldom caught by snakes, but this does occasionally happen. Such an instance is reported by Mr. Arthur Loveridge, who, while collecting in Kenya Colony, eastern Africa, captured a large black mamba, a highly poisonous cobra-like serpent that occasionally climbs trees. On opening its stomach, he found a freshly swallowed specimen of the big-eared orange-winged bat (*Lavia frons*). This bat hangs up by day among thorn trees or in the shelter of vine-covered bushes and, if approached, at once betrays its presence by the constant motion of its long sensitive ears. No doubt a tree-climbing snake would be quick to catch sight of this movement and stealthily glide within striking distance.

In Cuba it is well known to the natives that the Cuban boa (*Epicrates angulifer*) is a bat-catching snake. It reaches a length of fifteen feet or more and regularly frequents caves for the sake of the bats which roost there. The late William Palmer, whose notes are quoted by Miller (1904, p. 346), described a bat cave in Guanajay Mountain, the vertical opening of which was about twelve feet across and partly concealed by bushes. This cave was inhabited by thousands of bats of a species confined to the West Indies, *Phyllonycteris poeyi*, one of the leaf-nosed family and a fruit feeder. In early June the females were big with their single young, but later the little ones of different sizes were found scattered, hanging from the roof of the cave. On one side of the vertical opening of this cave grew a large tree, the roots of which descended like a stream into the cavity. Here, as Palmer was assured by the people living in the vicinity, the *majás* (as the Cubans call this boa) would coil themselves among the roots and make swift snatches at the bats as they flew out. He was told that the snake is frequently successful in securing the bats in this way. This account is corroborated by Dr. Thomas Barbour (1919), not only from the lips of a "wholly trustworthy" local naturalist, but also from his own experience. He describes a large cave at Maisi which he explored. Just within the entrance it opened into a large chamber whence a rapidly narrowing passage led to a second large hall. Here he and his companion heard a peculiar sound and found that

the whole floor of the cave was one seething mass of enormous cockroaches and that the noise was the result of the rubbing of one another as they struggled about. Large centipedes were moving back and forth across this living floor. Our lights showed a veritable inferno in miniature. Bats flew about in great clouds, the stench was overpowering and the chambers still further in were so fearfully hot that no entrance was possible. On our way out in the narrow passage between the first two halls a large majá was ensconced in a hole at about the level of one's shoulders and with several feet of his body projecting he was making vicious lunges at the passing and repassing bats which we had stirred up. We finally got him by the neck and with some labour hauled him free.

In the eastern tropics another snake of the colubrid type, *Coluber taeniatus*, found in India and Siam, is reputed to have a similar liking for bats and has become so adapted to cave haunting that its color tends to be pallid, like that of certain other animals which spend their lives in darkness. This snake is said to frequent the extensive Batu caverns of Selangor, living in part at least upon the many bats that frequent them.

Large trout sometimes catch bats, as Dr. C. H. Merriam has reported (in Murphy and Nichols, 1913, p. 10). Probably such captures are made at evening when many bats visit quiet pools and, flying low, skim the surface for a drink. The quick rush of a feeding trout is at times doubtless swift enough to intercept the bat.

Bats appear to have few other predaceous creatures to fear. In the warmer countries, however, where large spiders spread their strong webs, some of the small, weak-flying species are sometimes entangled. This was reported nearly a century ago by Dr. Theodore Cantor (1842), while stationed in medical capacity at Chusan Island, off the mouth of the Yangtse River, China. He wrote that the common small pipistrelle of eastern China is "frequently arrested in the strong web of two large spiders, *Epeira bilineata* and *heraldica* . . . which circumstance has given rise to the common erroneous belief that those and similar spiders feed upon bats." He believed the small bat was new and named it *irretitus* from the fact of its being thus netted.

Probably ants sometimes attack colonies of bats in the tropics, where, especially in parts of Africa, the dreaded driver ants are common. These will be found on the march in a narrow column which may sometimes be traced for hundreds of feet, when the vanguard deploys, swarming over trees, huts, or dwellings, pouring down into burrows, and spreading terror to every living thing in their foray. Writing of a sojourn in Nyasaland, Coudenhove (1925) describes the raids of driver ants — there locally known as "bambesi"— upon a colony of bats that lived between the corrugated iron and cloth ceiling of his house. The armies of ants would swarm up the posts of the veranda or drop to the roof from adjacent trees and attack the bats in their daytime quarters. On such occasions the adult bats would leave through their loopholes and fly out into the glaring midday sun, while the young were invariably killed or, if large enough, would scramble down the outside brick walls, only to be met at the bottom by other hosts. After seven months the bats and the author both abandoned the house.

Accidents sometimes overtake bats. I once saw the dried and shriveled body of a large flying fox or gray-headed fruit bat in

New South Wales resting by its outstretched wings across two electric wires on the outskirts of Kempsey. A large fig tree close at hand explained the matter. The bat, in coming to the tree at night for the figs, had endeavored to pass between the

Fig. 51—A gray-headed fruit bat (*Pteropus poliocephalus*) electrocutes itself in trying to reach a fig tree. Kempsey, New South Wales.

wires, but on striking both wings against them had created a short circuit and been electrocuted! Several cases are on record of bats that had evidently flown too near the hooked burrs of burdocks and, becoming hopelessly entangled, were unable to free themselves and perished. A still more curious disaster is reported by B. Campbell (1931) from Riverside County, California, on the edge of the Colorado Desert. A small reservoir, formed by damming an intermittent stream, was found in late December to have frozen to the depth of two or three inches, and in this ice were imbedded over forty Mexican free-tailed bats (*Tadarida mexicana*). Since there was no other standing water for miles about, Campbell supposes that the bats had come to drink at the surface but instead had struck thin ice and become stunned, later sinking more or less in, probably through slight melting at the warm part of the day.

# CHAPTER XIX

# THE PARASITES OF BATS

In a classic monograph published in 1853 Joseph Leidy, who was an authority both on fossils and on intestinal parasites, emphasized the fact that probably most of the higher animals during their lifetime support a fauna and flora within their bodies. Many of these parasites, if not unduly numerous, may cause no apparent harm to the host, while others may be distinctly harmful. Others again may even be beneficial. Thus, many quite harmless bacteria are regularly found within the mouths of healthy human beings, and Leidy gives a considerable list of the internal parasites of man. Bats are no exception to the rule that most, perhaps all, mammals may support such a fauna within themselves. These parasites are of two chief types: minute one-celled organisms which may be either plants (bacteria) or animals (Protozoa), and more highly organized forms, comprising various sorts of parasitic "worms," which, although of unpleasant association in the minds of most people, are none the less remarkable in their extreme degree of specialization for their strange mode of life. Many of these parasites pass through several stages of development, some of them in different hosts, and the several stages may bear almost no likeness to one another. In addition to these unseen companions, most mammals harbor a certain number of external parasites, chiefly mites and insects, all of which again show remarkable modifications in their structure to enable them more easily to survive under these special conditions.

The parasites of bats have only begun to be known, yet a summary catalogue of those reported up to 1930, published by Stiles and Nolan (1931), presents a formidable array. A perusal of this list brings out clearly that relatively few species of bats have been carefully studied, and this seems particularly true of tropical bats, among which one might expect to find the most parasites. Several European bats have been more thoroughly investigated, with the result that, while many individuals appear to be quite clean of parasites, the sum total of those known to occur in the species as a whole may be large. For example, the common greater horseshoe bat (*Rhinolophus ferrum-equinum*) has been found to harbor intestinal sporozoans of the genus *Eimeria*; a plasmodium of the genus *Grahamella*; stomach-worms of the genera *Lecithodendrium*, *Mesotretes*, and *Plagiorchis*; thread-worms of three genera; ticks and mites representing nine distinct genera; fleas of three different genera; and parasitic flies of three genera. The common large mouse-eared bat (*Myotis myotis*) is credited with a similar array in southern Europe, including a plasmodium resembling that of malaria, two sorts of trypanosomes, four genera of ticks and mites representing perhaps over a half-dozen species, two genera with four species of fleas, and four genera with eight species of parasitic flies (streblids and nycteribiids). Though some of the species credited are really synonyms of others, the variety of parasites is obvious. Bats of the genus Miniopterus, the long-fingered bat, with a wide range in the warmer parts of the Old World from southern Europe and the continent of Africa to Australia, seem especially infested by parasites, for at least the more conspicuous mites and parasitic insects usually abound in these bats. There are listed for the large European species, *M. schreibersii*: two blood parasites (a plasmodium and a trypanosome), two genera of stomach-worms, two of tapeworms, four of thread-worms, eight of mites and ticks, five of parasitic flies, but curiously none of fleas, as if the array were sufficient without them.

Phillips (1924a), who has given special attention to the ectoparasites of bats in Ceylon, points out a number of interesting facts. He finds the horseshoe and leaf-nosed bats generally free from these creatures, only rarely harboring a wingless fly or a nycteribiid. This he attributes to the bats' habit of hanging spaced apart in their caverns instead of in close contact with one another, so that there is less opportunity for the parasites to pass from one host to another. These parasites often show marked preferences for certain genera of bats as hosts. Thus, of the two families of parasitic flies, the wingless nycteribiids and the winged streblids, the fruit bats were found often to be victimized by the former, but in no instance by the latter. On the giant fruit bat (*Pteropus giganteus*) there were found in nearly every one examined from one to eleven large nycteribiids of the species *Cyclopodia sykesi*, while on the smaller species, the short-nosed fruit bat (*Cynopterus*), a smaller insect of the same genus occurs. Indeed, most of the known species of Cyclopodia are reported from fruit bats of the Old World, with at least one that occurs on several of the vespertilionids. In contrast, the false vampires of Ceylon were found to be often swarming with the small parasitic winged flies of the family Streblidae, but no nycteribiids.

It will be interesting to recall in brief review some of these bat parasites. Of the microscopic blood parasites, there are a number of records for those of the genus Plasmodium, the group to which the malarial organism belongs. Of the half-dozen or so different ones recorded from bats, the first to be made known was one discovered by Dionisi in 1899 and named by him *Plasmodium melaniferum*. It is known from Myotis (two species), Miniopterus, and Vespertilio of Europe. A second one, *P. murinum*, which he described at the same time, occurs in the blood of Vespertilio, Myotis, and a South African species of Eptesicus. One or two others have since been named from related eastern bats, while another, *P. pteropi*, occurs in fruit bats, with records from places as far apart as Australia (in *Pteropus gouldi*) and Africa (in the epaulet bat [Epomophorus]). In the latter case the organism may be the same as that named by Rodhain in 1926, *P. epomophori*, found in the last-named genus and in the hammer-headed bat (Hypsignathus), also of West Africa. Notwithstanding that these organisms are similar to the malarial parasites of man, it is not known that bats contract the disease or act as reservoirs for it. However, Dr. Richard P. Strong (1930) has described and beautifully figured a plasmodium from the blood of an African hollow-faced bat (*Nycteris grandis*) of Liberia, the only case found in various bats examined. These malarial organisms were fairly abundant, and the infected blood cell usually showed much enlargement. The same unfortunate bat also harbored blood parasites of the genus Grahamella and an undetermined trypanosome. These last are minute, one-celled structures, some species of which live in the blood stream of animals, others in plant fluids. They occur in three different forms, which probably represent stages in the life history of single species. In one stage they appear as blood parasites of more or less circular outline, a stage at first supposed to represent an independent kind of organism, and named Leishmania. In the second stage they have a long, slender, cigar-shaped body, with a lash or filament at one end, the motions of which propel the parasite, now known as a crithidia. The third type is the more typical trypanosome, resembling the last, but having in addition a transparent frill or membrane-like structure running the length of the body, and capable of aiding progress by its undulating motions.

It is these parasites that cause the dreaded sleeping sickness in man and the "nagana" or horse disease in Africa. Trypanosomes were first discovered in bats by Edmond and Etienne Sergent in 1905, while examining the white-edged pipistrelle (*Pipistrellus kuhli*) and the large Myotis, probably *M. oxyotis*, of Tunis and Morocco. They found what appeared to be two different kinds, one slender and ribbon-shaped with a short lash or propeller, and the other stouter. The first moved so rapidly that it was difficult to keep it in the microscope field, but the second was a much slower-moving type. In two cases both kinds were found in the blood of a single pipistrelle, though in others only one of the forms appeared in a given individual. These authors were inclined to believe that the two represented distinct species, which they named *Trypanosoma nicolleorum* and *T. vespertilionis*, respectively. They inoculated white mice, white rats, and young rabbits with these trypanosomes, but since, after three months, all the animals seemed perfectly well in the laboratory, they concluded that the parasites are non-pathogenic and relatively innocuous. Bats from these same colonies, if examined in winter or spring, showed none of the trypanosomes, which possibly are killed by exposure of their hosts to the relatively cool temperatures of those seasons. For Kalabuchov and Levinson (1935) have recently shown that trypanosomes of horse sickness (*T. equiperdum*), inoculated in the noctule bat (*Nyctalus noctula*) and *Pipistrellus nathusii*, not only do not develop if the bats are cooled to near the freezing point (3°–10° C.), but even disappear altogether from the blood. Unfortunately, such treatment is as yet impracticable for human beings! The Sergents report also finding forms of trypanosomes in bedbugs which, they say, came from the bat colony and were often seen crawling on the walls of the building. No connection, however, is made between the latter and any disease, although it is implied that these insects may act as vectors, to infect the bats.

Two genera and a number of species of trypanosomes have since been reported for bats, and it has been found possible to infect some of them experimentally with *Trypanosoma gambiense*, the organism of sleeping sickness. Bats from which species of these parasites are known include the African big-eared bat (*Lavia frons*) and two tropical American bats of the leaf-nosed family, the back-striped bat (*Vampyrops lineatus*) of Venezuela, and a Cuban species, probably Artibeus.

Three types of worms are known to inhabit the interior of the bodies of mammals, the trematodes or flukes, the cestodes or tapeworms, and the nematodes or hair- and thread-worms. Of the first, the liver fluke of sheep and cattle is perhaps the best known. These are small, an inch or less in length and leaf-shaped, or some may be nearly round and unsegmented. Their structure is simple: a mouth at the anterior end, a much-branched intestine filling the expanded body, with corresponding branches to make an excretory system, and finally a pair of suckers, or sometimes only a single one for attachment to the walls of the ducts of the host. It is thus a creature reduced to simplest terms, whose main functions are to hang on and to absorb food from its host. It reproduces by eggs and sperm and may be self-fertilizing. Great numbers of eggs may be produced, thus increasing the chances that some, in passing from the food canal of the host, may fall in a place favorable for development. These internal parasites have two hosts, the first usually an invertebrate, which, after infection by the trematode, may be eaten by a mammal or a bird, where the parasite then proceeds to develop through its second stage. Thus, the liver fluke of sheep first enters a snail, and then, after passing one stage there, escapes and attaches itself to grass stems in wet places, where the grazing sheep takes it in. The parasite thus enters the stomach and finally lodges in the sheep's liver, to start a new cycle.

A study of the index to bat parasites published by Stiles and Nolan in 1931 reveals an astonishing number of trematodes already reported for these mammals, representing no less than fourteen genera and over forty species. The differences between these genera are in minute details visible only with a microscope, and even the species are probably not all clearly defined. Yet a summary shows that these parasites have been found in twenty genera of bats representing eight of the seventeen recognized families. The most widely distributed genus of trematodes is known as Lecithodendrium, of which no less than twenty-three species have been described as parasitizing bats. They have been found in at least six of the seventeen families, including ten genera of vespertilionids, chiefly European, two of free-tailed bats or molossids, the Old World horseshoe bats, Rhinolophidae, the mouse-tailed bat, Rhinopomidae, the African big-eared bat, *Lavia*, of the family Megadermidae, and two genera of the family Emballonuridae or sheath-tailed bats. They occur, therefore, in both hemispheres and no doubt will be discovered in many other genera when further studies are made. Of American bats parasitized by this genus of flukes the red bat (*Lasiurus borealis*) and one of the small brown bats, *Myotis "subulatus"* (probably meant for *M. lucifugus*), are the only vespertilionids from which it is known, while Molossus and Peropteryx are the molossid and emballonurid hosts, respectively. Only two other genera besides Lecithodendrium, namely Plagiorchis and Dicrocoelium, are known from bats of both hemispheres; eight other genera are as yet reported from those of the Old World only, while three have not been found in bats other than New World species.

Some of the genera may be peculiar to particular types of bats. Thus one genus, Pycnoporus, with four species, has been found in bats of the genus Pipistrellus only, from Japan to Egypt and Europe. On the other hand, flukes of the third genus, Anchitrema, are found in bats of three different families, horseshoe bats, the big-eared bat of Africa, and sheath-tailed bats of the genus Taphozous. Another genus, Urotrema, is known from three other families of tropical America, including the fish-eating bats (Noctilionidae), the free-tailed bats (Molossidae), and the leaf-nosed bats (Phyllostomidae). This last was reported from the spear-nosed bat, *Phyllostomus*, of carnivorous habits, and is the only known record for the family. Still more recently, a new genus of cestode, Glyptoporus, has been discovered by Macy (1936) in the little brown bat in Minnesota. The bat most favored by the trematodes seems to be the Eurasian genus Nyctalus, including the common noctule bat of the Old World. This is known to be a migratory species, so that its wide-ranging habits may to some extent be correlated with the fact that no less than five genera of flukes have been reported from it. Another interesting point is that no flukes are reported from the flying foxes and their relatives comprising the family Pteropidae of the Old World tropics, nor are any known from the South American fruit-eating members of the family Phyllostomidae, although the insect-eating and carnivorous species of this latter group may be expected to show them, as in the case of the spear-nosed bat. The explanation probably is that the flukes parasitic on bats pass one stage of their existence as parasites of insects, especially those that live as larvae in water. The insectivorous bats, through feeding on these insects in the winged stages, devour the parasites at the same time, thus allowing the flukes to complete their life cycles in the bats as hosts. In proof of this, it has been shown that some of the species of the widespread genus of trematodes, Lecithodendrium, pass one stage as parasites of caddis flies, may flies (or ephemerids), stone flies (or perlids), and in the midges of the genus Chironomus, which swarm about ponds and marshes in the spring and are probably an important food item of bats in early summer. None of the many species of flukes occurring in bats is known to parasitize man, although he may act as host to related or congeneric forms.

Tapeworms or cestodes are less common than trematodes but have become even more thoroughly accommodated to a passive life within the intestine of the host. The adult tapeworm consists of a head or scolex, provided with a ring of hooks and suckers by which it attaches itself to the wall of the gut, and then buds off a long chain of segments, each one of which eventually develops sexual cells and is self-fertilizing. Tapeworms have no food canal but merely absorb nourishment from the digesting food of the host, in which they float. They have no sense organs, no blood system, no breathing system, but the general surface of the body suffices for all these purposes. The joints or segments that form the long, ribbon-like body increase in size from before backward, and the terminal ones at last reach maturity, break off, and pass down the intestine of the host to the exterior. Here they rupture, setting free the fertilized eggs, which, if swallowed by the proper intermediate host, develop in its intestine as embryos. These then bore a way through the intestinal wall, into the muscles or other parts of the host, which in turn falls a prey to the final host, and a new cycle starts. In the case of the tapeworm of man, the intermediate host is the pig. If one chances to pick up the eggs or embryos of the tapeworm in feeding, it retains them in its intestine until they have completed development to a bladder-worm stage, in which they bore into the muscles and become encysted, forming what is known as "measly" pork. If this is eaten by a human being, the cysts develop in his intestine and start the ribbon-like stage once again. Although tapeworms produce a large number of eggs, the chances of their reaching the proper hosts for their development are so small that the adults are comparatively rare. Indeed, Thomson says of the species infesting man that the chances are one in thirty-five million that the embryo will succeed in entering its human host and becoming adult, a slim chance indeed!

Tapeworms were first discovered in bats by Gmelin, a learned doctor and disciple of Linnaeus, who described as *Taenia vespertilionis* a small species from a European bat of an undetermined genus. Later, in 1819, the German naturalist Rudolphi found an allied species in the long-eared bat (*Plecotus auritus*) and a third in several other genera of vespertilionid bats of Europe.

In all, four species of tapeworms, Taenia, have been recorded from bats, including *Taenia taeniaeformis*, of man, but it seems likely that these reports will require revision as we become more discriminating. The bladder-worm stage to which formerly a separate generic name, Cysticercus, was given has been found in the big-eared bat, Schreibers's bat, and another of an undetermined genus. In a recent account Macy (1931) has reviewed the known tapeworms of the genus Hymenolepis, which are placed in a separate family from the Taeniidae, and are known to parasitize several genera of bats. One species, *H. moniezi*, is found in the Indian flying fox; a second, *H. acuta*, is reported from the tomb bat, *Taphozous perforatus*, of Egypt, one of the sheath-tailed family, as well as from five genera of European bats of the family Vespertilionidae; while a third tapeworm (*H. decipiens*) is recorded from Molossus and Eumops, of the Molossidae or free-tailed bats, and from Chilonycteris (of the Phyllostomidae or leaf-nosed family), all from Brazil. To these he adds a fourth, *H. christensoni*, discovered in the common little brown bat (*Myotis lucifugus*) of North America, the second genus in which these parasites have been found on this continent. It is a small tapeworm, with an average length of only 40 mm. In the case of insect-eating bats it seems likely that the insects on which they feed act as the occasional intermediate host, but how the Indian flying fox, a fruit-eating bat, becomes infected does not seem to have been discovered.

The third group of parasitic worms, some of which are found in bats, comprises the thread-worms or nematodes. As the name implies, these are small, whitish, and look like a bit of thread.

Many of the species pass their immature stages in an insect or a small crustacean, and the adult stage in a mammal by which the latter is eaten. Here they may become a danger to the host by blocking the lymph system or causing inflammation elsewhere. Some of the minute species such as Filaria pass the immature stages in the blood or bore into the tissues. Those of European bats have been most investigated, and a number of species are described from common vespertilionid bats, such as the long-eared, noctule, serotine, and the long-fingered bat (Miniopterus). One genus, Strongylacantha, is a parasite of the horseshoe bat (*Rhinolophus ferrum-equinum*), as well as of the long-fingered bat (Miniopterus) in Europe, while related genera are found in free-tailed bats (Eumops) and leaf-nosed bats (Phyllostomus, Carollia and Sturnira) of Brazil, as well as in the Egyptian tomb bat (Taphozous) — a wide distribution. A related type of worm, for which a special class, Acanthocephala, has been proposed, also has a double existence, spending its immature stage in a crustacean or an insect, and its adult life in a mammal. Stiles and Nolan record but a single instance of this type being found in bats, namely, the species *Prosthenorchis novellae*, reported from a Puerto Rican bat identified as Artibeus. Since, however, this is a fruit-eating species, one rather suspects an error in its identification, unless it accidentally had eaten an infected insect.

The external parasites of bats are no less remarkable than the internal, for many of them have evolved special means for survival. They include mites and ticks — distantly related to spiders — having eight legs in the adult state, and also various insects (six-legged) representing the four orders bugs, earwigs, flies, and fleas.

The mites and ticks found on bats are usually very small, with flattened and nearly circular or oval bodies, eight short legs at the small or head end, and sucking mouthparts which form a short stiff proboscis. This is buried in the skin of the host and serves not only for sucking blood but also for an anchorage. The young stages may have only six legs, so that these have at times been mistaken for insects and in one case an immature mite from a British bat was described as a new genus and species of louse, *Acanthophthirius etheldredae*, but the mistake was later rectified (Ferris, 1932), for no lice are known as parasites of bats. One of the first to give much attention to these bat parasites was a European naturalist, Kolenati, who in the 'fifties described a large number of species, now only in part recognizable, from the commoner bats of central Europe. Over forty genera of mites and ticks are listed by Stiles and Nolan. These include *Demodex*, some of which are minute forms living in the follicles at the base of hairs. Two species are known from the long-eared bat (*Plecotus auritus*) of Europe, and a third is reported from the South American spear-nosed bat (Phyllostomus).

Among the ticks, *Argas vespertilionis* is found on various Old World genera, such as Myotis, Barbastella, Pipistrellus, Nyctalus, Eptesicus, Miniopterus (of the Vespertilionidae), and Rhinolophus and Nycteris of Europe and Africa. The single record for a tropical American hare-lipped bat (*Dirias albiventer*) evidently arises from some error. One species of Ornithodoros has been found on a bat from Puerto Rico. Three species of Ixodes are found on horseshoe bats (Rhinolophus) in Europe, Africa, and China, as well as on some of the common genera just mentioned. Other ticks such as Haemaphysalis and Dermacentor are parasites of the common bats of Europe and Africa; while Amblyomma (on Dirias and Carollia) and Spelaeorhynchus (on Artibeus and Carollia) are known in the New World tropics on the leaf-nosed bats particularly. Mites of the family Spinturnicidae chiefly parasitize bats. They have short, bristly legs and are very small, living on the wing membranes. One genus, Ancystropus, is mainly a parasite of the fruit bats, Pteropidae, occurring on such widely separated genera as Pteropus and Macroglossus, Rousettus and Epomophorus of Asia and Africa; it occurs also on the African mouse-tailed bat (Rhinopoma). Mites of the genera Spinturnix and Periglischrus have been reported from many Old World species of bats, but only a very few from American species. One, *Periglischrus meridensis*, was lately described by Hirst (1927)

from the large fruit-eating bat, *Artibeus jamaicensis*, of Venezuela, while at the same time he recorded six species of Spinturnix from Old World bats. Thompson (1935) writes that
the mite, *Spinturnix murinus*, found on the whiskered bat
(*Myotis mystacinus*) and the serotine bat (*Eptesicus serotinus*)

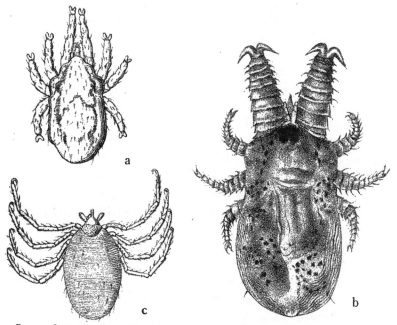

Fig. 52—Some external parasites of bats. (a) A mite (*Argas vespertilionis*) that lives on the
wing membranes of the mouse-eared and horseshoe bats of Europe; (b) an anchor mite
(*Ancystropus zelebori*) from the wing membranes of the rousette bat of Egypt; the anterior
pair of legs is greatly developed and provided with hooklike claws, whereby it anchors itself
to the skin of its host; (c) a slender-legged tick (*Ixodes flavipes*) found on the lower side
of the European horseshoe bats (Rhinolophus). All figures from Kolenati (1857), greatly
magnified.

in Great Britain, is a common species on all European bats,
while others, such as *Ceratonyssus musculi* and *Trombicula
autumnalis*, are often found on mice and voles as well. I have
found mites, perhaps Liponyssus, attached by the proboscis
on Old World specimens of Pipistrellus, either inside the ear
or on the face under the eye, sometimes, in the former situation,
in little groups close together. In such places, no doubt, they
are not easy for the bat to reach in cleaning itself.

Rodhain (1906) has reported a curious habit of an African

mite, related to the itch mite of man, which he calls *Teinocoptes epomophori*. It lives on the wing membranes of such fruit bats as Epomophorus, Epomops, Eidolon, and Micropteropus (all of small or medium size). The males are rare and do not penetrate the skin of their host; but the females, which are believed to live only about four weeks, move about when young, then after fertilization seek the hinder margin of the wings, and boring in, remain fixed in this position.

No less than four orders of insects are represented among the external parasites of bats, the Hemiptera or typical bugs, the Dermaptera or earwigs, the Diptera or two-winged flies, and the Siphonaptera or fleas. Many of these have departed very far from the usual habits and appearance of their group in developing special ways of adjustment to a parasitic life, such as short-cut methods of reproduction and means for clinging or attaching themselves in the hair and skin of the host.

Two families of hemipterous bugs are parasitic on bats. The first is that including the bedbugs (Cimicidae), loathsome insects in which the wings have been lost, perhaps as a result of their parasitic life, although very small vestiges of them remain; the body is as broad as long and, when not gorged, is much flattened for sidling into cracks and crevices from which these pests emerge to attack their host, retiring again after they have sucked its blood. Members of this group are found on birds and bats as well as on man, a very anomalous choice of hosts, but fortunately they are rare on the first two. Of bat bedbugs there are at present known four genera, Cimex, Cacodmus, Leptocimex, and Loxaspis. The first includes the ordinary bedbug, *Cimex lectularius*, parasitic on man, but the species known from bats are probably more or less specific upon these hosts. Thus *Cimex limai* has been described from "a bat" in Brazil; a second species, *C. vespertilionis*, is reported from two kinds of bats in Finland and England; and a third, *Cimex pipistrelli*, from the European pipistrelle. This last, according to Pringault, is the carrier of a blood parasite, Trypanosoma. A fourth species, *Cimex stadleri*, has recently been described from the mouse-eared bat in Germany.

On North American bats bedbugs are rare but have been found on the silver-haired bat (Lasionycteris), the long-legged bat (*Myotis volans*) of the Far West, and the twilight bat (Nycticeius) of the southern United States. On the first of these I once saw a bedbug attached behind the ear of a specimen captured on a fishing boat some distance from land in the Gulf of Maine, and Dr. Arthur A. Allen (1921) has figured a large brown bat (*Eptesicus fuscus*) from New York State with a bedbug attached behind each ear! The photograph was taken by flashlight immediately after the capture of the bat and before the insects had time to crawl off. This species, occasional on American bats in the temperate zone of the north, is *Cimex pilosellus*, which differs from the human bedbug in minute details. Thus the body is covered with longer though very small bristles, the second and third segments of the antennae are of equal length instead of the second's being the shorter, while the vestigial wings have the inner margin straight and longer than the scutellum, instead of rounded and shorter than that structure. That, in spite of their general similarity, the host preferences are quite different is attested by Dr. Allen, who writes that although in collecting the bats, "I was in the attic [where they roosted] for nearly two hours and saw them crawling all around, I received no bites, and careful examination of my clothes failed to reveal a single specimen." The tropical bedbug of man, *Cimex rotundatus*, has been reported by Kunhikannan (1912) in India as infesting the common yellow bat, *Scotophilus kuhlii*, which is often a house bat in that country; but this identification was probably an error, and he admits that his specimens were from a hollow coconut trunk at Tellicherry. At one time it was believed that the bedbug of man carries the organism causing the kala-azar fever of southeastern India, so that all of these insects are looked upon with suspicion from a medical standpoint, but the charge is not proved, and there is evidence now that a small sand fly is the vector. Two other related genera of these insects have been named: Cacodmus with three species from African bats of the genera Eptesicus, Pipistrellus, and Scotophilus; and Loxaspis (or Leptocimex) with two species from the African free-tailed bats (Chaerephon and *Mops angolensis*), as well as an African sheath-tailed bat, *Taphozous hildegardeae.*

The second family of hemipterous bugs parasitic on bats is the Polyctenidae. These differ in many ways from the bed-bugs, although they represent a related group. Like the latter, they have flattened bodies, but the abdomen is longer than it is broad, the head wide and triangular, and the legs are spreading and slightly bristly. The fore wings only are still represented by minute vestiges. As their name implies, most of them have a row of comblike points (ctenidia) projecting backward like a collar from the hind margin of the head shield and of the first abdominal segment. The use of these is evidently to catch in the hair of the host to aid in clinging on. The well-developed mouth-parts form a sucking proboscis by which they puncture the skin and suck blood. Jordan has described the remarkable method of reproduction. Unlike the bat bedbugs which infest the haunts of their hosts and probably crawl forth from their hiding places to feed upon the bats while they are roosting, the polyctenids stay with their hosts, hiding in their fur. As a provision for the future of their young and to insure their continuance with the host, the larvae hatch within the body of the female insect in an enlarged part of the oviduct, which thus forms a sort of uterus. Two young are hatched at a time and until they reach a nearly adult condition are nourished in this uterus by a remarkable development of the appendages on the front segment of the abdomen. These correspond to a pair of leglike structures which lengthen and attach to the wall of the uterus, thus simulating a placenta by which nourishment is drawn from the body of the parent insect. When the young are mature, they are "born" fully equipped to carry on an independent life like the adults.

There are five genera of these minute bugs, all peculiar to bats. Four are, so far as known, confined to the Old World, namely: Polyctenes, with one species reported from a free-tailed bat (Nyctinomus) of South China and from the false vampires, *Megaderma spasma ceylonicus* of Ceylon and *Lyroderma lyra* of India; Adroctenes, represented by a single species, *A. horvathi*, described by Jordan from an unidentified bat from Somaliland; Eoctenes, with some three species, of which *E. nycteridis* is a parasite of the African hollow-faced bats of the genus Nycteris, *E. intermedius* occurs on the genus Taphozous, in Africa and Sumatra, and *E. spasmae* on the false vampire and the small Far-Eastern fruit bat, Cynopterus. A fourth genus is Hypoctenes, again known from a single species, *H. clarus*, found on a molossid bat, *Mops thersites*, of western Africa. A single genus, Hesperoctenes, has been found on a few bats of the New World, and curiously, all of the five species that have been described are from free-tailed bats of the genera Eumops and Tadarida. Most of them are of tropical distribution, therefore, but Ferris (1919) has reported one of the species, *H. longiceps*, from the mastiff bat (*Eumops californicus*) of southern California, the first record of the genus in the United States. Why these curious little insects should be so partial to this group of bats is a puzzle, for the fur in the free-tails is unusually short.

A parasite of a wholly unexpected group was discovered by Jordan in 1909 in the shape of an earwig, representing the order Dermaptera. In these insects, which are remotely related to the Orthoptera or locusts, the abdomen ends in two sickle-shaped callipers or cerci. Some species are known as garden pests and are provided with wings. One group is parasitic on the giant rats (Cricetomys) of Africa, so that it may be less surprising to find that one, *Arixenia esau*, has become a parasite of a large free-tailed bat of Borneo, the so-called naked bat, *Cheiromeles torquatus*. Jordan discovered the new parasite in some specimens sent in alcohol and notes that they were tucked away in the hollow space under the wing, which forms here a sort of shallow pouch. In his account, however, he confuses this with the "gular sac," which is a gland in the middle of the throat. Of the four specimens secured, the largest measured 18 millimeters in total length but is even then still immature. The body is flattened, the legs are spreading, and the wings have disappeared in correlation with parasitic life. Jordan suggests that this earwig feeds on bat dung, and he mentions that an examination of the gullet showed microscopic remains of insects, among which a small fly was identifiable.

The most common external parasites of bats are perhaps the various minute flies, Diptera, of which two families are known, both belonging to the group Pupipara, so called because, instead of laying eggs, the females retain these within the abdomen until they hatch and become good-sized larvae, which are then "born" in an advanced state of development. This makes it unnecessary for the adult to seek out a suitable place for egg-laying and saves the young insect from having to develop apart from the host species, with the chances very great that it might never happen upon the kind of bat for which it is fitted. The two families are the Nycteribiidae and the Streblidae. The former are all wingless with a curious spidery appearance in the flattened body, minute head, and widespreading legs. The head folds back into a groove on the upper side of the thorax. Of the streblids many are winged, though in some the wings are small or even minute remnants. The head is not bent backward upon the thorax, and the eyes are reduced to mere vestiges or may be wanting.

An interesting point about the nycteribiids is that both in numbers of individuals and in variety of species and genera they are much more abundant in the Old World than in the New, with a center of abundance about the tropical parts of the Far East. Writing in 1924, Ferris says that only eight species of two genera are known from the western hemisphere but about sixty species from the eastern. Stiles and Nolan (1931) list eight genera and nearly ninety species in all, and others have since been described. Another significant fact is that many of these nycteribiids are peculiar to certain species or genera of bats. Thus, Eremoctenia is known only from the long-fingered bat (Miniopterus), which supports also various other parasites. A second genus, Archinycteribia, is found only on the large bare-backed fruit bats of the genus Dobsonia of the East Indies; Eucampsipoda chiefly parasitizes the trident bat, Asellia, and two genera of small fruit bats of the family

Pteropidae; while a third genus, Cyclopodia, includes at least fifteen described species, one only of which occurs on vespertilionid and megadermid bats, and all the others on fruit bats alone. The largest genus is Nycteribia with over forty species

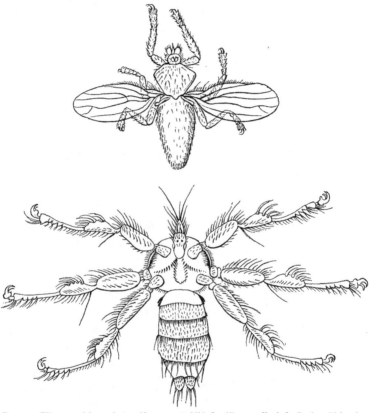

Fig. 53—Flies parasitic on bats. Above, a streblid fly (*Raymondia huberi*), in which wings are well developed, from the African horseshoe bat, *Hipposideros caffer*. Below, a wingless fly or nycteribiid (*Nycteribius latreillei*) seen from above, found on the large mouse-eared bat (*Myotis myotis*) of Europe. Both figures greatly magnified; after Kolenati (1857).

occurring in the warmer parts of both hemispheres, while another, Basilia, is said to have seven species in the New World and a single one in the Old. No doubt, however, the limits of the genera may be subject to further revision. These curious flies are found as far north as northern Germany and the British Isles, where two species occur, one of them a parasite of the greater horseshoe bat, itself a member of a warm-country group. In North America species have been described from a small brown bat (Myotis) and the big-eared bat (Corynorhinus) of southern California, from the cave bat (Antrozous) of Kansas, from the fringed bat (*Myotis thysanodes*) of New Mexico, from the free-tailed bat, *Tadarida cynocephala*, of New Orleans, and from a small brown bat, *Myotis austroriparius*, in Florida, localities which probably represent about the northerly limits of nycteribiids in the United States (Ferris, 1924).

Like the polyctenid bugs and some fleas, the streblid flies of certain genera have a comb or ctenidium of strong, backwardly directed spines on the under side of the flattened head to aid in clinging to the host. The group is only found on bats, although one or two species have been erroneously recorded from birds. Of the various genera described, Trichobius is among the best known; it has well-developed and functional wings, each with six simple, longitudinal veins. Closely related are the genera Pseudostrebla, Paratrichobius, Synthesiostrebla, and Speiseria, all of which are small yellowish flies mostly confined to bats of the American tropics, although one species comes as far north as Colorado in its partiality for the big-eared bat, Corynorhinus. Another American genus, Strebla, seems to be partial to leaf-nosed bats, but the others are found on these, as well as on other South American families of bats. Two winged genera are found in the Old World, Nycteribosca and Raymondia. In the former the eyes are vestigial, having only one facet. The half-dozen or more species now known have been found on a wide variety of bats in the eastern tropics. Thus, *N. alluaudi* occurs on the sheath-tailed bats of the genus Taphozous in Africa and Burma; *N. amboinensis* has been found in the East Indies on horseshoe bats of the genera Rhinolophus and Hipposideros, as well as on the long-fingered bat (Miniopterus); *N. buxtoni* is interesting, as it is known only from the small sheath-tailed bat, *Emballonura semicaudata*, of Samoa in the Pacific, while *N. rouxi* is parasitic on the curious long-tailed fruit bat, Notopteris, of the New Caledonian Islands.

Another, *N. gigantea*, is found on the large bare-backed fruit bat, Dobsonia, in the East Indian archipelago.

On the other hand, *N. kollari* appears to be much more general in its choice of hosts, for it is reported from bats of no less than five families in northern Africa, including the genera Rhinopoma, Nycteris, Asellia, Rhinolophus, Miniopterus, and Myotis. Of the genus Raymondia, in which the eyes are lacking and the wings are short, broad, and only five-veined, a recent review by Jobling (1930) recognizes but six forms, of which three are new. The species are found in Africa, India, and eastward into the Malay archipelago, and have been discovered on several genera of bats, including Nycteris, Cardioderma, Coleura, and Triaenops, as well as on Lyroderma of Ceylon. Still further reduction of the wings is found in the genus Aspidoptera, in which they lie flat on the back and do not reach beyond the first quarter of the length of the abdomen. Four species are recorded from South American bats of the families Noctilionidae and Phyllostomidae. Finally, in the genera Paradyschiria and Megistopoda the wings are lost altogether. The former is known only from bats of the Noctilionidae (the fish-eating hare-lipped bat and its smaller relative, Dirias), while the latter genus is apparently peculiar to leaf-nosed bats of the family Phyllostomidae. The streblids thus seem to be best developed as an American group of bat flies.

The most remarkable of the small parasitic flies infesting bats are those of the genus Ascodipteron, of which but a few species are known in the tropics of the Old World. The adult male, upon emerging from the pupal stage, resembles a small streblid fly and remains in this normal condition. But the female differs noticeably in the possession of a large proboscis, at the end of which are four series of minute chitinous blades, about fifteen in each rank, the individual blade somewhat crescent-shaped and sharp-edged. The female, after mating, seeks out as host some particular species of bat. Frederick Muir (1912), who has described the development of *Ascodipteron speiserianum*, found that this species is parasitic on the long-fingered bat, Miniopterus, in Amboina, and perhaps elsewhere in the Far-Eastern tropics. Having settled upon one of these bats, the female then cuts a small hole in the skin behind the bat's ear by means of the sets of blades at the end of her proboscis, and goes in head first through the opening, meanwhile shedding her wings and all but the basal joint of her legs. Here she ensconces herself, while her abdomen enlarges and actually engulfs the small head and thorax, so that they come to lie telescoped in a little pit at the front end of the abdomen. Here she lives, sustained presumably by juices sucked from the bat through the proboscis, and produces a small oval swelling externally, at the tip of which the abdomen of the insect appears as a small pearly-white protruding body. Here are the four spiracles or breathing pores of the parasite. When dissected out, it is a semi-transparent, flask-shaped object, four or five millimeters long, without visible head or thorax, for these have become engulfed in the abdomen. This body includes a large uterus, in which is contained a single larva that is fed on the contents of nutritive glands and grows to maturity within the body of the female. It is then ejected and falls to the ground as a pupa, from which presently the adult fly comes forth to begin the cycle over once more.

Since their proboscis is too weak to cut the skin of the bat, the males remain free-living and do not embed themselves in this way. A detailed account of this habit is given by Muir (1912), who concludes that the insect is really a streblid fly, as shown by the various structures, but that the female has undergone these profound changes in adaptation to her peculiar parasitic life. He describes a second species, *Ascodipteron australiansi*, from a long-fingered bat (Miniopterus) of northern Queensland. A third species, *A. phyllorhinae*, is perhaps the same as that found in the horseshoe bat of the Philippines, and there is a similar one found on these bats in Africa, of which the photograph here reproduced shows three embedded females in the fleshy part of the arm above the elbow of a small bat, *Hipposideros caffer centralis*, from Rutshuru in the eastern Belgian Congo. Three, lying side by side, seem to be all there is room for at this point, but I have examined some Philippine horseshoe bats which had in addition a single embedded female on each knuckle joint of the longer fingers. In one case Muir found two embedded females behind the left ear of a Miniopterus in Amboina. Because of this remarkable habit of the females in losing wings and legs and telescoping the head and thorax into the fore end of the abdomen, the Ascodipterons are regarded as forming a special subfamily of the Streblidae. It is interesting to see again that the long-fingered bat is especially subject to parasitism. Muir records that he found in a total of sixty of these bats no less than 28 Ascodipterons, 180 streblid flies of the species *Nycteribosca amboinensis*, and 2 genera of the wingless flies of the family Nycteribiidae, including 150 individuals of *Listropoda parilis* and 30 of *Penicillidia progressa*, a generous assortment. Monticelli has also described a new Ascodipteron from an African horseshoe bat, *Rhinolophus clivosus*.

Yes, bats have fleas! To most people fleas are fleas, but although they seem superficially much alike, with their compressed oval bodies, jumping legs, and sucking mouthparts, these wingless insects are in fact very diverse in the details of structure. Within certain limits they are far from indiscriminate in the choice of hosts, for different genera or species are usually more or less specific on particular mammals. No less than nineteen genera of fleas are listed from bats, and undoubtedly others will be discovered when more thorough search has been made for these pests. Some bats seem on the whole rather free of them. Thus, the fruit bats (Pteropidae) are known to harbor but few, for Stiles and Nolan list only two genera, Thaumapsylla and Archaeopsylla from the common rousette of northern Africa and the former again from the African straw-colored bat (Eidolon). The mouse-tailed bats (Rhinopomidae), a primitive group, sometimes carry a species of Ischnopsyllus, the most widespread genus of bat fleas, of which at least twenty-five species are known, most of them, however, from Old World bats of the family Vespertilionidae. Horseshoe bats (Rhinolophus) carry a few and, curiously, there is a single New World species peculiar to the small hare-

FIG. 54—Three ascodipterons embedded in the fleshy part of the forearm of an African horseshoe bat (*Hipposideros caffer centralis*), about thrice natural size. C. V. MacCoy, phot.

lipped bat, Dirias. This and three other species are the only members of this flea genus known from the western hemisphere. The three others infest two species of South American Myotis and the large brown bat (*Eptesicus fuscus*) of North America. The horseshoe bats are host to several genera of fleas, of which Leptopsylla is, so far as known, confined to the genus Rhinolophus, while others are more catholic in their tastes and are represented by related species on several Old World genera of bats. The Nycteridae, or hollow-faced bats, harbor at least two genera, one of which, Echidnophaga, is known only from *Nycteris grandis* of Africa, while a second, Rhinolophopsylla, from *Nycteris capensis*, belongs to a genus that parasitizes several other genera of bats, such as Rhinolophus, Myotis, Pipistrellus, and Barbastella of the Old World.

The sheath-tailed bats (Emballonuridae), which occur in the tropics of both the Old and the New World, seem to harbor few fleas. None is known from any of the species of the western hemisphere, but Taphozous, the genus including the tomb bats of the near East, is host to a genus of fleas, Chiropteropsylla, known from no other bat. Again, the only flea recorded from the leaf-nosed bats (Phyllostomidae) of the American tropics is a special genus, Rhopalopsyllus, found on a small fruit-eating species, *Sturnira lilium*. From bats of the world-wide family Vespertilionidae, eight genera with many species of fleas are reported. One of these, Myodopsylla, is found on the little brown bats of the genus Myotis in North America and has been reported also from a Pipistrellus in Manchuria, while another genus, Ischnopsyllus, and a third, Nycteridopsylla, likewise include species from both the Old and the New World. The free-tailed bats, Molossidae, are found in the tropics of both hemispheres and seem to harbor a number of fleas that are peculiar to them. The interesting point is that the genera are, however, limited to those of either the Old or the New World, indicating a very long period of separation between the two groups of bats. Thus, the flea genera Sternopsylla, Hormopsylla, and Hectopsylla are known from New World Molossidae only, the first from the "guano bat" (*Tadarida mexicana*) of Texas, the second from Tadarida and Eumops in Paraguay, the third from Tadarida and Molossus of South America. A fourth genus, Laguropsylla, is confined to the Old World molossids, and is known from five species parasitic on Mormopterus of Madagascar, Chaerephon of Java, India, and Tenasserim, and on Mops of West Africa. A most remarkable flea, *Rhynchopsyllus pulex*, found in Colombia, parasitizes the mastiff bat, *Molossus obscurus*. In its adaptation to a passive life it shows a parallel evolution to that of the ascodipterons, in that the female burrows into the skin, where it remains fixed, swells up, and casts off its legs as useless appendages.

No fleas are as yet recorded from several families of bats, such as the Megadermidae, Hipposideridae, Natalidae, and some others. It is interesting that certain genera of fleas have become peculiar to special *families* of bats; again, in the case of large genera with many species, these are in turn more or less characteristic of particular *species* of bats. In some genera of bats there are found more than a single kind of flea. Thus, the genus Pipistrellus is host to Ischnopsyllus, Myodopsylla, Nycteridopsylla, Rhinolophopsylla, and Xenopsylla, if identifications can be trusted, while the long-fingered bat (Miniopterus) is host to two genera, Araeopsylla and Xenopsylla. It is curious that fleas seem to be recorded from insectivorous bats chiefly, while the fruit-eating species appear to be largely free from them, yet this may be partly owing to limited search. Undoubtedly a better knowledge of these unwelcome parasites and their host species would reveal many interesting things. Fleas are very highly specialized, perhaps most nearly related to flies among other insects, for they still have a slender maggot-like larva, and the structure of the adult is also believed to show a certain likeness to that of the order Diptera. Their particular modifications for better living in the fur of their hosts include the loss of wings, the hardened chitinous exterior, the narrow compressed bodies which are expanded vertically instead of sidewise, the curious rows of comblike teeth on the fore part of the body to prevent them from falling out from the hair, and, finally, the perfection of the proboscis and sucking mouthparts for piercing the skin of the host and obtaining a meal of its blood.

Despite this seemingly long array of parasites, they are seldom very abundant, and one may often search carefully through the fur of bat after bat without finding a single one. Bats are usually very cleanly and spend much time in licking and combing their fur, so that the various devices that parasites have evolved to prevent their host from removing them doubtless are often effective and necessary. Nor need human beings be apprehensive lest bats bring vermin into buildings. Ordinarily they are clean enough, and any parasites they may have are probably in the main peculiar to themselves. On the other hand, if bats congregate regularly in buildings they may become offensive through the accumulations of dung in their sleeping places.

# CHAPTER XX

# BATS IN RELATION TO DISEASE

BATS at various times have been sadly maligned because of their supposed connection with certain diseases. Needless to say, there is very little truth in most of these beliefs, yet men refuse to give up these traditions. DeRennes (1924) tells of a marine engineer he met in Brittany, who firmly believed that the native bats of his country were dangerous creatures, whose nocturnal visits, being venomous, brought on pimples, boils, and other disorders! Probably, however, since the engineer himself was the victim of boils, tumors, and worse troubles, he pretended in this idea to find an excuse for his own condition. In another instance an innkeeper, living by the side of a stagnant pond, declared that microbes fell from the wings of bats and caused fevers among the members of his household! Doubtless the real danger here was from mosquitoes as carriers of malaria, but bats are so much more visible than mosquitoes that it was easier to blame them.

In recent years bats have come in for a certain amount of attention in relation to malaria, but, luckily or not, from another point of view. It is now well known that the immediate cause of this scourge of warm countries is a minute protozoan, a blood parasite which is transmitted to man by the Anopheles mosquito. In sucking blood, the mosquito punctures the skin and then injects from its salivary glands a secretion containing a substance that prevents the blood from coagulating in its stomach. One stage of the malaria organism is present in the salivary glands of infected mosquitoes, as a minute, needle-shaped body, which, making its way into the saliva, is injected into the blood of the victim. Here it penetrates and destroys a blood corpuscle and transforms into minute spores which, breaking forth, enter the blood stream and cause the fever. The various stages in the development of this organism have now been thoroughly worked out, enabling preventive measures to be taken, but in earlier times all this was quite unknown, and the discovery of the method of transmission by the Anopheles mosquito is one of the triumphs of modern science. Yet it was suspected long before. In his African explorations Stanley remarked that when he slept under a mosquito net he found himself much less liable to attacks of fever, although he seems not to have connected this with freedom from mosquito bites.

Curiously, Richard Burton many years previously had come very close to the great discovery. In his *First Footsteps in East Africa* he writes that while at Zayla, in Somaliland, about 1855, he found the Somalis were careful not to disturb the bats that took shelter by day in their houses, since they believed that the "fid-mer" or "evening fliers" keep off the flies and mosquitoes, which at certain seasons are a veritable plague in their country. The mosquito bites, they told him, bring on deadly fevers, a "superstition," Burton says, which "probably arises from the fact that mosquitoes and fevers become formidable about the same time!" Yet the "superstition" has now become a proved fact, although the evidence that bats play much part in reducing the mosquito hordes is small enough. For the Anopheles mosquitoes fly low and are probably very seldom taken by bats, although the statement is often made that they feed largely on these insects. The only direct evidence I have found that any bat eats mosquitoes is the statement of Hinton and Kershaw (1920) that the stomach contents of two specimens of the great-eared bat (*Lavia frons*) from the Dinka country of northeastern Africa consisted of mosquitoes and small flies.

Again, in a brief paper by the eminent entomologist, Dr. L. O. Howard (1922) the statement of a Mr. Seiss is quoted. He dissected a common brown bat from near Philadelphia and reported that its stomach was "full of mosquitoes." Partly on this evidence, no doubt, Howard, Dyar, and Knab, in their monograph on mosquitoes of North America, state that bats are important as mosquito destroyers and mention the suggestion made to them by Mr. A. C. Weeks, of Brooklyn, that bats might be bred artificially for the destruction of these insects and thus help to eliminate malaria. The same idea is quoted by Howard from another source. The plan of Dr. Charles A. R. Campbell, of San Antonio, Texas, for constructing bat towers has already been mentioned. To determine what part bats might play in mosquito destruction, F. C. Bishopp, of the U. S. Bureau of Entomology, collected a number of the bats from these roosts as they were returning from a night's feeding, and made many microscopic examinations, not only of the stomach contents, but also of the droppings accumulated beneath the roosts. He could identify only minute remains of moths and beetles. Further studies made by Storer (1926), who examined microscopically a quantity of droppings from the bat roost, only corroborate the conclusion that although immense numbers of injurious insects are eaten, there is no evidence that mosquitoes are anything more than a negligible element in the diet of these bats. It thus appears that bats as a possible means of reducing malaria are but a vain hope. Dr. E. W. Nelson (1926), who arrives at a similar conclusion, points out that even in localities where bats are plentiful the mosquitoes may be an unmitigated plague.

On the other hand, the recent investigations of Dr. Herbert C. Clark and Dr. Lawrence Dunn have definitely shown that one species of bat does play a part in the transmission of certain diseases in the American tropics. This is the vampire bat, *Desmodus rotundus* (and subspecies), which lives on the blood of other and larger mammals or of fowl, and in securing its meal may transmit certain diseases by its bite. In the process it first makes a small clean cut, with its bladelike front teeth, scooping out a small section, and then laps or drinks the blood as it wells out.

In Panama a common disease of horses and mules, known locally as "murrina," has in the past proved very deadly, killing great numbers of these animals. In 1909 Dr. S. T. Darling discovered its cause in a trypanosome or blood parasite, which he named *Trypanosoma hippicum*. Many attempts to discover an insect carrier of the disease gave only negative results. Dr. Dunn later found that, of a number of horses and mules that developed the disease, the majority had apparently become infected while in pasture and showed evidence of having been bitten by vampires. This clue led to his experimenting with this bat as a carrier. With much search he succeeded in discovering a colony of vampires in a cave in the vicinity and was thus enabled to carry out some experiments in 1932. In the first attempt six vampires were allowed to feed from the edge of the ear of a horse infected with the disease, from which it died eleven days later. The bats, however, showed no ill effects, nor were the organisms of the malady found in their blood. The work was continued, however, using infected guinea pigs as a source of food for the bats. In one case a bat was fed for three days in succession on the blood of an infected guinea pig, after which it was given blood from uninfected animals in order to test the period of incubation of the disease should it develop. On the eighth day its blood was found to be "positive," showing twenty trypanosomes of the disease to a droplet of blood. Having thus established the transmission of the disease organisms to the blood of the bat, he thereafter fed it on guinea pigs which, on being tested, were found to be uninfected. This continued for seventeen days, with the result that each of the guinea pigs bitten on the last twelve days became infected, evidently from the bite of the infected bat. This bat was then allowed to feed on a horse, the blood of which was found to be free from the trypanosomes, when, sure enough, after eight days microscopic examination revealed development of the infection in the blood of the horse.

After this almost conclusive proof of transmission by the bat's bite, further experiments along the same lines were continued, but with varying results, the bites sometimes producing infection, sometimes not. This was found to be largely owing to the bat's manner of feeding. Thus, if the blood welled up freely, the bat had merely to touch the tip of its tongue to the drop, to draw it into its mouth, giving little opportunity for transmission of the disease organisms. On the other hand, if the wound was in such a position on a surface that the blood had to be actively lapped from the cut, the chances of infecting the host became greatly increased. Ordinarily a bat would become gorged in twenty to thirty minutes. In another case a bat was fed for ten days on blood derived from an infected horse, and on the eighth day showed definite infection. Summing up the results of the experiments, we find that in five out of six cases the vampire was definitely shown to be the carrier of the horse disease caused by this trypanosome; these bats readily acquire the disease themselves by feeding on the blood of infected animals and show the organism in their blood after an incubation period of six to eight days; the disease proves fatal to the bats in nine to twenty-seven days, a period which in the wild state is long enough to permit them to spread it to other animals, particularly horses and mules. One is led to infer that the deadly trypanosomes are present in the salivary glands and are transmitted with the saliva.

In continuation of the experiments, it was found that of five different species of bats used, all were readily susceptible to the disease, which could also be induced in them either by direct feeding with infected blood or by passing it through a small rubber tube into their stomachs. Injections of infected blood produced the same result. Fortunately, the short but fatal course of the disease in bats indicates that they do not recover and act as further reservoirs for the trypanosomes, nor are any of the insectivorous or fruit-eating species likely to transmit it, since they do not attack other animals. On the other hand, Clark and Dunn (1933) have proved that cattle, pigs, sheep, and goats may carry a light infection of murrina for a long time, so that although these animals may eventually recover, they may meanwhile act as reservoirs for the disease and thus infect vampires that may attack them.

The blood-feeding habits of the vampire bat have brought it still further into disrepute as an agent in the spread of rabies in eastern South America. No one knows how this disease was first communicated to the bats; perhaps they became locally infected through lapping the blood of diseased livestock brought from the Old World. An excellent summary of the relation of vampires to this disease has lately been published by Dr. J. L. Pawan (1936), from whose account these facts are drawn. The malady is of a type different from the more familiar "hydrophobia," which we associate with the bite of "mad dogs." For the livestock bitten by infected vampires develop within a few days or longer the characteristic symptoms first of lassitude, then abundant salivation, with rapid emaciation and paralysis of the limbs and body. Death presently ensues, the time interval varying with different animals. The deadly virus is present in the salivary glands of the vampires and is transmitted by the saliva as the bats lap blood from the wound they inflict. Probably only a small percentage of the vampires in a given district is infected with rabies, but of this no definite figures are available. Such bats may probably be recognized by their abnormal behavior, resulting doubtless from their diseased condition. They become irritable, fighting with one another, and are driven to attack cattle and equine stock, as well as human beings, in full daylight, and perhaps also bite other harmless species of fruit- and insect-eating bats with which they may associate. Evidence of this last lies in the fact that in a few cases the brains and spinal cords of such fruit-eating genera as Artibeus and Carollia or the insectivorous ghost bat (Diclidurus) have, on examination, shown the presence of the Negri bodies characteristic of the disease. These species of course are harmless and do not communicate rabies, since they do not bite other animals.

As early as the eighteenth century de la Condamine recorded that in Ecuador and elsewhere in South America cattle were locally exterminated by bats. It now appears probable that these were vampires infected with rabies, which they transmitted through their bites. In 1908 a severe outbreak of disease occurred among the horses, mules, and cattle of the State of Santa Catharina and surrounding districts of southern Brazil. Over four thousand cattle and a thousand horses and mules succumbed. This disease was diagnosed by Carini in 1911 as a form of rabies, for he found in the affected animals the

characteristic Negri bodies that it produces in the brain and
spinal cord. Naturally it was at first thought that dogs were
the active carriers of the trouble. Yet, although a wholesale
destruction of dogs was undertaken in the hope of stopping
the ravages of the disease, this measure proved ineffectual, and
it became evident that some other agency than dogs was re-
sponsible for its spread. Carini specially noted that people
had observed vampires abroad and attacking animals by day
and that such animals subsequently died of the malady. Further, the trouble continued to spread up to 1920, among cattle
and horses of northern Argentina, Paraguay, Uruguay, and
Brazil, but dogs were only slightly affected and human beings
not at all.

In 1921 two investigators, Haupt and Rehaag, came to the
conclusion that vampires were the transmitting agents, and
this was later definitely proved by the brilliant work of Lima
(in 1934) in Brazil and by Pawan (1936) in Trinidad. "Bat-
proofing" by enclosing stables with fine wire netting was tried
and found to be efficacious. In one experiment two stables
were built thirty feet apart in a district of Trinidad where
rabies existed. The one, containing four cattle, was not thus
protected; the other, containing three mules and two horses,
was thoroughly screened. In the former, three of the cattle
died of rabies, while the animals in the latter remained un-
harmed. In another stable, carefully screened, the animals
contracted the disease, but by keeping watch it was found that
vampires crawled through a crack beneath a door and attacked
the livestock within.

Of the many tests made by Pawan the following is typical.
A vampire was found biting a cow in Malabou Village, Trinidad, at 7 A.M. Though repeatedly chased away, it returned
to attack the cow and was at length killed with a stick in the
act of biting. Paralytic rabies was present in the animals of
the district. The brain, spinal cord, and salivary glands of
the bat were at once dissected out, and on the next day an
emulsion made from them was injected into a healthy rhesus
monkey. Eight days later the monkey was screaming continu-

ously and would go into a violent rage when anyone approached its cage. On the following day the unfortunate monkey was salivating profusely and was unable to eat or swallow. Its death took place the same day. An examination of its brain showed the presence of the Negri bodies characteristic of rabies. Next, an emulsion of the dead monkey's medulla was injected into two calves.

Five days later calf no. 1 seemed unduly quiet, but was grinding its teeth continuously. There was an anxious expression in the eyes, and there were alternate backward and forward nervous movements of the ears, with repeated licking of the lips — evidence of commencing salivation. . . . [On the seventh day], these manifestations were more marked, especially the grinding of the teeth, and salivation became excessive. [Two days later] it was knocking its face and mouth against the wall, causing laceration and bleeding.

On the tenth day there was paralysis of the left front leg and quarters, and the animal was unable to rise from the ground. It died on the twelfth day. The Negri bodies were found in the brain. Calf no. 2, injected at the same time, was less resistant, and died in eight days, with the same manifestations.

Although in the Brazilian outbreak human beings were apparently unaffected with rabies and even dogs seemed immune, the case was different with the Trinidad strain. Persons bitten by infected vampires showed tragic results. Details of the early symptoms of the disease are tabulated in forty-seven cases by Dr. Pawan. According to the sufferers, its appearance was first noticed at intervals varying from two to six weeks from the time they were bitten, or in a few cases much longer, up to five or six months. Usually the bite had been inflicted on the foot, and the first indications of the disease were burning sensations, generally of the part attacked, though not invariably so, followed by paralysis of the legs. Another unexplained peculiarity is that in some cases rabbits injected with the virus from infected bats showed no Negri bodies in the brain and spinal cord on post-mortem examination, although they had developed the usual symptoms of paralytic rabies followed by death in one to three weeks.

In one case given by Dr. Pawan a boy was bitten on the foot by a vampire, which remained in the house in the morning, flying from room to room. During attempts to drive it out it flew straight at the master of the house and his wife, thereafter settling on the wall about ten feet from the floor, turning its head from side to side with its mouth wide open. When the lady passed under it, it again flew directly at her with open mouth. It was finally dispatched and given to Dr. Pawan, who at once gave the boy a course of anti-rabies vaccine and at the same time injected a rabbit as a test, with an emulsion from the bat. The boy remained well, but the rabbit died in seventeen days with all the symptoms of paralytic rabies.

As a result of his work, Pawan has been able to develop an immunizing vaccine. Rabbits injected with this in nearly every case survived inoculation with rabies. It is to be hoped that in the near future a vaccine can be prepared for immunizing cattle and horses. Since it is difficult to find and exterminate these bats, the best preventive seems to be to gather all cattle into stables or shelters of some sort at night and, by hanging lighted lanterns in the stalls, scare the bats away. Instances are known in Central America where vampire bats were such a source of annoyance to herds of cattle by night that it became necessary to move them to pasturage at a considerable distance away. In a later note Hurst and Pawan (1932) tell of an outbreak of rabies or "acute rabic myelitis" in Trinidad, and report negative results from an inoculation of the brains of the large fruit-eating Artibeus, as might have been expected, since these bats do not, like the vampires, feed on blood.

The possibility that vampire bats may at times transmit other diseases is not excluded, but the probability is that they are a relatively unimportant factor. Nevertheless, there is a little evidence that they are capable of carrying even a virus as well as a trypanosome, as the work on rabies has shown. In experiments carried on in South America by Kumm (1932), two species of free-tailed bats, *Molossus obscurus* and *M. rufus*, were exposed in captivity to the bites of the yellow-fever mosquito (*Aëdes aegypti*). However, attempts to transmit the virus to either the Molossus or to a vampire through the agency of these infected mosquitoes and to recover the virus from the bats proved negative. Yet by mechanically infecting vampires with yellow-fever virus, Kumm succeeded in two cases in obtaining its transmission. He admits, however, that these bats can hardly be considered a factor of importance in the spread of the disease among human beings. So far as cattle are concerned, the chief danger from the vampires' bites seems to be that the open wounds they make in obtaining blood become almost at once infested with fly maggots, as well as provide points of entry for bacterial infection.

Although, with all this evidence against it, the vampire bat seems to be from our point of view an unmitigated source of trouble, it is interesting to recall at least one account in which its blood-loving habit proved beneficial. It is related that in the early history of Mexico a monk was seized with a violent attack of fever and at evening was given over for dead by his associates. They withdrew for the night but on returning next morning to bury their brother were astonished to find him alive and on the road to recovery. It seems that his feet had been left uncovered and that during the night a vampire bat had entered the room, which, having bitten his toe and lapped his blood, had so reduced the fever that the sick man recovered!

# CHAPTER XXI

## THE CAVES OF YPORANGA

BAT collecting, like fishing, is fraught with a large element of luck as well as of skill, and there are almost as many means of effecting the one as the other. Many kinds of bats hide away so successfully by day as to elude all pursuit, but in the brief moments of dusk appear tantalizingly close at hand, offering an uncertain but sporting target to the naturalist with his shotgun and light charges of fine shot. Night after night I have taken a stand at the edge of some open space like the shore of a pond or a bare strip on the outskirts of a forest, gun ready cocked, facing the fading glow in the western sky, alert for a shot at some shadowy form flickering across the narrowing field of vision. Most species start flying when it is almost dark, but others do not appear until it is too late to see them at all. Again, some of the larger bats afford a relatively easy mark, flying high and steadily, while other smaller kinds are given to most irregular dashes with sudden and unexpected changes of direction, so that one pulls the trigger again and again just a wing-beat behind. Bats are fearless creatures and seem wholly unmindful of the fact that the loud explosion disturbing the sunset calm is directed toward them. Often they turn after the unsuccessful discharge to chase the falling gun wad in its parabolic course. Even if the shot reaches home and one has a fleeting glimpse of the small creature folding up and dropping like a plummet to the earth, it is not always easy to retrieve it, especially if the collector has not previously selected an open spot of ground or a placid bit of water whereon to drop his quarry. In the uncertain light, distances are deceptive, and a bat often falls close at hand that had seemed almost out of range when viewed against the sky.

Some collectors have had success in capturing bats by stretching a fine-meshed net across an opening among trees or over a brook where they are flying back and forth in pursuit of insects. A net set across a cave opening or fastened over a retreat under eaves or other holes may also yield excellent results. Dr. Josselyn Van Tyne (1933) has recounted his success in the tropics with a trammel net such as is used by the bird catchers of southern Europe. It consists of two long nets of dark linen twine, each some forty feet in length, stretched across a jungle opening or in the undergrowth of a forest. A third net of finer twine is rigged somewhat loosely between, making three thicknesses, so that a bat striking one of the outer nets goes partly through its larger meshes and becomes pocketed in the looser meshes of the inner net. With such a net in Guatemala he secured in the course of a month fifty-five bats of five species, chiefly of a small fruit-eating kind, previously known from relatively few specimens. In addition to bats, such a net frequently captured the shyer jungle birds, some of which, from their thicket-loving habits, very seldom are secured by collectors. Often, too, large flying beetles were taken and, becoming much entangled through their long-continued struggles, required some effort and patience to extricate. For this reason a linen fabric proved superior to one of silk that soon became hopelessly caught in every twig it touched.

Some of the smaller bats flit close to the ground or pass back and forth over the surface of ponds or small brooks. Stationed on a little promontory, one may often knock them down by frantically waving a switch with several long branches as they dart past. But in this type of pursuit luck is largely with the bat. I have sometimes tied a bit of cotton with a short string to the upper part of such a switch, hoping that the bat would see it and give pursuit, and so the more readily be knocked down. I have heard of fishermen, casting light flies at dusk for trout, hooking instead a passing bat that snapped up the bait, but in all the attempts I have made at bat fishing, I have never succeeded in landing the prey. Although they may occasionally "bite," they do not swallow the hook as a fish does but usually drop it or shake free at once. Perhaps a skillful fisherman could prevent this.

Hensel (1869) records a singular case in which numbers of the free-tailed bats, *Tadarida "brasiliensis,"* were evidently attracted by the presence of others of their kind to enter a glass vessel from which they could not escape. This bat, he writes, was very abundant at the hotel where he stayed in Porto Alegre, Brazil. One morning he found no less than 219 of these bats hanging in a room which they had entered through the open window. The proprietor of the hotel let them all be killed, since he believed they were to blame for the dilapidated condition of the building. His servant once had the clever idea of confining several living bats of this species in tall, open glass vessels and setting them in certain places in the hotel in the evening. Next morning there were in the three vessels 325 bats of this sort which had entered on hearing the cries of the ones already captured. None of them could scale the smooth glass walls. Those underneath were already dead, apparently crushed by the ones above. The uppermost part of the vessels was empty, for here the bats were able to fly out. How many others had come to the vessels and escaped could not be told.

Insect-eating bats will frequently check their course to chase a pebble thrown in the air near them, a habit which the old English naturalist Kerr (1792) says is sometimes taken advantage of by boys in catching some of the smaller species that fly near the ground. By throwing a small cluster of burrs into the air, the lads often succeeded in entangling the delicate wings, causing the bat to fall to the ground when it turned aside to pursue the moving object.

One of the most fruitful methods of collecting bats is to seek them out in caves or hollow trees. Many species, however, are not cave-dwellers and must be sought elsewhere. I recall a great hollow tree, a fallen giant, lying prostrate on the floor of a dense Liberian forest, within which a solitary bat regularly slept away the day. We disturbed it by chance while investigating the dark interior, which ran for fully fifty feet in the form of a narrowing funnel. The bat was usually roosting at some distance back from the entrance, yet seemed always alert. We tried at various times to circumvent it by stretching an inadequate net across the entrance, and then by crawling in on hands and knees with an electric light in one hand and a small collecting pistol in the other, attempting to get a shot as the bat hung suspended from somewhere in the dark interior. But always it eluded our efforts, suddenly darting out and under the net, or taking flight before the lethal weapon could be brought into action. No doubt this was one of the larger hollow-faced bats (*Nycteris grandis*), for we later secured one in a similar situation.

Better luck attended a memorable bat hunt in one of the pyramids at Gizeh. The importunate Arabs who haunt the locality offering their services as guides to tourists were much amused at the desire of a sedate white man to secure the "wit-wat" (Arabic for bat). One of them, nevertheless, eagerly bade us follow him. He led the way up the side of one of the lesser pyramids to the opening of the shaft that extended down at a steep angle into the blackness of the tomb of an ancient Pharaoh. I followed not less eagerly, armed with a collecting pistol, and presently found myself in the bowels of the earth, where a large rectangular chamber had been hewn from the solid rock below the base of the structure. Lighting a small candle-end, my guide pointed to the low ceiling, where I made out dimly a small gray form depending spider-like by all four feet from the rocky vault. The discharge of the pistol in the narrow quarters sounded with uncommon reverberation as a mouse-tailed bat (Rhinopoma) fell at our feet. I half expected the pyramid itself to collapse on top of us with the roar. Elated at this success, my guide excitedly beckoned me on. Feeling our way, we descended a still lower flight of rock-hewn steps and at once lost sight of the opening through which we had come. We were in complete darkness save for the flickering light of the small candle that made dancing shadows follow our footsteps with grotesque movements. A strange feeling of oppression came over me as we continued our descent down the narrow passage, a feeling that the walls might at any moment collapse behind us and hold us there forever. Yet, I recalled at once that since they had stood for four thousand years we might perhaps safely chance a few moments more. On we went, when presently a solid wall stopped our further progress. But my guide had been there before and, feeling with one hand in a fissure of the rock, presently drew forth another of the same species of bat. I followed his example and felt a thrill of excitement as small sharp teeth closed on one of my finger tips. Quickly withdrawing my hand, I seized another bat that had clung bulldog-like to my intruding member. Further search rewarded us with half a dozen of these extraordinary bats whose peculiarities rank them in a family by themselves. With the quarry safely secured, we felt our way back and shortly reached the main shaft whose distant opening made a spot of light far above us, and in a few moments more we were back in the light of day. No doubt generations upon generations of mouse-tailed bats have sheltered in these ancient tombs since the days of Kepheren. Only four hundred years before our visit old Pierre Bélon, whose work on ornithology published in 1555 stands as a milepost, had hunted these same bats here. He writes that "celles que se logent en la grande Pyramide d'Egypte, portent la queue longue comme font les Souris, & rendent les crotes aussi dures, & de meme façon," apparently the first published mention of this bat.

On another occasion a party of us were in the Bahama Islands investigating the open sea caves worn by waves at some former period in the limestone rock along shore. One of these recesses had a window-like opening at its farther end several feet above the floor on which we stood. This evidently led into another chamber, from the darkness of which came a confused chattering and bickering sound of many bat voices beyond. Climbing to the opening, I could dimly see by the aid of a small flashlight the walls of a dome-shaped cavern hung with multitudes of small bats. Without further ado I swung over the edge of the opening and let go, expecting a drop of a few feet to a solid floor somewhere below. Instead, I found myself nearly knee-deep in a large pool of semi-liquid bat guano, with the bats, now thoroughly disturbed, swirling about overhead or re-alighting on more distant walls. A few sweeps of a butterfly-net, however, soon gave us all the specimens we needed. These proved, on return to day, to be of the genus Erophylla, with curious round snouts, like little pigs, a type confined to the West Indies.

But bat hunts are not always attended by such success. Indeed, only a few days before we had drawn two complete blanks: one, after cutting a way with bush knives up a steep hill overgrown with scrub, to a cave reputed to be hung with festoons of bats, but which turned out to be completely empty; the other, owing to our arrival a few days too late, when a building was partly unroofed to clear out a large colony of mastiff bats that had found lodgment under the ceiling and nearly rendered the place uninhabitable. Many a "wild goose chase" have I made, lured to some distant cavern by lurid reports, only to find it tenantless.

One delightful week in midsummer saw a congenial friend and myself on a motor jaunt through the length of Vermont, with a view especially to investigating several caverns in the lime rock, where at various times others had reported "swarms of bats." Our first objective was the summit of Mt. Aeolus, up which we toiled in the heat of an August day. The dim trail led to the highest point, where, after a brief cast about, we found the entrance to the Cave of the Winds. After a steep descent over wet rocks slippery with a thin coating of mud, we reached the large vestibule or outer chamber. At the bottom the cavern narrowed, and several side passages opened off, apparently following fissures in the solid rock. One after another we explored these, wriggling along sideways or crawling on our stomachs as far as we could force our passage, but not a single bat did we find. Nevertheless, abundant remains of their skulls and other bones, as well as a small amount of guano, proved that at times they sojourned there. Miles farther on we reached the second cave, one that I had visited years before in winter with deep snow all around and found tenanted by a hibernating colony of hundreds of bats, representing four or five species. It was not easily found, but some farmers haying in a meadow near by knew the spot and directed our steps to it.

It was in a strange, rocky place amidst open maple woods, with a well-like entrance through which a small person could wriggle. But a projecting boulder partly blocked the way, so that one had to turn over and let oneself slide beneath it. Some twenty feet down, the sloping passage opened into a chamber high enough to permit of standing erect. It was here, on the previous occasion, that the winter colony was found, but now in midsummer the place was deserted and so were the other chambers, one of which could be entered only by lying flat and pushing oneself forward by the toes through a narrow round passage, humping along caterpillar fashion. It was disappointing, but we kept on, reaching late that afternoon the scene of our third attempt. This cave, when finally located, proved to be very different from the others, with an opening between piled-up boulders. Below this, one presently came upon a rude and now dilapidated ladder, by means of which the curious had at other times explored the place. With some difficulty we made the descent and found ourselves at the bottom of a vaulted dome, like Aladdin's cave without the jewels. Its ceiling seemed partly formed of crowded boulders that looked ready at any moment to crash down upon us. A thin coating of slime on the sloping floor made walking difficult, and, to our no small surprise, we found in the lowest corner a mass of still unmelted ice from the previous winter. As for bats, the object of our search, there was no sign whatever. Yet perhaps our investigations were not altogether fruitless, for even negative evidence has a certain value and in this instance showed that these caves are probably inhabited in winter only, for hibernation purposes.

When in a later year a kindly fate led the way to Australia on a scientific mission, I felt that a dream of years was about to be realized, namely, the chance to see the great roosts of fruit bats that at certain seasons congregate by thousands in dense and secluded swamps in the eastern part of that country. But it was not until the very last week of my stay that I was

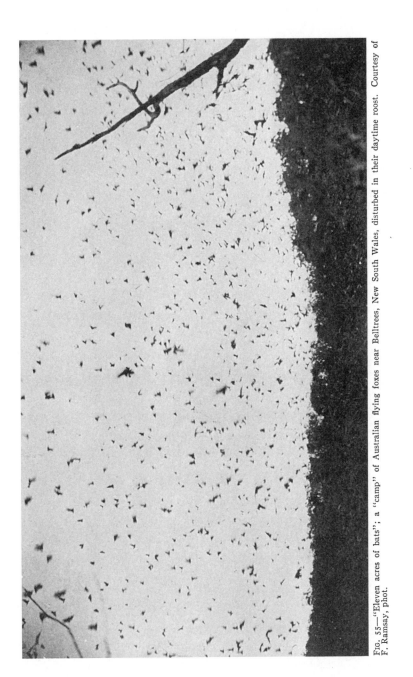

Fig. 55—"Eleven acres of bats"; a "camp" of Australian flying foxes near Belltrees, New South Wales, disturbed in their daytime roost. Courtesy of F. Ramsay, phot.

able to look for one of these great "camps," as they are locally called. At last, just before Christmas, a companion and I set forth for Kempsey on the coast of New South Wales, reputed to be a favored harbor of these great bats. On arrival, we made eager inquiries, and at length elicited information concerning a well-known "camp" some miles distant. The local taxicab was requisitioned forthwith, and the next day found us under way at an early hour, with lunch, cameras, firearms, and binoculars in expectation of the wonderful sight of "acres of bats" in their roost. By dint of many inquiries we eventually located the rough track through woods and pastures to a dense swamp of tall, slender, white-barked "tea-trees," in the tops of which, we were assured, the "foxes" would be discovered draped in profusion from the branches. Indeed, one person had even heard their bickering voices when he passed that way only a week before. The trail was getting hot! But alas, on reaching the swamp and penetrating its sodden depths from various sides, we regretfully learned that we were just too late, for the entire company had now abandoned the locality and passed on to parts unknown!

Undismayed, my friend and I now turned our attention to several caves in the "out back," where a certain road engineer had told us incredible swarms of small bats were to be found. A long forenoon's drive found us at length miles away, on the wrong side of Willy-willy Creek (native word for whirlwind), with a wooded hill beyond in which were several bat caves. So, having first disposed of lunch, we forded the stream and after long and diligent search through the thorny thickets found and explored their full extent. The bats were nowhere to be found, and most of the caves had long ago been dug out for the deposits of guano. Not to be outdone, we set forth again next day, along the same road, thirty miles over rough going, for a final attempt on another cave. At the very start the radiator of our car started a leak and caused several hours' delay, but at length we reached the last house on the road, where a steep and wooded cliff rose picturesquely above the little valley. At the house they told us that the cave was at the very top of the plateau and assured us in positive terms that it was "full of bats." The climb up proved a long and arduous one, in the course of which I brushed my forehead against a low-hanging bough of a nettle tree, leaving a stinging pain that lasted a full week thereafter. At last we reached the spot, where a broad well-like shaft led perpendicularly down into the ground, among boulders and limestone ledges. A short distance down, there was an improvised ladder made from a single tree trunk, with crossbars nailed on at intervals. Down this we proceeded, into the dark depths, stopping here and there in the descent to feel with one foot for a missing rung, and slipping carefully past the empty space to the next footing. This was a splendid cavern with several chambers, each one lower than the preceding, and joined by narrow sloping passages. The lofty walls disappeared in the darkness above, and the passages led away below. We spent an hour or more in these nether kingdoms and succeeded in startling only two small bats, whose wariness and skill eluded our utmost efforts to shoot or strike them down. We were a rather dejected lot as we drove back to town empty-handed over a long thirty miles of rugged road in a rocking Ford. However, the luck did change, for the climax of the hunt came with the discovery of a third cave that actually did "swarm" with bats, a large colony of old and young horseshoe bats, with a few of the long-winged Miniopterus, a rare and interesting sight as hundreds of them, disturbed by our invasion of their retreat, rushed back and forth from one large chamber to the other, or alighted in numbers against the side walls.

Another year found my wandering feet among the mountains of southern Brazil. With an intelligent school teacher as companion and in company with members of the staff of the Museu Paulista, we had spent a week collecting in a forest camp where a new roadway was under construction through a wilderness of wooded hills. In response to my inquiries concerning the possibility of bat caves, the museum curators were agreed in recommending a visit to the Caves of Yporanga, some days distant across the range. One of them had even been there in the course of geological exploration, and as usual he had found "swarms" of bats. Fired with zeal, my faithful friend agreed to accompany me on the quest, and we accordingly set forth along the mountain trail, lightly laden, sending on my collecting chest and other necessities in charge of a stalwart packer. Leaving other arrangements to my friend, who, as a native of the country, should know the methods of getting about, I set forth on the trail. For two hours and more we pushed ahead with many ups and downs, finally reaching at noon a beautiful spot where a clear brook formed a shaded pool in the forest.

"Une très belle place," remarked my companion, "pour nous rester et manger notre dejeuner!" (we conversed in French, for his English was nearly on a par with my Portuguese). "Oui," I replied hopefully, "et est-ce que nous avons du dejeuner?"

A faint smile flickered across his face, "Mais non."

For hours we plodded on, slipping, splashing, and climbing up and down one of the steepest, slipperiest, and altogether most miserable trails that has ever fallen to my lot, a crosscut as it later appeared, sometimes used by the country people. It was nearly sunset when at length we struggled down the other side of the mountain and came upon a wretched little shack with one or two unkempt men in its shelter. They had no food, so we plodded on once more, eventually reaching a small dwelling where a half-breed Japanese lived with his little family. They made us welcome, and the woman got us coffee, cornmeal cakes, and bacon, after which the two younger boys took us in their small dugout canoe down a winding forest stream. At length, reaching a village long after dark, we secured a barren room for the night in a rude public house. It was Sunday evening, and religious fervor was still unabated, for as we dropped gladly to sleep I could hear the strains of a hymn concerning the "agua da vida" coming from the barroom below. We started on again at five o'clock the next morning, without breakfast, wet, cold, and miserable. The heavy rains during the night had roused hundreds of tiny frogs to activity, and their tinkling chorus came from all sides as our boys continued to pole us down the river. At length we reached a junction where a number of Japanese settlers maintained a little farming community, and here we were courteously received by an elderly farmer, whose wife presently brought out a welcome cup of coffee. With this apology for breakfast, we now took to the forest trail that led on for some three hours overland to the main river, where the town of Sette Barras nestled on the hillside overlooking the stream, a cluster of some fifty houses mostly of wattle and daub construction and a single story high. In one of these we secured lodging for the night, and next morning set forth again in a dugout canoe with the addition of an outboard motor and a crew of two. All day it rained in torrents, but taking what comfort we might in our thin waterproof coats, we continued slowly upstream against the strong current from eight o'clock in the morning until five in the afternoon, with occasional halts by the riverbank to pour more gasoline into the hungry engine or to lunch on the cluster of small bananas that fortune had sent us. A humorous picture we must have made — our thirty-foot craft dingy and shelterless but sturdy, my friend and I seated on empty boxes in the center of its length, our two collecting cases between us covered with an inadequate tarpaulin; in the bow with his long fending pole an elderly Brazilian, draped in a heavy woollen shawl, wearing a battered felt hat of such picturesque shape as only a descendant of the Latin race can manage, while at the stern stood our youthful engineer holding his umbrella above him with one hand, with the other grasping his long steering oar.

Through all that miserable day we chugged over the muddy waters, no doubt presenting much the same forlorn appearance as the group of black vultures we passed sitting dejectedly over a dead calf by the riverside, their heads drawn down between their drooping shoulders, the picture of bedraggled misery. We were glad at length to reach the little village of Xiririca (pronounced "shirry-reeker"), an appropriate Indian word, signifying "the sound of rushing waters." It proved to be a cheery spot, and we found food and shelter, as well as a warm fire. Here we learned that the mail boat was due from

FIG. 56—Yporanga: the cave entrance.

FIG. 57—Yporanga: a chamber in the cave.

up-river in two days more and would carry us on the final stage of the journey to Yporanga, near the head of navigation of the river of the same name. For two long rainy days we awaited its coming, but the third day, dawning clear and glorious, brought the long-expected craft. It proved to be another long dugout hewn from a single great log, with a small outboard motor clamped to its overhanging stern. Unfortunately, some essential pin in its mechanism had become bent, occasioning the delay, so that it was not until nearly noon that this was finally repaired and the boat ready for the return journey. All that afternoon we pushed on up the turbulent stream, for it was much swollen with recent rains. Masses of floating wood and rubbish swirled by with occasional mats of water hyacinth. We made frequent stops, clinging to overhanging vines or clumps of stout reeds by the riverside while the boatmen tinkered the overworked engine or replenished its fuel.

The day was far spent when we at length drew up at a hospitable ranch where we were given supper and a comfortable lodging. The night was cold and damp, but we slept like tired dogs. Next morning the boatmen were early astir, and presently our host appeared with coffee, bread, and cheese. Gray dawn found us once more chugging up the racing stream, and so the morning wore on like another yesterday, when, on rounding a turn of the river, the little cluster of houses that was Yporanga came in view, with its entire population at the landing to welcome the overdue mail. An elderly Brazilian led us to the little inn of which he was proprietor, and through him we arranged for horses and pack mules to take us the following day to the caves, which still drew us on like a receding will-o'-the-wisp. Our transport was on hand promptly next morning, and after a sketchy breakfast we were off. The plan was to reach the caves after several hours' ride over mountain trails, spend the night farther on at a mining camp, and, after crossing a series of mountain ridges, reach a distant town, where we would close our long circuit. With our goods on the pack saddles of the mules, ourselves on the sure-footed horses, our guide riding silently ahead, we resumed the quest. Reaching a commanding ridge, we had a wide view of what lay ahead — a long series of steep hills and valleys over and across which the trail wound infinitely far ahead. At times the narrow mule-path hugged the edges of precipices where one could look almost directly down for hundreds of feet. In such places my steed had a way of walking on the outermost six inches of the trail, as if enjoying the downward view. Again and again I would rein him to the inner side of the path, but as persistently his feet would seek the outer rim. I seemed to be riding in midair, for his body hung out over the side, hiding the trail from my view, so that I could look over his rounded flank a very long way straight below. But at length I gave him free rein, recalling that if one foot lost its hold, he still had three more to keep him on the narrow way.

So we proceeded till noon, and at length reached a lonely ranch, where we stopped for rest and inquiries. Three stout lads here volunteered to lead us to the caves, at last close at hand. Leaving our horses, we soon reached a little valley with a narrow, rushing stream that disappeared at the base of a hill, beneath which it flowed, issuing forth again on the other side. An old and somewhat overgrown trail led up the steep cliff side, and in a few rods more we were at the wide mouth of the cavern. The men seemed reluctant to enter and gladly gave me precedence as with light in hand I descended into its dark depths. A sloping passageway soon brought me to a high, vaulted chamber, fairly dry, and completely dark. After a hundred feet or so it became narrower, and the rocky floor sloped away to a small stream which flowed off underground through a fissure. Every part of the great cavern was thoroughly searched, but there was no slightest indication of the fabled bats. It was completely empty! Yet hope was not wholly dead. It seemed there was a fine cavern on the other side of the great hill, and thither we made our way, scrambling over loose rocks and among tangled thickets, to the opening. Here the only passage within was by a long shelving ledge, affording a slippery foothold. We had come a long way for this opportunity, and the cave must be explored. So with the flashlight illuminating the dark walls, we made our way carefully along the ledge, until a vertical chasm below precluded further progress. A loose pebble dropped over the brink took several seconds before making a faint splash, far below, where, like "Alph, the sacred river," ran an underground stream, said to harbor blind fishes. But of the bats which we had come so far to find, and which should have been hanging in gay festoons on the walls, there was no slightest trace whatever.

Yporanga — "the beautiful waters" — so the Indians called them, but somehow they had lost their charm. Indeed, I have often thought that some strange fatality attends my bat hunts; or it may be that after all some wakeful genie keeps watch over the shadowy wings of the bats I seek.

In the foregoing pages I have shown that the many myths and superstitions about bats are mainly of interest as folklore and that our prejudices against them are largely unfounded; that far from being symbols of evil, they are by some men regarded as of good omen; and that, aside from the vampires of South America, "black sheep" of the tribe, they are for the most part useful animals. Their family tree has roots that extend far deeper into the past than do our own. In their many species and their various adaptive traits, they afford abundant examples of the evolution of structures. In the tropics, although the larger fruit-eating bats may at times come into competition with men for their favorite food, yet the native peoples of these regions often find the bats themselves toothsome morsels. The social habits of bats should again interest us, particularly those showing how by their very diversity these creatures are enabled to get along without interfering with one another. A shining instance of such racial tolerance is afforded by recent discoveries of ancient fossil remains of the bats Myotis and Rhinolophus, representing two distinct families, closely associated in the same deposits, an indication that, then as now, these genera got along together and lived in peaceful association in the same caves, a relation that has continued for millions of years since at least middle Tertiary days. Indeed, bats have something to teach us about good citizenship!

# BIBLIOGRAPHY

# BIBLIOGRAPHY

AITKEN, E. H., 1907. Do bats eat birds? Journ. Bombay Nat. Hist. Soc., 18: 190.

ALDROVANDUS, ULYSSES, 1681. Ornithologiae hoc est de avibus historiae. Libri XII. 4to, Bonn (see pp. 571–587).

ALLEN, ARTHUR A., 1921. Banding bats. Journ. Mammalogy, 2: 53–57, pls. 4, 5.

ALLEN, JOEL A., 1906. Mammals from the States of Sinaloa and Jalisco, Mexico, collected by J. H. Batty during 1904 and 1906. Bull. Amer. Mus. Nat. Hist., 22: 191–262, pl. 20–33.

    1911. Mammals from Venezuela collected by Mr. M. A. Carriker, Jr., 1909–1911. Bull. Amer. Mus. Nat. Hist., 30: 239–273.

    1916. Mammals collected on the Roosevelt Brazilian Expedition, with field notes by Leo E. Miller. Bull. Amer. Mus. Nat. Hist., 35: 559–610.

ALLISON, VERNON C., 1937. Evening bat flight from Carlsbad Caverns. Journ. Mammalogy, 18: 80–82.

ANDERSEN, KNUD, 1912. Catalogue of the Chiroptera in the collection of the British Museum. Vol. 1: Megachiroptera. 8vo, London, ci+854 pp., illus.

    1917. On the determination of age in bats. Journ. Bombay Nat. Hist. Soc., 25: 249–259, 1 pl.

    1917a. On the so-called colour phases of the Rufous Horseshoe-bat of India (*Rhinolophus rouxi*, Temm.). Journ. Bombay Nat. Hist. Soc., 25: 260–273, pls. 1, 2.

ANDERSON, A. R. S., 1899. Bats in Burmese caves. Natural Science, 14: 259–260.

ANDREWS, CHARLES W., 1900. A monograph of Christmas Island (Indian Ocean): physical features and geology, with descriptions of the fauna and flora by numerous contributors. 8vo, London, xvi + 337 pp., 22 pls., map.

ANTHONY, HAROLD E., 1918. The indigenous land mammals of Porto Rico, living and extinct. Mem. Amer. Mus. Nat. Hist., new ser., 2: 333–435, pl. 55–74, 55 text-figs.

BAILEY, VERNON, 1928. Animal life of the Carlsbad Cavern. Monographs of the American Society of Mammalogists. No. 3. 8vo, Baltimore, xiii + 95 pp., illus.

BAKER, JOHN R., and BAKER, ZITA (Mrs. J. R.), 1936. The seasons in a tropical rain-forest (New Hebrides). Part 3. Fruit-bats (Pteropidae). Journ. Linn. Soc. London, 40: 123–141.

BAKER, JOHN R., and BIRD, T. F., 1936. The seasons in a tropical rain-forest (New Hebrides). Part 4. Insectivorous bats (Vespertilionidae and Rhinolophidae). Journ. Linn. Soc. London, 40: 143–161, pl. 4.

BANKS, E., 1931. A popular account of the mammals of Borneo. Journ. Malayan Branch Asiatic Soc., 9: pt. 2, p. 1–139, 9 pls., map.

BARBOUR, THOMAS, 1919. The herpetology of Cuba. Mem. Mus. Comp. Zool., **47**: 69–213, 15 pls.

——— 1932. A peculiar roosting habit of bats. Quart. Review Biol., **7**: 307–312, 4 text-figs.

BARKOW, H. C. L., 1846. Der Winterschlaf nach seinen Erscheinungen im Thierreich dargestellt. 4to, Berlin, x + 525 pp., 4 pls.

BARRETT, S. A., 1933. Pomo myths. Bull. Publ. Mus. Milwaukee, **15**: 1–608.

BARTELS, M., 1908. Zur Lebensweise von *Eonycteris spelaea*, Dobs. Bull. Dépt. Agric. aux Indes Néerlandaises, Buitenzorg, no. 20, p. 13.

BATE, DOROTHY M. A., 1904. The mammals of Cyprus. Proc. Zool. Soc. London, for 1903, **2**: 341–348, text-fig. 43.

BÉLON, PIERRE, 1555. L'histoire de la nature des oyseaux, avec levrs descriptions, & naifs portraicts retirez dv naturel: escrite en sept livres. 4to, Paris (28), 381, (1) pp., illus.

BENEDICT, J. E., 1926. Notes on the feeding habits of Noctilio. Journ. Mammalogy, **7**: 58–59.

BIER, OTTO G., 1932. Action anticoagulante et fibrinolytique de l'extrait des glandes salivaires d'une chauve-souris hématophage (*Desmodus rufus*). Comptes Rend. Soc. de Biol., Paris, **110**: 129–131.

BLAKE, HENRY A., 1885. Note on the parturition of a West-Indian bat. Sci. Proc. Roy. Dublin Soc., (2) **4**: 449–450.

BLYTH, EDWARD, 1842. Notice of the predatory and sanguinivorous habits of the bats of the genus Megaderma, with some remarks on the blood-sucking propensities of other Vespertilionidae. Journ. Asiatic Soc. Bengal, **11**: 255–262.

——— 1844. Notices of various Mammalia, with descriptions of many new species. Journ. Asiatic Soc. Bengal, **13**: pt. 1, 463–494.

——— 1875. Catalogue of the mammals and birds of Burma. With a memoir, and portrait of the author. Journ. Asiatic Soc. Bengal, extra no., (2) **43**: pt. 2, xxiv, 167 pp.

BONHOTE, J. LEWIS, 1910. On a small collection of mammals from Egypt. Proc. Zool. Soc. London, for 1909, **2**: 788–798.

BREHM, CHR. L., 1827. Einige merkwürdige Beobachtungen über die Fledermäuse. Ornis, oder das Neueste und Wichtigste der Vogelkunde und Anziehendes aus der Thierkunde, Jena, no. 3: 17–29.

BURBANK, R. C., and YOUNG, J. Z., 1934. Temperature changes and winter sleep of bats. Journ. Physiol., London, **82**: 459–467.

BURT, WILLIAM H., 1934. The mammals of southern Nevada. Trans. San Diego Soc. Nat. Hist., **7**: 375–427, map.

CAHN, ALVIN, and KEMP, JACK T., 1930. On the food of certain owls in east-central Illinois. The Auk, **47**: 323–328.

CAMPBELL, BERRY, 1931. Bats on the Colorado Desert. Journ. Mammalogy, **12**: 430.

CAMPBELL, CHARLES A. R., 1925. Bats, mosquitoes and dollars. 8vo, Boston, viii + 262 pp., illus.

CANTOR, THEODORE, 1842. General features of Chusan, with remarks on the flora and fauna of that island (conclusion). Ann. Mag. Nat. Hist. (1) **9**: 481–493.

1846. Catalogue of Mammalia inhabiting the Malayan peninsula and islands, collected or observed by Theodore Cantor, M.D., Bengal Medical Service. Journ. Asiatic Soc. Bengal, new ser., 15: 171–203.

CARACCIOLO, HENRY, 1895. Bats. Journ. Field Nat. Club, Port-of-Spain, Trinidad, 2: 164–170.

CHAPIN, JAMES P., 1932. The birds of the Belgian Congo. Part I. Bull. Amer. Mus. Nat. Hist., 65: x + 756 pp., 10 pls., map.

CHAPMAN, FRANK M., 1892. Notes on birds and mammals observed near Trinidad, Cuba, with remarks on the origin of West Indian bird-life. Bull. Amer. Mus. Nat. Hist., 4: 279–330.

1932. A home-making bat. Natural History (New York), 32: 555, text-fig.

CHUBB, E. C., 1909. The mammals of Matabeleland. Proc. Zool. Soc. London, for 1909, 1: 113–125.

CLARK, HERBERT C., and DUNN, LAWRENCE H., 1932. Experimental studies on Chagas' disease in Panama. Amer. Journ. Tropical Medicine, 12: 49–77.

1933. Animal susceptibility to Trypanosoma hippicum, the equine trypanosome of Panama. Amer. Journ. Tropical Medicine, 13: 273–281, 1 text-fig.

CODINA, ASCENSIO, 1912. Pájaros y murciélagos que atacan a las libelulas (Neu.) (Carta abierta al Sr. Rene Martin.-Paris). Bol. Soc. Aragonesa Cien. Nat., Zaragoza, 11: 66–69.

COPE, EDWARD D., 1880. The Bad Lands of the Wind River and their fauna. Amer. Naturalist, 14: 745.

COTT, HUGH B., 1926. Observations on the life-habits of some batrachians and reptiles from the Lower Amazon; and a note on some mammals from Marajó Island. Proc. Zool. Soc. London, for 1926, 2: 1159–1178, pl. 1–6, map.

COUDENHOVE, HANS, 1925. My African neighbors. Man, bird, and beast in Nyasaland. 8vo, Boston, xiv + 255 pp., illus.

COURRIER, ROBERT, 1927. Etude sur le déterminisme des caractères sexuels sécondaires chez quelques mammifères à activité testiculaire périodique. Arch. de Biol., Paris, 37: 173–334, pl. 9–13, 10 text-figs.

COWARD, T. A., 1907. On some habits of the Lesser Horseshoe Bat (Rhinolophus hipposiderus). Proc. Zool. Soc. London, for 1906, 2: 849–855.

DALY, D. D., 1888. On the caves containing edible birds'-nests in British North Borneo. Proc. Zool. Soc. London, 1888: 108–116.

DANIELL, GEORGE, 1835. Observations on the habits of the pipistrelle, Vespertilio pipistrellus, and the noctule, Vespertilio noctula, in captivity. Proc. Zool. Soc. London, 2: 129–132.

DAWSON, WARREN R., 1925. Bats as Materia Medica. Ann. Mag. Nat. Hist., (9) 16: 221–227.

DELSAUX, E., 1887. Sur la respiration des chauves-souris pendant leur sommeil hibernal. Arch. de Biol., 7: 207–215, fig.

DERENNES, CHARLES, 1924. The life of the bat. Translated from the French by Louise Collier Willcox. sm. 8vo, 6 + 183 pp.; New York and London.

De Winton, W. E., 1901. On a new species of bat from the Soudan. Ann. Mag. Nat. Hist., (7) 7: 45–46.

Ditmars, Raymond L., 1935. Collecting bats in Trinidad. Four specimens of *Vampyrus spectrum* are exhibited for the first time. Bull. New York Zool. Soc., 38: 213–218, with illustrations.

Ditmars, Raymond L., and Greenhall, Arthur M., 1935. The Vampire Bat, a presentation of undescribed habits and review of its history. Zoologica, Sci. Contrib. New York Zool. Soc., 19: 53–76, pl. 5–7.

Dobson, George E., 1873. On the Pteropidae of India and its islands, with descriptions of new or little known species. Journ. Asiatic Soc. Bengal, (2) 42: pt. 2, 194–205, pl. 14, figs.

    1878. Catalogue of the Chiroptera in the collection of the British Museum. 8vo, xlii + 567 pp., 30 pls.; London.

    1881. On the structure of the pharynx, larynx, and hyoid bones in the *Epomophori*; with remarks on its relation to the habits of these animals. Proc. Zool. Soc. London, 1881: 685–693, 6 figs.

Dodsworth, P. T. L., 1914. Notes on some mammals found in the Simla district, the Simla Hill States, and Kalka and adjacent country. Journ. Bombay Nat. Hist. Soc., 22: 726–748, fig.

Dugès, Alfredo, 1906. Murciélago del genero *Ischnoglossa*. Mem. y Revista Soc. Cientifica "Antonio Alzate," 24: 117–119, figs.

Du Halde, J. B., 1738. A description of the empire of China and Chinese-Tartary, together with the kingdoms of Korea, and Tibet: containing the geography and history (natural as well as civil) of those countries. 4to, 2 vols.; London.

Dunckner, Georg, 1931. Gefangenschaft-Beobachtungen an *Myotis nattereri* Kuhl. Zool. Garten, new ser., 4: 17–27, 4 figs.

Dunn, Lawrence H., 1933. Observations on the carnivorous habits of the Spear-nosed Bat, *Phyllostomus hastatus panamensis* Allen, in Panama. Journ. Mammalogy, 14: 188–199.

    1935. Notes on the Little Bulldog Bat, *Dirias albiventer minor* (Osgood) in Panama. Journ. Mammalogy, 15: 89–90.

Eisentraut, M., 1934. Markierungsversuche bei Fledermäusen. Zeitschr. f. Morph. u. Oekol. d. Tiere, sect. A, 28: 553–560, 1 text-fig.

    1934a. Der Winterschlaf der Fledermäuse mit besonderer Berücksichtigung der Wärmeregulation. Zeitschr. f. Morph. u. Oekol. d. Tiere, sect. A, 29: pt. 2, 231–267, 8 text-figs.

    1935. Fledermauszug und Fledermausberingung. Ornith. Monatsber., 43: 22–25.

    1935a. Ergebnisse der Fledermausberingung. Ornith. Monatsber., 43: 150.

    1936. Ergebnisse der Fledermausberingung nach dreijähriger Versuchzeit. Zeitschr. f. Morph. u. Oekol. d. Tiere, 31: 1–26, 3 text-figs.

    1936a. Beitrag zur Mechanik des Fledermausfluges. Zeitschr. f. Wiss. Zool., 148: 159–188, 18 text-figs.

Feilden, H. W., 1889. Distribution of plants by frugivorous bats. Zoologist (3) 13: 179–180.

FERRAR, M. L., 1934. Daily flighting of Flying Foxes (*Pteropus giganteus* Brünn.). Journ. Bombay Nat. Hist. Soc., 37: 214–215.

FERRIS, G. F., 1919. Some records of Polyctenidae (Hemiptera). Journ. New York Ent. Soc., 27: 261–263, pl. 24.

1924. The New World Nycteribiidae (Diptera Pupipara). Ent. News, 35: 191–199, pl. 3.

FEYTAUD, J., 1913. Bull. Soc. d'Etude et de Vulgarisation Zool. Agric., Bordeaux, 12: 147.

FINCKENSTEIN, GRAF FINCK VON, and SCHAEFFER, HELMUT, 1934. Fledermauszug am Tage. Zool. Anzeiger, 106: 46–48.

FLOWER, STANLEY S., 1931. Contributions to our knowledge of the duration of life in vertebrate animals. V. Mammals. Proc. Zool. Soc. London, for 1931, 145–234.

FORMOSOV, A., 1927. [Note sur les passages des chauve-souris.] Compt. Rend. Acad. des Sci. URSS, 1927A, no. 17, p. 272–274 (in Russian).

FRAZER, J. G., 1910. Totemism and exogamy. A treatise on certain early forms of superstition and society. 8vo, London, 4 vols.

FRY, T. B., 1929. Report No. 46 (Supplementary) on the second, third and fourth collections from Toungoo, Burmah, made by Mrs. J. M. D. Mackenzie, I.F.S., between dates February 9, 1927 to March 2, 1928. Journ. Bombay Nat. Hist. Soc., 33: 636–652.

GATES, WILLIAM H., 1936. Keeping bats in captivity. Journ. Mammalogy, 17: 268–273.

GESNER, CONRAD, 1555. Historiae Animalium. Tiguri, fol., vol. 3.

GILE, P. L., and CARRERO, J. O., 1918. The bat guanos of Porto Rico and their fertilizing value. Bull. Porto Rico Agric. Exper. Sta., no. 25, 66 pp.

GLEADOW, F., 1907. Bats feeding on birds. Journ. Bombay Nat. Hist. Soc., 17: 1022.

GOLDMAN, E. A., 1926. [Review of C. A. R. Campbell's "Bats, Mosquitoes, and Dollars."] Journ. Mammalogy, 7: 136–138.

GOODWIN, GEORGE G., 1928. Observations on Noctilio. Journ. Mammalogy, 9: 104–113.

GOSSE, PHILLIP H., 1847. Brief notes on the habits of *Noctilio mastivus*. Proc. Zool. Soc. London, for 1847, 105–110.

GRANVIK, HUGO, 1924. On mammals from the eastern slopes of Mount Elgon, Kenya Colony. Mammals collected by the Swedish Mount Elgon Expedition 1920. Lunds Univ. Arsskr., new ser., sect. 2, 21: no. 3, 32 pp., 1 pl.

GREEN, E. ERNEST, 1907. Do bats capture and eat birds? Journ. Bombay Nat. Hist. Soc., 17: 835–836.

1910. A cannibal bat. Spolia Zeylanica, 7: 106.

GRIFFIN, DONALD R., 1934. Marking bats. Journ. Mammalogy, 15: 202–207, 1 text-fig.

GRINNELL, HILDA W., 1918. A synopsis of the bats of California. Univ. of California Publ., Zool., 17: 223–404, pl. 14–24, 24 text-figs.

GRINNELL, JOSEPH, 1910. A second record of the Spotted Bat (*Euderma maculatum*) for California. Univ. of California Publ., Zool., 5: 317–320, pl. 30.

GUTHRIE, MARY J., 1933. Notes on the seasonal movements and habits of some cave bats. Journ. Mammalogy, 14: 1–19, pl. 1.

1933a. The reproductive cycles of some cave bats. Journ. Mammalogy, 14: 199–216.

HAAGNER, A. K., 1921. Red Bat at sea. Journ. Mammalogy, 2: 36.

HAHN, WALTER L., 1908. Some habits and sensory adaptations of cave-inhabiting bats. Biol. Bull., 15: 135–193.

HALL, E. RAYMOND, 1930. A new genus of bat from the later Tertiary of Nevada. Univ. of California Publ., Bull. Dept. Geol. Sci., 19: 319–320, pl. 38.

HAMILTON, WILLIAM J., JR., 1933. The insect food of the Big Brown Bat. Journ. Mammalogy, 14: 155–156.

HAMLETT, G. W. D., 1934. Nema parasites in embryo bats. Biol. Bull., 66: 357–360, 5 text-figs.

1934a. Implantation und Embryonalhüllen bei zwei südamerikanischen Fledermäusen. Anat. Anzeiger, 79: 113–176, 2 text-figs.

HARI, PAUL, 1909. Der respiratorische Gaswechsel der winterschlafenden Fledermaus. Arch. f. Ges. Physiol., 103: 112–133.

HARPER, FRANCIS, 1927. The mammals of the Okefinokee Swamp region of Georgia. Proc. Boston Soc. Nat. Hist., 38: 191–396, pl. 4–7.

1929. Mammal notes from Randolph County, Georgia. Journ. Mammalogy, 10: 84–85.

HARTMAN, CARL G., 1933. On the survival of spermatozoa in the female genital tract of the bat. Quart. Review Biol., 8: 185–193.

HARTMAN, CARL G., and CUYLER, W. KENNETH, 1927. Is the supposed long life of the bat spermatozoa fact or fable? Anat. Record, 35: 39.

HELLER, FLORIAN, 1935. Fledermäuse aus der eozänen Braunkohle des Geiseltales bei Halle a. S. Nova Acta Leopoldina, Abh. K. Leop.-Carol. Deutsch. Akad. d. Naturforscher, Halle (2) 2: 301–314, 3 pls.

HENSEL, REINHARDT, 1869. Beiträge zur Kenntniss der Thierwelt Brasiliens. (Fortsetzung.) Der Zool. Garten, Frankfurt a. M., 10: 135–140.

HERLANT, MARC, 1934. Recherches sur les potentialités de developpement des oeufs obtenus par ovulation provoquée chez la chauve-souris en hibernation. Bull. Acad. Roy. de Belgique, cl. des sci., Bruxelles (5) 20: 359–366, 2 text-figs.

HERMANN, JOHANN, 1804. Observationes Zoologicae quibus novae complures, aliaeque animalium species describuntur et illustrantur. 8vo, Paris, viii + 332 pp.

HEUGLIN, TH. VON, 1861. Beiträge zur Fauna der Säugethiere N.O.-Afrika's. Nova Acta Acad. Caes. Leop.-Carol., Halle, 29: no. 8, 1–24, 1 pl.

1877. Reise in Nordost-Afrika. Schilderungen aus dem Gebiete der Beni Amer und Habab nebst zoologischen Skizzen und einem Führer für Jagdreisende. 8vo, Braunschweig, 2 vols., illus.

HIBBARD, CLAUDE W., 1934. Notes on some cave bats of Kansas. Trans. Kansas Acad. Sci., 37: 235–238.

HILLER, DR., 1858. Vespertilio als Feinschmecker und Systemverächter. Entomol. Zeitung, Stettin, 19: 223–226.

HINTON, M. A. C., and KERSHAW, P. S., 1920. On a collection of mammals from the Dinka country, Bahr-el-Djebel. Ann. Mag. Nat. Hist. (9) **6**: 94–101.

HINTON, M. A. C., and LINDSAY, H. M., 1926. Bombay Natural History Society's mammal survey of India, Burma and Ceylon. Report no. 41, Assam and Mishmi Hills. Journ. Bombay Nat. Hist. Soc., **31**: 383–403.

HIRST, STANLEY, 1927. Notes on Acari, mainly belonging to the genus Spinturnix von Heyden. Proc. Zool. Soc. London, for 1927, pp. 323–328, 13 text-figs.

HOLMBERG, UNO, 1927. Mythology of all races. 8vo, Boston; see vol. 4, p. 7.

HOWARD, L. O., 1922. Mosquitoes and bats. U. S. Public Health Service, Public Health Reports, reprint no. 715, pp. 1789–1795.

HOWELL, A. BRAZIER, 1920. Contribution to the life-history of the California Mastiff Bat. Journ. Mammalogy, **1**: 111–117, pl. 5–6.

HOWELL, A. BRAZIER, and LITTLE, LUTHER, 1924. Additional observations on California bats; with observations upon the young of Eumops. Journ. Mammalogy, **5**: 261–263, pl. 30.

HOWELL, ARTHUR H., 1908. Notes on diurnal migrations of bats. Proc. Biol. Soc. Washington, **21**: 35–38.

HUEY, LAURENCE M., 1925. Food of the California Leaf-nosed Bat. Journ. Mammalogy, **6**: 196–197.

1926. Bats eaten by Short-eared Owl. The Auk, **43**: 96–97.

HUGUES, ALBERT, 1913. Sur les migrations des chiroptères. Compte Rend. 41e Sess. Assoc. Franç. Av. Sci., Nîmes, for 1912, Notes et Mém., 411–413.

HURST, E. WESTON, and PAWAN, J. L., 1932. A further account of the Trinidad outbreak of acute rabies myelitis: histology of the experimental disease. Journ. Pathol. and Bacteriology, **35**: 301–321, pl. 31–37.

HUTTON, THOMAS, 1872. On the bats of the north-western Himalayas. With notes and corrections in nomenclature by Prof. W. Peters, C.M.Z.S. Proc. Zool. Soc. London, for 1872, 690–714.

HUXLEY, THOMAS H., 1865. On the structure of the stomach in *Desmodus rufus*. Proc. Zool. Soc. London, for 1865, 386–390, 1 text-fig.

JAMESON, H. LYSTER, 1909. On a collection of mammals from South Africa. Ann. Mag. Nat. Hist. (8) **4**: 455–474.

JEX-BLAKE, G. J., 1931. Notes on poisoning fruit bats (*Epimorphus* [sic] *wahlbergei*). Journ. East Africa and Uganda Nat. Hist. Soc., 1931: 179–182.

JOBLING, B., 1930. A revision of the genus Raymondia Frauenfeld. (Diptera, Pupipara, Streblidae.) Parasitology, **22**: 283–301, 10 text-figs.

JORDAN, K., 1909. Description of a new kind of apterous earwig, apparently parasitic on a bat. Novitates Zool., **16**: 312–326, pl. 16–18.

KALABUCHOV, N., 1933. Anabios in mammals at temperatures below 0°. The action of low temperatures on bats (Chiroptera). Bull. Soc. des Naturalistes, Moscou, Biol., new ser., **42**: 243–255 (in Russian with English summary).

KALABUCHOV, N., and LEVINSON, L., 1935. Effect of low temperature upon trypanosomes (*Trypanosoma equiperdum*) in mammals. Nature (London), **136**: 553.

KELLER, OTTO, 1909. Die antike Tierwelt. Erster Band: Säugetiere. 8vo, Leipzig, xii + 434 pp., 3 pls., 145 text-figs.

KERR, ROBERT, 1792. The animal kingdom, or zoological system, of the celebrated Sir Charles Linnaeus; Class I. Mammalia: (etc.) 8vo, London, pp. 1–12 (13–40), 1–651.

KERSHAW, P. S., 1922. On a collection of mammals from Chiromo and Cholo, Ruo, Nyasaland, made by Mr. Rodney C. Wood, with field-notes by the collector. Ann. Mag. Nat. Hist. (9) **10**: 177–192.

KILLINGTON, FREDERICK J., 1932. Neuroptera as the prey of bats. Journ. Entom. Soc. of South of England, **1**: 28–29; also in Hope Reports, 1933, vol. 19.

KIRK, JOHN, 1864. List of Mammalia met with in Zambesia, east tropical Africa. Proc. Zool. Soc. London, for 1864: 649–660.

KOLENATI, F. A., 1857. Die Parasiten der Chiropteren. 8vo, Dresden, 51 pp., 4 pls.

KOLMER, WALTER, 1926. Ueber die Augen der Fledermäuse. Verhandl. Zool.-Bot. Ges. Wien, **74–75**: 29–31.

KORMOS, THEODOR, 1930. Beiträge zur Praeglazialfauna des Somlyöberges bei Püspökfürdö. Journ. Trimestr., Sect. Zool., Soc. Roy. des Sci. Nat. de Hongrie, **27**: 57–62.

KUHL, HEINRICH, 1817. Die deutschen Fledermäuse. 8vo, Hanau, pp. 1–67, pl. 22–25.

KUMM, H. W., 1932. Yellow fever transmission experiments with South American bats. Ann. Tropical Med. and Parasitol., **26**: 207–213.

KUMMERLÖWE, H., 1929. *Plecotus auritus* L. in der Gefangschaft. Zool. Garten, **2**: 106–112.

KUNHIKANNAN, K., 1912. The bedbug (*Cimex rotundatus*) on the Common Yellow Bat (*Scotophilus kuhli*). Journ. Bombay Nat. Hist. Soc., **21**: 1342.

LANG, HERBERT, and CHAPIN, JAMES P., 1917. The American Museum Congo Expedition collection of bats. Part II. Notes on the distribution and ecology of Central African Chiroptera. Bull. Amer. Mus. Nat. Hist., **37**: 479–496, text-fig. 16.

LEA, ARTHUR M., 1922. One year's food of an owl near Adelaide. Journ. of Agric., Adelaide, South Australia, for 1922: 938–943, 4 text-figs.

LELAND, CHARLES G., 1891. Gypsy sorcery and fortune telling. 8vo, New York.

LE SOUEF, A. S., BURRELL, HARRY, and TROUGHTON, ELLIS LeG., 1926. The wild animals of Australasia, embracing the mammals of New Guinea & the nearer Pacific Islands. 8vo, London, 388 pp., illus.

LINSLEY, JAMES H., 1842. A catalogue of the Mammalia of Connecticut, arranged according to their natural families. Amer. Journ. Sci. (1) **43**: 345–354.

LOVERIDGE, ARTHUR, 1923. Notes on East African mammals, collected 1920–1923. Proc. Zool. Soc. London, for 1923, **2**: 685–739, map.

LYON, MARCUS W., JR., 1903. Observations on the number of young of the Lasiurine bats. Proc. U. S. Nat. Mus., **26**: 425–426, pl. 17.

1931. The Vampire Bat. Science, new ser., **73**: 124–125.

MACGILLIVRAY, JOHN, 1860. On the habit of *Notopteris macdonaldii*, Gray. Ann. Mag. Nat. Hist. (3), **6**: 152.

MACY, RALPH W., 1931. A key to the species of Hymenolepis found in bats and the description of a new species, *H. christensoni*, from *Myotis lucifugus*. Trans. Amer. Microscop. Soc., **50**: 344–346, pl. 35.

1936. A new genus and species of trematode from the Little Brown Bat and a key to the genera of Pleurogenetinae. Proc. U. S. Nat. Mus., **83**: 321–324.

MATHIS, J., 1929. Vom Leben der gemeinen Fledermaus. Zeitschr. Morph. u. Oekol., **13**: 706–721, 1 text-fig.

MATTHEW, W. D., 1915. Climate and evolution. Ann. N. Y. Acad. Sci., **24**: 171–318, 33 text-figs.

1917. A paleocene bat. Bull. Amer. Mus. Nat. Hist., **37**: 569–571, 1 text-fig.

MCCANN, C., 1931. On the fertilization of the flowers of the Sausage Tree (*Kigelia pinnata*, DC.) by bats. Journ. Bombay Nat. Hist. Soc., **35**: 467–471, 3 text-figs.

1933. The Brown Hawk-owl (*Ninox scutulata* Raffles) feeding on bats. Journ. Bombay Nat. Hist. Soc., **36**: 1002–1003.

1934. Notes on the Flying-fox (*Pteropus giganteus*, Brünn.). Journ. Bombay Nat. Hist. Soc., **37**: 143–149, 1 pl.

MEARNS, EDGAR A., 1898. A study of the vertebrate fauna of the Hudson Highlands, with observations on the Mollusca, Crustacea, Lepidoptera, and the flora of the region. Bull. Amer. Mus. Nat. Hist., **10**: 303–352.

MERRIAM, C. HART, 1888. Do any Canadian bats migrate? Evidence in the affirmative. Proc. and Trans. Roy. Soc. Canada, Ottawa, for 1887, **5**: sect. 4, 85–87.

MERZBACHER, L., 1903. Untersuchungen an winterschlafenden Fledermäusen. I. Mittheilung. Das Verhalten des Centralnervensystems im Winterschlafe und während des Erwachens aus demselben. Arch. f. Gesammte Physiol., **97**: 569–577.

MILLER, GERRIT S., JR., 1897. Migration of bats on Cape Cod, Massachusetts. Science, new ser., **5**: 541–543.

1897a. Description of a new bat from Margarita Island, Venezuela. Proc. Biol. Soc. Washington, **11**: 139.

1898. List of bats collected by Dr. W. L. Abbott in Siam. Proc. Acad. Nat. Sci. Philadelphia, for 1898: 316–325.

1904. Notes on the bats collected by William Palmer in Cuba. Proc. U. S. Nat. Mus., **27**: 337–348, pl. 9.

1907. The families and genera of bats. Bull. U. S. Nat. Mus., no. 57, xvii + 282 pp., 14 pls., 40 text-figs.

1918. Three new bats from Haiti and Santo Domingo. Proc. Biol. Soc. Washington, **31**: 39–40.

MOHR, CHARLES E., 1933. Observations on the young of cave-dwelling bats. Journ. Mammalogy, 14: 49–53.

MOHR, ERNA, 1932. Haltung und Aufzucht des Abendseglers (*Nyctalus noctula* Schreb.). Zool. Garten, new ser., 5: 106–120, 9 text-figs.

MOLLER, W., 1932. Das Epithel der Speiseröhrenschleimhaut der blüten-besuchender Fledermaus *Glossophaga soricina* im Vergleich zu insektenfressenden Chiroptera. Zeitschr. f. Mikroskop. Anat. Forsch., 29: 637–653, 6 text-figs.

MOONEY, JAMES, 1900. Myths of the Cherokee. 19th Ann. Rept. Bureau Amer. Ethnol., pt. 1: 3–548, 20 pls.

MOSELEY, H. N., 1879. Notes by a naturalist on the "Challenger" being an account of various observations made during the voyage of H.M.S. "Challenger" round the world in the years 1872–1876, etc. 8vo, London, xvi + 620 pp., illus.

MUIR, FREDERICK, 1912. Two new species of Ascodipteron. Bull. Mus. Comp. Zool., 54: 349–366, pl. 1–3.

MURIE, ADOLPH, 1935. Mammals from Guatemala and British Honduras. Univ. Michigan Mus. Zool., Misc. Publ., no. 26, 30 pp., 1 pl., map.

MURPHY, ROBERT C., 1917. Winter activity of the Brown Bat, *Vespertilio fuscus* (Beauvois), at Brooklyn, N. Y. Science, n. s., 45: 565–566.

MURPHY, ROBERT C., and NICHOLS, JOHN T., 1913. Long Island Fauna and Flora — I. The bats (Order Chiroptera). Science Bull. Mus. Brooklyn Inst. Arts and Sci., 2: 1–15.

MURRAY, ANDREW, 1869. [Bats used as food in Old Calabar.] Proc. Zool. Soc. London, for 1869: 530.

NAKANO, O., 1928. Ueber die Verteilung des Glykogens bei den zyklischen Veränderungen in den Geschlechtsorganen der Fledermaus, und ueber die Nahrungsaufnahme der Spermien in dem weiblichen Geschlechts-wege. Folia Anat. Japon., Tokyo, 6: 777–828, 1 pl., 25 text-figs.

NELSON, E. W., 1926. Bats in relation to the production of guano and the destruction of insects. Bull. U. S. Dept. Agric., no. 1395:1–12, 4 text-figs.

NORRIS, THADDEUS, 1874. The use of bats. Amer. Sportsman, 4: 90.

NORTON, ARTHUR H., 1930. A Red Bat at sea. Journ. Mammalogy, 11: 225–226.

OSBURN, W., 1865. Notes on the Chiroptera of Jamaica. Proc. Zool. Soc. London, for 1865: 61–85.

OSGOOD, F. L., 1936. Melanistic pipistrelles. Journ. Mammalogy, 17: 64.

OSGOOD, WILFRED H., 1932. Mammals of the Kelley-Roosevelts and Dela-cour Asiatic Expeditions. Field Mus. Nat. Hist., Zool. Ser., 18: 191–339, pl. 9–11.

PAWAN, J. L., 1936. The transmission of paralytic rabies in Trinidad by the Vampire Bat (*Desmodus rotundus murinus* Wagner, 1840). Ann. Tropical Med. and Parasitol., 30: 101–129, pl. 4, 2 text-figs.

PAYN, W. H., 1933. Kestrel taking bat. British Birds, 27: 204.

PETERS, JAMES L., 1929. An ornithological survey in the Caribbean low-lands of Honduras. Bull. Mus. Comp. Zool., 69: 397–478.

PHILLIPS, W. W. A., 1922. Notes on the habits of some Ceylon bats. Journ. Bombay Nat. Hist. Soc., 28: 448–452.

1923. Further notes on some Ceylon bats. Journ. Bombay Nat. Hist. Soc., **29**: 154–156, 2 pls.

1924. A guide to the mammals of Ceylon. Spolia Zeylanica, Ceylon Journ. Sci., sect. B, **13**: 1–63, 5 text-figs.

1924a. Ecto-parasites of Ceylon bats. Spolia Zeylanica, **13**: 65–70.

1927. The maternal instinct in the dwarf pipistrelle (*P. mimus mimus*). Journ. Bombay Nat. Hist. Soc., **32**: 211–213.

1927a. The colour change, and sexual differences in colour in the Long-armed Sheath-tailed Bat (*Taphozous longimanus*). Journ. Bombay Nat. Hist. Soc., **32**: 371–372.

POOLE, EARL L., 1932. Breeding of the Hoary Bat in Pennsylvania. Journ. Mammalogy, **13**: 365–367.

PORSCH, OTTO, 1932. Crescentia — eine Fledermausblume. Oesterr. Bot. Zeitschr., Wien, **80**: 31–44, pl. 9–10.

1932a. Das Problem Fledermausblume. Anzeiger Akad. Wiss., Wien, no. 3, 2 pp.

POULTON, E. B., 1929. British insectivorous bats and their prey. Proc. Zool. Soc. London, for 1929, **1**: 277–303.

PRATER, S. H., 1914. Notes on Wroughton's Free-tailed Bat (*Otomops wroughtoni*). Journ. Bombay Nat. Hist. Soc., **22**: 788.

PRIMROSE, A. M., 1907. Bats feeding on small birds. Journ. Bombay Nat. Hist. Soc., **17**: 1021–1022.

PRYER, H., 1884. An account of a visit to the birds'-nest caves of British North Borneo. Proc. Zool. Soc. London, for 1884: 532–538.

RATCLIFFE, F. N., 1931. The flying fox (Pteropus) in Australia. Bull. Council for Sci. and Industr. Research, no. 53, 81 pp., 2 pls.

1932. Notes on the fruit bats (Pteropus spp.) of Australia. Journ. Animal Ecology, **1**: 32–57, 4 pls.

REVILLIOD, PIERRE, 1916. A propos de l'adaptation au vol chez les Microchiroptères. Verhandl. Naturf. Ges., Basel, **27**: 156–183.

1917. Contribution à l'étude des chiroptères des terrains tertiaires. Première partie. Mém. Soc. Paléontol. Suisse, **43**: 1–60, pl. 1, 13 text-figs.

1917a. Fledermäuse aus der Braunkohle von Messel bei Darmstadt. Abh. d. Grossherzoglich Hessischen Geol. Landesanstalt zu Darmstadt, **7**: no. 2, 159–196, pl. 1, 4 tables.

1920. Contribution à l'études des chiroptères des terrains tertiaires. Deuxième partie. Mém. Soc. Paléontol. Suisse, **44**: 61–130, pl. 2–3, 46 text-figs.

1922. Contribution à l'études des chiroptères des terrains tertiaires. Troisième partie et fin. Mém. Soc. Paléontol. Suisse, **45**: 131–195, pl. 4, 24 text-figs.

ROBIN, H. A., 1881. Recherches anatomiques sur les mammifères de l'ordre des chiroptères. Thèses présentées à la faculté des sciences de Paris. 8vo, Paris, and Ann. des Sci. Nat., Zool. (6) **12**: no. 2, 1–180, pl. 1–9.

RODHAIN, J., 1906. Nouvelles observations sur les Sarcoptides psoriques parasites de rousettes africaines, au Congo. Revue Zool. Africaine, **14**: 212–216, 1 text-fig.

ROLLINAT, R., and TROUESSART, E. L., 1896. Sur la reproduction des chauve-souris. Mém. Soc. Zool. de France, 9: 214–240.
——— 1900. Sur le sens de la direction chez les chiroptères. Comptes Rend. Soc. Biol., Paris, for 1900: 604–607.
ROTH, W. E., 1915. An inquiry into the animism and folk-lore of the Guiana Indians. 30th Ann. Rept. U. S. Bureau Ethnol., 103–386.
——— 1924. An introductory study of the arts, crafts, and customs of the Guiana Indians. 38th Ann. Rept. U. S. Bureau Ethnol., 25–745, illus.
RULOT, HECTOR, 1901. Note sur l'hibernation des chauve-souris. Arch. de Biol., 18: 365–375.
RYLEY, KATHLEEN V., 1913. Bombay Natural History Society's mammal survey of India. With field notes by the collector, G. C. Short-ridge. Journ. Bombay Nat. Hist. Soc., 22: 283–294, 1 pl.
SANBORN, COLIN C., 1931. Protection against Vampire Bats. Journ. Mammalogy, 12: 312–313.
SANSOM, G. S., 1932. Notes on some early blastocysts of the South American bat Molossus. Proc. Zool. Soc. London, for 1932: 113–118, 2 pls.
SAUNDERS, W. E., 1930. Bats in migration. Journ. Mammalogy, 11: 225.
SCHÖBL, JOS., 1871. Die Flughaut der Fledermäuse, namentlich die Endigung ihrer Nerven. Arch. f. Mikroscop. Anat., 7: 1–31, pl. 1–5.
SCHWEPPENBURG, H. GEYR VON, 1923. Ziehende Fledermäuse. Ornith. Monatsber., 31: 39.
SCLATER, P. L., and SPEKE, J. H., 1864. On the mammals collected and observed by Capt. J. H. Speke during the East-African expedition. With notes by Capt. J. H. Speke. Proc. Zool. Soc. London, for 1864: 98–106, pls. 12, 13.
SEAGER, H. W., 1896. Natural history in Shakespeare's time, being extracts illustrative of the subject as he knew it. 8vo, London, viii + 358 pp., illus.
SELER, EDUARD, 1904. The Bat God of the Maya race. Bull. Bureau Amer. Ethnology, Smithsonian Inst., no. 28: 231–240, text-fig. 49–53.
SERGENT, ETIENNE and EDOUARD, 1895. Sur les trypanosomes des chauves-souris. Comptes Rend. Soc. Biol., Paris, 58: 53.
——— 1921. Formes leishmaniennes chez les punaises de chauve-souris. Comptes Rend. Soc. Biol., Paris, 85: 413–415, 1 text-fig.
SHERMAN, H. B., 1930. Birth of the young of Myotis austroriparius. Journ. Mammalogy, 11: 495–503, pl. 26.
SHORTT, J., 1863. [On the fishing propensities of the Pteropus of India.] Proc. Zool. Soc. London, for 1863: 438–439.
SILVER, JAMES, 1928. Pilot Black-snake feeding on the Big Brown Bat. Journ. Mammalogy, 9: 149.
SPALLANZANI, LAZARO, 1784. Dissertations relative to the natural history of animals and vegetables, translated from the Italian, etc. 8vo, London, 2 vols.
SPERRY, CHARLES G., 1933. Opossum and skunk eat bats. Journ. Mammalogy, 14: 152–153.

SPILLMANN, FR., 1927. Beiträge zur Biologie des Milchgebisses des Chiropteren. Abh. Senckenberg. Naturf. Ges., Frankfurt a. M., 40: 249–255.

STADLER, H., 1922. Wandernde Fledermäuse. Naturwiss. Wochenschr., 37: 649–652.

STANĚK, V. J., 1933. K. topograficke a srovnavaci anatomie sluchoveho organu nasich chiropter. Ceske Akad. Ved a Umoni, for 1933, 67 pp., 9 pls. (on the inner ear of bats).

STILES, CHESTER W., and NOLAN, MABELLE O., 1931. Key catalogue of parasites reported for Chiroptera (bats) with their possible public health importance. Bull. Nat. Inst. of Health, U. S. Treasury Dept., no. 155, pp. 603–742.

STIRTON, R. A., 1931. A new genus of the family Vespertilionidae from the San Pedro Pliocene of Arizona. Univ. of California Publ., Bull. Dept. Geol. Sci., 20: 27–30, 2 text-figs.

STORER, TRACY I., 1926. Bats, bat towers and mosquitoes. Journ. Mammalogy, 7: 85–90, pl. 11.

STRONG, RICHARD P., 1930. The African Republic of Liberia and the Belgian Congo. 8vo, 2 vols., illus. (See vol. 2, Medical and Biological Observations.)

SWINHOE, ROBERT, 1870. Catalogue of the mammals of China (south of the River Yangtsze) and of the island of Formosa. Proc. Zool. Soc. London, for 1870: 615–653.

TENNENT, SIR J. EMERSON, 1861. Sketches of the natural history of Ceylon with narratives and anecdotes illustrative of the habits and instincts of the mammals, birds, reptiles, fishes, insects, &c. . . . London, 8vo, xxiii + 500 pp., illus.

THOMAS, OLDFIELD, 1888. On a collection of mammals obtained by Emin Pasha in equatorial Africa, and presented by him to the Natural History Museum. Proc. Zool. Soc. London, for 1888:3–17, pls. 1, 2.

1902. On the mammals collected during the Whitaker Expedition to Tripoli. Proc. Zool. Soc. London, for 1902, 2: 2–13, pl. 1.

1908. The missing premolar of the Chiroptera. Ann. Mag. Nat. Hist. (8) 1: 346–348.

1921. Bats on migration. Journ. Mammalogy, 2: 167.

THOMAS, OLDFIELD, and HINTON, M. A. C., 1923. On the mammals obtained in Darfur by the Lynes-Lowe Expedition. Proc. Zool. Soc. London, for 1923, 1: 247–271.

THOMPSON, GORDON B., 1935. The parasites of British birds. IV. — Records of bat parasites. Entomologists' Monthly Mag., 71: (ser. 3: 21) 143–147.

TICKELL, S. R., 1842. Remarks on Pteropus edulis, Geoffroy. Calcutta Journ. Nat. Hist., 3: 29–36, pl. 3.

TOMES, R. F., 1858. A monograph of the genus Kerivoula. Proc. Zool. Soc. London, for 1858: 322–338, pl. 66 (Mammalia).

TROUGHTON, ELLIS LE G., 1931. The habits and food of some Australian mammals. Australian Zoologist, 7: 77–83.

VAN TYNE, JOSSELYN, 1933. The trammel net as a means of collecting bats. Journ. Mammalogy, **14**: 145–146.

WARD, HENRY L., 1904. A study in the variations of proportions in bats, with brief notes on some of the species mentioned. Trans. Wisconsin Acad. Sci., Arts and Letters, **14**: 630–654, pl. 50–54 (graphs).

—— 1905. The number of young of the Red Bat. Bull. Wisconsin Nat. Hist. Soc., **3**: 181–182.

WETMORE, ALEXANDER, 1936. Hibernation of the Brown Bat. Journ. Mammalogy, **17**: 130–131.

WHITAKER, ARTHUR, 1905. Notes on the breeding habits of bats. The Naturalist (London), for 1905: 325–330, pl. 22.

WHITMEE, S. J., 1874. [Habits of *Pteropus whitmeei* in Samoa.] Proc. Zool. Soc. London, for 1874: 666–667.

WILDER, BURT G., 1875. Bats and their young. Pop. Science Monthly, **7**: 641–652, 11 text-figs.

WILLEY, A., 1904. Crows and Flying Foxes at Barberyn. Spolia Zeylanica, **2**: 50–51.

WINIWARTER, H. DE, 1926. Modification de la muqueuse laryngée et trachéale pendant l'hibernation, chez les chiroptères. Comptes Rend. Soc. de Biol., Paris, **94**: 405–406.

WOOD, J. G., 1870. Bible animals; being a description of every living creature mentioned in the Scriptures from the ape to the coral. 8vo, New York, xxix + 652 pp., illus.

WOOD JONES, FREDERIC, 1925. The mammals of South Australia. Part III. (Conclusion) containing the Monodelphia. 8vo, Adelaide, So. Australia, pp. 271–458, illus.

WRIGHT, EDWARD P., 1868. Notes on the bats of the Seychelle group of islands. Ann. Mag. Nat. Hist. (4) **2**: 436–438.

WROUGHTON, R. C., 1914. Bombay Natural History Society's mammal survey of India, Burma and Ceylon. Report No. 15 [Kumaon]. Journ. Bombay Nat. Hist. Soc., **23**: 282–301.

—— 1915. Bombay Natural History Society's mammal survey of India, Burma and Ceylon. Report No. 16 [Dry zone of central Burma and Mt. Popa]. Journ. Bombay Nat. Hist. Soc., **23**: 460–480.

—— 1915a. Bombay Natural History Society's mammal survey of India, Burma and Ceylon. Report No. 18 [Ceylon] & 19 [Bengal, Bihar, Orissa]. Journ. Bombay Nat. Hist. Soc., **24**: 79–110.

YERBURY, J. W., and THOMAS, OLDFIELD, 1895. On the mammals of Aden. Proc. Zool. Soc. London, for 1895: 542–555.

YOUNG, CHUNG-CHIEN, 1934. On the Insectivora, Chiroptera, Rodentia and Primates other than Sinanthropus from locality 1 at Chaikoutien. Palaeontologia Sinica, (C) **8**: no. 3, 160 pp., 10 pls., 51 text-figs.

ZONDEK, BERNHARD, 1933. Action of folliculin and prolan on the reproductive organs of the bat during hibernation. Lancet, **225**: 1256–1257.

# INDEX

# INDEX

A CATALOG OF SELECTED

# DOVER BOOKS

IN ALL FIELDS OF INTEREST

# A CATALOG OF SELECTED DOVER
# BOOKS IN ALL FIELDS OF INTEREST

CONCERNING THE SPIRITUAL IN ART, Wassily Kandinsky. Pioneering work by father of abstract art. Thoughts on color theory, nature of art. Analysis of earlier masters. 12 illustrations. 80pp. of text. 5⅜ x 8½. 23411-8

ANIMALS: 1,419 Copyright-Free Illustrations of Mammals, Birds, Fish, Insects, etc., Jim Harter (ed.). Clear wood engravings present, in extremely lifelike poses, over 1,000 species of animals. One of the most extensive pictorial sourcebooks of its kind. Captions. Index. 284pp. 9 x 12. 23766-4

CELTIC ART: The Methods of Construction, George Bain. Simple geometric techniques for making Celtic interlacements, spirals, Kells-type initials, animals, humans, etc. Over 500 illustrations. 160pp. 9 x 12. (Available in U.S. only.) 22923-8

AN ATLAS OF ANATOMY FOR ARTISTS, Fritz Schider. Most thorough reference work on art anatomy in the world. Hundreds of illustrations, including selections from works by Vesalius, Leonardo, Goya, Ingres, Michelangelo, others. 593 illustrations. 192pp. 7⅛ x 10¼. 20241-0

CELTIC HAND STROKE-BY-STROKE (Irish Half-Uncial from "The Book of Kells"): An Arthur Baker Calligraphy Manual, Arthur Baker. Complete guide to creating each letter of the alphabet in distinctive Celtic manner. Covers hand position, strokes, pens, inks, paper, more. Illustrated. 48pp. 8¼ x 11. 24336-2

EASY ORIGAMI, John Montroll. Charming collection of 32 projects (hat, cup, pelican, piano, swan, many more) specially designed for the novice origami hobbyist. Clearly illustrated easy-to-follow instructions insure that even beginning papercrafters will achieve successful results. 48pp. 8¼ x 11. 27298-2

THE COMPLETE BOOK OF BIRDHOUSE CONSTRUCTION FOR WOODWORKERS, Scott D. Campbell. Detailed instructions, illustrations, tables. Also data on bird habitat and instinct patterns. Bibliography. 3 tables. 63 illustrations in 15 figures. 48pp. 5¼ x 8½. 24407-5

BLOOMINGDALE'S ILLUSTRATED 1886 CATALOG: Fashions, Dry Goods and Housewares, Bloomingdale Brothers. Famed merchants' extremely rare catalog depicting about 1,700 products: clothing, housewares, firearms, dry goods, jewelry, more. Invaluable for dating, identifying vintage items. Also, copyright-free graphics for artists, designers. Co-published with Henry Ford Museum & Greenfield Village. 160pp. 8¼ x 11. 25780-0

HISTORIC COSTUME IN PICTURES, Braun & Schneider. Over 1,450 costumed figures in clearly detailed engravings—from dawn of civilization to end of 19th century. Captions. Many folk costumes. 256pp. 8⅜ x 11¾. 23150-X

THE STORY OF THE TITANIC AS TOLD BY ITS SURVIVORS, Jack Winocour (ed.). What it was really like. Panic, despair, shocking inefficiency, and a little heroism. More thrilling than any fictional account. 26 illustrations. 320pp. 5⅜ x 8½. 20610-6

FAIRY AND FOLK TALES OF THE IRISH PEASANTRY, William Butler Yeats (ed.). Treasury of 64 tales from the twilight world of Celtic myth and legend: "The Soul Cages," "The Kildare Pooka," "King O'Toole and his Goose," many more. Introduction and Notes by W. B. Yeats. 352pp. 5⅜ x 8½. 26941-8

BUDDHIST MAHAYANA TEXTS, E. B. Cowell and others (eds.). Superb, accurate translations of basic documents in Mahayana Buddhism, highly important in history of religions. The Buddha-karita of Asvaghosha, Larger Sukhavativyuha, more. 448pp. 5⅜ x 8½. 25552-2

ONE TWO THREE . . . INFINITY: Facts and Speculations of Science, George Gamow. Great physicist's fascinating, readable overview of contemporary science: number theory, relativity, fourth dimension, entropy, genes, atomic structure, much more. 128 illustrations. Index. 352pp. 5⅜ x 8½. 25664-2

EXPERIMENTATION AND MEASUREMENT, W. J. Youden. Introductory manual explains laws of measurement in simple terms and offers tips for achieving accuracy and minimizing errors. Mathematics of measurement, use of instruments, experimenting with machines. 1994 edition. Foreword. Preface. Introduction. Epilogue. Selected Readings. Glossary. Index. Tables and figures. 128pp. 5⅜ x 8½. 40451-X

DALÍ ON MODERN ART: The Cuckolds of Antiquated Modern Art, Salvador Dalí. Influential painter skewers modern art and its practitioners. Outrageous evaluations of Picasso, Cézanne, Turner, more. 15 renderings of paintings discussed. 44 calligraphic decorations by Dalí. 96pp. 5⅜ x 8½. (Available in U.S. only.) 29220-7

ANTIQUE PLAYING CARDS: A Pictorial History, Henry René D'Allemagne. Over 900 elaborate, decorative images from rare playing cards (14th–20th centuries): Bacchus, death, dancing dogs, hunting scenes, royal coats of arms, players cheating, much more. 96pp. 9¼ x 12¼. 29265-7

MAKING FURNITURE MASTERPIECES: 30 Projects with Measured Drawings, Franklin H. Gottshall. Step-by-step instructions, illustrations for constructing handsome, useful pieces, among them a Sheraton desk, Chippendale chair, Spanish desk, Queen Anne table and a William and Mary dressing mirror. 224pp. 8⅛ x 11¼. 29338-6

THE FOSSIL BOOK: A Record of Prehistoric Life, Patricia V. Rich et al. Profusely illustrated definitive guide covers everything from single-celled organisms and dinosaurs to birds and mammals and the interplay between climate and man. Over 1,500 illustrations. 760pp. 7½ x 10⅛. 29371-8

Paperbound unless otherwise indicated. Available at your book dealer, online at **www.doverpublications.com**, or by writing to Dept. GI, Dover Publications, Inc., 31 East 2nd Street, Mineola, NY 11501. For current price information or for free catalogues (please indicate field of interest), write to Dover Publications or log on to **www.doverpublications.com** and see every Dover book in print. Dover publishes more than 500 books each year on science, elementary and advanced mathematics, biology, music, art, literary history, social sciences, and other areas.